The Complete
HOYLE'S GAMES

Revised and updated by
LAWRENCE H. DAWSON

Wordsworth Editions

First published as *Hoyle's Games Modernized* by Routledge & Kegan Paul,
London, 1950.

This edition published 1989 by Wordsworth Editions Ltd,
8b East Street, Ware, Hertfordshire, under licence
from the proprietor.

Copyright © Routledge & Kegan Paul Ltd 1950.

ISBN 1-85326-942-5

Printed and bound in Great Britain by Mackays of Chatham.

PREFACE

EDMUND HOYLE first published his " Short Treatise on Whist " in the year 1742 ; in 1748 came the eighth edition, including in it 'chapters on Quadrille, Piquet, and Backgammon ; and a few years later he put out his final edition —the 11th—with an additional Chapter on Chess.

It is from such beginnings that the present compendium of over eighty games and varieties takes its source as well as its name ; and it has been the object of the editor to maintain the high standard set by the original, so that the good old phrase " according to Hoyle " should keep its universal significance and imply that he who plays the game according to the rules and suggestions here given will not only always play absolutely correctly, but will have the best chance of success.

There have been so many editions of " Hoyle," both in England and in America, since the death of its first compiler at the ripe old age of 97, in 1769, that it would be well-nigh impossible to say what the precise number of this one would be ; but its more recent forbears are those published under the editorship of the well-known expert, Professor Hoffman, towards the close of the last century, the revision of this which appeared in 1909 and to which Mr. Ernest Bergholt added certain chapters in 1913, bringing the total number of games treated to thirty-two, and the edition of 1923, prepared under the present editorship, in which were included all of these games with, in the cards section alone, some thirty that had not before appeared in the English " Hoyle," and in the later sections a further fifteen. Among the card games treated then for the first time may be mentioned Auction, Contract, Boston, Hearts, Coon-Can, Cassino, Faro, Monte, and Pelmanism ; Petits Chevaux, Sandown, and Minoru were new to the games of chance, and Volunteer Snooker to the Billiards section.

In 1934 the sections on Whist and Auction (pp. 9-38), for which the present editor is solely responsible, were entirely re-written ; and by 1942—in the thick of the second World War—another new edition became necessary, largely on account of the phenomenal advance during the intervening years in the study and play of Contract, as well as various changes in the Laws. For this the editor was indebted to J. T. Bolton, Esq., a well-known expert on many games and branches of sport ; but by 1949 more changes promulgated by the international authority had rendered this to some extent out of date, and so made necessary the rewriting of the earlier part of the article and revision of the score-table at p. 59. For many of the other card games (to p. 192) we are indebted to Major H. S. Browning's " How to Play Cards " (Routledge & Kegan Paul, Ltd.), and would note that the laws of Poker given in this section are those under which the game is played by leading players in this country, and consequently may be accepted as the standard Laws of English Draw Poker. We are further indebted to Major Browning for the chapters on Roulette and Trente-et-Quarante ; to Mr. Ernest Bergholt's " New Book of Patience Games " and his little manual on " Solitaire " ; to Mr. H. F. Lewis's book on Dominoes ; and to Messrs. F. H. Ayres, Ltd., for assistance and permission with reference to Sandown.

Chess made its first appearance in " Hoyle " nearly 200 years ago, but Chess today is not quite the same as then, and we are glad to be able to take advantage of the present edition to include the latest of many revisions ; the number of diagrams has been doubled, the illustrative games much increased, and many of the modern Openings have been treated for the first time. The editor takes full responsibility for this section, and would like to express his indebtedness to the excellent revisions of Hoffer's "Chess" and Cunnington's "How to Play Chess" by J. du Mont, Esq., late editor of *The British Chess Magazine*.

The section on Billiards and other games on the billiard table was much augmented and largely re-written with the assistance of the late George Richmond, Esq., better known as "Spider" and formerly Billiards editor of the "*Pink 'Un*"; and we are grateful to A. Stanley Thorn, Esq., Secretary of the Billiards Association and Control Council, for permission to quote from the latest official Rules. The rules of most of the games played on "the board of green cloth" have undergone modifications in recent years, while Snooker has been gaining vastly in popularity; we are, therefore, glad to be able to include the latest rules governing their play.

With the inclusion for the first time in 1942 of the all-conquering Darts and a selection from among its many variations, and the ever popular Shove-ha'penny with, in the present edition, an article detailing the play and pleasures of Rummy, it may fairly be claimed that the "Hoyle" of today provides a thoroughly up-to-date and comprehensive manual of Indoor Games.

L.H.D.

CONTENTS

PART I

CARD GAMES

ALPHABETICAL CONTENTS

HOYLE'S GAMES

THE WHIST FAMILY

WHIST

WHIST, the venerable parent of all card games played with the full pack, the cards ranking from Ace high to Deuce low, scoring being by tricks and honours—or by tricks only—and one suit being trumps, is still very widely played in spite of the vast, and comparatively modern, popularity of Auction and Contract—to say nothing of " Solo." At the clubs and in the family circle it still finds a following ; while, were it not for the variety known as " Progressive Whist," organizing secretaries of charities up and down the country would have an even harder time of it in raising funds than they have at present. We, therefore, especially as the only legitimate descendant of the original "Hoyle," which was first published by Edmond, of that name, in 1742, and was confined to Whist, make no apology for still placing it in the forefront of *Hoyle's Games Modernized*.

Whist is a partnership game for four players, two against two. The players cut (or draw) for partners, those cutting the two highest cards playing against those cutting the two lowest, the player with the lowest card being first dealer and having the choice of cards and seat. For this purpose—and this purpose only—the Ace counts low ; ties (except in the case of the two highest) cut again ; if two " tied " players are the lowest these play together and cut again for first deal ; if three players tie they cut again ; but in all cases of re-cutting the position of an " original high " or " original low " who does not have to re-cut remains unaffected. Next, the cards are shuffled (dealer having the right to the final shuffle), cut (by dealer's right-hand adversary), and then dealt from left to right.

one at a time and face downwards, the last card being dealt face up to show the trump suit and remaining exposed until it is dealer's turn to play to the first trick, when he takes it into his hand.

As might well be expected in the case of a game with such a long and honoured life as Whist, its Rules are many, and precise ; a large portion of them, however, deal with what might be called the minutiæ of the game—giving, almost in the language of an Income Tax demand note, detailed instructions as to the procedure to be adopted in every circumstance that possibly can—but very rarely does—arise, and so forth. They are easily obtainable in pocket form so we are not reprinting them here in full, giving from them, instead, all the essentials and everything that is necessary for a thorough understanding of the way in which the game should be played.

To begin with the DEAL—which commences with the player who cut the original lowest card and passes to the left until the completion of the rubber. There must be a new deal by the same dealer if (i) during the deal or the play of the hand the pack proves to be incorrect ; (ii) if any card—except the last—be faced ; and (iii) if any player takes up another player's hand. This is the strict rule ; but in many circles by previous agreement the exposure of a card during the deal may be overlooked, in which case the exposed card cannot be " called " during play. A player dealing out of turn should be stopped before the trump card is turned ; if he is not the deal stands, and the game proceeds as though no mistake had been made. A dealer who misdeals loses the deal ; unless, during dealing, he had been interrupted by an opponent or during the deal an opponent had touched the cards and dealer's partner had not. Any player during the play of the hand may ask dealer to name the trump *suit*, but not the trump *card ;* and a player naming the latter during play may be penalized by a call for his highest or lowest trump, which he is bound to play unless such play would cause him to revoke.

This brings us to an important point in Whist—the REVOKE. It is a revoke when a player, holding one or more cards of the suit led, plays a card of a different suit, and the penalty for it is at the option of the adversaries, who, at the end of the hand, may either take three tricks from the revoking player and add them to their own tricks, or deduct three points from his score, or add three to their own score (the adversaries being allowed to consult as to which penalty they will exact) ; the penalty cannot be divided—that is, a player cannot add one or two to his own score and deduct one or two from the revoking side ; and it can be enforced for as many revokes as occur in the hand. Further, under no circumstances can a player win the game by the result of the hand during which he has revoked ; he cannot score more than four. From all of which it will be seen what a very serious matter a revoke at Whist is.

Cards Exposed or Played in Error :

An " exposed " card is one accidentally—or otherwise —shown or named by the player holding it ; all such cards are liable to be " called " by the other side and must be left or placed face upwards on the table ; similarly a player who, under the impression (or otherwise) that the result of the game is not open to doubt, lays his cards face up on the table, exposes them. The opponents may call an exposed card at any time during the play, and it must then be played, unless this would cause the player to revoke.

If a player play top card to an incomplete trick and then leads winning cards again without waiting for his partner to play, the latter may be called upon to win any of these tricks, and the other cards thus improperly played are treated as exposed cards.

If third player plays before second, fourth may play before his partner ; but if fourth play before second and third he may be called on to win or to lose the trick. If any player omits to play to a trick and the error is not discovered till he has played to the next the adversaries may claim a new deal ; should they not do so the surplus card is considered to have been played to the imperfect trick, but does not constitute a revoke therein.

Except in the case of a revoke partners may not consult as to exacting a penalty or as to which to exact when there are alternatives ; if they do so they lose their right to a penalty—as does also a player who demands an unauthorized penalty.

PLAY AND SCORING :

The deal being properly completed, each player picks up his cards and—for his own convenience—sorts them into suits. The player to the left of the dealer (the " elder hand ") now " leads," that is, plays any card he chooses, and the rest follow in turn, each playing a card of the same suit if holding one ; when all have played the player of the highest card of the suit led—or of the highest trump, if the suit has been trumped—takes the trick and leads to the next. This continues until all thirteen tricks have been played.

The object of the Whist player is to win the " Rubber," and a rubber consists of three " Games," or " Hands," of thirteen tricks each, each game consisting of five points, which are scored as follows :—(i) By tricks ; each trick above six (the " book ") made counts 1 point ; (ii) By " Honours " ; Ace, K, Q, and J of the trump suit are the honours ; a side holding all four (how divided is of no consequence) score 4 points ; holding three, 3 points ; and below three nothing ; but partners who at the commencement of the deal held a score of 4 towards game cannot score at all for honours. It will be seen from this that a score of 8 tricks (2 above the book) and 3 honours gives " Game."

Though 5 points constitute a game the *value* of the game varies with the points scored by the adversaries ; thus, if the adversaries have not scored the winners gain a " treble " (game of 3 points), if they have scored less than 3 the winners gain a " double," and if 3 or 4 points the winners gain a " single." The winners of the rubber are also awarded 2 additional points ("rubber points") ; when the first two games of a rubber are won by the same side the third is not played ; and when three games are played the value of the losers' game is deducted from the gross number of points gained by the winners.

The ultimate *value* of a rubber, therefore, depends largely upon the value of its component games. For instance : AB have won two singles and YZ a treble. Here the points scored by AB are 1 + 1 + 2 (rubber) = 4, but from them are deducted 3 for YZ's treble, the nett value of the rubber being 4 − 3, or 1. This is the smallest value a rubber can have, the highest being 8 points (3 + 3 + 2), which are made when two trebles are scored by the winners and nothing by the losers.

How to Play :

The first step to becoming a good Whist player, after making oneself thoroughly acquainted with the Rules, is to learn the leads that long experience has proved to be the best. The original lead should be from the strongest (*i.e.*, the longest) suit—the one possible exception being when the hand contains three cards in three suits and four in the other, this being "trumps": here it may be unwise to lead from trumps, but even here it can be held that in the long run nothing will be lost by such play.

When holding *in plain suits*—

A, K, Q, J—lead (1st) K, (2nd) J.
A, K, Q—(1st) K, (2nd) Q.
A, K, and others—(1st) K, (2nd) A.
A, K (only)—(1st) A, (2nd) K.
K, Q, J, and 1 small—(1st) K, (2nd) J.
K, Q, J, and 2 or more—(1st) J, (2nd) K if 5, Q if more.
A and 4 or more small—(1st) A, (2nd) 4th best of those left.
K, Q, and others—(1st) K, (2nd, if K wins) 4th best of those left.
A, Q, J, with or without 1 small—(1st) A, (2nd) Q.
A, Q, J, with 2 or more—(1st) A, (2nd) J.
K, J, 10, 9—(1st) 9, (2nd, if A or Q falls) K.
K, J, 10—10.
Q, J, 10, 9—(1st) Q, (2nd) 9.
Q, J, and 1 small—(1st) Q.
Q, J, and 2 or more—4th best.

When holding *in trumps*—

A, K, Q, J—lead (1st) J, (2nd) Q.
A, K, Q—(1st) Q, (2nd) K.
A, K, and 5—(1st) K, (2nd) A.
A, K, and less than 5 small—4th best.
And if holding none of these combinations lead the 4th highest from the longest suit.

For subsequent leads, also, the principle indicated above must be followed, remembering always that the object of opening up a suit is eventually to win a trick or tricks in the suit, so that once the K or Q has become the established winner this naturally would be led out. Later on in the hand the saving of the game may be vital, or the winning of it in sight, when in either case it might be the obvious play to lead an ace at once to make certain of the trick. But the leader (and all players when leading) must be careful not to play a card—even his best—which one adversary can trump and the other discard to. This lead, as a rule, is certain to cause loss, and the situation can always be known provided the conventional leads are stuck to ; but before showing this by example, we must touch on the play by the original leader's partner. The conventional play for him, and for all players when in similar situation, is most important and allows of no variation. *Win with the smallest and return the highest.* This means that third player, when holding cards of equal value, must play the smallest and, if he wishes to return the suit, must lead the highest. Thus a player holding A, K, Q of the suit opened will win with the Queen, and lead back the Ace—that is, of course, if it is advisable to return that suit. Or should the third player hold J, 10, 9 of his partner's suit, he will head the trick with the 9, and when leading the suit back play the J. Under other circumstances the leader's partner must play his highest card in the suit, and return the highest if he originally held three of the suit, and the lowest if more.

Now we can see how the correct original lead combined with correct play by third in hand will, as a rule, indicate the position of remaining cards of the suit.

Original leader has Q, 9, 8, 6, 2, and correctly leads the 6 ; his partner plays the A and returns the 3 ; second player replies with the K, original leader plays the deuce, and fourth player a small one. The position is now clear. Original leader's partner holds no more of the suit—he cannot possibly have held more than three originally (had he held remaining unseen cards, viz., J and 10, by convention he would return the J, or had he held one of them, he would have led it back, being the highest of three). Thus his 3 is single ; further, this player having observed that his partner led the 6 and then played the 2, knows for certain that his partner holds exactly three more of the suit, the 6 being his fourth best.

Note that there are two exceptions to this play : (*a*) When leader's partner holds A, Q in his partner's suit (a " compulsory finesse ") he plays his Q, finessing against the K, and if it wins returns the A, when the fall of the cards to these two rounds will show leader the exact position of the remaining cards ; and (*b*) When A and K only are held in the suit led, win the trick with A and lead K back, and leader will know that that is the extent of your holding in that suit. Leader's partner *must* give this signal—the adversaries *may* do so if they wish to ruff on the third round; it is only employed when holding A, K cards (not K, Q, or Q, J, etc.).

Further, it should not be assumed that the suit *must* be returned at the first opportunity. One may wish to show his own suit first, when he becomes an original leader, and must lead according to the usual convention; and it is often wiser to open your own suit, if you have one worth trying to establish. The immediate return of your partner's suit may tell him that no more are held, and that you want to trump on the third round.

WHEN TO PLAY TRUMPS:

It is a universally established rule that trumps should be led when five or more are held, and none but the most expert player should ever depart from it. A player holding five trumps or more should " call " trumps at the first opportunity. The " call " is the most important convention at Whist; it is made by playing an unnecessarily high card and following it with a lower. Thus, second player holds 10, 6, 3 in the suit led. To trick one he plays the 6, to the next he drops the 3. He has called for trumps and his partner, when he gets the lead, must comply—the Ace, if held, must be played at once; otherwise the highest of three and the lowest of four. A call for trumps cannot be made with honours, because with such cards the player may have to play the high before the low cards in ordinary play. Thus second player holds Q, J, 2 of the opened suit: by rule he must play his J and his 2 next time. This would not be a call for trumps. Players must distinguish between the " call " and the ordinary play of cards in their correct order. Again, no player (except the expert) is justified in refusing to lead trumps when his partner has called. Perhaps he may be anxious to keep his trumps for ruffing; he should not do so; he must obey the command of his partner, who very likely himself holds the cards his partner is anxious to ruff.

The player having started or called for trumps would not keep on leading them if he finds them awkwardly placed in the adversaries' hands: he must be guided by circumstances. For instance, if an adversary should call for trumps, the player holding five should not lead them, since that would be playing the adversaries' game. When holding three trumps, a doubtful card should be ruffed, when holding more it should be passed, since one player will at once know his partner's numerical strength in trumps by noticing whether he ruffs or passes. There are occasions, too, when even a winning card would not be trumped—this when a player is very strong in trumps, and it is to his advantage not to weaken his hand by ruffing. This is tantamount to a call for trumps, and the partner, as a rule, should play trumps when he gets the lead. The minimum strength on which one should lead or call for trumps is four with two honours, and some outside strength either in leader's hand or marked in partner's. If you are weak in trumps you should not force your partner—*i.e.*, lead a card that will take a trump from him —unless he has shown that he wants you to do so.

DISCARDING :

The discard may be grouped under three heads :—

(1) When trumps have not been led nor called for by adversaries, discard lowest of weakest suit.

(2) When adversaries have indicated strength in trumps either by leading or calling, discard lowest of strongest suit.

(3) When partner has led trumps, discard lowest of weakest suit, except when holding all the top cards in a suit, when winning card should be thrown away to show partner that you hold the others. But when partner has indicated strength in trumps, doubtful cards should be ruffed, irrespective of trumps in hand.

These are the general lines on which a hand at Whist should be played, but each rule must be varied according to circumstances, and it is in recognising the exceptions that good players show their superiority over the slaves of the book.

The most obvious cases when play must vary arise when the state of the score demands the playing of a *coup*. Suppose that three more tricks are necessary either to win or save a game : a player holding A, K, and two small trumps, would trump a doubtful card immediately, thus making the three necessary tricks certain. Again, you have to win two tricks and hold the A and Q of trumps : each player has three cards, but who holds the K of trumps is uncertain, though you know your left-hand adversary holds nothing but trumps. Your right-hand adversary leads a winning card in a plain suit. *You must not trump.* Your left-hand adversary *must*, and then lead up to your A, Q, when you make both no matter who holds the K. These are obvious *coups*. A more difficult one is when, with three cards left, you hold K, J, and small one of a suit led, the A being gone, but cannot place the Q. The K should not be played, since then the next lead would have to be made from J and small : play the small card, when the lead may come back to you fourchette of K, J, and you win both, unless you require but one trick to win, when play the K at once.

It is the play to the last four or five tricks that really counts, and by then the player who has followed the play should be able to place most of the unseen cards fairly accurately. A note must be made of the state of the score ; take no risks if the game is in danger, make sure of winning it at the earliest opportunity, but take any risk if that is the only way of saving the game. Thus, suppose adversaries held the four honours, risk all to win the odd trick ; even if you lose the lot, you are no worse off than in failing to win seven.

The notes to the play of the following hand bring out some important points. A and B play Y and Z ; Z deals and turns up 4 D : the hands held are :—

B—H, A, Q, 2 ; D, Q, 9, 6, 3 ; C, 9, 2 ; S, K, 9, 6, 5.
Y—H, 8, 4 ; D, K, 10, 8, 7, 2 ; C, A, J ; S, Q, 10, 7, 4.
Z—H, 10, 5, 3 ; D, 5, 4 ; C, K, Q, 10, 8, 7, 6 ; S, A, 8.
A—H, K, J, 9, 7, 6 ; D, A, J ; C, 5, 4, 3 ; S, J, 3, 2

Trick	A	Y	B	Z	Tricks Won A-B	Tricks Won Y-Z	Trick	A	Y	B	Z	Tricks Won A-B	Tricks Won Y-Z
1	7 H	8 H	Q H	3 H	1	–	5	J S	A S	K S	A S	3	2
2	6 H	4 H	A H	5 H	2	–	6	A D	8 D	6 D	5 D	4	2
3	J H	2 D	2 H	10 H	2	1	7	K H	10 D	Q D	8 S	5	2
4	J D	7 D	3 D	4 D	3	1	8	3 C	A C	9 C	Q C	5	3

The winning card in each trick is *underlined*.

Trick 1.—A leads fourth highest of longest suit ; Y, with five trumps, starts a call for trumps with an unnecessarily high card ; B takes the compulsory finesse of Q, from A, Q.

Trick 2.—B, having nothing worth opening, returns partner's suit. Y's call is now complete.

Trick 3.—All remaining Hearts are now marked in A's hand.

Trick 5.—A must not play Hearts now, since one adversary will ruff and the other discard, and it would put his partner in an awkward position. He leads the *highest* of three cards. Z, of course, covers with Q, 10, and small.

Trick 6.—Z, of course, must go on with trumps : the fall of the cards has told their position—Y started with five and remains with two, as also does B. This is known from the first round of trumps when Y led his 7 (now seen to be his lowest), therefore he held four only after trumping Trick 2. As Z could not cover the 7 and has now led the 5, it is clear that *he holds no more.*

Trick 7.—The fall of the cards here should be studied. A correctly goes on with Hearts since it will force the strong adversary and must establish one trump in his partner's hand—no matter what the two remaining trumps are. Y, of course, must trump, though he expects the over-ruff. Z discards from his weakest suit.

Trick 8.—Y's play here is excellent. B leads Clubs (higher of two) for two reasons. He dare not lead Spades, since he remains with second best, and must wait for that lead to come from elsewhere, and further, he wants to put his partner in to go in with his Hearts, when he (B) must make his remaining (and losing) trump. The Club is the best chance. Z plays Q by convention, but his partner overtakes the trick—a dangerous proceeding, but Y is an excellent player and knows what he is about. The 9 must be B's best Club, and Z's strong suit. Playing the Q second in hand, and B not being able to cover, marks Z with the K. The position of the 10 and others is doubtful, but if Y does not play the A now, he must block his partner suppose he holds this 10. Thus nothing can be lost by the overtake, and further, it is necessary to gain the lead to extract B's remaining trump. Y now leads K of trumps and then J of Clubs, which Z, in his turn, overtakes with the K, and Y Z make the rest.

AUCTION.

THE development of Auction from Whist was gradual, and took place by way of the now extinct game, " Bridge," which had wide popularity in the closing years of the last and the opening years of the present century. Laws of Auction Bridge, as it was originally called, were first officially issued in England in 1908 ; these were subsequently revised at various dates, and the game is now played under the Code issued by the Portland Club, the Whist Club of New York, and the Commission Française du Bridge in 1932.

The main points in which Auction differs from Whist are :—

(a) The trump suit is not left to chance.

(b) The scoring generally is more complicated, the suits have different values, viz., the value of each odd trick (i.e., each above six) is :—

When Clubs	arc trumps .		.	.	6
,, Diamonds	,, ,,	.	.	.	7
,, Hearts	,, ,,	.	.	.	8
,, Spa les	,, ,,	.	.	.	9
and when there are no trumps		.	.	.	10

(c) It does not follow that the side scoring the greater number of points wins the rubber.

(d) The game can be won on any deal only by the side having the play of the hand, and cannot be lost by that side.

(e) One hand is exposed, becoming dummy, and is played by the partner of the player to whom it was dealt

The preliminaries are practically as at Whist : that is, two complete packs of 52 cards are used and are dealt (see p. 21) by four players who draw for partners—a shuffled pack being spread face downwards, each drawing a card and exposing it when all have drawn.

As soon as the deal is completed the " Auction " commences, its object being to obtain the privilege of playing the combined hands of declarer and dummy by making the highest bid. The dealer opens it either by making a declaration or by passing, in which case he says " No bid." By his declaration, bid, or call the caller undertakes to make the number of odd tricks mentioned in the suit he names trumps, or in No-trumps, as the case may be.

Each player in succession to the left must now call or pass, and the auction continues until a call has been passed by the three following players, the player who has made the final bid (which is necessarily the highest) and his partner become the declaring side, the player who first bid the suit (or No-trump) in which the hand is to be played is the Declarer, his final bid the Declaration, and his partner Dummy.

"Highest bid" needs a little explanation. A bid, which is one of the three possible calls (the others being a Pass, and a Double or Redouble) is an offer to contract that if the hand is played in the suit (or No-trump) named the Caller's side will win at least as many odd tricks as are specified ; after the dealer the eldest hand (dealer's left-hand adversary) has next bid, then dealer's partner, then the next player, and then dealer again, and so on ; but each player in his turn must bid something higher—*i.e.*, of greater scoring value—than the previous bid—or pass, or double the previous bid. When two bids are of equal scoring value, the bid that involves more tricks outbids the other : for instance, 3 Hearts (24) are overcalled by 4 Clubs (24), for although the score is the same in each case the Club call involves a greater number of odd tricks. During the auction any player may in his turn double the preceding bid of an opponent or redouble one that has been doubled by an opponent, making the scoring value of odd tricks in the suit named worth double (or quadruple, as the case may be) their usual value ; but doubling in no way affects the value of the bid for the purpose of the auction, nor the right of the player whose bid has been doubled (or redoubled) to bid again. Thus ; say the bid of 2 Hearts is doubled and redoubled ; that makes the declaration, if won, worth 32 a trick, but the bid remains worth 16 only and could be overcalled with 2 Spades ; and there is nothing to prevent the caller of a redoubled suit playing for safety by "switching over" to such a call himself.

The auction over, we come to the play, the object of which is to win—first the game, second the rubber. Game is won by the side that first scores 30 points for tricks declared and won, and the rubber by the side that first wins two games, the winners of the rubber adding a bonus of 250 to their score. The trick points are as stated above (p. 19) ; these, when the declaring side has been successful, are entered below the line drawn across the scoring-block, all other scores are entered above the line and come in only at the end of the rubber when the difference between the two complete totals is the number of points won and lost. Should the declaring side fail to fulfil the contract, that is, make the number of tricks specified in the declaration, they score nothing below the line but their opponents score 50—above the line—for each trick by which they fail (the under-tricks), or 100 if doubled, and 200 if redoubled ; if the declarer has been doubled and makes good his declaration he scores 50 bonus points and another 50 for each trick made over and above his declaration, while if he fails the adversaries score 100 for each under-trick, and these bonuses are doubled if the declaration has been redoubled.

Ace, K, Q, J and 10 rank as Honours in a suit declaration and the four Aces in a No-trump ; they are scored by either side holding them and are not affected by doubling and redoubling. For the scores *see* the Table on p. 37.

Either side winning all thirteen tricks scores 100 for Grand Slam, or winning twelve tricks 50 for Little Slam ; but if the side has contracted to make seven odd tricks and makes six only it cannot score a Little Slam.

Before discussing the considerations that should influence bids and the play of the hand generally, we give the ruling on various questions that arise, the authority being the above-mentioned Laws of 1932.

THE DEAL :—Unlike Whist, at Auction the deal goes to the player drawing the highest card, Ace counting *high*, and cards of equal value ranking by suit, Q or 4 of Hearts, for instance, beating Q or 4 of Clubs ; the dealer of the first hand of a rubber has the choice of seat and pack, and thereafter each player to the left deals in turn. Further, a deal is not lost through a misdeal, nor by dealing with a pack containing a faced card, nor by exposing a card ; in any such case dealer must deal again with the same pack, as also if he should deal out of turn and be stopped before the last card is dealt. A new deal may also be demanded in the case of certain irregularities in the bidding and for the omission to play to a trick (*see below*).

THE AUCTION :—If in bidding a slip of the tongue is made and the bid is immediately amended the revised bid stands ; if an insufficient bid is made and the caller corrects it in the same suit before player on his left has called or any player has drawn attention to the irregularity, he is not penalised and the corrected bid stands, as also if the next player calls before the irregularity has been noticed , but in the case of an insufficient bid that is not corrected the player on the left of the offender may allow it to stand (when it ranks as a sufficient bid) ; or he may treat the number of tricks named as raised sufficiently in the same denomination to overbid the previous bid (or to seven, whichever is the lower), in which case the offender's partner must pass in his next turn unless an opponent has overbid or doubled ; or he may close the auction, when the bid next before the offending bid becomes the declaration, including any double or redouble that may have been made.

There is no penalty for an out-of-turn *pass*, nor is there for an out-of-turn *call* if the player on the offender's left has called before it has been noticed, and in either case calling proceeds in the ordinary way ; but if a call is made before bidding has started, when it is the turn of the offender's partner or of his opponent on the left, that opponent may either claim a new deal or ignore the irregularity—in which case the bidding proceeds. If a player calls when it is the turn of the opponent on his *right* that opponent has his call and the bidding proceeds, but the offender's partner must pass at his next call.

A new deal may be demanded by the player on the left of a player who has made an impossible or illegal bid or double ; alternatively, this player may ignore the call, in which case the call is treated as a " pass," or he may hold a bidder of eight or more tricks to a bid of seven ; and he may allow an illegal double or redouble to stand. If one of the declarer's opponents makes a bid (not a pass) after the auction is closed, declarer may call a lead from offender's partner when it is first the turn of the latter to lead.

At any time before the opening lead any player may have all the calls repeated, but afterwards he may only ask what is the contract and whether—but not by whom— it was doubled or redoubled.

If before the auction is closed a player exposes a non-honour card, not meaning to lead it, the eventual declarer may, if an opponent of the offender, treat the card as though exposed during play (*see* p. 24), or disallow offender's partner leading the exposed suit on his first lead ; if the exposure is an honour, or more than one card, or any card with intent to lead, the player on offender's left may claim a new deal.

IRREGULAR PLAY :—If an opponent plays to an out-of-turn lead it must be treated as a correct lead ; but if declarer is the offender either opponent, before it is covered, may require him to lead from the correct hand, in which case he must lead from the same suit if able to do so. If he leads from either hand when it is an opponent's turn either opponent may ask him to take the card back, but he may not do so without being so asked.

If an opponent leads out of turn the declarer may, before playing to the trick from either hand, call a suit from the offending side when first an opponent has the lead, treating the card led out of turn—if it is not an opponent's turn to lead—as an exposed card until it is an opponent's turn to lead ; or he may treat the card wrongly led as an exposed card, and if it is still in this case when it is next the turn of the offender's partner to lead, forbid the lead to be made in that suit : or he may treat the card as a card led in turn.

If declarer plays to an opening lead by the wrong opponent he becomes Dummy and his partner Declarer.

If in playing to a trick one of declarer's opponents plays when it was his partner's turn or leads to the next trick or exposes a card before his partner has played to the trick in progress, declarer has the option of requiring the offender's partner either to win the trick (even by trumping), to lose it, or to discard from a given suit—always providing that the player cannot be required to revoke. But if declarer plays a card from either hand out of turn, after having led from the other hand, fourth hand may play before second and no penalty can be exacted.

A player holding a surplus card through omission to play to a trick is penalized as follows :—If he, not being Dummy, has led or played to a trick subsequent to the offence the declarer—or the opponent on the declarer's left, as the case may be—may demand a new deal ; if this is not done (and, also, if Dummy is the delinquent) the offender must at once withdraw a card from his hand, whenever possible one which could have been played to the defective trick.

EXPOSED CARDS :—An exposed card is one dropped face upwards on the table, but one dropped elsewhere in such a manner that its face can be seen only by an opponent (also one held in such a manner) is not technically " exposed." The two last cards held by an opponent of declarer are also exposed if before he had played to the twelfth trick his partner has shown his last card, and so is any card that a player holds if he has indicated by word of mouth that he holds it.

We have already (pp. 22-23) explained the procedure in the case of a card exposed during the auction ; after its close, if an opponent of declarer exposes a card that card is left face up on the table and declarer may call upon its owner to lead or play it whenever it is his turn, provided that this would not entail a revoke. Note that no penalty attaches to declarer or his partner for exposing a card after the auction is closed.

DUMMY'S RIGHTS AND DISABILITIES :—Dummy has the same rights as any player, except that he does not play his hand and he may not make any suggestions regarding the play to declarer (though if asked by him he may say which hand has the lead). He may not call attention to an opponent's revoke, out-of-turn lead, or exposure of a card ; but he may question declarer with regard to a suspected revoke by him, though if he does so after having intentionally seen a card in any other hand declarer may not withdraw his card.

If Dummy in any way suggests the play of a card the opponent on his left may (provided no revoke would arise) call upon declarer to play or not to play that card ; while if he calls declarer's attention to any irregularity on the part of an opponent declarer is debarred from enforcing the penalty attached thereto. He may call attention to the wrong gathering of tricks and to certain faulty play, as the playing of the wrong number of cards to a trick and the playing by declarer of two cards from one hand and none from the other ; he has the same right to see a trick before it is turned and quitted as the other players ;* and he may consult with his partner as to the revoke

* The penalty for unlawfully looking at a quitted trick is that the declarer—or the opponent on his left, as the case may be—may say which suit is to be led when it is next the turn of the offender's side to lead.

penalty, may take part in discussions, and may correct an erroneous score, a misstatement of fact, or an opponent's erroneous claim to a penalty.

THE REVOKE :—At Auction an established revoke (*see* p. 10) is penalized by the transfer of two tricks from the revoking side to the other side at the end of the hand (the trick itself remaining as played), and one trick for any subsequent revoke by the same side in the same hand ; but no trick won before the first revoke, nor any trick transferred from the other side under this rule, shall be transferred.

A revoke does not become " established " until—the offender or his partner leads or plays to the next trick, if the revoke was made in *playing* ; or, the offender's partner plays to the trick, if it was made in *leading*. Until it is established it is open to the player to correct his revoke by playing (or leading) a correct card ; if revoker is an adversary, declarer may either treat the card played in error as an exposed card or may call on the offender to play the highest or lowest held in the correct suit ; if declarer himself is the offender and has revoked from his own hand, the player on his left may, after he has played to the trick, call upon him to play in its place the highest or lowest held in that suit, while if declarer has revoked from dummy there is no penalty ; and no penalty attaches to a card played to a trick after a revoke which has been corrected—it cannot be treated as an exposed card.

How TO BID :—There are three main considerations in the bidding for trumps, (a) to get the declaration for yourself, (b) to prevent your opponent getting it, and (c) to give information. The first two might seem to run concurrently but, as will be seen, this is not so. Having first call you could always get the declaration by bidding Grand Slam in No-trumps ; this, of course, would be an absurdity, but when opponent is bidding against you, you should, however, bid up the maximum trick value of your hand, sometimes with the object of getting the declaration yourself, sometimes to keep opponent out. There are occasions when you must call above your trick value—as, for instance, to make your opponent overcall himself, though, of course, you are overcalling on your own account and may be left to struggle with a hopeless contract. This is where judgment tells, to know how far an adversary will be pushed—this is where the real skill in Auction comes in. As an example, your opponent is twenty-two and his bid of 1 Heart is in ; at all costs outbid him, since 1 Heart will give him game ; he is sure to bid up to 2 or 3, and in this he may fail, when you not only save the game but get a bonus.   The converse of this situation requires attention ; suppose the score is love all and your opponent is in the bid with 1 Club or Diamond—the game is not in much danger in this declaration, he has to score five odd to win it, so it might be unwise to disturb the bid.   At the same time you would not allow your adversary to walk over in 1 Club or Diamond if you happened to hold a potential game-winner yourself ; always bearing in mind that if you do make an effort for the declaration you are thereby opening up the bidding to the other side to get away into a suit that may hurt.   Say, as fourth caller, you hold 3 small Spades, 3 small Hearts, 2 small Clubs, and Ace, K to five Diamonds, and the adversary holds the call with 1 or 2 Clubs, you should not overcall in Diamonds, although it would be perfectly legitimate on your holding.   If you do he may switch to Spades, Hearts or even No-trumps, and go game. Therefore leave him alone to make what he may in Clubs —he will hardly make game.   If, however, in the same situation the call against you is 1 Spade, Heart, or No-trump, then bid 2 Diamonds without hesitation ; not that you expect good results, but you must try to shift your opponent from his dangerous call—or make him bid beyond his strength.   Against a No-trump bid, always call two in a suit if it is not your own lead—and, as a rule, if it is.   Here you score in two ways, you push the adversary and at the same time tell your partner what suit to open.

This giving and obtaining of information is the third of the main considerations mentioned above.   Many players would be inclined to rank it first, for one's first duty is to discover the best way of co-operating with one's partner in the main business of making game and winning the rubber ; and, as the only way is by bidding, one's first call should be for an informational more than for a trick-getting purpose, and should therefore be made according to the conventions.   Conventional bids are solely for the purpose of giving information ; they apply to the first round of bidding only, and if the state of the hand (taken in conjunction with preceding bids) is such that it is impossible for you to make one of them then, and then only, may the declaration of No Bid be made. And do not forget that a first bid especially must be *sound;* that is, the information that it conveys, whether positive or negative, must be absolutely reliable—though it need not be complete—and, further, that declarer must be prepared, if necessary, to fulfil the contract. Even with a hand that is good for 5 or 6 Spades some players will always refuse—except when the state of the score calls for a pre-emptive or shutting-out bid—to bid more than 1 on the first round ; that is perfectly all right, for there is nothing misleading about it, but it would be perfectly all wrong to call 1 on 8 or even more to the J, because that is tantamount to announcing that you hold, if not Ace and K of the suit, then either Ace *or* K with another honour and at least one quick trick in an outside suit.

The conventional bids, for use in first round bidding only, are as follows :—

A bid of ONE in any suit shows that declarer holds one of the following :—

Trumps	Headed by—	Outside Strength
Four	3 Honours, J low	1 sure quick trick
Four	A, K and Q	None necessary
Five or more ...	A or K and Minor Honour	1 sure quick trick
Five or more ...	A and K	None necessary

The bid of TWO in a MINOR suit shows that declarer holds at least 5 trumps to the A, K, Q, with insufficient outside strength for a No-trumper.

The bid of TWO in a MAJOR suit (Hearts or Spades) shows long trumps headed by A or K, and at least 6 tricks if the specified suit is trumps.

THREE or more bid in a MINOR suit signifies that declarer expects to make game if the hand is played with the trumps specified.

THREE bid in a MAJOR suit shows 7 sure tricks in declarer's hand, and a bid of FOUR 9 sure tricks with the specified suit as trumps.

A bid of ONE NO-TRUMP shows that declarer holds either (a) the four suits all stopped, (b) three suits stopped—one of them with an Ace, (c) three K-Q or K-J suits, or (d) five solid Clubs or Diamonds with at least one outside Ace.

A bid of TWO NO-TRUMPS indicates a holding of 6 or more solid Clubs or Diamonds with at least an Ace or guarded K in two other suits.

The basic principles in bidding for trumps are that the cards, and certain combinations of cards, have a definite average value as trick winners and that the total of these values held gives the average playing value of the hand ; all bidding is based on averages.

There are 13 tricks to be played for at each deal, so if each player has his fair share of strength his hand will be worth 3¼ tricks. Now if dealer sees 4 tricks in his hand he ought to be able to make a call of 1 because, as there are 9 tricks left and we are justified in assuming that they are equally divided between the remaining players, his partner will have 3, giving 7 tricks between the two hands, and this is the lowest possible bid.

There are three distinct classes of calls, and these must be thoroughly understood if success is to be attained :— (1) The free, or voluntary bid ; (2) the assist, or the supporting bid ; and (3) the forced bid.

(1) A free bid is one made when the opponent has not yet spoken, and to make it, it is necessary to hold considerable strength in the suit named. Strength means high cards—honour strength. The minimum in Spades or Hearts is 5 headed by K Q, or 4 to Ace K : to call Diamonds or Clubs, at least Ace, K, Q to 5, or Ace, Q, 10 to 6—or similar strength—but in all cases the top honours must be there.

Remember that a free bid informs partner that caller can make tricks in that suit, and remember, too, that a bid in a major suit is an attacking bid, and in a minor suit defensive or informatory. If you hold 5 to the Ace K in Hearts or Spades bid 1, for if the cards are evenly distributed you will exhaust the trumps in the third round and make four tricks in that suit. Similarly, with the same holding in a minor suit you would also call 1 ; but, whereas in the former case your partner will take you out only if he is unable to help, here you *invite him* to do so. Hence it is argued that, as it is unlikely that a Club or Diamond call will be left with the declaration, length in a minor suit is much less important than strength, and a player holding an average hand with, say, 4 Clubs or Diamonds to the Ace K J, should call it and so show his partner his strength.

In a hand that looks like a No-trumper the " Robertsonian rule," in helping one to decide whether or not to call it, as slightly amended by Mr. Ernest Bergholt in his

" Auction Bridge " (Routledge & Kegan Paul, Ltd.), is of great service. An Ace—not being a singleton—counts 8, a guarded K 5, Q 3, J 2, and 10, if of independent value, 1 ; a singleton Ace is valued at 3 only, an unguarded K at 2 and Q at 1. On this system 19 points in a hand gives an average holding and is, therefore, the very minimum on which one can, in the absence of favourable information from previous bids, call a No-trump ; and it is rarely advisable to do so under a count of 22.

Experts are still undecided, but opinion leans to making the No-trump call on a very minimum of all-round strength ; some players will risk it on J and 10 in Hearts, Q, J, 9 and 8 in Diamonds, K and 6 of Clubs, and 10, 9, 8 and 7 of Spades—though the count gives a total of only 15—the idea being to tell partner that you have something, though it fails a suit call, and also to get first run at the call yourself. But as first caller you must not declare a No-trump without a genuine No-trump hand, and to be justified in calling it as fourth hand you should have at least 20 per cent. above that.

The most difficult hand to declare is one that is really worth calling a suit on—but does not contain the necessary high honours. Thus, six Hearts to the 10, with, say, Ace and 2 of Spades, K, Q, 3 and 2 of Diamonds, and a small Club is surely likely to be successful in Hearts, yet you must not call it ; such a call would deceive partner. Some players call 2 Hearts on this holding, to inform partner that the suit is sound, but has no high honours. Our advice, however, is to pass, and to call 2 on the second round. The hand on which to call 2 or 3 tricks straight off is the hand which calls for silence from partner—it is a " preemptive " call. With Ace, K, J, 10, 8, 4 Hearts : K, J, 10, 9, 2 Diamonds ; Ace, Q Clubs—call 3, or even 4 Hearts ; shut partner out, tell him to keep quiet !

(2) The supporting bid, or " assist," is a raise in your partner's call, usually—but not necessarily—after it has been overcalled. If you have a better game-going suit of your own you will, of course, call it and await events ; if not, and you are strong enough to raise, you will do so. Strength in the trump suit is not essential but you *must* hold outside strength, and you *must* hold more than the 3 tricks with which your partner credited you when he called 1.

In valuing your hand for supporting purposes in suit declarations, guarded trump honours, guarded side-suit K's, and all side-suit Aces count both as tricks and raisers ; singletons in side-suits also count as raisers, and blank suits and singleton side-Aces each as two raisers if you have at least 3 trumps with which to ruff. Remember that in the " assist " a raiser is just as important as a sure trick, that Q's and J's cannot be counted as raisers whether guarded or not (except in No-trumps), and that you must never raise if you hold 3 trickless suits, not even if your strong suit is trumps. Side-Q's do not count because their chance, if it comes at all, comes too late to save the hand. To give an instance : Dealer has bid a Heart, 2nd player a Spade, and you, as 3rd hand, hold Ace, J, 9 and 3 other Hearts ; Q, J Clubs ; Q and 2 small Diamonds ; and Q and 1 small Spade. If with your 6 trumps to the Ace you raise to 2 and your partner happens to have called on 7 trumps with no side trick—which would be quite in order—your opponents may make six tricks with the top honours of Spades, Diamonds and Clubs before you can start on the trumps and you will be down ; if, however, you had been bare of a suit the assist would have been justified ; your trumps would have come in at once, which is why, as we have already mentioned, a blank suit is counted as worth 2 raisers if trumps are held.

Put briefly : if you have not less than 5 values (that is, tricks and raisers) you should assist once, with 6 twice, and with 7 three times ; and if declarer has rebid his hand without help from you, you should then assist if you have 4 values, if he has rebid twice with 3, and if three times, you should do so with only 2. Raising partner from 2 to 3 is the same as raising him from 1 to 2 ; do not refuse to raise if your hand justifies it, for, if you do you may deceive partner ; and resist the temptation to make a raise that is unjustifiable merely in the hope of saving game or rubber. It is your partner who is bidding, and any bluffing or taking of risks must be left to him, for if he gets the declaration it is your hand that will be exposed, not his.

To assist a No-trump call the same general principles apply, with the important exception that ruffing is ruled out. Here length is strength, singletons and blank suits are worthless, and *all* guarded honours count as tricks and raisers. We take it for granted that the No-trump bidder has a stopper in any suit that an opponent has previously called ; but you yourself, before supporting him with a raise, must make certain that you also have a guard in such a suit ; without it the risk is too great and it would be wiser to shift to 2 in a major suit, if you can, when it would still be open to partner to rebid his No-trumper without increasing the contract. Indeed, it is almost axiomatic that one partner, both on strength and on weakness, should, when his holding justifies it, call two in a suit and " take out " the other's No-trump. The hand cannot be too strong for this, but it can be too weak. Thus, on Ace, K, Q to 5 Spades ; Ace, Q and small Heart ; Q, J and 10 Diamonds, take out the No-trump with 2 Spades ; but on 5 or 6 Spades to the J and no other court card, leave the No-trump alone—the hand is too weak. If, however, the Spades are headed by the Ace the switch-over should be made. This is a sort of safety-valve to guard the No-trumper, who, as we have seen, can always go back to two No-trumps if the suit call does not fit in with his holding.

(3) The forced bid. Any except a free bid is a forced bid. After dealer's free bid, 2nd player must try to prevent dealer getting the declaration on a one-bid call, and if dealer has passed and 2nd hand has bid, 3rd hand is then in the same position. Sometimes a forced bid is also a forcing bid, in that the intention is to make opponents overcall ; such a case occurs when, 2nd hand having passed dealer's bid of 1 Heart, 3rd hand raises it to 2 Hearts. The difference between an original free bid and a forced bid is of great importance when it is a question of assisting, for if your partner has passed on the 1st round his 2nd round bid of two or more may be made merely with the intention of forcing opponents, and in any case his passing when he had the opportunity of calling will have told you that he does not hold original bidding strength and that, consequently, your own strength must be considerably greater than in the ordinary way before you can safely raise his bid.

DOUBLING AND REDOUBLING :—The beginner must be very careful about doubling. High contracts become possible from the nature of the game itself—that is to say, given an intelligent understanding of the early bidding, a high contract can be framed with every likelihood of fulfilment. Therefore, even though it may seem an easy business to defeat opponents who have undertaken to make a great number of tricks, it may not be nearly so easy as it looks. Don't double a contract just because it is a high one—only double when you hold such stoppers as make success practically certain, and never double when the suit called is the only one you can defeat or when holding only one strong suit. Remember that if your hand is good enough for a call of 5 Hearts because you have a very long and strong Heart suit, and the adversary has called 5 Spades over you, the chances are that you will not make a trick in Hearts, for most likely the 5 Spade call has been made because one or other of your opponents can ruff Hearts.

It is always dangerous to double a call that will not bring opponents to game if you had not doubled—such as 3 or 4 Diamonds or Clubs when their score is under 12. 18 is not game, neither is 28 ; but 36 and 58 *are*. Opponent probably had a good reason for his call, and it is quite possible that he will pull it off even though you feel certain of defeating him, as the following example of a hand actually played will show :—

    Z—S, J, 10, 9 ; H, 8, 7, 6 ; D, K, Q, J, 10, 9, 8 ; C, K.
    A—S, A, Q, 3, 2 ; H, Q, J, 10, 9 ; D, A ; C, A, 6, 5, 4.
    Y—S, o ; H, A ; D, 7, 6, 5, 4, 3, 2 ; C, Q, J, 10, 9, 8, 7.
    B—S, K, 8, 7, 6, 5, 4 ; H, K, 5, 4, 3, 2 ; D, o ; C, 3, 2.

Z bid 2 Diamonds, A no, Y 4 Diamonds, B no ; and on the second round Z called " No bid," A doubled the 4 Diamonds, and the auction closed. The double looked a certainty—yet, of course, Z made 5 odd tricks.

In addition to the possibility of materially assisting opponents to go game by doubling, another danger is that as a double reopens the bidding, opponents, with the information they now have, may shift from a shaky call to a suit in which the combined hands may be strong ; and this gives rise to the strongly-advocated maxim that one should never double anything unless he can double everything. This sounds sweeping, but there is no doubt about its good sense ; for unless one is prepared to double again, no matter to what suit opponents switch over, the double will be wasted—and worse, because without it you may have been points to the good. A bad double is more expensive than a bad bid : opponents can go game or rubber on the former—and very often do.

You need not hold high trumps to double, but you *must* have at least the book in your hand, and you *must*, as has been said, be prepared to double any call. Remember, too, that if you are on bidder's right you need greater strength than if you are on his left ; but it is nearly always better to win the game yourself than to double opponent. If your opponents can play you will not get them down more than a trick or two—game to your side is worth more than that. Therefore, if you see game in your hand go for it and don't bother about doubles—even though partner is the doubler. In that case, if the double looks doubtful and the game likely, take him out into his own or your suit, for unless you score at least 300 the double has misfired.

The cautions we have given about doubling apply also, and much more strongly, to redoubling ; and especially we would warn the novice *never* to redouble unless he is ready to redouble all round. If you have been doubled and have any doubt about winning you naturally will not redouble ; while if you are certain of pulling it off you must then consider the possibility of your redouble sending opponent back to his suit. In the hand given above you will have noticed that A's double of 4 Diamonds closed the bidding. Y and Z were quite right not to redouble, for had they done so it would have made A and B think—and B would probably have thought to the tune of 4 Spades and, of course, would have got away with it. Never redouble even on a certainty unless you know opponents cannot take advantage of your warning.

There still remains the INFORMATORY DOUBLE. This is an immediate double by the opponent on declarer's left, and is intended only as an invitation to partner to take the caller out with the best call he can make ; it shows a good all-round hand, but one whose strength is insufficient for a two-bid—or for a No-trump if a suit has been called. For instance : dealer bids 1 Spade and player on his left holds only 2 small trumps with the A, K, Q of Hearts, and K, Q and 2 small in both Diamonds and Clubs. He cannot call two of anything, and if he says " One No-trump " and is left with it, Spades are certain to be led up to him and he will be lucky if he makes more than five tricks. So he doubles, knowing that his partner will take him out in two of any suit other than Spades, or with a No-trumper if he holds a guarded Spade honour.

The Informatory Double code has been brought to a high pitch of efficiency in America ; in England the system in most general use is confined to the following rules :—

(1) A double of " One " of a suit or of " One No-trump," is an Informatory Double, whether doubler or doubler's partner has previously bid or not.

(2) A double of " Two " of a suit is informatory unless doubler or doubler's partner has previously bid.

(3) A double of " Three " of a suit or of " Two No-trumps " is always business.

The Play of the Hand.

When playing the hand the Auction player must keep in mind first, the fulfilling of his contract, and after that see about winning the game. In most cases once dummy has exposed his cards, declarer will be able to foretell the result to within a trick or two ; and the result, probably, will depend on a finesse. The previous bidding, of course, must be remembered, as this will help to place the adverse high honours in the foreign suits.

On general lines, when there are trumps they should be extracted at the first opportunity, not failing, however, to utilise dummy's little trumps to ruff losers before doing so. Next, long suits, if any, in dummy or declarer's hands, or in both, should be established, the player being careful to retain cards of entry in the correct hand as otherwise declarer may have to lead away from, instead of up to, his own or dummy's tenaces, and so on, to the utter ruin of the hand.

Every hand dealt needs careful play by declarer—the very good hand to slam, the medium hand to squeeze the contract home, perhaps by bringing in a thirteenth card or by forcing the adversary to unguard a K or Q, and the bad hand to save as much as possible out of the wreck. Success at Auction is due to the extra tricks won on one hand and saved on another. Most players can win tricks with Ace and K—good players make them with tens and nines. Declarer should play the hand according to circumstances as follows : If the contract plainly is hopeless, get as near to it as possible ; if the contract looks possible, make it certain ; if the contract is certain, try for game : if game is certain, win a slam.

A hand by way of example :—

Z has the declaration with a call of 4 Spades ; he holds—S A. 10, 8, 7, 6, H 6, 5, 4, D Q, 10, 9, C A, K ; A leads a Heart, dummy shows—S Q, J, 9, H A, D K, 8, 7, 6, 4. 2, C Q, 3, 2, and at a glance Z sees 9 certain tricks, viz., 4 Spades, 1 Heart, 1 Diamond, and 3 Clubs. To make them his first consideration must be to keep a card of entry in dummy to bring in the Q of Clubs. If Z can catch the K of Spades his contract and game is certain. To catch the K it must lie with B, and Y must lead trump through him. So dummy wants another card of entry : while if Z uses one of dummy's trumps to ruff a Heart, he has a chance of small slam.

All this is obvious. After winning with the Ace of Hearts, the correct play from dummy is a Club ; Z plays away his Ace and K and then leads a Heart. Here the thoughtless player will stumble, for he will trump with the 9, which may prove fatal to his slam. Dummy must trump with an *honour*, play his Q of Clubs, on which Z throws his last Heart, and then dummy leads his other trump honour, which, unless covered by B, declarer runs. If it wins, dummy goes on with his 9 of trumps, and if not covered, declarer can *now overtake* with the 10 and play the Ace, which should catch the K. He leads one more round of trumps, hoping to get a Diamond discarded, when if this suit plays luckily for him the only trick he loses is the Ace of Diamonds. The play of this hand is simple, yet it contains many points worthy of the novice's attention.

Dummy has few privileges, but those he has (*see above*) he should exercise. Most important is to ask invariably whether declarer has a card in a suit he renounces ; but if he has looked at any of the other hands he loses this privilege and if, in spite of the rule, he *does* ask the question and it is found that declarer could have followed suit, the revoke is still established. Some players object to being asked this question, regarding it as a slur on their play. In this they show their ignorance—all good players insist on dummy putting the question ; and, of course, no good dummy will look at the other player's hands if only to avoid losing this advantage. This questioning one's partner holds good, too, on defender's side—one should ask the other ; it is the fault of the revoking player's *partner* that the revoke is not corrected.

The defenders—the side playing against the contract—should make it their first objective to save the game ; their second to get the adversary under. The opening lead is the most difficult ; nine times out of ten it is advisable to lead the suit one's partner has made a call in (if he has called in two suits, the one named first), and the highest card should be led. The exception is when leader himself holds a strong suit—it is often wiser to open this before touching partner's suit. Holding Ace, K and but 1 small in a suit, lead the King and then partner's suit—to open from a suit of 5 to the J in preference to partner's suit would be bad play. In the same way it is generally wiser to return partner's lead before touching your own. The main principles to play on are :—

1. Avoid establishing winners in dummy.
2. Remove dummy's cards of entry.
3. Force the hand that is strong in trumps—
4. But try to prevent dummy getting off his little trumps in ruffs.
5. Unless for a special reason, do not lead a card that partner can ruff, if he will be overruffed.
6. Never lead a card which one opponent can trump and the other throw away on.
7. Don't finesse against partner.
8. Try not to block partner's suit.

The cards should be played in the orthodox manner, *i.e.*, win the trick with the lowest card possible, return the highest held in the suit. Always lead from the top of a sequence—not an intermediate card. Playing false cards does not pay—it always deceives your partner, rarely your adversary.

Against a No-trump declaration the same line of play should be adopted ; but an exceptionally strong suit must be held to open it in preference to partner's suit. And partner's suit should be persevered with whenever opportunity occurs unless, of course, it is plainly hopeless. Branching from suit to suit is fatal—the more suits opened the better for declarer, it clears the air for him, and probably is exactly what he wants. Hold up the winning card of declarer's suits as long as possible, especially in dummy's long suits—don't, however, hold winners so long that they never make.

It is in leading against a No-trumper that what is known as the " Eleven Rule " comes in specially useful—though it is also relied on in leading to a suit declaration when partner has made no bid. Stated briefly it is as follows :—
" Subtract the number of pips on the card led from 11, and tne remainder gives the number of cards higher than that

TABLE OF SCORES.

TRICK SCORE (below the line).	Undbld.	Dbld.	Redbld.
For each Odd Trick :—			
When Clubs are trumps	6	12	24
When Diamonds are trumps	7	14	28
When Hearts are trumps	8	16	32
When Spades are trumps	9	18	36
When played in " No Trumps "	10	20	40

PENALTY SCORE (above opponents' line).			
For each undertrick	50	100	200

PREMIUM SCORE (above the line).			
For making the contract	—	50	100
For each overtrick	—	50	100

For *Honours :—

*Honours and Slams are scored by either side by which they can be claimed.

When played in a trump suit—

5 Honours in one hand	10 times the trick value.		
4 in one and 1 in the other ...	9 "	"	"
4 " " " 0 " " " ...	8 "	"	"
5, divided 3 and 2...	5 "	"	"
4, divided	4 "	"	"
3 (divided or not)...	2 "	"	"

When played in " No Trumps "—

4 Aces in one hand	100
4 Aces divided	40
3 Aces (divided or not)	30

For *Little Slam ... 50   For *Grand Slam ... 100

For Rubber 250

For one Game in Unfinished Rubber 125

led that are not held by leader " ; its essence being that the leader plays *the fourth highest card of his longest suit*. This is one of the most useful of the conventions, and thorough : and, while it will help the declarer also to place the highest cards of the suit, it often enables leader's partner (who, of course, by the time he comes to play has seen dummy's hand as well as his own) to save an honour and still prevent opponents winning the trick.

The following example is given as typical play against No-trumps, and as proof of the importance of hammering away with partner's suit :—

A holds—S J, 10, 2, H K, 8, 7, 6, 4, D 5, 3, 2, C 4, 2 ; and dummy—S K, 6, 5, 4, H Q, 2, D K, Q, 6, C 8, 7, 6, 5. The score is love all ; Z has the declaration with 1 No-trump and A leads the 6 of Hearts—his partner having made no call. Dummy plays the 2, B wins with Ace, Z plays 3. B returns 9 Hearts, Z plays 10, A plays *he 4*, allowing dummy to win the trick with his Q.

The play is correct. A holds no card or re-entry. If he puts up his K now he will never make another trick, since declarer is marked with J. But his partner (B) is also marked with another, therefore if he (B) gets in and leads this Heart, as he should, A wins 3 tricks right off, and the game is saved. It is true that by this play A may never make his K, but that chance must be taken, for to save the game at all B must hold a winner somewhere and, given a winner, A and B score 4 tricks in Hearts against 2 if A plays K to the 2nd trick. Had A held a probable card of entry he ought to have played K at once, and gone on with the suit.

To conclude with a piece of advice that is, to our readers, perhaps more obvious than necessary : if you wish to become a competent Auction player take every opportunity of watching good players, and of playing with them. Study the " Auction " columns appearing in the Press ; and make yourself perfect in the Laws ; but of Auction it is almost more true than it is of any game—except, perhaps, Chess—that one cannot become a master without matching oneself against masters. Problems, the various treatises, " Bridge talks," and the Sunday papers all help, but, in the long run, only *Experientia docet*.

CONTRACT

CONTRACT may be roughly described as an elaborated form of Auction : it originated in France as " Plafond " shortly before the War of 1914–18, but did not achieve popularity until about 1926, by when our American friends had taken it in hand and altered it almost beyond recognition.

Before going into details of the Laws, which were drawn up internationally by the Portland Club of London, the European Bridge Club, and the National Laws Commission of America, or its actual play we will point out the main feature that differentiates the game from Auction, namely that, whereas in Auction one can make game without having bid for game, in Contract one cannot. In Contract it is only the odd tricks *bid and won** that score towards game, and the effect that this seemingly small divergence has upon the calling is tremendous. Apart from this, and the differences in the auction itself and the scoring mentioned later, there is practically no difference between the two games—until we come to the vexed subjects of " Systems " and " Conventions "— unless we include " Vulnerability," for explanation of which see p. 44.

Dealing and similar preliminaries are the same as in Auction, but in the auction a call of 3 of any suit overbids a call of 2 of any suit or no-trumps, with the values in the order—Clubs (low), Diamonds, Hearts, Spades (high). Note too, that if a player changes a call practically in the same breath the last call stands ; if there is any pause the call is void, and if the first call was improper it is treated as such, while if it was proper either it stands (at the caller's choice) and his partner passes at his next turn, or he may substitute some other proper call and his partner passes for the rest of the auction. The caller of an insufficient bid may either make a sufficient bid or pass : there is no penalty if his revise is the lowest sufficient bid in the same suit, but if it is not his partner must pass whenever it is his turn to call, as also if the offender has passed when (in this latter case only) if the

* Note that for scoring purposes tricks transferred as a penalty for an established revoke count as tricks bid and won.

offending side become defenders declarer may require or forbid the opening lead of any specified suit.

It is in the bidding that the Auction player will first find himself at sea, partly because only odd tricks *bid and won* count to game, and partly because of the wide difference in the scoring of tricks, premiums or bonuses, and penalties. Scoring is on a considerably higher scale, and consequently stakes are usually lower ; if 2s. 6d. a 100 satisfies you at Auction you will be wise to drop to 10d., or even less, at Contract.

SCORING. The various scores—with " doubles " and " redoubles," are fully tabulated at p. 59. Each game of a rubber is complete in itself and is won by the side which first scores 100 for odd tricks bid and won ; and the rubber, as at Whist, is won by the side that scores two games. Trick scoring (the only points entered " below the line " and counting towards game) is simpler than at Auction, but note that for a No-trump call it is 40 for the first and 30 for each subsequent trick above " book." From " love " game can only be made with 5 in Diamonds or Clubs, 4 in Hearts or Spades, and 3 in No-trump. Points entered " above the line " (the " premium score ") are as follows :—

OVERTRICK POINTS. A side winning tricks above those contracted for takes for each the same score as would have been taken had it been contracted for ; if doubled and the side is invulnerable 100, and if doubled and vulnerable 200, for each trick over, both of these being doubled if the contract had been redoubled.

UNDERTRICK POINTS. A side that falls short of fulfilling its contract scores nothing for tricks over " book " (if any), while the opponents take (a) if the contract was not vulnerable, 50 for each undertrick (i.e., trick under the contract) when not doubled, and when doubled 100 for the first, and 200 for each subsequent undertrick ; (b) if the contract was vulnerable, the same points as in the not vulnerable doubled contract if not doubled, and if doubled or redoubled twice or four times these respectively. Thus, if a not vulnerable side is left in with a call of 5 Spades, undoubled, and makes only 2, it scores nothing for tricks and its opponents 150 above the line ; if the side were vulnerable and the call had been doubled opponents would score 800—200 for the first and 300 each for the second and third undertricks.

HONOUR POINTS. The scoring for Honours—Ace, K, Q, J, 10—is (a) in a Trump suit, 100 for four held in one hand, 150 for five held in one hand, and (b) in a No-trumper, 150 for all four Aces in one hand.

SLAM POINTS. 500 for a Little Slam bid and won when not vulnerable, 750 when vulnerable ; and for Grand Slam 1,000 not vulnerable, and 1,500 vulnerable. Note that the caller of a Grand Slam who fails by one trick scores nothing for his Little Slam ; while a Little Slam caller scores only the Little Slam, plus the overtrick, if he makes Grand Slam.

RUBBER POINTS. A side winning the rubber on the first two games takes 700 ; for two games out of three 500. For an unfinished rubber the winners of one game take 300, and if one side only has a part score in an unfinished game it takes 50 points.

THE WINNING SIDE. When the rubber is finished the trick and premium scores of each side are totalled ; the side having the larger total is the winner of the rubber, and the difference between the two totals represents the number of points by which it has won.

Procedure in cases of irregularities, the revoke, dummy's rights, etc., is similar to that in Auction, but the following divergencies should be noted.

If any card be prematurely led during the auction offender's partner must pass the following round, also if an Ace, K, Q, or J is exposed ; otherwise there is no penalty. If, during play, declarer exposes his hand claiming or conceding one or more tricks he must lay his cards face up and make clear his intended line of play ; whereupon either defender may face his hand and suggest a play to his partner. Should a defender then require play to continue declarer leaves his cards face up and may make no play inconsistent with his statement ; he may not (unless he has so announced, or holds no other card) lead a trump if either defender has one, and he may not finesse either in the suit led or in trumping the suit led.

For a first revoke the penalty is the transfer of two tricks made after (and including) it : there is no penalty for a subsequent revoke in the same suit by the same player, nor for one made from dummy's hand. Dummy may question any player about a revoke, and draw attention to or try to prevent irregularities, if he has not seen a card in any other player's hand ; if he *has* he may still draw attention to a defender's irregularity without penalty, but if he warns declarer about the lead either defender may choose the hand from which the lead shall come ; and if in such case he questions declarer about a revoke and the revoke card is withdrawn either defender may require declarer to play his highest or lowest correct card.

If declarer leads from the wrong hand and attention is called to it the card is withdrawn and a correct lead— if possible in the same suit—is made ; if a defender leads in contractor's turn the card led becomes a penalty card, and if in the other defender's turn declarer may forbid the lead of that suit or may treat the card as a penalty card—in which case any card may be led. If a defender improperly exposes his remaining card or cards declarer may treat the remaining cards of either defender as penalty cards.

HOW TO BID

As it is only the points for tricks *bid* which count towards game the bidding is of paramount importance ; points for overtricks, though they are included in your rubber-total, do not help towards scoring games. Without a firm understanding of this and all that it implies no one will ever make a Contract player : and we repeat—*You must contract to make a game before you can make it*. It is true that the score for overtricks—tricks in excess of the contract, not (as in Whist) tricks in excess of the " book " —does count in the end ; but as you get 700 if you win a rubber in two games, or 500 if you win it in three, overtrick points are generally of minor importance. The deduction from this is that players should always aim at bidding the full value of their combined hands.

Contract has become wedded to bidding " conventions " of various kinds and of varying degrees of popularity ; facetious sceptics still insist that the best is the " Oldham," but while it is true of Contract that the vast majority of tricks are won with the honour cards, it is equally true that the conventions have advanced the bidding to a scientific level undreamed of in the days of Auction.

First and foremost the idea of conventions was to advance the bidding, as between partners, to such a call as would give them game ; and their study and use were greatly fostered by the high awards obtainable, especially by the making of Slams. In the early days the bonus for Grand or Little Slam, when vulnerable, was 2,250 and 1,500 respectively, and 750 and 500 if the side was non-vulnerable. Such rewards fostered the habit of going for a Slam whenever there seemed the slightest possibility of its being made, even though when the time came to play the hand it was obvious that the bonus could only be secured if one or two cards happened to be on the right side. As the Table on p. 59 will show, the Little and Grand Slam bonuses when vulnerable have been cut down considerably. By the time the change was made, however, the big bonus germ had infected many players, and the systems which, in addition to building up a game call are supposed to help the possible lead up to the proper calling of the Little or the Grand Slam, have become part and parcel of the game. It is now not going too far to say that real Contract cannot be played—and is not played—without conventions of some sort. Hence the first thing which players sitting down to a rubber talk about—unless they know through constantly playing together—is the convention they are going to follow ; the partners agree as to the convention they are playing, and this knowledge is passed on to the opponents. It is claimed by experts that when bidding is finished in accord with the particular convention or conventions being followed, it is possible for declarer to " place " correctly practically every card which matters ; so one must pay the closest possible attention to the whole of the bidding. As in Auction, the rules state that up to the opening lead being made any player may call for the whole of the bidding as it has been carried on ; it is not a sign of weakness to ask how it is going or has gone, it is a sign of the desire to be fully armed.

All sorts of objections were lodged by newcomers to Contract against the use of the more or less complicated conventions. The stock argument was that it was equivalent to kicking one's partner under the table—an impression soon dissipated and in any event never to be accepted literally. In the first place any convention being played is known—or at least should be—to the opponents ;

hence the " kick " is above, not below, board. Further,
rudimentary "conventions" have been practised by
players of Whist, and still more so at Solo, right down the
ages. Indeed all bidding, no matter what the game, is
"conventional," and in Contract all that has happened
is that the rough and ready conventions have been
smoothed out and considerably elaborated. They are—
once again—meant as a way of getting the maximum
points out of two combined hands—first to get a game
bid and secondly to " examine " the possibility of a Slam.
Consider an extreme case, to drive home the necessity of
getting full value from two hands. Partners who have
bid 3 No-trump make a Grand Slam when vulnerable.
They score 100 for their contract and 120 for overtricks.
If, in the same vulnerable position they had bid the
grand slam they would have made 1,500 additional points.

As we have again mentioned the word " Vulnerable "
it will be convenient if we here interpose a little more
on this exclusive feature. Put shortly, all it means is
that if you have won a game you are " Vulnerable " for
the rest of that rubber, if you have not you are not. If
you are vulnerable the penalties you incur for failing to
make your contract are heavier than they would be if
you were not vulnerable. That is all quite simple and obvious to anyone who considers the scoring Synopsis (*see* p. 59)
for a minute. But—the player who is familiar with its
effects must pardon the writer for insisting upon the
point—the word " Vulnerable " seems to have an unduly
deterring effect upon nearly all beginners and, further,
to hamper the calling of many who have had some
experience of the game. For what do the rules mean ?
Nothing more than this : if the vulnerable bidders (not
doubled) fail to make their contract their opponents score
100 points for each trick under contract—an increase of
50 per trick. If they are doubled then, of course the
penalties increase, as shown. The increasing penalties
were introduced to prevent players having a cheap dash
in an effort to win the rubber, and equally to make
" flag-flying "—an attempt to save the rubber by making
a deliberate overbid—an expensive pastime. In this it
has succeeded ; but for many players it has been too
successful. They seem to fear the extra penalties and
the risk of being doubted to such an extent that they do

not take reasonable chances. It should be remembered that with reasonable prospects of winning the rubber, which means the addition of 500 or 700 to the caller's score, they should not shrink from the possibility of being one trick, or even—on occasions—two tricks, down. It may be said that when you are vulnerable you should naturally and properly put the brake on your bidding. Agreed : but do not put it on too hard, for if you do you may have a nasty skid ! Vulnerable or otherwise, the trick values of any hand remain the same.

There are other points that the beginner, and the unwary, would do well to bear in mind. Besides rules, there are " proprieties " in Contract, and these must be observed. The heinousness of such obvious misdemeanours as indicating the strength—or otherwise—of your hand, or of disguising it, by the tone or manner in which you bid need not be insisted upon : such faults should be suppressed by the natural instinct of the player, and in any case this is not a Guide to Etiquette. But there are some points in the rules which leave room for a certain amount of discretion : for instance, the Declarer who touches a card of Dummy's hand " unless for a purpose other than play either manifest or mentioned " may be compelled to play it. The spirit of that rule should be strictly insisted upon ; but it may happen that a player moves one card to get at another without declaring his intention. To insist upon the letter of the law in such a case is to kill the spirit of the game. It is also advisable to make a note of the fact that a revoke cannot effect the making of a contract once it has been made. If a declarer, having bid one, makes 7 tricks, revokes on the 8th and loses the rest, his making of the contract is totally unaffected by the exaction of the penalty. Long observation has shown that these general remarks are likely to be useful to the novice—and others.

The importance of the " original bid," meaning the first bid, can hardly be exaggerated. The dealer, who has the first opportunity of calling, has the first chance of telling his partner where his strength lies, of indicating the possibilities of securing game or, at least, something towards it. Obviously this opportunity should be exploited to the utmost. But how? To give an all-embracing and quite impeccable answer to such a question is, of course, impossible ; there are still differences of opinion : the state of the game or the rubber is another factor and, as will be shown later, the form which the original bid takes varies—or should do—to a much greater extent in Contract than in Auction. The original bid— as indeed all bidding—must, if the foundation of success is to be soundly laid, give as nearly as possible an accurate indication of the " telling " cards held.

To take by way of a start, what might be termed orthodox holding : it is generally agreed that in order to make an original bid a player must hold $2\frac{1}{2}$ to 3 " quick tricks," and preferably five of the suit called. The meaning of this statement will be obvious to any card player, but, to avoid any misunderstanding, we may say that a " quick trick " is a card that is certain, or practically certain, to win on the first or second time that the suit to which it belongs is led. Aces are obviously quick tricks ; Ace, K of the same suit represent two quick tricks ; and K, Q of the same suit are equal to one quick trick. But it must be borne in mind that Ace, K, Q of a suit are not 3 quick tricks, because unless they are of the trump suit there is a chance of at least the Q being trumped. A guarded K is counted as a $\frac{1}{2}$-trick. This method of estimating the value of a hand is not, however, mathematically correct. A guarded K is actually worth rather more than $\frac{1}{2}$ when one is making an original call, because if one's partner holds the Ace the K will make ; if the opponent on the right has the Ace, the K is practically certain to make, while even if the opponent on the left holds it it may still make a trick. But for practical purposes this method of sizing up the value of a hand is very useful.

To proceed : It is advisable to make an original bid on such a hand as the following :—Ace, K, x x, x Spades ; x, x, x Hearts ; K, x, x Diamonds ; K, x, Clubs. This is worth 1 Spade. Your objective is to win or, failing that, to prevent your opponents winning. By bidding 1 Spade you have at least told your partner something : if he has a good hand he will raise you, while if he has a poor one your opponents will take the initiative and the hand will be played in another suit. And even so you have a fairly useful defensive hand.

Here is a hand of similar value on which it is equally

advisable to bid :—K, Q, x, x, x Spades ; x, x Hearts ; Ace, x, x Diamonds ; K, Q, x Clubs. This is above average strength, and a call of 1 Spade is not only indicated but necessitated.

This 2½ to 3 quick trick foundation for an initial call is perfectly sound. It is based upon the fact that 8 of the 13 tricks are usually won by the higher cards, and that therefore the caller's hand will probably win 4 or more tricks. But Contract Bridge demands discretion—that is why it is so fascinating—and there are many combinations that may place the dealer, who, of course, is the first to bid, in an awkward position. He may, for instance, hold :—Ace, x, x Spades ; Ace, x, x Hearts ; K, x, x Diamonds ; x, x, x, x Clubs. Here we have 2½ quick tricks right enough, but all the same most players would refrain from calling on it, because there is no real suit, though with another combination of similar quick trick value, such as :—x, x Spades ; Ace, Q, x, x Hearts ; x, x, x Diamonds ; Ace, J, x, x Clubs—1 Heart may safely be bid. Similarly with—K, J, x, x, x Spades ; Q, x Hearts ; Ace, x, x Diamonds ; Q, x, x Clubs—you will not go far wrong with 1 Spade, although many expert players will maintain that it is safer to pass on such a hand. If the partner holds cards which justify him bidding, a second opportunity of telling about this hand is sure to arise. If the partner has little or nothing of value, this last quoted hand may not be worth much.

If you have a choice between bidding 1 of a suit or a No-trump it is advisable to bid the suit. It is dangerous to bid on a long suit without top honours unless you have support in the other suits ; 6, or even 7, of a suit headed by K or Q do not, unless supported, justify an original bid. The quick tricks are missing. Unless you have outside strength you are practically certain to be overcalled—and then your long suit is useless for defensive purposes. As an original call is generally assumed to signify that the caller holds a certain number of quick tricks for defensive as well as for attacking purposes, one cannot call on length alone—one *must* have strength. As total value, Ace, Q, or Ace, J, 10, or K, Q, 10 of same suit are each assumed to be worth a trick and a half.

For practical purposes this is all that need be said about initial bids by the dealer. If the dealer passes, the second player bids on lines similar to those described—still leaving systems out of consideration for the time being. If two players pass it is generally agreed that the third player must hold a slightly stronger hand than those described in order to justify his bidding, and a fourth player, after three passes, should be stronger still. These general suggestions will be slightly modified by the state of the score and by whether caller is, or is not vulnerable.

The first bid gives the next player something to go upon, and it is generally easier to make the second bid than the first. The second caller (unless first has passed) is entitled to bid on weaker hands. For instance ; after a bid of 1 Spade you might call 2 Diamonds on—x Spades ; K, J, x, x, Hearts ; K, J, x, x, x, x Diamonds ; x, x Clubs. This would not justify an original Diamond call of 1, because it is so weak in defensive cards ; but directly your opponent has opened the bidding you are entitled to do anything you can to upset his scheme and give your partner an indication of the value of your own hand. The calling of the second hand does not imply the values that the calling of the first one does. Your partner will allow for this and bid accordingly. This understanding leads directly to the " Jump " call. If your opponent has bid 1 Heart and you call 1 Spade, what you are doing is to tell your partner that you have some strength in Spades and a prospect of upsetting the chances of your opponent's getting a game score. That applies to every call which barely overcalls the bidder on your right. 2 Clubs over 1 Spade comes into the same category. But if you have a strong hand you should bid 1 more than the simple overcall. For instance : an original call on—x, x Spades ; Ace, K, x, x, x Hearts ; K, x, x Diamonds ; Ace, x, x Clubs would be 1 Heart. But if an opponent has called 1 Spade you will, on an average, profit by calling—not 2, but 3 Hearts. It is not so much a question of your scoring 3 Hearts, although you have a very fair prospect of doing that or something better ; the point is that you have disturbed your opponent's calling and told your partner how you stand. This is the " Jump " bid, of which average players do not take sufficient advantage.

The partner of original caller will take into account an opponent's intervening call but, in the absence of such, he, knowing that his partner has opened on a minimum of 2½ quick tricks and a suit of probably five, can give support if he holds 1½ quick tricks and a biddable suit. If this suit is higher than that which his partner bid and he holds only the minimum he will bid *one* of his own suit ; if his suit is a lower one he may bid *two* of it. If his distribution is unfavourable he may bid one No Trump.

The Jump bid operates in various ways. If a caller bids 1 Spade, and his partner " jumps " him by calling 3 of any other suit he must realize that this is an indication of exceptional strength, probably in the suit bid, and consequently proceed to raise the bidding until a game or Slam score is reached. Calls such as these are sometimes known as " Pre-emptive bids," and sometimes as " Conventions." Actually the " Jump " belongs to neither of these categories ; but there are certain " Conventions," or " Conventional bids," to which we can now turn.

CONVENTIONS

No attempt can be made here to deal with all the various systems or conventions and their ramifications. The range is too wide for one thing, and for another there is no universally accepted acceptation of the same convention, while the particular situation—the score or the state of the rubber—may be put in as a third minor reason for hesitancy in being dogmatic as to how the bidding should be started and how it should be followed up according to the cards held by the partner. Duplicate Bridge has often proved that when really expert players are operating, that is players with full knowledge of the use of conventions, the same final bid is arrived at despite the use of conventions differing considerably in detail. Here is the point to be borne in mind—the reason why conventions and systems have been devised and used at all is to enable the players to get the best possible maximum bid out of the cards—to arrive at a game call, if that is possible, and secondly to help them to estimate the chances of a more or less safe Little or Grand Slam bid.

The various conventions have been given titles which, to a greater or lesser extent, explain themselves. Perhaps the most popular—that is the most generally favoured by players of average ability—is known as the " Forcing Two." The chief reason for its popularity is that it tells the simple truth, as distinct from conventions or systems which, when one thing is said, something different is meant. A cursory examination of the Forcing Two may be worth while ; it is so called because the player making the original bid of 2, forces his partner —in the unlikely event of an intervening bid—to call something which will keep the bidding open. Experience demonstrates that the hand which starts the bidding with 2 of a suit should hold $5\frac{1}{2}$ quick tricks. Two Ace K suits, an Ace suit and a K in the remaining suit count the $5\frac{1}{2}$, as do two Ace K suits and a K Q suit. The left hand opponent of the player making the opening bid is not likely to overcall, so it is then up to the partner to call— he must do so to keep the bidding open for his partner. A hand devoid of quick tricks calls for a 2 No-trump response, leaving the original caller with the very definite knowledge that he cannot rely on effective help. It is therefore up to him to decide whether he can safely go to game on his own hand. A positive response from his partner immediately opens up the possibility of a Slam. Presupposing the first of the holdings quoted above, to give such a response the partner must—obviously—hold the other Ace—remember the caller holds three—and a Queen. The first decision to be arrived at mutually is the best trump suit. Consider an original call of 2 Hearts. The caller's partner holds, say, 4 Hearts to the Q—or may be even only 3 to the Q J, plus the other cards which justify a positive response. The first response to the Forcing Two 2-heart call is 3 Hearts. The suit the hand will be played in is thus established. After this the convention merely asks that information shall be passed from one partner to another ere the small or big Slam is reached. Very simple, of course, with given hands, but providing difficulties when hands near enough to be tempting and yet not quite solid enough to be safe, have been dealt.

Some players will take a Forcing Two chance on 5 quick tricks and a bit. Here is a typical example. Only the hands of the callers are given in detail as the opposition holding does not matter. Dealer had Spades A, K, x, x, x, Hearts A, x, Diamonds A, K, x, and Clubs x, x, x. Taking a chance with the 5 quick tricks only, the dealer called 2 Spades. His partner held Spades 10, x, x, x, Hearts Q, 10, x, x, Diamonds Q, x, x, and Clubs A, K. The positive response under the Forcing Two convention was completely justified. A 3 Spades response decides the suit, followed by 4 Diamonds from the original caller, 5 Clubs from his partner—showing no losers in that suit— 5 Hearts as the next reply, and thus to 7 Spades. The call almost inevitably fails, as a Heart must be lost. The Grand Slam failed because the declarer " took a chance " on 5 quick tricks when 5½ was the minimum for safety. Exchange in the hands of original declarer K of Hearts for the Ace, give him the Ace of Clubs and his partner the Ace of Hearts and the K of Clubs, and an ordinary distribution makes the bidding of a Grand Slam a matter of calm confidence, and the making of it almost a certainty.

This example is typical of a particular and not very complicated system. It has the merit of being, to a large extent, natural. The opening call tells partner more or less accurately what is held : the partner in his turn announces support and the giving of information continues afterwards on natural lines. There are variations, of course. Here is an " artificial " variation, widely adopted and known as a " Slam Convention." It is the bidding of a suit to show that the caller has no loser in the suit an opponent may have called. Opening bidder calls 1 Spade. His left hand opponent calls 3 Hearts. Over this comes the call 4 Hearts from the partner of the original caller. Such a call is meant to indicate—and should only be used to this end—that caller No. 3 has no losing trick in the suit called against him. It would be justified by the holding of a singleton Ace of Hearts, or if the hand is completely void of Hearts.

Mention of this kind of bid leads us by a straight path to the consideration of a system different in essentials from that already dealt with. It is known as the " One Club " or the " Big Club." By an original call of one Club a strong hand is indicated ; but the artificiality of the convention lies in the fact that the player making it *may not have a Club in his hand.* He has, however, some trick-making cards, though possibly not sufficient to justify a hint of a game or a Slam call in any particular suit. The proper response from partner is laid down in the system. If he has a worthless hand—that is to say a hand without quick tricks—he must make a 1 Diamond call. That, again, is the negative response.

But if the partner has a fairly good hand—holding, say, 2 quick tricks, then he can bid accordingly. Also he can bid confidently, knowing that his partner would not have bid an original one Club unless in possession of some quick tricks. Between the two partners there can be built up at least a game bid, and possibly a Slam. In the latter event there would, by players using this convention, be "jumps" here and there. It will be noticed that the first objective of this convention is to keep the bidding open for the player who, by his call, has made original mention of the fact that he has a good hand.

Scores of books have been published dealing with various systems or conventions and it will be appreciated that no attempt at even a bare outline of all of them can be attempted here. There are systems which depend on methods of counting Aces, Kings, Queens and so on, with "points" added, in the counting, for extra cards in the trump suit over the normal holding. Nothing like finality is agreed upon in respect of the use of any system : indeed, the differences of opinion as to the cards which call for a particular response have made Contract the most controversial of all card games.

"Inquests" apart, one hotly debated topic connected with conventions may fairly be mentioned here, even by a writer who is hesitant to give a definite and complete answer. Suppose at the start of a rubber, two partners announce that they are playing this or that convention. At some stage of the rubber—for what may seem to the bidder very good reasons—he makes a call which, as events show, is not in accord with the convention. Can such a player be accused of deliberately misleading or, if the stronger word be permitted, cheating? According to the convention, he announces, when making his bid, that he holds certain cards. Actually he doesn't hold those cards. It is argued by some players that such departure from the agreed convention is not "playing the game." There is, however, an important, if not wholly complete, reply which can be given : that while the player departing from the convention may succeed in deceiving the opposition, he is also deceiving his partner—giving him false information. Such deception, in practice, is the short cut to points piled up against the "false" bidder and his partner. The international

Laws deal partly with the point in these terms :

" It is improper to employ, without explaining its meaning to the opponents, a convention in calling or an unusual convention in play, the significance of which may not be clear to them. When applied to a call the term ' convention ' covers a call designed to convey an arbitrary or artificial meaning or used by a player with the assurance that his partner will not accept it in its natural sense. It is necessary that a convention so used should be fully understood by the other side, and players using convention calls should be ready to reply fully to a proper inquiry by an opponent as to their meaning or use. Should it be necessary to make such an inquiry during the auction, the partner of the player who has made the convention call should reply."

Certain major points will be obvious even to the novice from the rough details of the systems previously explained. The fact that to a considerable extent they rule out the " psychic bid " is clear. It is inadvisable, save in exceptional circumstances, and without running the risk of heavy penalties, to take a chance when playing any of the established or agreed conventions. The other major point is that, as they have been explained here, the Systems make no provision for a call from part-score. Although the objective of the bidding at Contract is to work up at least a game bid, it naturally follows that many calls are made, and the contract duly carried out, which do not add up to a game. And, of course, a part-score—say 40—is extremely valuable. How then to distinguish between calling in an effort to complete a game already partly won, and calling which aims at a Slam bonus ? The accepted procedure is simple. A call of 2 Hearts with the part-score standing at 40 should be regarded by the partner as merely an attempt to complete a game. If the original caller has a hand of more than game possibilities from a part-score, he then makes an overcall : That is to say 3 Hearts would be an invitation to his partner to keep the bidding open. Equally, of course, a response to a call which, if made, would be sufficient to give partners game, means that the caller holds more than an average hand ; that is one with Slam bonus possibilities.

In the previous paragraph the phrase " psychic bid " was used, and it would be as well to make some further allusion to this type of bidding. The perils having been stressed, it is still true that from time to time opportunities

arise for the use of what is known as the " psychic bid "
which, broadly speaking, is a call that is not justified by
the actual cards in the hand. If it is admitted that there
are such phenomena as " psychic " card players—that
is, players who can sense the general disposition of the
cards in the hands as yet undisclosed—then there should
surely be a handicapping system attached to Contract, for
obviously such players would possess an almost over-
whelming advantage. The player who bids " falsely "—
i.e., makes a call not justified by the holding or the
previous bidding—and finds his partner possessing length,
even if not strength, in that particular suit may afterwards extol his psychic powers, whereas what has actually
happened,was that he had an astonishing piece of good luck.

No, it must surely be admitted that the old-fashioned
word " bluff " comes much nearer to a correct description
of bidding not justified by the cards, and that " psychic "
is merely a fancy term that, through the dictate of fashion
or some mistaken notion of gentility, has gradually
supplanted it. However, despite all the systems and
conventions and the " musts " and " must nots " which
have become part and parcel of Contract, the game
would be less worth playing if a bluff bid could never
be tried, and it would be strange if such a bid did not
produce gratifying results now and then. After all,
if you know your opponents—as a good player very
quickly does—then it is part of the game to play those
opponents in addition to playing the cards. The one
general qualification with regard to the bluff bid is that it
is specially dangerous—not to say suicidal—without
some trick-making cards in the hand. As illustration,
take a classic instance from an actual big match play
bidding, in which the players may be camouflaged as our
old friends North and South opposed to East and West.

North deals and, with a fairly good all round hand,
guarding pretty strongly 3 suits but without a real
biddable suit, he made a justifiable call of 1 No-trump.
His left hand opponent, East, held nothing of consequence
save 7 Clubs to the four top Honours and a singleton
useless Spade. The mind of East worked rapidly. There
was, in all probability a Spade game bid in the two
opposing hands, and if he called the Clubs it was a virtual
certainty that, as neither of his opponents could have a

guard in view of his own holding, they would switch from the No-trump call to a suit. So East called 2 Spades. The effect was exactly as anticipated. South had Ace, Q of Spades and a couple of small ones, plus good support in Diamonds and Hearts. Hence, holding the Spades which had been called against him, South gave his partner this information by bidding 2 No-trumps. West passed ; and North, thus encouraged, went on to 3 No-trump. East now doubled, but the opposition, firmly convinced that East was relying to some extent on his Spades to justify the double, stayed where they were. And East, with the lead, proceeded to make 7 tricks off the reel in Clubs, putting the 3 No-trumper down by 3 tricks, when his opponents could have made a comfortable game in Spades. A bluff successfully carried through by East to his own and his partner's satisfaction ! It is worth noting that the same hands, duplicated at another table, were played in 4 Spades ; and 5 were made because there, in reply to the No-trump bid, the holder of the 7 Clubs to the four top Honours bid the Clubs, thus showing the red light to the opposition. A good, if extreme, example of a bluff, with precious little of the " psychic " about it, though many would dub it a " psychic bid."

Further opposition calls arise out of the foregoing for consideration. If a player holds a good hand against a call of 1 of a suit, but is without sufficient strength or length in any other suit to justify him in overbidding, he doubles the original call. This is known as the *informatory double* (or *informatory raise*), and is a demand for a call from partner. It means that the caller has a prospect of winning the hand if his partner bids his strongest suit, and doubling an original call of 2 is frequently used to convey the same information, so also is the overbidding in a suit originally called. These informatory doubles, if made on a call of 1 trick may be taken for granted, if on a call of 2 it is better to have an understanding before starting play. Many good players fight shy of the informatory double for this reason. When one partner responds—as he must—the " informatory doubler " may only have a vague idea of his partner's holding. The best suit—which has to be called—may be only 4 to the Queen—or even of less value than that.

Naturally, many bids are made in Contract as actually

played, not with any intention of asking the partner to continue bidding or even in the hope of upsetting the bidding of opponents, but with the idea of telling the partner something about the strength of one's own hand, and such information must be utilized as soon as play commences. A call of 2 of a suit over 1 No-trump may be of this character , it indicates strength in that suit and helps the partner to decide what to lead in the fight to prevent their opponents making their contract. It should be noted, however, that such bids are occasionally made to deceive. Having a weak hand, and being practically certain that the opponents will make a game call, a player may intervene with a call of 2 or 3 of a suit without having strength in it. If the partner holds the K the declarer may have to finesse against it, and the misleading bid will very likely induce him to finesse against the wrong hand. It is not often that this form of deception is indulged in, but it is useful to bear the possibility in mind, and it illustrates how the calling affects the actual play.

THE PLAY OF THE HANDS.

The apparent simplification of the play through the information broadcast by the bidding, as already mentioned is largely counteracted by the necessity for extreme accuracy in the play itself owing to the fact that the winning or the losing of a single trick may very well result in an enormous difference in the score. There is no other card game in which one trick may be of such value. The winning of the 13th trick in a Grand Slam declaration, for instance, may mean scoring not only the points for the tricks and the rubber, but also 1,500 for the Grand Slam ; while if it is lost the declarer not only forgoes any possibility of scoring at all but is penalized into the bargain for failing to make contract. Furthermore, he leaves the fate of the rubber still in doubt. Correct bidding is of such outstanding importance that the necessity for correct play is often apt to be underestimated. Actually, it cannot be overestimated. Even leading experts make blunders in play at times. Take the following instance which occurred in an important match ; the holdings were :—

A—S, x, x ; **H**, Ace, Q, 10, 9, 7 ; **D**, Ace, J, 10, x,
   x ; **C**, x.
Y—S, Ace, K, J, x ; **H**, J, 5, 3, 2 ; **D**, x ; **C**, 10, x, x, x.
B—S, x, x, x ; **H**, K, 8, 6, 4 ; **D**, x ; **C**, Ace, Q, x, x, x.
Z—S, Q, 10, x, x ; **H**, nil ; **D**, K, Q, x, x, x, x ;
   C, K, J, x.

The call in both rooms was 4 Hearts, and in one of them
it was doubled. In one room after Y had played K, Ace
of Spades, A (declarer) got the lead, and then led his
Club, finessed with Dummy's Q, and finished 1 trick down.
There was no need for this finesse. In the other room the
declarer took this trick with his partner's Ace and then
cross-ruffed the Clubs and Diamonds and made his
contract. This gave the winning team an advantage
of 740 points. That "last trick," which may be so
valuable if a Little Slam or Grand Slam has been called,
has emphasized the importance of end play. So we may
insert a note on the "Squeeze"—the principle of which
is this : By playing winning cards a player forces the
opposing side to discard and thereby strip themselves of
winning cards or guards to high cards. In many cases
a player will deliberately play with the intention of thus
defeating his opponents, and, obviously, if he persists in
leading so that his opponent or opponents are compelled
to discard valuable cards, he is "squeezing" them without doing any harm to himself.

Here is a simple illustration of the Squeeze. The game
is being played in No-trumps, and the cards left are :—
   A—S, x ; **H**, x ; **D**, nil ; **C**, x.
   Y—S, Q, J ; **H**, nil ; **D**, Q ; **C**, nil.
   B—S, K, 10 ; **H**, nil ; **D**, J ; **C**, nil.
   Z—S, x ; **H**, 10 ; **D**, x ; **C**, nil.
Now if A leads a Club Y is squeezed. If he discards his
Diamond Dummy (B) plays the 10 S ; then A leads a
Spade and B makes K S and J D. If, on the other hand,
Y discards a Spade, Dummy drops the Diamond, and the
result is the same. The idea has been elaborated and
many complicated hands have been won by its means ;
but the subject is too involved for discussion here.

From end play we may revert, for a moment, to beginning play. Experience tells most emphatically that
in Contract opposition play is particularly important,
especially when the calling suggests that the position so

far as the opponents to the call are concerned is pretty
hopeless, as in the case, say of a Little or Grand Slam bid
against. Consider this point in connexion with the lead—
it is one often overlooked. If the opponents, by the use
of systems, conventions, and demand-bidding have gone
to 7 Hearts, to give an example, it must be presumed
that they hold all the cards in Hearts which are of any
importance, and that nothing can stop them making
Hearts tricks. East, with the lead, has 2, or perhaps 3,
small Hearts. Experience teaches that he is likely to do
the least possible harm by leading Hearts, and he may
do some good to his side—such as, for instance, taking
out of Dummy one Heart which might otherwise be used
to trump possible losers in North's hand. By the lead
of any other suit East might well help his opponent to
discover the situation of an odd Queen which he must
find in order to make his Grand Slam.

Take another case. Playing against a Grand Slam bid
there is a natural tendency, in making the first lead, to
play an Ace if East happens to possess one. But such a
lead might prove disastrous. The Grand Slam should
not have been called if there was an Ace missing in a suit
of which both the bidders held one loser. Suppose
East succumbs to the temptation to play his Ace of
Diamonds. When Dummy goes down he finds, to his
consternation, that Dummy has the remaining four
Honours in that suit, and that Dummy's partner is able
to trump the Ace which has been hurriedly led. The other
Honour tricks in that suit are set up, to be used in due
course to enable the declarer to discard other possible
losers. If the player with the opening lead had not been
in such a hurry to make a trick with his Ace the declarer
would have been left with the task of guessing whether
the missing Ace, which he must get rid of to establish the
other winners in Diamonds, was on his right or his left—
a ticklish procedure. "When in doubt lead trumps"
has often been advised in regard to card games : ex-
experience proves that it is a good stand-by for this
comparatively newly developed game of Contract.

TABLE OF SCORES

Trick Score (below the line)	Undbld.	Dbld.	Redbld.
For each Odd Trick bid and won in—			
Clubs or Diamonds, each	20	40	80
Hearts or Spades, each	30	60	120
No-trump { first	40	80	160
{ each subsequent	30	60	120

Penalty Score (above opponent's line)	NOT VULNERABLE			VULNERABLE		
	Undbld.	Dbld.	Redbld.	Undbld.	Dbld.	Redbld.
1st undertrick ...	50	100	200	100	200	400
Each subsequent	50	200	400	100	300	600

Premium Score

	NOT VULNERABLE			VULNERABLE		
Each overtrick ...	trick value	100	200	trick value	200	400
Making Contract	—	50	50	—	50	50
Little Slam, *if bid*	500			750		
Grand Slam, *if bid*	1000			1500		

Honours, in one hand—		Rubber points—	
4 of trump suit ...	100	2-game rubber ...	700
5 ,, ,, ,, ...	150	3-game rubber ...	500
4 Aces, when playing " No Trumps "	150	1 game of unfinished rubber	300

SOLO WHIST

SOLO WHIST has features in common with common with both Whist and Napoleon, and as both these games are described in the present volume, it will only be necessary to briefly state the points of resemblance. Like Whist, it is played with the full pack of fifty-two cards, which range in value from ace, highest, to deuce, lowest ; the last or fifty-second card being turned up to fix the trump suit. Tricks are made as at Whist, and form the basis of the score. The affinity to Napoleon is traceable in the various calls that the players make, and in the further fact that every hand is a separate game, upon which stakes are won and lost. Solo Whist, however, possesses special features of its own—viz., that the partnerships or combinations are always changing round after round, and that there is a special call named Misère,* which is a declaration to *lose* the whole of the thirteen tricks.

DESCRIPTION OF THE GAME :

The objects of Solo Whist are—to make eight tricks out of the thirteen in conjunction with a partner ; to make five or nine tricks out of your own hand against the other three players in combination ; or to play your own hand so as to avoid taking a trick, however strenuously your three adversaries may endeavour to force you to do so.

The cards are dealt round to the four players, *three cards at a time*, until there are only four remaining. Then these are dealt singly, the last card being turned up as the trump, and being the property of the dealer. The eldest hand, *i.e.* the player on the dealer's left, has the first call. He can *propose*, *i.e.* ask for a partner with the object of making with that partner eight of the thirteen tricks ; he can call a *solo*, which is a declaration to make five of the thirteen tricks without having a partner ; he can declare *misère*, *i.e.* to lose all the thirteen tricks—in this phase of the game all the four suits are equal, the trump suit being .annulled ; or he can call *abondance*, when, making whatever suit he likes trumps,

---

* Misère is also played in Napoleon. *See* p. 139.

and declaring the suit before the first card is led, he endeavours to make nine tricks out of the thirteen. The call of *abondance* is, however, superseded by any other player declaring to make *abondance* in trumps, *i.e.*, with the trump suit as it stands.

Further than this, he may call an *open misère*, or *misère ouverte*, thereby undertaking not only to lose all the thirteen tricks, but to expose his own cards on the table as soon as the first trick is played to and turned. Or—the supreme call of all—he may announce his intention of taking the whole thirteen tricks by saying, "*Abondance declarée*." In this case, as in the simple *abondance*, he names his own trump suit, and in the case of this declaration, and this only, he leads, wherever he may chance to sit, the original lead to the first trick in all other cases coming from the eldest hand.

There are thus six things the eldest hand may do after he has examined his cards, and in showing what the eldest hand can do we have explained what the various calls are. Recapitulating them in due order of value, they are —proposition and acceptance when two players (wherever they sit), undertake to make eight of the thirteen tricks against the other two in partnership ; a solo, where the caller to win must take five tricks at least, the suit originally turned up being trumps ; the misère, the abondance, and the two exceptional calls, which have already been sufficiently described. The eldest hand may not, however, have cards that would justify his attempting either of the things specified. In that case he says, " I pass " ; and here it may be observed that, in the case of the eldest hand, and to the eldest hand *only* who has passed, there is extended the privilege of accepting a proposition made by the second, third, or fourth players, such proposition, of course, not having been previously accepted or superseded by a higher call.

The second hand, whose turn it now is to declare, may accept a proposal if one has been made, may propose if the eldest hand has passed, or may make any better call than the eldest hand has made. Of course, an *inferior* call is nugatory, *i.e.* a player cannot call a solo if a previous hand has called a misère. The higher call always supersedes the lower one, but a player, having once called, can, if he is over-called, increase his call up to the highest limit—the abondance declarée.

The third hand can accept a proposition if one has been made and has not been accepted or superseded, can propose if no proposition or higher call has been made, or can make any call superior to those previously declared.

The fourth player—the dealer—may accept a proposition coming from any quarter under the previously announced stipulations ; or he may propose, in which case only the eldest hand can accept ; or he may make an independent call, provided it is better than any preceding call.

The matter may be thus illustrated : suppose the eldest hand passes, the second proposes, the third and fourth pass, and the eldest hand accepts, then—calling them A, B, C, D, according to their order at table—A, B would be partners against C, D, and would be obliged to make eight of the thirteen tricks. They would occupy their original seats and play in their proper order, B following A to the first trick, and the regular progression from left to right being observed all through the hand. Again we will suppose that A proposed, B passed, C called misère, and the fourth player (D) called an abondance. The calls of A and C would be superseded, unless, indeed, A should call an abondance in trumps, which would supersede the abondance of D in a plain suit ; or C should call a misère ouverte, which would supersede the other calls ; though D would still have the option, if his hand were strong enough to justify it, of making the supreme call of abondance declarée. We will assume that D's call of abondance was left unchallenged, and in that case he would then, but not before, announce the suit that he made trumps, and A, the player on his left, would lead out for the first trick, A, B, and C playing together in concert, but not, of course, being allowed to see each other's cards, or in any way to acquaint each other with the cards held, except by the legitimate and proper means afforded by the play of the hand. D's object is now to make nine tricks unaided, and the aim of his opponents is to score more than four tricks between them. Sometimes, indeed, an abondance, like a solo or a proposition, succeeds with two or three tricks to spare. These are called " over-tricks," and are paid for according to an agreed-upon scale. On the other hand, any tricks short of the number required by the caller are known as undertricks, and are paid for by the caller in the manner we will shortly describe.

Before passing to other matters, it is necessary to draw attention to some important facts to be impressed upon the memory : (1) that no player, after having " passed," can make an independent call or a proposition ; (2) that only the eldest hand can accept a proposition after having once passed ; (3) that a superior call always annuls and supersedes a call of inferior value ; and (4) that a player having once made a call, may increase it to anything up to the supreme call. It should be understood that a caller, in increasing his declaration, can make any higher call he chooses. Thus, should he propose, or even accept, and be overcalled by a solo, he would be at liberty to at once call an abondance declarée, and " skip " all the declarations of intermediate value.

In the case of all the players passing, the cards are thrown up, and there is a fresh deal by the next player in rotation. It is sometimes arranged, however, rather than throw up a hand that has been dealt to play what is called a general misère. This is very simple in its form, but by no means so easy to play as it appears to be. There are no trumps. The tricks are led and followed to in the usual way, and the player who takes the last or thirteenth trick pays an agreed stake, equal as a rule to the stake of a solo, to each of his adversaries. Generally speaking, the big cards are thrown away, but it is often necessary to keep one or more leading cards to force through a suit in which you may be dangerous.

THE STAKES :

These are proportioned to the value of the calls ; that is to say, they progress from low to high, just as the various calls progress from low to high. It is customary, and distinctly advisable, to play Solo Whist for small regular stakes. One form of the game is known as " six, twelve, and eighteen." This means that propositions and solos are paid for at 6d. each, misères at 1s., and abondances at 1s. 6d. The proposition and acceptance being played and succeeding, the partners receive 6d. each if they make eight tricks, and 1d. each for every trick over eight. If they, however, make a " slam," that is to say, get the whole thirteen tricks, they would receive 1s. 4d., that is, double for the over-tricks—five over-tricks at 2d. each = 10d., and 6d. for the original declaration. Should they fail to make eight tricks, they pay their opponents 6d. each, and 1d. for each under-trick, that is, every trick under eight. It will be seen that they can each win the 6d. exactly, but if they lose they must lose 7d. each, or more. It is quite understood that, in the case of a proposition and acceptance, each partner only receives or pays once—that is, suppose A and B are playing against C and D, A pays to or receives from C, and B pays to or receives from D. This pro-position is the only joint call, all other phases of the game being individual calls, in which one player, the declaring hand, pits himself against the other three. In these cases, therefore, the stakes are paid to or by every one of the three adversaries.

The lowest of the individual calls, the solo, would there-fore earn him who made it 1s. 6d., or more—that is, the three sixpences, with over-tricks or not, as the case might be ; and in the event of his failing to make five tricks, it would cost him 1s. 9d., or more, that is, three sixpences, with 3d. (or more) for the under-tricks.

The misère costs 1s., neither more nor less, therefore the caller risks losing 3s. in calling misère. If he makes the declaration, he receives 1s. from each of the others ; if he fails, he pays 1s. each. There are in this case no over or under-tricks, the misère having to be played right out to win, and being defeated directly the caller has to take a trick.

Next in importance comes the abondance, in which the stake is 1s. 6d., and it is not uncommon here to double the value of the over-tricks, but not of the under-tricks. This must be a matter of arrangement. A player making ten tricks would, with double over-tricks, receive 1s. 8d from each, and, if he only made eight tricks, would pay 1s. 7d. each. An abondance in trumps is of the same money value as another abondance, though the trump call supersedes the call in plain suits. With it we reach the limit of ordinary calls ; but it should be said that the misère ouverte is double the price of the ordinary misère, and the abondance déclarée double the price of the ordinary abondance. There are no under-tricks at the call of an abondance déclarée, as the caller is beaten directly he loses a trick.

You can make the stakes whatever you like, only it is well to preserve the proportions just laid down. Thus you can have propositions and solos 1d., misères 2d., and abondances 3d. ; or you can make them 1s., 2s., and 3s. respectively, with 3d. each for over-tricks. We need scarcely say that you can substitute sovereigns for shillings, but not to the advantage of the game in general company.

A DIGEST OF THE LAWS :

Solo Whist is not yet fortunate enough to possess an established code of laws having universal authority. Probably the best and fullest rules for the game are those given in *Solo Whist and Auction Solo*, by Abraham S. Wilks (Routledge & Kegan Paul, Ltd.), from which little text-book we give here an epitome of the more important provisions.

The cards must be shuffled by the player on the dealer's left ; the dealer may then shuffle if he likes, and the pack is cut by the player to the right of the dealer.

A fresh deal is necessary if a card is exposed or faced in the pack, of if there is a misdeal. This new deal is by the same player, and there is no penalty.

The trump card must be left exposed on the table until after the first trick is turned and quitted, but the dealer may play it to the first trick if he can legally do so.

When the trump card has been taken up, it must not be named, although—except when a misère is being played—any one may ask, and must be told, what is the trump suit.

There is no penalty if the caller of a solo, misère, or abondance exposes any or all of his cards, the exposure being in this case to his own disadvantage. There are, however, penalties if any one playing *against* a single caller, or for or against a proposition, exposes any of his cards.

If a card is exposed by one of the adversaries of a misère or misère ouverte, the misère-caller can immediately claim the stakes, and is regarded as having won the declaration, the stakes being paid by the offender for himself and his partners. The misère-caller can enforce the same penalty if a card is led out of turn against him, or if a revoke is made against him, or, indeed, if any one follows suit out of turn.

It should be said that an exposed card is a card that is placed face upwards on the table, or the face of which can be seen by any of the players except him to whom the card belongs. The aggrieved party can demand that the card be played or not be played, *i.e.* he can say, " Follow suit or play the ———— " (naming the exposed card), and this demand can be repeated as long as the exposed card remains unplayed. If the exposed card is a trump, and trumps are not led, the adversary may say, " Follow suit or pass the trick," when the holder of the exposed card must not trump, but must renounce a card of another suit if he cannot follow.

The offender cannot be prevented from throwing away an exposed card if he has not a card of the led suit, or from leading it when it is his turn to lead, except against a solo or abondance, when he may be repeatedly prohibited from leading it. When the suit exposed is led by someone other than the offender, the adversary may say to him who exposed the card, " Play "—or " Don't play that card " ; or he can make him play either the highest or lowest of his suit to the lead.

A suit cannot be called for exposing a card ; the penalty known as calling a suit is exacted when a man leads out of his turn.

If a player does lead out of his turn, the card may be treated as an exposed card by the adversaries if they choose, or they may call a suit from either the man who exposed the card or his partner when next either of them has to lead ; and any such demand must be complied with, under penalty of a revoke.

In exacting any of these penalties, the partners against whom the offence has been committed may decide which of them shall exact the penalty, but must not consult, save in the case of a revoke, as to what that penalty shall be.

Where a man follows suit out of turn, i.e. plays before one of his partners who ought to have played before him, that partner can be compelled to play his highest or lowest of the suit, or to trump or not to trump at the adversaries' option.

If all the four men have played to the trick before any irregularity is discovered, there is no penalty. This, however, does not apply to a revoke.

Now, as to revokes. No revoking player or partnership can win a declaration.

The penalty for every revoke is the loss of three tricks from the score of the revoking side.

A revoke is established when the trick containing it is turned and quitted, i.e. is covered up and turned over, and the hand has left it. The offender or his partner leading, or following the lead, to the succeeding trick, also establishes a revoke.

If, after the three tricks for a revoke are taken from the score of the offending side, he or they still have enough tricks to win the declaration, then he simply loses the declaration—*i.e.* supposing a solo-caller revokes, and he has made eight or nine tricks, he would, after the penalty was paid, have made enough to win the solo. He then only pays 6d., at the stakes which we have been explaining, to each of his opponents.

If, however, the forfeiture of the tricks brings the offender's number down below the score required by the declaration, then for each trick short the agreed-upon price of an under-trick must also be paid.

The actual offender pays the stakes in all cases of a revoke, except in the instance of a proposer and acceptor, who, being voluntary partners, pay the fine between them.

If a revoke is suspected, those who wish it may, at the close of the hand, examine all the tricks for proof of their assertion ; and if the other side do not allow this examination to be properly made, the revoke is established.

It is essential, after a misère is defeated, that the opposing hands be instantly exposed to prove that no revoke has been made.

In case of a revoke on both sides, the deal is void.

In order to prevent revokes as far as possible, the rule should be stringently observed of calling a player's attention to the fact that he renounces upon or trumps a led suit. The general question is, " You have no spade, partner ? " or whatever the suit may be to which he has not followed. These remarks do not apply to a misère, because in the case of that declaration an exposed card is as fatal as a revoke itself.

If one man proposes, and another man, not hearing or not noticing, also says, " I propose," the second declaration cannot be amended to an acceptance, but any other player may accept, or the original proposer may amend his call to anything better.

In the same way, a player may call one thing when he intends something else. If he correct himself instantly, it is courteous to let the change be made ; but he cannot claim this indulgence.

What we have said about improper calls applies with increased strength to improper remarks or suggestions.

As a general rule, it may be said that any remark made conveying an unfair intimation to partners entitles the other side to throw up the cards and demand a fresh deal.

As at Whist, however, a player may ask for the cards on the table to be " placed " when it is his turn to play, just as he may ask to see the last trick, or to know what suit is trumps.　This demand to see the last trick holds good at all declarations except a misère.

A trick once turned in a misère must not be looked at or referred to ; but in the other phases of the game, any player at the table, whether it is his turn to play or not, may ask to see the last trick, and must be shown it, but he can never see more than eight cards, and if there are no cards on the table he can only see the last trick.　He can never see two tricks that have been turned.

Should the cards be improperly divided, the declaring hand or hands win the stakes if their own cards are correct, and any person or partnership with the incorrect number of cards must, whatever has happened, lose the stake, unless the error is discovered before the first call is announced.

There are two varieties of the game that must be just mentioned before dismissing the subject.　These are Solo Whist for five players, and Solo Whist for three players.

Where the table consists of five, one man stands out every round, the person chosen being he who sits to the dealer's right.　The person standing out neither pays nor receives on that round.

Solo Whist for three players is not quite so simple. There is in this no proposal and acceptance, the solo being the lowest call.　There are two very good ways of playing, the best being to throw out the twos, threes, and fours from the various suits, and to turn up the fortieth card as trump, but not regarding that card as belonging to any individual.　The tricks, of course, consist of three cards each.　The other plan is to play with three suits only, leaving the fourth suit out altogether. The former method, however, makes the more scientific game.*

* For more detailed information on Solo Whist and its allies see A. S. Wilks's *Solo Whist and Auction Solo* (Routledge & Kegan Paul, Ltd.).

PIQUET

PIQUET is generally regarded as the best of card games for two players.

It is played with a pack of thirty-two cards, which is called a " piquet pack," all below the seven being excluded The cards rank in Whist order—ace, king, queen, knave, ten, nine, eight, seven.

The score is made partly by combinations of cards held in the hand, and partly by points marked in the course of play.

THE DEAL :

The two players cut for deal, and in this cutting the ace ranks the highest. The player who cuts the higher card has the choice of first deal. After this the players deal alternately.

It is customary to use two packs of cards, and the first dealer has the choice which pack he will use. Each player has a right to shuffle both his own and the adversary's pack, the dealer shuffling last. After this the pack is " cut to the dealer " by the adversary, as at Whist.

It is customary to call the non-dealer the " elder hand."

The dealer must deal the cards by two at a time, or by three at a time, giving the top cards to his adversary, the next to himself, and so on, until each has twelve cards.

The eight cards that remain (called the " stock ") are placed face downwards between the players.

There are no trumps in this game.

DISCARDING AND TAKING IN :

Before anything else is done, each player has a right to reject some of his cards, and take others in their place.

The elder hand begins. He has the privilege of discarding from his hand any number of cards not exceeding five (he *must* discard at least one), and taking a corresponding number from the top of the stock. If he does not take all his five, he may look at those he leaves,, concealing them, however, from the other player.

The dealer may then discard and replace in like manner, taking the cards from the stock in the order in which he finds them. He is bound to discard one, and he may, if he pleases, take all that remain, or any number of them. He may look at any cards of his own portion of the stock he leaves behind ; but if he does, the elder hand may demand to see them too, after playing his first card, or naming the suit he intends to play.

CALLING :

The hands being thus made up, the elder hand proceeds to declare or " call " the scoring combinations he may hold, in the following manner. There are three things in the hand that may be scored, namely (1) the *point;* (2) the *sequence;* (3) the *quatorze* or *trio.*

(1) The *point* is scored by the party who has the most cards of one suit. The elder hand states how many he has. If the dealer has not so many, he says " Good," and the elder hand scores one for each card ; if the dealer has more, he says " Not good," and the elder hand, scoring nothing, passes on to the next item. If the dealer happens to have the same number, he says " Equal," and then the elder hand must count and declare the number of the pips—the ace counting eleven, the court cards ten each, and the others what they are. The highest number of pips makes the cards " good," and invalidates those of the other party. If the number of pips are equal, neither scores.

(2) The second item is scored by the party who has the best *sequence,* that is, the greatest number of consecutive cards, not less than three, of the same suit, or, if an equal number, those of the highest rank. Thus, ten, nine, eight, seven are better than ace, king, queen ; but ace, king, queen are better than king, queen, knave ; and so on. A sequence of three cards, no matter what, counts three ; of four cards, four ; beyond this ten are added, so that a sequence of five cards counts fifteen ; of six cards, sixteen ; and so on. The elder hand declares his best sequence. If the dealer has a better, he says " Not good " ; if only inferior ones, he says " Good." In the latter case the holder scores not only for the *best* sequence, but for every other he holds in his hand ; all

the opposite party may hold being invalidated. If the best sequences are equal, neither scores.

(3) The third item is called the *quatorze*, from the fact that four aces, four kings, four queens, four knaves, or four tens in one hand, if " good," score fourteen. Three of either kind (called a *trio*) score three. In deciding which party is to score, the higher cards are better than the lower, but any four like cards take precedence of the best three. Thus four tens are better than three aces ; but three aces are better than three kings, and so on. The elder hand names his best quatorze or trio, to which the dealer says " Good " or " Not good," as the case may be ; and, as with the sequence, the one who has the best scores all others he may hold, while those of the opponent are all destroyed.

The point and sequence, when scored by either party, must be shown to the other, if asked for.

THE PLAY :

The items in the elder hand thus being counted, the holder lays down one card, thus beginning the " play." The dealer plays to this ; but, immediately before doing so, he calls and counts all *he* has to score in his hand.

The play, the object of which is to gain tricks, follows the ordinary Whist rule ; the second player being obliged to follow suit, if he can, and the best card winning. If he cannot follow suit, he loses the trick, throwing away any card he pleases.

The scoring of the play is peculiar. The first player to every trick counts one for the card he so plays ; but if the second player wins the trick, he also counts one. The player who takes the last trick counts an extra one for it.

If either player wins more than six tricks, he scores *ten* " for the cards," as it is called. If the two players win six tricks each, there is no score " for the cards " on either side.

EXAMPLE :

What has been above described constitutes the simple or ordinary game. There are some additional scores for extraordinary cases ; but before we mention them it will be well to illustrate the foregoing directions by an example of an imaginary hand, which will show that although the description may appear complicated, the practice is very easy.

A and B play at Piquet, B being the dealer, and A the elder hand. B deals out the following cards:

To A.

Spades—nine, seven
Hearts—ace, nine, eight
Clubs—knave, ten, seven
Diamonds—knave, ten, nine, eight

To B

Spades—queen, ten, eight
Hearts—queen, knave, seven
Clubs— ace, king, queen, eight
Diamonds—king, queen

After the deal the stock contains cards in the following order:

Ace of diamonds (top card)
Nine of clubs
Seven of diamonds
Ace of spades
King of hearts

_____

King of spades
Ten of hearts
Knave of spades (bottom card)

A has a poor hand, and must take all his five cards, in the hope of improving it. He must keep his diamond suit entire; so he discards the nine and seven of spades, the nine and eight of hearts, and the seven of clubs, taking in the five upper cards from the stock.

B's is already a good hand with the quatorze of queens —which he knows must be " good "—a fair chance for the point, and other favourable cards for trick-making. But he discards the ten and eight of spades and the seven of hearts with the hope of improvement, taking in the three remaining cards of the stock.

The two hands are then as follows: A (elder hand) has ace of spades, ace and king of hearts, knave, ten, nine of clubs, and ace, knave, ten, nine, eight, seven of diamonds. B (dealer) has king, queen, knave of spades; queen, knave, ten of hearts; ace, king, queen, eight of clubs; and king and queen of diamonds.

The following conversation may be supposed to take place:

A :   My point is 6.

B :   Good.

A (shows his diamonds, or says,—in diamonds ; and then adds) : My best sequence is the quint to the knave of diamonds.

B :   Good.

A :   I have also a tierce to another knave (shows knave, ten, nine of clubs, or says,—in clubs)

A :   And I have three aces.

B :   Not good.

A :   Then I score 6 for the point, 15 for the quint sequence, and 3 for the tierce, making 24.

He then plays ace of diamonds, and says : 25.

B :   I score 14 for four queens, and three for three kings—total 17.

B (plays queen of diamonds, and repeats) : 17.

A (plays seven of diamonds) : 26.

B (taking it with king) : 18.

B (leads ace of clubs) : 19.

A (follows with knave) : 26.

B (plays king of clubs) : 20.

A (ten of clubs) : 26.

B (queen of clubs) : 21.

A (nine of clubs) : 26.

B (eight of clubs) : 22.

A (throws away king of hearts) : 26.

B (leads king of spades) : 23.

A (takes it with ace) : 27.

A (now leads knave of diamonds) : 28.

B (anything) : 23.

A (ten of diamonds) : 29.

B (anything) : 23.

A (nine of diamonds) : 30.

B (anything) : 23.

A (eight of diamonds) : 31.

B (anything) : 23.

A (ace of hearts) : 32.

B (his last card) : 23.

A :   Then I score 1 for the last trick—33, and 10 for the cards ;* that makes me in all 43.

B :   And I score 23.

* A having made seven out of twelve.

A note is made of these numbers, and the next deal is proceeded with. We shall hereafter explain how the final score is made up from the results obtained in the successive hands ; but before doing this it will be well to complete the description of the scoring elements.

Piquet is remarkable for containing certain *extraordinary chances*, some of them of great scoring value. These are four in number, namely, the *Carte Blanche*, the *Repique*, the *Pique*, and the *Capot*.

CARTE BLANCHE :

If the hand originally dealt to either player contains neither a king, a queen, nor a knave (no picture card, in fact, whence the name), it entitles the holder to score ten.

As soon as the player is aware that he has this, he is bound to inform his adversary ; and after the adversary has discarded, he is bound to show his carte blanche by counting the cards, one by one, on the table.

The score for a carte blanche takes precedence of all other scores.

REPIQUE :

When either player can score thirty or more by the contents of his hand alone, before his adversary can score anything, he gets what is called a repique, which enables him to add *sixty* to his score.

Thus, if the elder hand finds himself with, say—

A good point of five - - - - - -	5
A good quint sequence - - - - -	15
A good quatorze - - - - - -	14
	34

such a combination will enable him (if the dealer does not hold carte blanche) to score ninety-four.

PIQUE :

When the elder hand counts something less than thirty in hand, but can make it up to thirty by *play* before his adversary counts one, he adds *thirty* on this account to his score. This is a pique. It is obvious that a pique can never be gained by the dealer, as his adversary always counts one for the first card he plays.

CAPOT:

If either of the players gain *all* the tricks, he scores *forty* for them, instead of ten for the majority. This is called a *capot*.

Pique, repique, and capot are not infrequent; but the occurrence of carte blanche is exceedingly rare, occurring only about once in nine hundred deals.

An an example of how these extraordinary chances tell, suppose that the elder hand, after discarding, should find himself with four major tierces in his hand, the dealer having only three cards of each suit, including at least one knave, so as to prevent a carte blanche: the elder hand would then score as follows:

In the hand—

Point - - - - - - - - -	3
Four tierce sequences - - - -	12
Three quatorzes - - - - - - -	42
	57
Add for the repique - - - - - -	60

In play—

Twelve cards, all winning - - - - -	12
For the last card - - - - - -	1
For the capot - - - - - - -	40
Total score for one hand - - -	-170

When it is considered that in some hands the score may be nothing, and that it may vary in all degrees between these, the variety obtainable will be strikingly evident.

THE FINAL SCORE:

Be it noted that to count a *pique* or a *repique* the scores shall be reckoned in the following order of precedence—viz. :

1. Carte Blanche.
2. Point.
3. Sequence.
4. Quatorze and trio.

Thus a Carte Blanche having been declared, neither pique nor repique can be scored. Or, say either player holds a good point with two good quatorzes but no sequence, while the opponent does hold a sequence—the repique cannot be counted. Or, say eldest hand counts point 6 with seizieme 16, plus a quint 15, he counts a repique, despite his adversary's 14 Aces. But should he hold a point of 6 with a quint, plus a quart major plus a quart minor=29, his adversary's trio of queens stops the pique.

The Final Score:

It is only necessary to discuss the *Rubicon Game*, the game of 100 or 101 points being in disuse.

The players play six deals, forming what is called a " partie." The scores made by each player in each deal are registered on a card, and at the end of the partie they are added together. The partie is won by the player who has made the highest aggregate score. The winner then deducts his adversary's score from his own, and 100 is added to the difference, which makes the number of points won.

Thus, suppose A has scored in the six deals 120 points, and B 102, A wins 120—102+100=118 points, for which he has to be paid.

But there is another condition, namely, the establishment of 100 as a " Rubicon." The law says that, if the loser fail to reach this amount, the winner reverses the rule, and instead of *deducting* the loser's score *adds* it to his own.

Thus, if A has scored 120, and B only 98, A wins 120+98+100=318, although the loser is only four short of his former score.

Another method of scoring is to make the *partie* four deals instead of six, the amount scored by each player on the *first* and *last* deals being doubled.

In the former method of scoring it is advantageous to get the first *senior* hand : in the doubling game it is better to have it last, since this gives the player a greater opportunity of discarding to the score.

Under both methods, should neither side have reached the requisite 100 points, two further hands are played and the score added to those already marked. In the doubling game, neither of these additional scores is doubled.

APPLICATION OF SKILL :

The skill required in Piquet applies to the rejection of cards from the original hand, and to the subsequent play, both of which offer excellent scope for intelligence and judgment. It would be impossible, in the short space at our disposal, to enter into all the complicated considerations which influence this matter. These, therefore, must be studied in larger works on the game, such as the excellent treatise on the game by " Cavendish,"published by Messrs. De La Rue & Co.

ÉCARTÉ

THE game of Écarté is played with what is known as the Piquet pack of thirty-two cards. The relative value of the cards is the same as at Whist, with one exception, viz. that the king is the highest card, the ace ranking between the knave and the ten. Thus the knave can take the ace, but the ace can take the ten.

Trumps, as at Whist, are the most powerful cards. A seven of trumps can take the king of another suit.

LAWS OF ÉCARTÉ:

The laws of Écarté, as accepted by the principal clubs in London and elsewhere, are as follows. We here quote them as given in " Cavendish on Écarté,"* a standard authority on the subject. Any reader who desires to become a skilful player cannot do better than procure and study this work.

The Club Code laws are—

1.—Each player has a right to shuffle both his own and his adversary's pack. The dealer has the right to shuffle last.

2.—The pack must not be shuffled below the table, nor in such a manner as to expose the faces of the cards, nor during the play of the hand.

3.—A cut must consist of at least two cards, and at least two must be left in the lower packet.

4.—A player exposing more than one card when cutting for deal must cut again.

5.—The player who cuts the highest Écarté card deals, and has choice of cards and seats. The choice determines both seats and cards during the play.

6.—The cut for deal holds good even if the pack be incorrect.

7.—If in cutting to the dealer a card be exposed, there must be a fresh cut.

* De la Rue & Co.

8.—The dealer must give five cards to his adversary and five to himself, by two at a time to each, and then by three at a time to each, or *vice versa*. The dealer, having selected the order in which he will distribute the cards, must not change it during that game ; nor may he change it at the commencement of any subsequent game, unless he inform the non-dealer before the pack is cut.

9.—If the dealer give more or less than five cards to his adversary or to himself, or do not adhere to the order of distribution first selected, and the error be discovered before the trump card is turned, the non-dealer, before he looks at his hand, may require the dealer to rectify the error, or may claim a fresh deal.

10.—The hands having been dealt, the dealer must turn up for trumps the top card of those remaining.

11.—If the dealer turn up more than one card, the non-dealer, before he looks at his hand, may choose which of the exposed cards shall be the trump, or may claim a fresh deal. Should the non-dealer have looked at his hand, there must be a fresh deal.

12.—If, before the trump card is turned up, a faced card be discovered in the pack, there must be a fresh deal.

13.—If the dealer expose any of his own cards the deal stands good. If he expose any of his adversary's cards, the non-dealer, before he looks at his hand, may claim a fresh deal.

14.—If a player deal out of his turn, or with his adversary's pack, and the error be discovered before the trump card is turned up, the deal is void. After the trump card is turned up, it is too late to rectify the error, and if the adversary's pack has been dealt with, the packs remain changed.

15.—If, after the trump card is turned up, and before proposing, or, if there is no proposal, before playing, it be discovered that the non-dealer has more than five cards, he may claim a fresh deal. Should the non-dealer not claim a fresh deal, he discards the superfluous cards, and the dealer is not entitled to see them.

16.—If, after the trump card is turned up, and before proposing, or, if there is no proposal, before playing, it be discovered that the non-dealer has less than five cards, he may have his hand completed from the stock, or may claim a fresh deal.

17.—If, after the trump card is turned up, and before the dealer accepts or refuses, or, if there is no proposal, before he plays, it be discovered that he has dealt himself more than five cards, the non-dealer may claim a fresh deal. Should he not claim a fresh deal, he draws the superfluous cards from the dealer's hand. Should the dealer have taken up his hand, the non-dealer is entitled to look at the cards he draws.

18.—If, after the trump card is turned up, and before the dealer accepts or refuses, or, if there is no proposal, before he plays, it be discovered that the dealer has less than five cards, the non-dealer may permit the dealer to complete his hand from the stock, or may claim a fresh deal.

19.—If a fresh deal be not claimed when the wrong number of cards are dealt, the dealer cannot mark the king turned up.

20.—If the non-dealer play without taking cards, and it be then discovered that he has more or less than five cards, there must be a fresh deal.

21.—If the dealer play without taking cards, and it be then discovered that he has more or less than five cards, his adversary may claim a fresh deal.

22.—If a king be turned up, the dealer is entitled to mark it at any time before the trump card of the next deal is turned up.

23.—If either player hold the king of trumps, he must announce it before playing his first card, or he loses the right to mark it. It is not sufficient to mark the king held in hand without announcing it.

24.—If the king be the card first led, it may be announced at any time prior to its being played to. If the king be the card first played by the dealer, he may announce it at any time before he plays again.

25.—If a player, not holding the king, announce it, and fail to declare his error before he has played a card, the adversary may correct the score, and has the option of requiring the hands to be played over again, notwithstanding that he may have abandoned his hand. If the offender win the point he marks nothing; if he win the vole he marks only one ; if he win the point when his adversary has played without proposing, or has refused the first proposal, he marks only one. But if the adversary himself hold the king, there is no penalty.

26.—If a player propose, he cannot retract ; nor can he alter the number of cards asked for.*

27.—The dealer, having accepted or refused, cannot retract. The dealer, if required, must inform his adversary how many cards he has taken.

28.—Each player, before taking cards, must put his discard face downward on the table, apart from the stock, and from his adversary's discard. Cards once discarded must not be looked at.

29.—If the non-dealer take more cards than he has discarded, and mix any of them with his hand, the dealer may claim a fresh deal. If the dealer elect to play the hand, he draws the superfluous cards from the non-dealer's hand. Should the non-dealer have taken up any of the cards given him, the dealer is entitled to look at the cards he draws.

30.—If the non-dealer asks for less cards than he has discarded, the dealer counts as tricks all cards which cannot be played to.

31.—If the dealer give his adversary more cards than he has asked for, the non-dealer may claim a fresh deal. If the non-dealer elect to play the hand, he discards the superfluous cards, and the dealer is not entitled to see them.

32.—If the dealer give his adversary less cards than he has asked for, the non-dealer may claim a fresh deal. If the non-dealer elect to play the hand, he has it completed from the stock.

33.—If the dealer give himself more cards than he has discarded, and mix any of them with his hand, the non-dealer may claim a fresh deal. If the non-dealer elect to play the hand, he draws the superfluous cards from the dealer's hand. Should the dealer have taken up any of the cards he has given himself, the non-dealer is entitled to look at the cards he draws.

34.—If the dealer give himself less cards than he has discarded, he may, before playing, complete his hand from the stock. If the dealer play with less than five cards, the non-dealer counts as tricks all cards which cannot be played to.

---

* The elder hand may " propose," *i.e.*, ask for cards, as often as he pleases. If the dealer is not content with his own hand, he will give cards, but after the first proposal, it is entirely at his own option whether or not to do so.

35.—If a faced card be found in the stock after discarding, both players have a right to see it. The faced card must be thrown aside, and the next card given instead.

36.—If, in giving cards, any of the non-dealer's are exposed, he has the option of taking them ; should the non-dealer refuse them, they must be thrown aside and the next cards given instead. If the dealer expose any of his own cards, he must take them.

37.—If, after giving the cards, the dealer turn up a card in error, as though it were the trump card, he cannot refuse another discard. If another be demanded, the non-dealer has the option of taking the exposed card.

38.—If the dealer accept when there are not sufficient cards left in the stock to enable the players to exchange as many cards as they wish, the non-dealer is entitled to exchange as many as he asked for, or, if there are not enough, as many as there are left, and the dealer must play his hand ; the dealer is at liberty to accept, conditionally, on there being cards enough in the stock.

39.—A card led in turn cannot be taken up again. A card played to a lead may be taken up again to save a revoke or to correct the error of not winning a trick when able, and then only prior to another card being led.

40.—If a card be led out of turn, it may be taken up again, prior to its being played to ; after it has been played to, the error cannot be rectified.

41.—If the leader name one suit and play another, the adversary may play to the card led, or may require the leader to play the suit named. If the leader have none of the suit named, the card led cannot be withdrawn.

42.—If a player abandon his hand when he has not made a trick, his adversary is entitled to mark the vole. If a player abandon his hand after he has made one or two tricks, his adversary is entitled to mark the point. But if a player throw down his cards, claiming to score, the hand is not abandoned, and there is no penalty.

43.—If a player renounce when he holds a card of the suit led, or if a player fail to win the trick when able, his adversary has the option of requiring the hands to be played again, notwithstanding that he may have abandoned his hand. If the offender win the point he marks nothing ; if he win the vole, he marks only one ; if he win

the point when his adversary has played without proposing, or has refused the first proposal, he marks only one.
Should the card played in error be taken up again prior
to another card being led (as provided by Law 39), there
is no penalty.

44.—A player may call for new cards at his own
expense, at any time before the pack is cut for the next
deal. He must call for two new packs, of which the dealer
has choice.

45.—If a pack be discovered to be incorrect, redundant,
or imperfect, the deal in which the discovery is made is
void; all preceding deals stand good.

46.—The game is five up. By agreement, the game
may count a treble if the adversary has not scored; a
double if he has scored one or two; a single if he has
scored three or four.

47.—A player turning up a king, or holding the king of
trumps in his hand, is entitled to mark one.

48.—A player winning the point is entitled to mark
one; a player winning the vole is entitled to mark two.

49.—If the non-dealer play without proposing, and fail
to win the point, his adversary is entitled to mark
two. If the dealer refuse the first proposal, and fail to
win the point, the non-dealer is entitled to mark two.
These scores apply only to the first proposal or refusal in
a hand, and only to the point, the score for the vole being
unaffected.

50.—If a player omit to mark his score, he may rectify
the omission at any time before the trump card of the
next deal is turned up.

51.—An admitted overscore can be taken down at any
time during the game.*

We will now suppose, by way of illustration, that A and
Y play a game of Écarté.

Two packs of different colour or pattern, say a red and
a white pack, are used. From these packs the cards
from two to six are extracted. A and Y cut for deal;
A cuts the knave, Y the ace. A therefore deals, as knave
is in this game higher than ace.

The cards having been shuffled, A gives the pack to Y

* For some further rules, defining the position and obligations of
bystanders betting on the game, see the work of "Cavendish,"
referred to at p. 78.

to be cut. A then deals three cards to his adversary, three to himself, then two to his adversary, and two to himself, and turns up the king of spades. " I mark the king," says A (see Law 22).

A does not look at his cards, but waits to see what his adversary will do. Y looks at his hand, and says, " I propose." A looks at his hand, and finds in it queen, knave, ace of spades, the ace of diamonds, and the eight of hearts. A has the trick now to a certainty, and cannot lose it by accepting, the low heart being the weak point in his hand. The hand of Y was ten of spades, king of hearts, ten and seven of diamonds, and nine of clubs. Y takes three cards ; A takes two. Y takes in the king of diamonds, the seven of spades, and the seven of hearts ; A takes in the nine and eight of spades, and must win the vole.

Y now deals, and turns the nine of clubs as trumps. A looks at his hand, and finds in it the king and ace of diamonds, the eight and seven of hearts, and the ten of spades. A proposes. Y looks at his hand, and finds king, queen, knave of spades, eight and seven of clubs. " Play," says Y, and he wins the vole. Score : Y= 2 ; A=3.

With such a hand as Y held, to accept the proposal would have been wrong, the chances being in his favour.

A now deals, and turns knave of diamonds. Y looks at his cards, and finds they consist of queen, ten of diamonds, ten and eight of clubs, and eight of hearts. He elects to play without proposing. A's hand consists of knave of clubs, ace, knave, ten of hearts, and eight of diamonds. Y may now win or lose the point, according to the cards he leads.

If he led queen, then ten of diamonds, he would lose the point. If he led ten of clubs, he would win the point. The reader should place the cards and play out these hands.

We will suppose that Y played correctly and won the point ; the game stands at 3 all.

It is now Y's turn to deal. We will suppose that he does so, and wins the point ; the game is then, Y=4 ; A=3.

A now deals, and turns the nine of diamonds. Y's hand consists of queen, knave of diamonds, king, queen, ace of spades. Y elects to play. A looks at his hand, and finds in it the king, ace of diamonds, the ace of hearts, the king of clubs, and the eight of spades.

Y must win the game if he plays correctly ; but, being anxious to win more tricks than are necessary, he loses it by reckless play. Y leads king of spades on which A plays eight of spades, *without marking the king*. A does this because Y, having played without proposing, will lose two if he lose the point. To mark the king will be useless, if Y win the point ; hence A conceals from Y the fact of his holding the king. Y plays incautiously, and leads as his second lead queen of diamonds ; A wins with king of diamonds, and leads king of clubs, which Y trumps, and leads queen of spades, which A trumps, and leads ace of hearts, which wins the game.

If Y had followed his first lead with queen of spades, he must have won the game ; but, imagining that A could not hold the king because he did not mark it, he played feebly, and lost the game.

This example will give some idea of the play of a hand, and of the different results which follow the correct and incorrect play of even five cards.

JEUX DE RÈGLE :

Great stress is laid by scientific Écarté-players on what are termed Jeux de règle, that is, hands which ought to be played without " proposing " or " accepting." When the cards held by a player are so good that he cannot fail to win three tricks unless his adversary hold two trumps, it is the rule to play without proposing. It is easy, by an examination of the five cards, to perceive at once how the trick must be won, unless the adversary hold two trumps. Here are a few examples :

King, queen, knave of spades, eight of hearts (trumps), eight of diamonds. Lead king of spades ; if not trumped, follow with queen, etc.

With three trumps, play without proposing. Likewise with two trumps, if the other cards belong to one suit, or with two cards of one suit, one of which is the king or queen.

Play if holding only one trump, provided the other cards are four of one suit, one being a king ; or three cards of one suit, one being a king or queen, and the fifth card being a king or queen.

Play with no trump if three queens are held, or four court cards.

When playing these hands (and they apply mainly to the leader) it is important to remember the disadvantage that follows leading from a suit of two when one is a high, the other a much lower card, and the advantage of leading from a suit of two when these are in sequence.

Take the following hands as examples:

A holds queen of clubs, queen of diamonds, queen and eight of hearts, and eight of spades, the ten of spades being turned up as trump.

Y holds king and nine of hearts, nine and seven of diamonds, and nine of spades.

If A lead the queen of hearts, he must lose the point, no matter how Y plays. If, however, he lead either of his single queens, he *may* win the point, if Y, after winning the queen of clubs, lead the king of hearts.

Again, A holds queen, ten, of spades; knave, ten, of hearts; ten of diamonds; diamonds being trumps.

Y holds knave, seven, of spades; seven of hearts: and knave, eight, of diamonds.

If A lead the queen of spades, he loses the trick. If he lead knave and then ten of hearts, he wins the trick.

From these examples it will be evident that cards in sequence, or single cards, are better as leads than one high card, and then a small one of a two-card suit. Also it is desirable that the adversary should be the leader when the third lead occurs.

What is called being " put to a card," is, if possible, to be avoided.

The dealer has the option of refusing or accepting; before doing either, he should not only consider well the cards in his hand, but the state of the score.

It is not unusual for a player who may hold the trick for certainty to propose in the hopes of being refused, in order that he may, by winning the trick, score two. If this occurred at the score of three, the results would be fatal.

As a general rule, refuse if only two cards can be discarded. A king or a trump should not be discarded in the first instance.

With three trumps, refuse, unless the king of trumps is one of the three, when there is a great chance that the cards taken in may enable the vole to be won.

With only one trump and one king, no matter what the other suits may be, if not having a card higher than a ten, accept. But with one trump, two queens guarded, or a king and queen guarded, refuse. Although in many cases, where it is the rule to play, it is two to one in favour of the player winning the point, it must not be imagined that he will always win. He may win twice out of three times, but it is possible for the adversary to hold exceptionally good cards, and to win the point against the *jeu de règle*. For example, A holds queen, ace, and seven of hearts (trumps), king of spades, king of diamonds, and, of course, plays without proposing. Y holds king, knave, nine, and eight of hearts, and nine of clubs, and must win the point ; but for A to propose would have been wrong, his hand being strong enough to win four times out of five.

EUCHRE

EUCHRE may be played either as a two-, three- or four-handed game, the latter being the most popular form. For greater facility of explanation, however, we will commence with the two-handed game.

Euchre is played with the " piquet " pack of thirty-two cards, consisting of the ace, king, queen, knave, ten, nine, eight and seven of each suit. The above is their rank in play, subject to the qualification that the knave of the trump suit for the time being is known as the " Right Bower," and takes temporary precedence of all other cards. The knave of *the opposite suit of same colour* (*e.g.*, of diamonds when hearts, or of spades when clubs are trumps) is known as the " Left Bower," and ranks next in value. The Left Bower is considered for the time being to belong to the trump suit, so that if this card is led, the trump suit, and not its own, must be played to it.*

TWO-HANDED EUCHRE:

The players having cut for deal, five cards are dealt (by twos and then threes, or *vice versa*, at the pleasure of the dealer) to each player. The eleventh card is turned up by way of trump. If the non-dealer thinks his hand good enough, with the suit of the turn-up card as trumps, to make three tricks, he says, referring to that card, " I order it up." This fixes that suit as trumps. The dealer discards the worst card of his own hand, placing it face downwards under the pack, and the turn-up card is thenceforth considered to form part of his hand. He does not, however, actually take it into his hand until the first trick has been played.

* A still higher trump is sometimes by agreement introduced in the shape of a blank card, backed like the rest of the pack, which in this case consists of thirty-three cards. This is known as the " Joker," or " Best Bower," and takes precedence even of Right Bower. If the " Joker " chance to be turned up, the card next in order decides the trump suit.

If the non-dealer does not consider his hand good for three tricks, or is of opinion that he would be likely to gain by a change of the trump suit, he says, " I pass," and the dealer examines his own cards from the same point of view.   If he thinks his hand is good enough with the subsisting trump suit to make three tricks, he says, " I take it up," and proceeds to place, as before, one card under the pack.   If he does not think his hand safe for three, he says, " I turn it down," and places the turn-up card below the rest of the pack.   This annuls the trump suit, and the non-dealer has now the option of saying what suit shall be trumps.   He considers what will best suit his hand, and says, " Make it hearts " (or otherwise, as the case may be), accordingly.

If he decides to " make it " *of the same colour* as the previous turn-up card (*e.g.,* spades in place of clubs, or hearts in place of diamonds), he is said to " make it next."   If otherwise, to " cross the suit."

If, even with the privilege of making the trump what he pleases, he doubts his ability to win three tricks, he again " passes," and the dealer " makes it " what best suits him.   If he too has such a bad hand that he thinks it safer to " pass " again, the cards are thrown up, and the deal passes.

The trump suit having been " made " by the one or the other player, the non-dealer leads a card, and the dealer plays to it, the two cards constituting a " trick."   The second player must follow suit if he can, subject to the qualification that (as already stated) if the Left Bower be led, a trump must be played to it.   The higher card wins, trumps over-riding plain suits ; and the winner of the trick leads to the next.

The player who has " ordered up," " taken up " (save in obedience to order), or " made " the trump, thereby tacitly undertakes to win at least three tricks.   If he makes less than this number, he is " euchred," and his opponent scores " two."   If he makes three tricks he wins " the point," and scores one.   Four tricks are no better than three, but if he make all five he wins a " march," which scores two.   The non-challenging player is not under any obligation to win, but scores if his adversary fail to do so.

Five points constitute " Game."

FOUR-HANDED EUCHRE :

Where four players take part, two play in partnership against the other two, partners facing each other, as at Whist. Five cards having been dealt to each, and the twenty-first turned up by way of trump, the elder hand (*i.e.*, the player to the left of the dealer) declares whether he will " order up " the trump card or " p∪ss." In the latter event, the option passes to the dealer's partner ; but he expresses it in a somewhat different manner, inasmuch as he is dealing with a friend instead of an enemy. If he thinks his hand good for two or more tricks he says, " I assist." This is considered a call to his partner (the dealer) to take up the trump, which he does accordingly, he himself having no choice in the matter. If the second player passes, the option rests with the third player, who " orders it up " or passes, as his hand may warrant. In the latter case the dealer decides for himself whether to take it up to turn it down. If the trump has either been ordered up or taken up voluntarily by the dealer, the play proceeds as in the two-handed game. If, on the other hand, the dealer " turns it down," the players, beginning with the elder hand, are invited in succession to " make it " what they please ; the challenging party in either case being bound, in conjunction with his partner, to make three tricks, under penalty of being euchred.

A player with an unusually strong hand may elect to " go alone." In such case his partner turns his cards face downward on the table, and leaves the " lone hand," as he is termed, to play the game singly against the two opponents.

If a player " going alone " is lucky enough to win all five tricks, he scores *four* (instead of three) for the " march " ; but if he make three or four tricks only, he scores one for the point in the ordinary manner.

THREE-HANDED EUCHRE :

Here each plays for his own hand. The value of the march and point are the same as in the two-handed or four-handed game, but if the challenging player is euchred, each of his adversaries scores two points. If this should carry them both " out," the elder hand is the winner. To avoid this, which is hardly a satisfactory termination for the younger hand, another method of scoring is sometimes adopted, the points for the euchre being *deducted* from the score of the euchred player, who is " set back " accordingly. Should he have made no points towards game, he is considered to owe the points for the euchre ; so that a player, standing at love when euchred, has seven points to make before he can win.

MARKING THE SCORE :

The method of scoring at Euchre is somewhat peculiar. The score is usually kept by means of spare playing cards, a three and a four (of any suit) being used by each side. The " three " face upwards, with the " four " turned down upon it, indicates *one* (however many pips may chance to be exposed). The " four " face upwards, with the " three " turned down upon it, indicates *two*. The face of the " three " being uppermost counts *three;* and the face of the " four " being uppermost counts *four*.

Another method of keeping the score is by means of a cross × chalked at the outset of the game on the table beside each player. " One " is scored by rubbing out the centre of the cross, leaving the four arms still standing, and these in turn are rubbed out, one for each point which the player becomes entitled to score.

The hints for play which follow are borrowed, with slight modification, from the American Hoyle. They refer more especially to the four-handed game.

HINTS FOR PLAY

PASSING AND ORDERING UP :

No prudent player will order up the trump unless his hand is sufficiently strong to render his chances of success beyond reasonable doubt. There are cases, however, when there would be no imprudence in ordering up upon a light hand. For instance, supposing the game to stand four and four, and the elder or third hand to hold an ordinarily good show of cards in the trump suit as turned up, with nothing better in any other suit, then it would be proper to order up, for, should the trump be turned down, your chance of success would be lost. If you are euchred, it does but give the game to those who would win it anyhow in some other suit.

If the player is elder hand, and a suit should be turned in which he receives both bowers and another large trump, and he has also two cards of the suit corresponding in colour, it is his best policy to pass ; for the obvious reason that if the dealer's partner should assist, he would be enabled to euchre the opposing side, and, if the trump were turned down, his hand would be just as good in the next suit.　Having in such case the first opportunity of making the trump, he could " go alone," with every probability of making the hand and scoring four.

Elder hand holding the Right Bower, ace or king, and another small trump and a card of the same colour as the trump suit, should pass ; for if his adversaries adopt the trump, he will, in all probability euchre them ; and if they reject it, he can make the trump next in suit, and the chances of scoring the point are in his favour.

As a general rule, the elder hand should not order up the trump unless he has good commanding cards, say Right Bower, king and ten of trumps, with an ace of a different suit, or Left Bower, king and two small trumps. The player at the right of the dealer should hold a very strong hand to order up the trump, because his partner has evinced weakness by passing ; and if the opposing side turn down the trump, his partner will have the advantage of first call to make a new trump.

ASSISTING :

Two court cards usually form a good " assisting " hand, but where the game is very close it is advisable to assist, even upon a lighter hand.　If, for instance, the game stands four and four, the first hand will naturally order up if the suit turned is the best in his hand.　The fact of his having passed is, therefore, an evidence of weakness.

When, as dealer, and assisted by your partner, you hold a card next in denomination to the card turned up (whether higher or lower), play it as opportunity offers. If, for instance, you turn up the ace, and hold either the Left Bower or king, when a chance occurs play the Bower or king, and thus inform your partner that you have the ace remaining.　The same policy should be adopted when your partner assists and you have a sequence of three trumps, the trump card being the smallest of the three.

In such a situation, play the highest card of the sequence ; this will inform your partner that you hold the remainder of the sequence, and enable him to shape his play accordingly.

As a general rule, always assist when you can win two tricks.

TAKING UP THE TRUMP:

What constitutes sufficient strength to take up the trump is a matter of considerable importance to the player. The object being to make a point, there must, of course, be a reasonable probability of securing three tricks, but the decision should, to a certain extent, depend upon the position of the game. If the dealer should be three or four towards game, while the opponents are one or two, the trump might be turned down, and the chances of winning the game still be not materially reduced ; but if the position should be reversed the dealer would be warranted in attempting the hazard upon a light hand, as the prospects of defeat would be no greater than by adopting the opposite alternative. It is generally accepted as sound that three trumps, backed by an ace of another suit, are sufficient to attempt a point. If the game stands four all, it is better to take up the trump on a small hand than to leave it for the adversaries to make. With the game three all, it is necessary to be very cautious in adopting the trump with a weak hand, because a euchre puts the opponents out.

MAKING THE TRUMP:

Should the dealer turn the trump down, the eldest hand has the privilege of making it what he pleases, and the rule to be generally followed is, if possible, to make it next in suit, or the same colour as the trump turned. The reason for this is evident. If the trump turned should be a diamond, and the dealer refuse to take it up, it is a fair inference that neither of the bowers is in the hands of your opponents ; for if the dealer's partner had held one of them, he would in all probability have assisted ; and the fact of the dealer turning down the trump also raises the presumption that he had neither of them. Then, in the absence of either bower, an otherwise weak hand could make the point in the same colour. For reverse reasons, the partner of the dealer would " cross the suit," and make it clubs or spades ; for, his partner having evidenced weakness in the red suits, by turning a red card down, it would be but fair to presume that his strength was in the black suits.

Be careful how you make the trump when your adversaries have scored three points, and, as a general rule, do not make or order up a trump unless you are elder hand or the dealer's partner.

THE BRIDGE :

If one side has scored four, and the other side only one, such position is known as the " bridge," and the following rule should be observed :

To make the theory perfectly plain, we will suppose A and B to be playing against C and D, the former having scored four, and the latter but one. C having dealt, B looks at his hand, and finds he has but one or two small trumps ; in other words, a light hand. At this stage of the game, it would be his policy to order up the trump, and submit to being euchred, in order to remove the possibility of C or D playing alone ; for if they should by good fortune happen to succeed, the score of four would give them the game. If B were to order up the trump, the most that could be done by the adversaries would be to get the euchre, and, that giving but a score of two, the new deal, with its percentage, would in all probability give A and B enough to make their remaining point and go out. If, however, B has enough to prevent a lone hand, he should pass, and await the result. The Right Bower, or the Left Bower guarded, is sufficient to block a lone hand.

The elder hand is the only one who should order up at the bridge, for if he passes, his partner may rest assured that he holds cards sufficient to prevent the adversaries making a lone hand. If, however, the elder hand passes, and his partner is tolerably strong in trumps, the latter may then order up the trump to make a point and go out ; for, by the eldest hand passing, his partner is informed that he holds one or more commanding trumps, and may therefore safely play for the point and game.

The elder hand should always order up at the bridge

when not sure of a trick ; the weaker his hand, the greater the necessity for doing so.

PLAYING ALONE :

If your partner announce that he will play alone, you cannot supersede him and play alone yourself, but must place your cards upon the table face downwards, no matter how strong your hand may be.* In order to avail yourself of the privilege of playing alone, it is necessary to declare your intention of so doing distinctly, and in plain terms thus, " I play alone " ; if you fail to do this, and the adverse side makes a lead, you forfeit all claim to the privilege. You must also make the announcement in good time ; if you neglect to do so, and the adverse side make a lead, or if you yourself lead before declaring your intention of playing alone, you lose the right, and your opponents may compel you to play with your partner.

In playing a lone hand, it is a great advantage to have the lead. The next best thing is to have the last play on the first trick. The elder hand or the dealer may, therefore, venture to play alone on a weaker hand than either of the other players.

When your opponent is playing alone, and trumps a suit led by yourself or your partner, take every opportunity to throw away cards of that suit upon his subsequent leads.

When, opposing a lone hand, you find that your partner throws away high cards of any particular suit, you may be sure that he holds high cards in some other suit ; you should, therefore, retain to the last your highest card of the suit he throws away in preference to any other card, short of an ace.

DISCARDING :

When the dealer takes up the trumps before the play begins, it is his duty to discard or reject a card from his hand in lieu of the one taken up. We will suppose that the ten of hearts has been turned up, and the dealer holds the king and Right Bower, with the ace and nine of clubs, and king of diamonds. The proper card to

---

* Under the more modern practice the player having the later call can play alone in place of his partner. Only a very strong hand, however, would justify his doing so.

reject would be the king of diamonds. There would be
no absolute certainty of its taking a trick, for the ace
might be held by the opponents ; whereas, retaining the
ace and nine of clubs, the whole suit of clubs might be
exhausted by the ace, and then the nine might be good.
If the trump were one of the red suits, and the dealer
held three trumps, seven of spades and seven of hearts,
it would be better for him to discard the spade than the
heart ; for, as the dealer's strength is in the red suit, the
probabilities are that the other side will be correspondingly
weak, and the heart would therefore be better than the
spade.

Where you have two of one suit and one of another to
discard from, always discard the suit in which you have
one only, for then you may have an opportunity to trump.

Leading :

Where the dealer has been assisted, it is a common
practice to lead through the assisting hand, and frequently
results favourably ; for in the event of the dealer having
but the one trump turned, a single lead of trumps exhausts his strength, and places him at the mercy of a
strong plain suit. It is not, however, always advisable
to lead a trump ; for, if the elder hand holds a tenace, his
duty is to manœuvre so as to secure two tricks ; but this
is an exceptional case. The proper lead must be determined by the quality of the hand, and the purpose to be
accomplished. The elder hand, holding two aces and a
king, with two small trumps, would, of course, lead
trump through the assisting hand ; for the only hope of
securing a euchre would be dependent upon the success
of the non-trump suits, and they can only be made available after trumps have been exhausted.

Where the dealer takes up the trump voluntarily, the
elder hand is, of course, upon the defensive, and to lead
a trump under such circumstances would be disastrous.

Should your partner have turned up the Right Bower,
lead a small trump as soon as you can ; by so doing you
will be sure to weaken your adversary's hand.

When your partner makes the trump, or orders it up,
lead him the best trump you hold.

When you hold the commanding cards, they should be
led to make the " march " ; but if you are only strong

enough to secure your point, cards of other suits should be used.

When opposed to a lone hand, always lead the best card you have of another suit, so that the possibility of your partner's retaining a card of the same suit with yourself may be averted. If the card you lead is of an opposite colour from the trump, so much the better ; for if a red card should be trump, and an opponent plays alone, the chances are against his holding five red cards. Besides, if the lone player did hold five red cards, it would, in like proportion, reduce the probability of your partner having one of the same suit, and give him an opportunity to weaken the opposing player by trumping.

The exception to the above rule is when you hold two or three cards of a suit, including ace and king, and two small cards in other suits ; in this case your best play would be to lead one of the latter, and save your strong suit, for your partner may hold commanding cards in your weak suits, and you thus give him a chance to make a trick with them, and if this does not occur, you have your own strong suit as a reserve, and may secure a trick with it.

When playing to make a lone hand, always lead your commanding trump cards first, reserving your small trumps and other suit for the closing leads. When you have exhausted your commanding trumps, having secured two tricks, and retaining in your hand a small trump and two cards of another suit, lead the highest of the non-trump suit to make the third trick, then your trump. For instance, suppose that hearts are trumps, and you hold the Right and Left Bowers and ten of trumps, and ace and nine of spades ; lead your bowers, then the ace of spades, following with the ten of trumps and nine of spades. The reason for playing thus is obvious. You *may not* exhaust your adversaries' trumps by the first two leads, and if either of them chanced to retain a trump-card superior to your ten, by leading the latter you would, in all probability, be euchred on a lone hand.

Holding three small trumps and good plain cards, and desiring to euchre your opponents, lead a trump, for when trumps are exhausted you may possibly make your commanding plain suit cards.

When you make the trump next in suit, always lead

a trump, unless you hold the tenace of Right Bower and ace, and even then it would be good policy to lead the bower, if you hold strong plain-suit cards.

When you hold two trumps, two plain cards of the same suit, and a single plain card of another suit, lead one of the two plain cards, for you may win a trick by trumping the suit of which you hold none, and then, by leading your second plain card, you may force your opponents to trump, and thus weaken them. With such a hand it would not be good play to lead the single plain card, for you might have the good fortune to throw it away on your partner's trick, and ruff the same suit when led by your opponents.

When your partner has made or adopted the trump, it is bad play to win the lead, unless you possess a hand sufficiently strong to play for a march. If your partner assist you, and has played a trump, and you have won a trick and the lead, do not lead him a trump unless you hold commanding cards, and are pretty certain of making the odd trick or a march, for your partner may have assisted on two trumps only, in which case such lead would draw his remaining trump, and, in all probability, prove fatal to his plans.

Having lost the first two tricks and secured the third, if you hold a trump and a plain card, play the former, for, in this position of the game, it is your only chance to make or save a euchre.

There are only two exceptions to this rule, viz., when you have assisted your partner, or when he has adopted the trump and still retains the trump card in his hand. In the former instance you should lead the plain card, trusting to your partner to trump it ; in the latter case you should also lead the plain card, unless your trump is superior to your partner's, and your plain card is an ace or a king, in which case you should play a trump, and trust to the plain card to win the fifth trick.

The reason for this play is manifest. If your opponents hold a better trump than you do, it is impossible to prevent their winning the odd trick, and, therefore, the euchre or point ; but if they hold a smaller trump, your lead exhausts it, and you may win the last trick with your plain card.

This position frequently occurs in the game, and we recommend it to the attention of the novice.

CONCLUDING HINTS:

Never lose sight of the state of the game. When the score is four all, adopt or make a trump upon a weak hand.

When the game stands three to three, hesitate before you adopt or make a trump upon a weak hand, for a euchre will put your adversaries out.

When you are one and your opponents have scored four, you may risk trying to make it alone upon a weaker hand than if the score were more favourable to you.

When you are elder hand, and the score stands four for you, and one for your opponents, do not fail to order up the trump, to prevent either of them from going alone. Of course, you need not do this if you hold the Right Bower, or the Left Bower guarded.

When playing second, do not ruff a small card the first time round, but leave it to your partner. Throw away any single card lower than an ace, so that you may afterwards ruff the suit you throw away.

When your partner assists, and you hold a card next higher than the turn-up card, ruff with it when an opportunity occurs.

When third player, ruff with high or medium trumps, so as to force the high trumps of the dealer.

When your partner leads the ace of a plain suit, and you have none, do not trump it ; but if you have a single card, throw it away upon it.

When second hand, if compelled to follow suit, head the trick if possible.

When you cannot follow suit or trump, throw away your weakest card.

NOTE.—There is no English Code of Laws for Euchre. The accepted American Code was compiled in 1888 for the Somerset Club, Boston, Massachusetts, by Messrs. H. C. Leeds and James Dwight.

COLONEL (COON-CAN FOR TWO PLAYERS)

COLONEL is two-handed " Coon-Can." An ordinary pack of 52 cards is used, and both players receive 10 cards each, dealt face downwards one at a time. The deal is determined by the cut—Ace counting lowest ; lowest deals. The remaining cards are termed the stock pack, the top card of which, called the optional card, being turned up.

The object of the game is to get rid of all one's cards by making sequence flushes, threes and fours of a kind, the player who first gets rid of his cards scoring the value of the cards left in his opponent's hand.

A sequence must be of at least three cards and all of the same suit—say, 5, 6, 7 of Diamonds—and these may be laid out, as may be threes or fours by the player when it is his turn to play. Once a sequence is put out, either player in his turn may add one or more suitable cards to it—or the fourth of its kind may be added to exposed threes.

The non-dealer having sorted his cards into potential sequence flushes, threes, etc., may pick up the " optional " card, or if that does not suit his hand, the top card of the stock pack. Now he " declares," that is, he exposes any sequences, threes or fours he has, and he may declare as many of these at one time as he happens to hold. Next he discards from his hand the card apparently most useless to him. This card is placed face upwards to the dealer's left of the stock pack.

The dealer plays next, drawing a card in the same way as the non-dealer, but he has also the option of taking in the latter's discard if it suits him.

So the game proceeds, each player alternately drawing a card (either the top card of the stock pack or the last discarded card), declaring and discarding ; the discard being placed face upwards on the top of the previous discard.

The player must " declare " before he discards. The other player is in play immediately the discard has been made. *The declaration is optional*, and this is where *play* at the game comes in. As soon as a sequence is declared, either player may add to it, thus getting rid of his single cards—just as by declaring a trio the opportunity is given to the opponent to play the fourth.

The ideal is to pack one's own hand with sequences and trios, and to declare the complete hand at a single go. The danger is that the opponent may pack his hand first, leaving you with all your ten cards to count against you. Judgment must be brought to bear to guard against this, as for instance if you observe that the opponent picks up your discard, you must be careful not to discard a card that will pair, or one that will help him to form sequences; or if you notice that he does not discard the card drawn in, and so appears to be packing his hand, then it is time for you to declare and to lessen your liability.

The value of the cards is ace, king, queen, knave and ten, 10 points each—the others their face value in pips— so if your hand consists mainly of count cards, it is dangerous to keep these too long; if, however, your sequences, trios, etc., are among the smaller values, not much harm can come to you.

Any trio of " ten " cards, or sequence containing two " ten " cards should be declared at the first opportunity— while the one-ended sequence, *i.e.*, *ace*, 2, 3, 4, or ace, king, queen, may be declared early on, since there is only one card to fit it. (Round the corner sequences are not played.)

If your hand is not shaping well towards sequences, try to pack your hand with small cards, then " challenge." Either player may " challenge " at any time prior to the stock being used up; his opponent can accept or reject the " challenge." If accepted, the hand of fewest pips wins, the winner scoring the whole number of pips in opponent's hand without deducting his own. If the whole stock pack is used up, both players lay out what they hold, and the player holding the least value in pips wins, and adds to his score the number of his opponent's pips less those in his own hand.

Each deal may be considered a complete game—or so many points up may be played, or a running score kept and settled up at any time.

CRIBBAGE

CRIBBAGE is primarily a game for two players, though it may also be played by three, or even four persons; in the latter case, two playing against two, as at Whist. Of the two-handed game there are three varieties, known, from the number of cards dealt to each player, as " five-card," " six-card," and " seven-card " cribbage. The number of points to be made in the first case is 61; in the second, 121; and in the third, 181. If the loser has made less than half the specified number of points, he is " lurched," and pays double the agreed stake.

The score is marked by means of pegs of ivory or bone, on a special board. There is on either side of the board a double row of holes, thirty in each, divided, for convenience in counting, into sets of five. The board is placed cross-wise between the players, and both start from the same end (which should be that to the left of the first dealer), each travelling up the outer and down the inner row (once round in the " five-card," twice in the " six-card," and thrice in the " seven-card " game), terminating with the " game-hole " at the end from which they started. In scoring, the hinder peg for the time being is advanced the requisite number of points beyond the foremost.

We will commence with the five-card game.

The pack of fifty-two cards is used, and the players cut for deal, the lowest dealing. For this and for " sequence " purposes, the cards rank in regular order from ace (lowest) up to king (highest), but in counting court cards count as tens.

The pack having been shuffled, the non-dealer cuts, and his opponent deals, one at a time, five cards to each player. Meanwhile, the non-dealer scores three holes, known as " three for last," and regarded as a set-off for the advantage of first deal. The undealt portion of the pack is placed face downwards between the players. Each player now " lays out " two of his cards (placed face downwards to the right hand of the dealer) to form what is called the " crib." The principles which govern the " lay out " will be discussed later.

The crib having been laid out, the non-dealer cuts, by lifting off the upper half of the pack. The dealer turns up the card left uppermost and places it on the top of the pack. This card is known as the " start." Should it chance to be a knave, the dealer is entitled to " two for his heels," and scores two points.

The score depends partly upon the course of play, and partly upon the player's holding certain combinations of cards. These latter are scored at the close of the hand.

The scores which may be made in course of play are as under :—

PAIRS.—A player playing a similar card to the card last played by his adversary (as a king to a king, or a seven to a seven) is entitled to score two for a *pair*.*

PAIRS-ROYAL. If the first player in the case last supposed can follow with a third card of the same description, he scores *six* for a *pair-royal*.

DOUBLE PAIRS-ROYAL.—If the second player replies with a fourth card of the same description, he scores *twelve* for a *double pair-royal*.

SEQUENCES, or RUNS.—Three or more cards of any suit but forming a regular numerical succession (as two, three, four ; knave, ten, nine), count one for each card to the last player. The sequence need not be played in regular order, so long as the cards exposed for the time being form an unbroken series. Thus, suppose that A plays a five, and B a four. If A now plays either a six or a three, he is entitled to score a run of three (three points). We will suppose that he plays a three. If B can play either a six or a two, he will be entitled to score *four* ; and if A can then add another card at either end, he will score *five*. Suppose, again, that A has played a five and a three, and B a two and a six. If A now plays a four, he is entitled to score five for the complete sequence. The highest number that can be scored for a sequence is *seven*, for ace, two, three, four, five, six, seven. Ace, king, queen, do not count as a sequence.

* Court cards, though they all count as of the same value—*i.e.*, " ten "—retain their distinctive rank for pairing purposes. Thus a knave can only be paired with a knave, and so on.

FIFTEEN OR THIRTY-ONE.—A player whose card makes, with those already exposed, the number *fifteen*, scores two. If either player makes *thirty-one*, he scores two in like manner. If, when the cards on the table approach thirty-one, the player whose turn it is can go no further without passing that number, he says, "Go." His opponent then plays any other card or cards up to that limit. If they make thirty-one exactly, he scores two ; if not, he scores one for "last card," *i.e.*, the last card played. This (at five-card cribbage) terminates the hand.

The hand being over, the players, beginning with the non-dealer, proceed to "show," *i.e.*, turn up their cards, and reckon how many points they may contain conjointly with the turn-up card, which is regarded as belonging, for this purpose, to the hand of each player, as also to the "crib" of the dealer. The first point noted is the *fifteens* they may contain, *two* points being reckoned for each, and the cards being combined in every possible way to make that number. Thus three fives and a ten or court card make (apart from their value under other aspects) four fifteens (technically spoken of as "fifteen eight "*), each of the fives forming one fifteen with the ten, and the three fives united forming another.

The next thing to be noted is the presence of any pairs, pair-royal, or double pair-royal. Thus, in the case supposed, the player, after claiming "fifteen eight," would go on to say "and six for a pair-royal, fourteen."

If all the three cards in the hand are in sequence (independent of suit), three points are reckoned for this, or if the three form a sequence with the turn-up card, four.

If three of the cards are in sequence, and the fourth is a duplicate of one of them, such fourth card is regarded as making a fresh sequence with the other two, the "double run," as it is called, scoring six points. Besides this, the holder is entitled to two for his "pair" (the two duplicate cards), bringing the total value (irrespective of "fifteens ") up to eight.

Where (as in crib at five-card, or hand or crib at six-card Cribbage) five cards have to be reckoned, it may happen that three are in sequence, and that the other two

---

* A single fifteen is spoken of as fifteen two, two fifteens as fifteen four, three as fifteen six, and so on. Four (fifteen eight) is the largest number of fifteens that can be made with four cards.

are duplicates of one of them. In this case they constitute a treble run of three (nine points) and a pair-royal (six points), total fifteen.

If the three cards of the hand are all of one suit, the player scores three points for a *flush*. If the turn-up is of the same suit, four points.

If the hand chance to contain a *knave of the same suit as the turn-up card*, the holder is entitled to score one point, " for his nob."

The non-dealer having scored his points, as above indicated, the dealer proceeds to score any points, first in his hand, and then in the crib, in like manner. There is only one distinction, viz., that, in counting crib, a flush is not reckoned unless the " start " is of the same suit as the rest. In this case the flush is worth five points (one for each card).

The following table indicates the method of counting some of the more important combinations (including the start) of the hand at five-card Cribbage :—

		Points.
Four fives (*Fifteen eight and a double pair-royal*)		20
Three fives and a ten (*Fifteen eight and a pair-royal*) - - - - - - -		14
Two fives, a four, and a six	*Fifteen four, pair,*	
Two fours, a five, and a six	*a double run of*	
Two sixes, a four, and a five	*three* - - -	12
Three threes and a nine		
Three sixes and a nine		
Three sixes and a three		
Three sevens and an eight	*Fifteen six and a*	
Three eights and a seven	*pair-royal* - -	12
Three nines and a six		
Three sevens and an ace		
Two eights, a six (or nine), and a seven	*Fifteen four,*	
	pair, and	
Two sevens, a six, and an eight	*double run*	
Six, five, and two fours	*of three* -	12
Two fives and two tens or court cards of like denomination (*Fifteen eight and two pairs*) -		12
Two nines and two sixes (*Fifteen eight and two pairs*) - - - - - - -		12
Two fives, a ten, and a court card (*Fifteen eight and a pair*) · - - - ·		10

Two sixes, a seven, and an eight (*Fifteen two,*
    pair, and double run of three)   -   -   -   10
A five and any three court cards in sequence, or
    ten, knave, queen (*Fifteen six and run of*
    three)   -   -   -   -   -   -   -   9
Any sequence of three cards, with a duplicate of
    one of them, but no " fifteen " (*Pair and*
    double run of three)   -   .   .   .   -   8

Where the four cards of the hand (or all four of the
crib, and the start) are of the same suit, the value of the
flush (four or five, as the case may be) must be added.
Where either includes a knave of the same suit as the
start, one " for his nob " will be scored in addition.

A study of the foregoing table should be a material aid
to the player in discarding for " crib." If he is dealer,
he desires the crib to be as productive as possible ; if non-
dealer, the reverse. On the other side, he desires to
retain such cards as shall be likely to score best in his hand,
and these two objects frequently clash. From this it
will be seen that success at cribbage, therefore, depends
largely upon knowing what is best to discard for one's
own or one's opponent's crib, and what best to retain in
one's own hand.

We will first examine the question from the dealer's
point of view. Both hand and crib belong to him, but
the hand consists (including the start), of *four* cards only,
while the crib has *five*. The possible combinations of five
cards are so numerous that space will only permit us to
give examples of a few leading hands. The highest
possible score is twenty-nine, which is made by three fives
and a knave, with a fourth five, of the same suit as the
knave, turned up by way of start.*

The mode of reckoning is as follows : the four fives, in
four combinations of three, score fifteen eight. Each of
them again scores a fifteen in conjunction with the knave,
making eight more. To these are added twelve for the
double pair-royal, and " one for his nob," making twenty-
nine.

* If the knave and start be of different suits, the score is twenty-
eight. With four fives in the crib, and the knave turned up, the
value of the show will be twenty-eight only, but the dealer will
already have scored " two for his heels," so that the total value is
thirty.

Two fives, two fours, and a six	*Fifteen eight, two pairs, and a run of three four times repeated -*	24
Two fives, two sixes, and a four		
Two fours, two sixes, and a five		
Two sevens, two eights, and a nine		

Four threes and a nine (*Fifteen twelve and a double pair-royal*) - - - - - 24

Three fives, a four and a six (*Fifteen eight, a pair-royal, and a run of three thrice repeated*) - 23

Three fours, a five, and a six	*Fifteen six, a run of three thrice repeated -*	21
Three sixes, a four, and a five		
Three sevens, an eight, and a nine		
Three eights, a seven, and a nine		

Four twos and a nine	*Fifteen eight and a double pair-royal*	20
Four threes and a six		

Two sixes, two sevens, and an eight	*Fifteen four, two pairs, and run of three four times repeated -*	20
Two sevens, an eight, and two nines		
Two eights, a seven, and two nines		

Three tens, or court cards of like denomination and two fives	*Fifteen twelve, pair-royal, and pair -*	20
Three threes and two nines		
Three sevens and two aces		

Three threes and two sixes* (*Fifteen ten, pair, and pair-royal*) - - - - - 18

Three fours, three, and five (*Fifteen two, pair-royal, and run of three thrice repeated*) - - 17

Three tenth cards in sequence and two fives (*Fifteen twelve, pair, and run of three*)† - 17

* The score is made up as follows. Each of the sixes combines with each nine to make a fifteen, giving fifteen four. Again, each of the threes combines with the two sixes, bringing the score to fifteen ten. The pair and pair-royal make it eighteen.

† If the three tenth cards make neither pair nor sequence, the score will be fourteen only.

Any three cards in sequence, with duplicates of
two of them, but no " fifteen " (*Two pairs
and run of three four times repeated*)　-　　-　16
Any three cards in sequence, with one of them
thrice repeated, but no " fifteen " (*Pair-royal
and run of three thrice repeated*) -　　-　　- 15

As for combinations of minor value, their name is
legion.

With four cards only, the general average is very much
lower, as will have been seen from the table on p. 105.

A comparison of the foregoing tables shows that the
crib at five-card Cribbage is likely to be much more
important than the hand, and this furnishes us with a
safe principle for the guidance of the player in laying out.
In the case of the dealer, he should lay out for crib such
cards as are most likely to form valuable combinations,
even though he may, to some extent, sacrifice the scoring
value of his hand. Conversely, it is to the interest of
the non-dealer to lay out such cards as are likely to " baulk
the crib," as it is termed, even though he may to some
extent injure his own hand in doing so. On close
examination of the tables, it will be found that the cards
most likely to help the crib are *pairs*. If the other three
cards chance to be in sequence, they are worth, standing
alone, three only, but the addition of duplicates of either
of the series will bring their value (for runs and pair-
royal) up to fifteen, independently of any other points they
may contain. Or suppose, with six as start, that the
dealer has thrown out a four and a five, these are worth
five only ; but if the non-dealer had been rash enough to
throw out a pair, either of fours or sixes, the score would
run up to twenty-one. If the non-dealer had thrown out
a pair of fives, it would have been twenty-three.

Next to a pair, two cards forming a fifteen, or two
cards in sequence, are most likely to help the crib, and
should therefore be preferred by the dealer, and eschewed
by the non-dealer—the more so, if they chance to answer
both conditions—*e.g.*, a seven and eight. Next to cards
in sequence come cards only one or two points apart, as
the cards of the opposite player may fill up the gap, and
convert them into sequence cards. Of single cards, a
five is the most likely to score, inasmuch as there are

sixteen tenth cards to four of any other denomination, and the chances of its forming part of one or more fifteens are therefore considerable. The cards which are least likely to make for crib are king and ace, inasmuch as nothing save queen, knave can convert a king into a sequence card, and nothing save a two and three can convert the ace into a sequence card. The best cards for the non-dealer to throw out are therefore a king or ace, and some second card so far removed from the first that the two cannot form part of the same sequence. King or queen, with nine, eight, seven, six, or ace, are good " baulking " cards ; likewise two or ace, with seven, eight, nine, or ten. The non-dealer should never throw out a knave if he can help it, as the start may cause it to score a point for " nob." In like manner, the non-dealer should avoid laying out two cards of the same suit, as he thereby runs the risk of a flush in crib.

In the play of the hand the guiding principle should be to give to the adversary the fewest possible opportunities of scoring. Bearing this in mind, it will be seen that the best card to lead at the outset is an ace, two, three, or four, as the second player cannot make fifteen, and the chance of doing so will revert to the first player. A five, on the other hand, is a very bad lead, inasmuch as, from the greater number of tenth cards in the pack, it gives the second player the best possible opportunity of making fifteen. If the leader holds duplicates of ace, two, three, or four, one of them is a very good lead ; for if the second player should pair, the leader will have the opportunity of making a pair-royal. Failing pairs, if the leader hold two cards which together make five, *i.e.*, two and three, or ace and four, it is good to play one of them, when, if the adversary play a tenth card, the leader will be enabled to make fifteen. Likewise, if the leader hold a six and a three, a four and a seven, or a three and a nine, the first card of the couple is a safe lead, for if it is paired, the second will make fifteen. On the other hand, should the second player play a tenth card to the lead, the first player may pair it with perfect safety, for no pair-royal can be made without overpassing the limit, thirty-one.

As regards the second player, he will generally do well to make fifteen if he can. If a low card, *i.e.*, a four or less has been led, he has no choice, in the majority of cases, but to leave the fifteen to his adversary ; but he should carefully avoid playing such a card as will enable the adversary to score not merely the fifteen, but a pair or sequence in addition. On a four led, for instance, it would be very unwise to play either a six or a five, as in such cases respectively, a five or six played by the first player would give him both fifteen and a sequence. On a three it would be equally wrong to play a six ; on a seven a four ; on a nine a three, or on an ace a seven ; for a like card played by the first player would give him both fifteen and a pair. Again, it is in general unwise for second player to play a close card (*i.e.*, next or next but one to the lead), as he thereby gives the adversary the chance of a " run." If he is in a position to continue the run, he may, of course, play a close card with impunity. The points of " five " and " twenty-one " are to be avoided, as a tenth card played by the adversary will in such case make him fifteen or thirty-one. Similarly, it is bad play to make fourteen or thirty (*i.e.*, one short of fifteen or thirty-one) with an *ace;* to make thirteen or twenty-nine (*two* short) with a *two;* twelve or twenty-eight with a *three;* eleven or twenty-seven with a *four;* as in either of such cases, should the adversary be able to pair, he will thereby score four holes. The only exception is where the player chances to hold two deuces or aces, in which case it will be worth while to make twenty-nine or thirty respectively with one of such cards, on the chance of the opponent holding no deuce or ace, in which case the first player will himself gain the advantage of the double score.

Some discretion is needful in pairing the card first led, as the first player may be aiming at a pair-royal, and the temporary gain of two points may be counter-balanced by six to the adversary. Where, however, the player holds two of the card led, it may be paired without hesitation. The chances are much against the dealer's being in a position to make a pair-royal, and if he should, it can be capped (unless the card be over seven) by the double pair-royal of the last player.

A further point to be considered, in deciding whether to make a pair or sequence, is the state of the score. It is calculated that the non-dealer, at five-card cribbage, should make, on an average, *six* in hand and play ; the dealer *eleven*, or a shade more, in hand, play, and crib. When each has dealt once, they should stand abreast at seventeen to eighteen, and so on throughout the game. The player who has maintained this average is said to be " home," and a player who is in this condition at an advanced state of the game, should run as few risks as possible ; should avoid pairing, play wide cards to avoid sequences, and so on. This is known as " playing off." If, on the other hand, he is behind his proper position, his chance of winning will depend, in a great degree, on his making more than the average number of points in play. In such case, he should embrace every opportunity of making a fifteen, a pair, or a sequence, even at the risk of giving opportunities to the enemy. This is known as " playing on." As there are sixteen tenth cards in the pack, and ten out of fifty-two are dealt, the probabilities are in favour of the players holding originally three between them, and this probability should be borne in mind, as the so doing will often help the player to a thirty-one. Suppose that the leader starts with queen, and that the other player has no tenth card, but has a seven and a four, an eight and a three, or a nine and a two. In such case it is good policy to play the seven, eight, or nine. If the first player again plays a tenth card, the second will be enabled, with his small card, to score thirty-one. If the second player have no tenth card in his own hand, the probability of his opponent holding more than one is proportionately increased.

It may be useful to illustrate these elementary principles by the play of a couple of imaginary hands. Let us suppose that A (elder hand) has the queen and six of hearts, nine of clubs, eight of diamonds and seven of spades. And B (dealer) the ace and ten of hearts, ten of clubs, five of spades, and four of diamonds.

It will be observed that A has four cards, six, seven, eight, nine, in sequence, of which either the six and nine or the seven and eight will form a fifteen. His fifth card, the queen, does not and cannot score with either of the others. Obviously the queen should form one card of his lay-out. Of the four remaining, he will naturally keep three in sequence. Which shall he throw out, the six or the nine? The six in one respect is preferable, inasmuch as it cannot be brought into sequence with the queen, whereas the nine might possibly be so. On the other hand, the six is of the same suit as the queen, and might help towards a flush. He decides, therefore, to throw out queen, nine, retaining the six, seven, and eight.

B's proper course is clearly to throw out the ace of hearts and four of diamonds, retaining the two tens and the five, which are good for six points, viz. fifteen four and a pair, and with a five or ten start would be worth twelve. On the other hand, should there be one or more tenth cards in the crib, the four and ace will give them a scoring value.

The cards are cut, and B turns up the queen of clubs.

A leads the seven of spades, saying, " seven." This is his best lead. If B should play an eight making fifteen, A will be enabled to continue with the six, and so score a run of three.* But B cannot make a fifteen, and it is therefore his best policy to go beyond that point. He plays the ten of hearts, saying, " Seventeen," or more shortly, " '-teen." A has no card which will score, and he therefore plays his highest, as the nearer he gets to thirty-one the fewer chances does he leave his opponent of getting closer to that number. He plays the eight of diamonds, saying, " Twenty-five." B plays the five of spades—" Thirty." " Go," says A. B scores one for last card, and the play of the hand is at an end.

The cards are turned up, and A counts his hand. The start has left him " no better." He scores fifteen two for the seven and eight, and three points for the run— five in all.

B is rather better off. With the start he has fifteen six and a pair—eight in all. In crib the start has helped him considerably. Without it he had fifteen two only— the ace and four combining with the queen of hearts; with the start he has six—fifteen four and a pair. The nine is useless.

A having taken his three points as non-dealer, the score stands eight to fifteen. It is now A's turn to deal, and the cards fall as follows : B has king and eight of hearts,

* In the case supposed, it would be very unwise for A to pair the eight, as, in the event of B's holding a second eight, he would make a " pair-royal " and " go " simultaneously.

seven of spades, eight of diamonds and three of clubs. And A (dealer) five and nine of diamonds, three of spades, ten of hearts and six of clubs.

B throws out the king of hearts and three of clubs ; A, the six of clubs and nine of diamonds. The cards are cut, and the six of diamonds is turned up.

B leads the eight of hearts. This is a safe lead, for, if A scores fifteen, B can pair them ; if A pairs, B can make a pair-royal. A, not being able to do either, plays the ten of hearts, making eighteen. This prevents all possibility of B's making fifteen ; and should B play a tenth card, A's three will make thirty-one. There is a possibility of B's playing a nine, and so making three for the run, but this risk must be taken. Should he do so, A will in all probability score one for last card ; but B, having only a seven and an eight, plays the latter, making twenty-six. This is a shade the better card, inasmuch as it brings the score one point nearer thirty-one. As it happens, the choice was unfortunate, for A, having a five, is able to make thirty-one exactly, scoring two points accordingly.

The cards are shown : B scores fifteen four, a pair, and a run of three twice over—twelve in all. A has in hand fifteen two only ; but in crib he has fifteen six and a pair, making eight in all.

The game now stands—A 20, B 27. Both have made their full average in the two deals ; but B's seven points ahead give him a decided advantage, and, on the principle already explained he will do well to " play off " during the remainder of the hand.*

Six-Card Cribbage.

In this form of the game *six* cards are dealt to each player. Two being laid out for crib, four are still left in hand, and the scores accordingly average very much higher than in the five-card game. The only material difference of procedure is that in the six-card game the scoring of three extra points by the non-dealer is omitted,

* There is no authoritative code of Cribbage Laws, and there is considerable divergence of opinion on sundry minor points. For the rules generally accepted, the reader may be referred to the pocket guide to the game by " Rawdon Crawley, Bt." (Thos. De La Rue & Co., Ltd.).

both players being considered to start on an equal footing ; and secondly, that the cards, instead of being thrown
down as soon as thirty-one or the nearest possible
approach to it, is reached, are played out to the end.
The player who failed to score for the " go " leads again,
giving the adversary the opportunity to make fifteen, or
pair him if he can. Each plays alternately as before, the
player of the " last card " scoring " one " for so doing.
If there is only one card left after the " go," the leader
still scores it as " last card." The general principles
laid down as to five-card cribbage apply equally to the
six-card game, save that in the latter, as hand and crib
consist of the *same number* of cards, the non-dealer is no
longer under the same compulsion to baulk the crib, even
to the destruction of his own hand. The two objects—
preserving the hand and baulking the opponent's crib—
are in this case on the same level, and either may legiti-
mately be preferred, as the nature of the hand may render
desirable.

In consequence of the greater facility of scoring, it is
customary to play six-card cribbage twice round the
board, *i.e.* to make the game 121 points.

Seven-card Cribbage.

Seven-card cribbage is played in the same manner as
the six-card game, save that *seven* cards are dealt to each
player, two being thrown out for crib, and *five* left in
hand, or, with the start, six. With such a largely increased number of possible combinations, very high
scores are frequent, and for this reason it is customary to
make the game three times round the board, *i.e.* 181
points.

Three-handed Cribbage :

When three persons play, five cards are dealt to each,
one card of each hand being laid out for crib, with one
card from the top of the pack to complete it. The start
is then cut for in the usual manner. The player to the
dealer's left has first lead and first show, and deals in
the succeeding hand.

The score is usually marked on a triangular board,
open in the centre, or the ordinary cribbage-board may be

furnished with a supplementary arm, turning on a pivot, and duly provided with holes, to keep the score of a third player.

FOUR-HANDED CRIBBAGE :

Where four persons engage in the game, two play as partners against the other two, each pair sitting facing each other. Partners and deal are cut for, as at Whist, the two lowest playing against the two highest, and the lowest dealing. Five cards are dealt to each player, and each puts out one for the crib, which belongs, as in the two-handed game, to the dealer. The player to the dealer's left has the lead, and each of the others play to it in rotation. No consultation is allowed during the play, but partner may assist partner in counting his hand or crib. One partner scores for both. The cards are played right out, as in the six-card game.

The score is usually twice up and down the board, *i.e.* 121 points.

At all games of Cribbage the player who first pegs out wins the game, when the hands are abandoned.

POKER

THERE are several varieties of Poker, such as "Stud," "Whiskey," and "Straight" Poker and so on, but it will be sufficient for our purpose to attempt a description of Draw Poker; the laws herein given represent the recognised rules under which the game is played by the leading players in this country, and may therefore be accepted as the standard laws for English Draw Poker.

Draw Poker—or simply Poker—is played with an ordinary pack of 52 cards. Any number up to eight can play, but seven is really the maximum, for when eight play the dealer deals himself out and takes no part in that hand. Five or six is said to be the best number.

Each player receives five cards, dealt one at a time, and in turn has the option of " coming in " or of not playing. Those that come in put so many chips into the pool (or " pot "), and can then discard any number or all of their cards and receive in exchange (face downwards) an equal number. Only one exchange is allowed, and after the " draw " as it is called, the player whose turn it is " bets "; that is he stakes so many chips that his hand will defeat the hands of each one of the other players. Then each player in turn may pass or put into the pot the same number of chips as the bet to " see " it, or may " raise " the previous bets, that is he bets a still larger sum that he holds the best hand, and so on round the table, each player in his turn " passing," " seeing," or " raising," until finally there is no further raise. Then the player who is seen or "called" shows his hand, and if it is best he takes the pot. Failing him, the player who actually does hold the best hand wins, but only the winner and the " called " hand need show their cards.

Suppose A, B, C, D, and E are all " in," the phraseology of the betting would go :—

A : " I bet one chip " (puts up one chip).
B : " I see one chip " (puts up one chip).
C : " I see and raise five " (puts up six chips).

116

D : " I see six " (puts up six chips).

E : " I see and raise ten " (puts up 16 chips).

A : " I pass " (throws up his hand).

B : " I see 16 " (puts up 15, making 16 with the one already bet).

C : " I retire " (throws up his cards).

D : " I see and raise ten " (puts up another 20—making 26 in all—6 his first see, a further 10 to see E's raise, and a further 10 his own raise back).

E : " I see " (puts in another 10).

B : " I see " (puts in another 10).

B shows his hand (all five cards) and calls " three aces."

E : " Beats me " (throws away his cards without showing them).

B : " I have a flush " (shows it and takes the pool).

Had B not been able to beat three aces he would have thrown away his cards without exposing them. Theoretically the best hand wins, but this is not always so. To explain this it is necessary to go more fully into the details of the game, which we now proceed to do.

The values of the Poker hands in order of merit are :

1. *Straight Flush.* 5 cards of the *same* suit in sequence (a combination of the Straight and the Flush).

2. *Fours* (four of a kind). 4 cards of the same denomination, e.g., 4 queens, 4 sevens (and 1 indifferent card).

3. *Full Hand.* 3 cards of the same denomination with 2 cards of the same denomination, e.g. 3 tens and 2 fours ; 3 kings and 2 nines, etc.

4. *Flush.* All five cards of the same suit, e.g., 5 hearts, 5 spades.

5. *Straight.* All 5 cards in sequence, e.g., knave, 10, 9, 8, 7 ; ace, 2, 3, 4, 5 ; or ace, king, queen, knave, 10, in different suits.

6. *Threes.* 3 cards of the same denomination, e.g., 3 aces ; 3 sixes (and 2 indifferent cards).

7. *Two pairs*, e.g., 2 queens and 2 twos ; 2 eights and 2 fives (and 1 indifferent card).

8. *One pair.* Any two cards of the same denomination (and 3 indifferent cards).

9. *Highest card.* Ace high (no pair).

With similar hands highest card wins, e.g., Flush knave high beats Flush 10 high; Straight to queen beats Straight to knave; Pair eights and king next beats pair eights with queen next, etc. With Full Hands the higher threes win, e.g., 3 threes and 2 fours are better than 3 twos and pair aces.

If the hands are identical the pool is divided.

Any hand in which the best combination of its kind is held is known as a " pat hand," and it is the object of the player to turn his holding as dealt him into a " pat hand " by changing such cards as are useless for others that will " improve " his hand, if possible to a pat, but failing that to something better than he now holds. Thus a player on the deal holds the ten of diamonds, and the ten of clubs, and ace, king, queen of spades. This is a Poker hand representing " pair-tens," the ace, king, queen of spades being worthless, and these good *looking* cards would be thrown away in hopes of drawing another ten, when the hand is " threes "—a most excellent Poker hand. If two tens are drawn the hand becomes " four of a kind," a " pat hand," and practically unbeatable—or the " pair-tens " may turn into a " full " on the draw by getting a third ten and another pair or by picking up " threes."

A player with queen, knave, ten, nine of spades and ace of hearts holds nothing at Poker—ace high. He draws one card, throwing the ace. Should he draw the king or eight of spades he has made the best possible—a straight flush—or if he draws a spade of any kind he has a flush, the fourth best possible. Thus " a four straight flush," as this kind of holding is called, is the very best hand to draw to—although as dealt it is worthless. So with two pairs originally, the bad card is thrown away in hopes of making a Full by drawing a card of the same denomination as either of the pair held ; and so on.

A limit is set in the amount of the bet. This does not mean that the betting cannot be increased after the " limit " has once been bet. It represents the amount to which a player is limited at any moment when it is his turn to bet. The betting can always be increased by the limit by any player in his turn. This is sometimes and erroneously called " unlimited " Poker. " Unlimited "

Poker would mean that any one player could bet an unlimited amount in any one bet, which of course would turn the game into an absurdity ; if the betting were limited to one bet of the limit it would be equally an absurdity at Poker.

The player on the left of the dealer, known as the " age," puts so many chips into the pot—this is called the " ante," and it must be a small proportion of the limit—the smaller this proportion the better the game ; it is usual nowadays to make the ante about one-tenth of the limit, though one-twentieth part would be better. One shilling ante with one pound limit makes an excellent game of (small) Poker.* This amount is the smallest amount the Age can ante, but at Poker proper he is allowed to ante any sum up to half the limit. The player sitting on the left of the " age " having looked at his cards, is now asked by the dealer if he plays. If he does he puts into the pot *twice* the amount of the ante : if not he throws his cards face downwards on to the table, and so on round the table, the " age " being the last to declare whether he plays or not. Then the dealer, *beginning with* the " age " asks each player in turn how many cards are required—so the dealer, if he is a player, is the last to draw. The players having exchanged their cards—only one draw or exchange of cards being allowed —the betting begins.

The first bet is with the player sitting on the left of the age, and he can bet any sum from the amount of the ante up to the amount of the limit. If he does not think his hand worth betting on he throws up his cards, face downward, and the player on his left has next bet ; if he does not care to bet, the player on his left has the right, and so on round the table, the ante man having the last bet, and if it so happens that nobody before the ante man has made a bet, that player collects the pot without making a bet or showing his cards. As soon as one player makes a bet the player on his left can " see " the bet or raise him or drop out, and so with each player in his turn. Suppose one or more players simply " sees " or " calls."

* It is the one flaw in the game of Poker that it must be played for stakes of some importance—and the higher the stakes the better the game. £10 limit is better Poker than £1 limit. But at *all* stakes the proportion between limit and ante must be maintained.

the bet ; the cards of the original betting hand are exposed, and if they are the best they win the pool. If any of the other " callers " have something better he takes the pool, and so the best hand of those that saw the bet wins. We will now suppose that one of the players in addition to seeing the previous bet " raises " it. He puts into the pot the amount of the original bet plus the amount he raises, which may be the limit or any part of it. Now any player wishing to call this raise must put in a similar amount, and further, if he chooses, he may raise again the limit or any part of it, and so with all players in turn until the last raise is seen, when the best hand wins as before—or if no player sees the last raise, the player who made it takes the pot plus all previous bets without showing his hand. In this case of course it does not follow that the best hand has won. The raiser may hold nothing at all, but has succeeded in frightening the others out by the amount he bets. This is called " bluffing," which is the Poker term for " betting as though you had them." The players who fail to see a raise retire for that hand, but have to sacrifice any bet or bets they have previously made. Money once put into the pot can never be withdrawn.

We will now give an example of one hand at Poker. The game is nearly always played with chips, and we will say that one white chip (=1/-) is the ante, that blue represent 2/6, red 5/-, and a yellow 10/- is the limit. There are five players and A deals, B on his left ante's one chip. A deals five cards *one at a time* to each player, and asks C—on B's (the age's) left—if he plays. We will say that C holds no pair or combination of cards that is worth drawing to, so drops out. D holds " a pair kings," and three indifferent cards and comes in, putting two whites into the pot. E, holding pair tens and pair threes (two pairs) and one indifferent, also comes in and puts up two white. A, the dealer, with 3, 4 of diamonds, 5 of clubs and 6 of hearts and one indifferent card—say king of clubs—comes in on " a four straight with two openings " for two whites. B, the ante man, plays on ace, king of hearts, and three indifferent cards. Of course he holds nothing at present, but being already one white in for his ante thinks it worth while to " make good his ante," *i.e.*, puts in one more white, and to chance the draw to ace, king. He draws three cards, and has the luck to draw another ace and another king, making " two pairs ace up," a very good hand. C is not playing and D draws three cards to his pair-king, but fails to improve. E draws one to his two pair, and drawing a three improves his hand to " a full of threes." A draws a deuce, making " a straight, six high."

The betting now starts with D, who puts up one white on his pair kings. E, on his full, raises 5/- only, not wishing to frighten the opposition out, and puts in one white plus one red. A, thinking his straight good enough, raises this the limit, so puts in one white plus one red plus one yellow. B fancies his two pair ace up must have a chance and " sees," so puts up an equal amount to A—one white, one red, and one yellow. D sees he is beaten and retires, but E naturally raises again—this time the limit—so puts in *two* more yellow (one to make up A's raise of a yellow, and one more to raise him). A, feeling that E must be very strong, is afraid to raise him again, so puts in one more yellow to " see." B is now sure that either E or A, and probably both, can defeat his two pair, so refuses to see, and retires, sacrificing his white, red and yellow chip. E being seen, shows his full, which wins, being a better hand than A's straight. B collects the cards, and deals the next hand, C becoming the ante man.

This is a typical deal at Poker, but it may vary in many ways from a financial point of view. Thus B—the age—could have ante'd a blue, or a red chip, instead of a white, when each playing coming in would have had to put up two blues or two reds. Or C could have " straddled " B's ante—that is he could have doubled the ante *before* looking at his cards, when each player would have had to pay double the amount of the " straddle " to come in. And D could have re-straddled C—that is doubled the amount of C's straddle—before looking at his cards. But these " blind " ante, straddle, or re-straddle can never exceed half the limit, since it can never cost more than the limit to come in in the first instance. The age passes from the ante man to the straddler, and on into the re-straddler if there be one. This means that the last straddler gets the last option of coming in, and the last bet. This is most important, because the " last to speak " is in the best position at the table, and without this advantage there would be no object in straddling blind. Again, any player in any position at the table, after seeing his cards, can raise the " come in " by the limit or any part of it, and he can be raised and re-raised indefinitely by the following players before the draw—but these raises do not shift the position of age as in the case of the straddle and re-straddle. It is sometimes arranged that a limit is put to this class of raise before the draw, but that is not true Poker. In America, for instance, " the chief betting is done before the draw," which means that players raise the " come in " on the value of the cards as dealt, thereby pushing off the weaker hands so as not to risk the luck of the draw.

We give an example of these variations. A deals. B is the ante man for one blue (2/6) ; C straddles, putting in one red (5/-). If 10/- is the limit D cannot re-straddle. D then is the first to speak and plays for two red ; E also comes in ; A, holding threes " cold," raises the limit, making it two red and one yellow to play. B, holding two good pairs, comes in for this price, and C holding but one pair retires and loses his straddle of one red. D, who held a " pat " flush, but did not like to expose his strength as first player, not only comes in, but raises the limit, so E, if he wants to play, has to put up another yellow, which he does. B is in the same position but notions that his two pairs are well beat before the draw, and does not fancy his chance of improving as worth another yellow, so refuses to " make good," and retires. The game is now between D and E. D, of course, on his pat flush refuses to draw, and E draws two cards to his threes. D bets the limit, and E not having improved his threes, plays D correctly for a pat, so he refuses to see, and throws up his threes ; D takes the pot. In this case D would always be first better, and C, the straddler, would always have last bet, but as he did not come in that privilege reverted to B again, the raises on the part of A and B not interfering with the position of the age in any way. Here D does not show his cards, nobody having called him, so in reality he might have won on nothing at all, just by playing the same game, raising, drawing, and betting " as though he'd got them."

THE JACK POT:

The Jack Pot is a variation of the ordinary game and is played under conditions pre-arranged by the players. A usual method for determining the Jack Pot is to play one whenever the dealer holds " the buck "—a token which is thrown into the first pool and is taken by the winner. When it becomes the deal of the player who holds the buck, he declares a Jack Pot, and the winner of it takes the buck. By this method there must be a " Jack " once in every round, and there might be one on every deal, for there is no reason why the buck should not be won by the next to deal every time, and so go round and round the table. Another method is to have a jack after certain events, such as the appearance of a full or better, or when nobody plays, or when there is no betting. This must be decided on by the players, or by custom— but should depend to an extent on the number of players —thus with six or seven players a buck should be used—with a smaller number no buck should be used but when there is no betting or seeing a jack may be played.

In Jack Pots there is no age or ante. Each player tits up so many chips to form a pool, and the dealer, beginning with the player on his left, asks each player in turn if he can " open the pot." Once the pot is opened, the dealer does not ask the following players if they can open, but if they will " play in the pot." To *open* the pot, a pair knaves or something better than a pair knaves must be held, but anybody, once the pot has been opened, can " come in " on anything at all. Cards are exchanged as at the ordinary game, the opener starts betting, and the game proceeds in the usual way, the best hand winning the pot—or, of course, the player whose bet is not called. The opener of the pot must show his whole hand whether his bet is seen or not, or even if he subsequently retires from the pot. The tit-up to the pot by each player should be not more than a quarter of the limit, but the pool itself may be opened for any amount up to the limit, and once the pot is opened raising and re-raising is allowed before the draw by any player whether he holds openers or not. Should the pot not be opened, the deal passes to the next player on the left, and each person puts into the pot an amount equal to the ordinary ante by way of a " sweetener."

The rules specially applicable to Jack Pots are as follows :—

(1) A player to open must be dealt the openers or better. He may not open on four to a straight, or flush on chance of filling. Should he do so, even if he fills, he is liable for the penalty of false opening, and cannot take the pot.

(2) The opener of the pot may discard one of his openers to draw for a superior hand. Thus holding two queens and four hearts, he may discard one queen and draw for the flush, but before *doing so he must declare that he is splitting his openers*, and keep the discarded queen near him to show at the end of the hand. In the same way an opener on two pairs may throw one of the pairs and draw for threes.

(3) A player holding openers need not open the pot ; nor having once opened, need he stay in to see any subsequent rises.

(4) The opener under all circumstances must show his whole hand.

(5) If a player opens a pot without openers or better, under no conditions can he win the pot, and he must leave therein anything he has opened for plus any bets, raises or calls he is liable for.

(6) Should a false opener win the pot—*i.e.* be entitled to lift it, had he not made a false opening—he must replace the pot in its entirety and add thereto from his own chips its original value plus all coming in chips of other players, but not the amount of any bets made. This pot is played for without any tit-up by the other players. It can be won by the false opener.

(7) Should any other player win the pot, he lifts it ; and in this case the false opener puts up as a fresh pot the entire value of the pot plus all coming in chips and any bets, raises or calls made by himself, but not those bets, raises or calls made by other players. The new pot is then played for without any tit-up from the other players. It can be won by the false opener.

(8) A false opener may correct his mistake any time before cards are drawn, when any other player in his turn may open, provided he holds openers. But the false opener must leave his opening chips in the pool ; the other players withdrawing theirs. The false opener may not play for the pot on that hand, otherwise the hand is played out in the ordinary way.

(9) Players having thrown in their cards on a false opening may not pick up their discarded hands should the pot be opened by some other player. They may of course come in and draw five cards.

Hints on Play :

Each player should pay particular attention to and make a mental note of the number of cards drawn by the other players. This is the first guide to what the hands consist of, and on general lines it may be assumed that a player

drawing	3 cards	held	originally	one pair.
,,	2 ,,	,,	,,	threes.
,,	I ,,	,,	,,	2 pairs, or 4 to a flush or 4 to a straight, or fours.
,,	0 ,,	,,	,,	a pat, full, straight or flush.

The subsequent betting should prove the genuineness of these original holdings, and it will also give an indication whether the player has improved on the draw. For instance a two-card buyer bets the limit, and in turn is raised the limit by a one-card buyer. The latter should know that the two-card buyer holds threes, yet he raises him the limit, proving that on the buy he has filled, and can now beat threes. Therefore if the two-card buyer has not improved he must recognise that he is second best and should not waste further chips to see the raiser. *The first rule at Poker is to be able to put down three aces.* But in addition to this the psychology of each player must be studied, information must be gathered from the play whether a man is a bold or a timid player, whether he bets the limit only with sense, or whether he bets only because he has no sense, whether he never draws false, whether by tone or gesture he gives an indication of having improved or not, whether he is a hardened bluffer, or perhaps careless as to what other players draw. So in the example just given our two-card buyer may be one who makes a habit of false drawing two cards to a pair only, when it would be assumed that he does not hold threes, and then the one-card buyer might safely raise him on two pairs or on a bluff with nothing at all. Again the one-card buyer might be known as an unobservant player, who did not notice the other fellow's draw of two cards, and consequently being a dashing player would raise the limit for sure on two pairs—then the two-card buyer should see the raise, or might even raise once more and have the best of the odds. But if both these players had been playing poker, the one-card buyer has the winning of the pot, and two-card buyer would lay down. The good player must never earn a reputation for anything at Poker, except that he is a good player, which means that he must not be known as either timid, bold, careless, or a hardened bluffer.

Further, the player must learn either by study or experience the winning chances of each hand both before and after the draw, and he must invest his chips accordingly, that is if his Poker chance of winning the pot is three to one against him, he would be foolish to invest his chips against a possible win of only an equal number of chips. There should be at least three times as many in the pot. The average pair or threes is eights; two pairs knaves and sixes; pat hands average one full against nine flushes and 12 straights (leaving fours and straight flushes out of the question). Holding anything better than the average the player has a mathematical advantage—the hands otherwise being equal. For instance two players hold pat hands—one a flush. This hand is by Poker mathematics the better of the two, and should meet (and beat) as the other pat a straight twelve times against nine, and (be beaten) by a full one time in nine.

With two players, the player holding pair nines has the advantage and should bet on them; two pair queens up will beat any other two pair on the average, and so on. Again the odds against improving a hand must be considered. It is over four to one against filling a four flush, and nearly five to one against filling a four straight with two ends. It is rare that the pot gives these odds against the coming in chips, and some good Poker players never play on such hands. These players may be considered stone wallers perhaps, but it must be remembered that even if the hands fill, they do not of necessity win, but having filled they must be " bet," then if they lose they cause vexation. These hands are called " bobtails " and should be looked upon with great suspicion.

All these considerations (with yet one or two more) must enter into the Poker player's calculations, and when it is said that if a player can thoroughly grasp one of them he is not altogether a bad player, while the player who gets well hold of any two is above the average, it will be seen what a wonderful Poker player is he who understands and applies them all to each hand dealt and played. And there are a few such Poker players—and they win the chips.

Poker is popularly and legally a gambling game. As a matter of fact there is no gamble in Poker—it is a game of pure skill, requiring more science than any other card game yet invented. It is a game of mathematics (combined with judgment of character), and so sure as the laws of chance assert themselves so surely will good play win at Poker.

The most important laws at Poker are :—

1. The cards must be shuffled by the player on the dealer's left and cut by the player on his right.
2. The cards must be dealt one at a time.
3. If 2 cards are turned up in the deal, there must be a new deal.
4. Each player, including the dealer, must announce in a sufficiently loud voice for everyone to hear how many cards he draws, or if he draws none.
5. No player after he has been given the number of cards asked for can be called upon to name the number he took.
6. Each player must discard, and throw to the deadwood face downwards, the number of cards he wishes to exchange before drawing the required number of cards. The discard may not be

looked at afterwards.   (See splitting openers in Jack Pots.)

7. If a card is exposed in the draw, the player cannot accept that card.   He takes those not exposed, and after all the other players have made their draw, another card is given in place of the exposed card.

8. The bottom card of the pack may not be given in the draw.

9. If there are not sufficient cards in the stock to complete a draw, the number there are—less the bottom card, are taken, the balance being given from the other players' discards, which shall be shuffled.

10. No player may declare to come in, bet, see or raise out of his turn.   Nor may a player throw up his hand out of turn either on the " come in " or after the draw.   But players not coming in, or not betting, seeing, or raising, shall immediately throw their cards to the deadwood when their turn to speak comes round.

11. The dealer is responsible for the pot.   And he must see that each ante, straddle, or re-straddle (if any), is correctly marked.   Ask each player in his turn if he comes in, and if so see that the player tits up correctly ; is responsible that the bets are made in correct order, and that all chips for bets, raises, and calling are duly put up by the players concerned.   The dealer in fact rules the table for his deal.

12. If a player having been dealt six cards picks them up, he cannot play on that hand (he may come in and draw five cards).   But if he does not pick them up, he can call upon the dealer to take back one of the cards, and the hand is good. If a player be dealt and picks up four cards he may call on the dealer to give him a fifth card, and the hand is good.

13. If a player after the draw finds he has more than five cards he cannot win the pot under any circumstances, even though he bets and is not seen. The pot in this latter case is left and re-played for.   But a player holding less than five cards

can win the pot if he bets and is not seen. He cannot, however, win the pot if his bet is seen, and it is discovered he has less than five cards.

14. If a player be given more cards than he has asked for, he can call upon the dealer to rectify the error provided he has not picked up any of the cards so given him. If he has been given too few cards, the error can be rectified any time before the betting begins.

Poker Maxims.

It is unwise to come in on hands that plainly are inferior before the draw. So pair-eight being the average pair, it is not worth putting chips into the pot on a smaller pair ; nor even on a pair-eight if there are any players in before you and others to come in after you— the certainty being that these players hold better than pair-eights. In the same way when you know there are threes against you either by a raise before the draw or by the betting after the draw, you should not see on less than three eights—average threes being eights of course.

Never raise but always see a one-card buy. A one-card buy which has filled will see and raise your raise and beat you—if he has not filled he won't see you—so your raise is simply asking for trouble. On the other hand he may be putting up a bluff—therefore see him once on average one-pair.

Never be certain of winning because you hold a good hand—the other fellow, if he is betting, may hold better, and you will lose your chips if you play him for a fool all the time, unless you know he is a fool always. No hand is certain of winning the pot at Poker ; if you hold a straight flush ace high so may another player, in which case you only halve it ; so remember money talks, and nothing talks so loudly at Poker as Poker chips.

Bet your hand to the maximum and don't wait for somebody else to bet it for you. If you have filled bet a limit, not one white on chance of finding an obliging adversary willing to raise. Try by deduction not to *hope* you have the best hand, but to be pretty confident that you have ; you can always be confident that you have

E

worst hand—that is the time to get out or bluff. Money is
made at Poker by saving it, so if for this reason only don't
make good your ante, straddle or re-straddle when you
have no business in the pot. The fact that you have lost
one chip to the pot does not justify you in losing two.
Bluffing all the time does not pay, even if you win all the
time. It pays to bluff now and again and to be found out
sometimes. Next time the other fellow will think you
are bluffing when you're not, and you'll get your money
back with interest. Three main principles to bear in
mind always are—(1) The pot is as much yours as anybody else's before the cards are dealt ; (2) after looking
you can tell it is not yours this time after all, or that you
are in position to assert your right to it ; (3) after the
draw that it ought to be yours or (being guided also by
the betting) that the other fellow has the bulge. Play
accordingly and you'll win.

Odds against Improving Hands (roughly).

A four straight flush (2 opening)

			to a straight flush	23 to 1
,,	,,	,,	to simple flush ...	4 to 1
,,	,,	,,	to simple straight	5 to 1

(or say 7 to 4 against any improvement).

Against filling a straight (one opening, *i.e.*, ace,
king, queen, knave, ten, or 9, 8, 7, ten,
5, etc.)   ...   .   11 to 1

,,   ,,   with two openings ...   5 to 1

Against filling a flush   ...   .   4 to 1

,,   improving 1 pair to 2 pairs ...   ...   5 to 1

,,   ,,   ,,   threes   ...   ...   7 to 1

,,   ,,   ,,   a full   ...   ...   98 to 1

,,   ,,   ,,   fours   ...   ... 359 to 1

(or say 2½ to 1 against any improvement of 1 pair).

Against improving 2 pairs to a full   ...   ...   11 to 1

,,   ,,   threes   ,, ...   15 to 1

,,   ,,   ,,   fours   ...   ...   23 to 1

(or say 8½ to 1 against any improvement to threes).

It will be noticed that it is easier to fill a flush than a
straight, yet the former is the better hand. The reason

is that the *pat* straight and the four-card straight occur more frequently than the pat or four-card flush. When dealt a hand that allows of either drawing (say 2, 3, 4, king of hearts and five of another suit) draw for the flush always.

The above odds are theoretically (in round figures) correct. But after a pack has been played with for a little time, pairs are picked up far more often than theory admits. This is because the cards are not shuffled, and pairs get stuck together, most players pairing the cards in their hands, before throwing them to the deadwood. The cards should be well shuffled at Poker, if the chances are to keep honest.

SURPRISING FACTS IN POKER MATHEMATICS:

There being threes out cold against your big two pairs cold you should discard the small pair and draw three cards.

If a player in front of you stands pat, and you hold a pat straight 5 high, draw four cards to the ace.

To come into a Jack Pot on pair tens or smaller pair and ace king, you should discard your pair and draw three to ace, king.

Playing on pair fives or smaller pair and an ace or king, hold the kicker (ace or king) and draw two. On pair sixes or better, throw the kicker and draw three.

The odds are rarely good enough to play on a four straight, and not often sufficient for a four flush. There is a fascination however in drawing to these hands, which possibly justifies the expenditure. Actually your chances of winning are better on a draw to ace, king, queen, knave, or 10 of different suits.

You should raise the limit before the draw on a four straight flush with two openings. If the hand doesn't improve, however, lay down.

In Jack Pots, being *first* to come in after the pot has been opened, raise the limit in pair kings or better. The object is to push off weaker hands on your left that might come in on small pairs.

The most scientific book on the game is *Draw-Poker*, by Major Hoffman, of U.S. Army (Routledge & Kegan Paul, Ltd.) ; also *Poker*, by Frank Arnold and Herbert Johnston (same publishers).

LOO

Loo is played in divers fashions, but there are two leading varieties, known as " three-card " and " five-card " Loo respectively. There is no limit in either case to the number of players, but six or seven make the better game.

THREE-CARD LOO:

The full pack of fifty-two cards is used, the cards ranking as at Whist. The dealer, having been selected,* places an agreed number of counters (either three or some multiple of three) in the pool. Three cards are dealt, one by one, to each player, also an extra hand, known as " miss." The card next following is turned up, and fixes the trump suit. The dealer then asks each player, beginning with the elder hand, whether he will play or " take miss." The player looks at his cards. If he holds a good hand, he will elect to play ; if otherwise, he has the option of either " taking miss," *i.e.* taking the extra hand in place of his own, or of " passing," *i.e.* throwing up his hand altogether for that round. If miss be declined, the same offer is made to the next in rotation ; but so soon as miss is taken, the remaining players have only two alternatives—viz. either to play the cards they hold, or to pass. A player who has taken miss is bound to play. The cards he has discarded, as also those of any players who pass, are thrown face downwards in the middle of the table, and no one has a right to look at them.

Should one player take miss, and all the rest throw up their cards, he is entitled to the pool. Should only one player have declared to play, and not have taken miss, the dealer may play either his own cards or take miss on his own account, but if he does not care to do either, he is bound to take miss and play for the pool, *i.e* the proceeds of any tricks he may make remain in the pool, to abide the

* This is usually done by dealing a preliminary round, face upwards, the first knave turned up entitling the holder to the deal.

result of the next round. In the event of all save the dealer " passing," the dealer is entitled to the pool.

The elder hand (as among those who have declared to play) now leads a card. If he has two trumps he is bound to lead one of them. If he holds the ace of trumps he is bound to lead it, or if an ace be turned up, and he holds the king of the same suit, he is bound to lead the latter. If only two persons have declared to play, and the leader holds two or more trumps, he must lead the *highest*, unless his highest trumps are in sequence or of equal value,* when he may lead either of them. (With more than three declared players the last rule does not apply.)

The other players play in rotation to the card led, subject also to certain fixed rules, viz., each player must follow suit, if possible, and he must " head the trick," *i.e.* play a higher card to it, if able to do so. If unable to follow suit, he is bound to trump, or if the trick be already trumped, to over-trump, if practicable.

The winner of each trick leads to the next. He is under the same obligations as the original leader, and is further bound to lead a trump, if he has one. This latter obligation is briefly stated as " trump after trick."

The hand having been played out, the pool is divided, in the proportion of one-third to each trick. Suppose, for instance, that five persons have played ; that one of them has taken two, and another one trick. The first takes two-thirds, and the second one-third. The remaining three players are " looed," *i.e.*, mulcted in the same amount as was originally placed in the pool, and these " loos," as they are called, with a like contribution from the new dealer, form the pool for the next hand. It may, however, happen that only three players declare to play, and that each of them takes one trick. In such case no one is looed, and the only fund to form the pool for the next round is the contribution of the dealer. The next hand in such case is known as a " single," and it is a usual, though not invariable, rule, to make it what is called a " must," meaning that every one, whatever his cards, is bound to play. This necessarily produces as many loos (less three) as there are players, and

---

* As, for instance, where the player holds the seven and nine of trumps, the eight having been turned up ; the seven and nine are then of equal value.

consequently a full pool for the next hand. In the case of a " must " there is no miss.

In circles where the interest of a game is gauged by the amount of money that changes hands, the payment for a loo is sometimes made equal to the amount which may chance to be in the pool for the time being. Playing upon this principle, the amount of a loo tends constantly to increase, until the occurrence of a single (*i.e.* three players only declaring to play, and each taking one trick) brings it back to its normal proportions. Loo in this shape is known as " unlimited." Under such an arrangement pence grow to pounds with startling rapidity, so much so, indeed, that no prudent player will ever sit down to the game in this form, and even among the most reckless it is customary to fix a *maximum* beyond which no further advance shall be permitted.

Five-card Loo :

In this case five cards are dealt to each player, the card next following being turned up by way of trump. There are, therefore, five tricks to be contended for, and the contributions to the pool are made divisible by *five* accordingly. There is, in this case, no miss, but each player (beginning with elder hand) may discard as many cards as he pleases, the dealer replacing them with a like number from the remainder of the pack. It is at the option of each player either to play or to pass, but having once drawn cards he is bound to play. The discarded cards are thrown face downwards in the centre of the table.

There is in this case a variation, in the fact that the knave of clubs, known as Pam, is made a sort of paramount trump, taking precedence even of the ace of the trump suit. The rules as to leading, following suit, and heading the trick, are the same as at the three-card game. If, however, the ace of trumps be led, and the holder pronounces the formula " Pam, be civil," the holder of the latter card is bound to pass the trick, if he can do so without a revoke.

Special value is in this game given to a flush, *i.e.* five cards of the same suit, or (which are regarded as equivalent) four cards of the same suit and Pam. The holder of such hand at once turns up his cards, and "looes the board," *i.e.* wins every trick as of right, without playing his hand, even though stronger individual cards were in the hands of other players. No one is in this case allowed to throw up his cards, and all save the holder of the flush are looed. Should more than one player hold a flush, a flush in trumps has priority over one in a plain suit. As between two flushes in trumps, or two in plain suits, that consisting of the better cards wins.* The holder of the losing flush, or of Pam, if in the hand of one of the losers, is exempt from payment. In other respects the game resembles three-card loo.

Some players at either game maintain what is termed " club law," meaning that whenever a club is turned up by way of trump, everyone is bound to play. In such case there is no miss or drawing of cards.

THE LAWS OF LOO.

These may be briefly stated as follows :

1.—Each player has a right to shuffle at the commencement of a deal, the dealer shuffling last. The cards shall then be cut by the player to the right of the dealer. To constitute a valid cut, there shall be at least four cards in each portion of the pack.

2.—The cards shall be dealt one at a time to each player (with one card extra in each round for miss).† This having been done, the card next following on the pack shall be turned up as trump. If a card be found faced in the dealt portions of the pack, the cards shall be reshuffled and recut, and there shall be a fresh deal by the same dealer.

3.—If the dealer—
    (1) Deals without having the pack cut ; or again shuffles after the pack has been duly cut ;
    (2) Exposes a card in dealing ; deals too many or too few cards to any player ;

* Sometimes the preference is given to the elder hand, irrespective of the value of the cards.

† The words between brackets apply of course to three-card loo. Sometimes the dealer is allowed, after dealing one card to each player, to deal three together for a miss, but the practice is irregular.

At five-card Loo the *Écarté* method of dealing (first by threes, and then by twos, or *vice versa*) is sometimes adopted.

(3) Misses a hand or deals a hand or part of a hand additional ;

(4) Or otherwise commits any irregularity in dealing, it is a misdeal, and the dealer forfeits a single to the pool. The cards are again shuffled and cut, and there is a fresh deal by the same dealer.

4.—Players shall declare whether they play or pass in strict rotation, beginning with the elder hand.

5.—Any player declaring before his turn, or looking at his cards before it is his turn to declare, forfeits a single to the pool.

6.—Any player looking at miss before he has declared to take it, or exposing a card or cards of another player, forfeits a single to the pool, and must retire from the game for that round.

7.—The dealer, taking miss against one player only, must declare before doing so, whether he plays for himself or the pool. In the latter case he cannot be looed ; but the proceeds of any trick he may make are left in the pool, to abide the result of the next hand.

8.—If no one declares to play, the dealer is entitled to the pool.

9.—A player having the lead, and holding the ace of trumps (or king, ace being turned up), is bound to lead it.

10.—A player having the lead, and holding two trumps, is bound to lead one of them.

11.—A player having the lead, and holding two trumps, other than in sequence or of equal value, is bound (when there are two players only), to lead the highest.

12.—Every player is bound to follow suit if able to do so.

13.—Every player is bound to head the trick if able to do so.

14.—Every player winning a trick, and still holding one or more trumps, is bound to lead a trump.

Any player committing any infractions of Laws 9, 10, 11, 12, 13, or 14, must leave in the pool any tricks he may make, and forfeit to the pool four times the amount of a single.

15.—If a player, having declared to play—

(1) Exposes a card before it is his turn to play, *or*

(2) Plays a card out of turn, *or*

(3) Plays a card before all have declared, *or*

(4) Exposes a card while playing, so as to be named by any other declared player,

he shall be compelled to throw up his cards, and to forfeit a single to the pool.

16.—In the case of a revoke, it is in the option of any player, other than the offender, to require that the cards be taken up and the hand played again.

17.—All penalties of a single shall be deemed to belong to the existing pool ; all higher penalties and proceeds of tricks left by way of penalty in the pool to the pool next following.

IRISH LOO :

Another and most excellent variation is what is known as Irish or Draw Loo.

This is three-card Loo, but any player coming in may draw any number of cards up to three. He can only effect one exchange of cards however. This of course makes the game more exciting and gives the speculative player greater scope for coming in.

The same laws as those in ordinary Loo hold good, but to make the game even more lively what is known as " Club Law " is usually introduced. This means that whenever clubs are trumps everybody must come in. There is no " miss " in Irish Loo, but the dealer is bound to defend the pool against a solitary opponent.

Irish Loo should always be limited—otherwise owing to the greater number of " players," the pool reaches most extravagant figures. A certain Irish Lord is reported to have lost £10,000 at one sitting at half-crown *unlimited* Irish Loo—six players.

NAPOLEON

NAPOLEON is played by any number of players from two to six with a full pack of 52 cards, ranking as at whist. Ace highest and deuce lowest. The process of calling is as follows :—

Each player receives five cards, dealt singly. The players declare in their turn how many tricks they think they can make. The eldest hand—that is, the player to the dealer's left—has the first call, and every one after him can declare by increasing his call, up to the limit, " Nap," which is a declaration to take all the five tricks. Whoever makes the highest call has all the other players pitted against him, and leads out—that is to say, he puts a card face upwards on the table in front of him, the playing of that card determining the trump suit, as whatever suit is first led by the caller is trumps by virtue of the lead. The players then follow in order, it being imperative to follow suit if possible, but, except for this, any card may be played.* There is no rule as to heading a trick or playing a trump after a trick, or indeed any restriction whatever beyond following the led suit if you can, under penalty of a revoke for trumping or discarding when holding a card of the suit called for. The highest card of the led suit takes the first trick, and the winner leads a card to the second trick, the cards played not being packed or gathered together, but being left face upwards in front of their owners. The winning card is alone turned down. The winner of the second trick leads to the third, and so on, the declaration succeeding or failing according as the caller makes or fails to make the number of tricks that he declared. It matters nothing whether he makes two or even three tricks more than he declared to make ; he is only paid for the number that he originally announced, and even if he does not take a trick, he simply pays for the number he called.

It is a level-money transaction all round ; that is to say, if a man calls three at " penny Nap," he receives 3d.

* A call of one trick is not recognised, and with a small party not less than three should be declared.

138

from every other player if he makes the three tricks, and pays 3d. to every other player if he does not make three tricks. But if he calls Napoleon (five tricks) he receives 1od. if he wins, and only pays 5d. if he loses. We may say here that in most places where penny Nap is played, the 1od. and 5d. are raised to 1s. to win and 6d. to lose, on the plea of making it even money. The round being over and the stakes paid, the deal passes in the usual way to the person to the left of the last dealer, and so on.

This is the old simple form of Napoleon, and it is what most people understand by the game. It is without complication of any kind, and the skill it requires is of two sorts—first, to judge the value of a hand with due regard to the number of players and any calls that may have been made previously ; and, next, how to play the hand—whether as caller or as one of the combination against the call—to the best advantage.

THE VARIATIONS :

Here we may first note the call of " Wellington," which is a superior call to Napoleon, inasmuch as it supersedes the latter. As in the Nap call, the player undertakes to make the whole five tricks, but at double the Nap stakes. Thus, if the caller of Nap receives 1s. or pays 6d., on a Wellington he would receive 2s. or pay 1s. Wellington can only be called over Napoleon, that is, it cannot be declared unless " Nap " is declared before it.

Another innovation is an adaptation from Solo Whist, and is called " Misery." It is on the principle of the Misère, when, there being no trumps, the caller has to lose the whole five tricks, while his opponents, of course, endeavour to force him to take a trick. At some tables trumps, determined in the usual way by the initial lead, are recognised ; but this feature is quite foreign to the original Misère. If trumps are recognised the caller should invariably lead a single suit—*i.e.* a suit consisting of one card only. This declaration ranks between the calls of *three* and *four*, and is paid for in the same way as a call of three is paid for ; that is, at our stakes, to win would be to receive 3d. from each of the other players, and to lose would be to pay 3d. to each.

Another variation is to allow a player, who has called Nap to exchange if he will the top card of the pack for one of his own. This is called " Peep Nap."

" Purchase " or " Écarté " Nap, however, is unquestionably the most interesting form of Napoleon.   After the
dealer has dealt, and before anybody starts calling, the
dealer goes round again in turn, and serves out fresh cards
from the pack in exchange for as many cards as the
players may wish to throw away from their original hands.
For every fresh card so exchanged the player has to pay
one penny (or more, according to the stakes) into the
pool.   He must not exchange cards more than once in
each round, but he can then purchase any quantity up to
five.   The cards thrown away are not shown, nor used
again till the next deal.   The dealer must sell to each
player in turn, and to himself last, after which the calls
start from his left in the usual way.   In view of the extra
number of cards brought into the game, Purchase Nap
should be confined to a table of not more than four players,
and for the same reason the calls should be made on much
stronger hands than at ordinary Nap.

A declaration once made stands, and cannot be recalled.

A player at Purchase Nap, having once bought fresh cards
or refused to buy, cannot subsequently amend his decision.

When there is no calling it is customary to play the
next hand for double stakes.   This is called a " double
header," and it remains so until a hand is called and won.

Anyone who has trumped a suit, or renounced upon
a suit before all the five tricks have been played out, and
so made or defeated a declaration, must immediately show
his remaining cards to prove that he has not revoked.   So
stringent is this rule, that if he should refuse to show
them, he is held to have revoked, and a revoke entails the
following penalties :—

On the revoke being discovered, the cards must be
taken up and replayed properly—that is to say, players
must follow suit, if they can ; and always remember that
a revoke is just as much a revoke if you throw away a
card of another suit, holding a card of the suit led, as
if you trumped under the same circumstances.

The hand having been replayed, the offender pays the
stakes for himself and every one of the other players to
the caller, if the call succeeds.   If the call fails, he pays
the stakes to every other player, except the caller.

A revoke proved against the caller himself entails the
immediate penalty of the loss of the stakes ; that is to say,

if a man calls three and revokes, it matters not how many tricks he makes, he must pay (at penny Nap) 3d. to every one of his opponents.

If a card is exposed in the pack or in dealing, or if there is a mis-deal, or if the pack is shown to be faulty, or if the cards are dealt without being cut, there should be a fresh deal by the same player.

Any player can demand a fresh deal if any one of these faults is committed, but the demand must be made before the hands are looked at ; otherwise the deal must stand.

After all the calls have been declared, should a player discover that he has too few or too many cards the game must be played out, and if the number in the superior caller's hand be correct he takes the stakes, if he succeeds in making his call good, but neither receives nor pays if he fails. Should the caller, however, hold a wrong number in his hand, he neither receives nor pays if he wins, but pays if he fails. When a Nap is declared, the game must be played out subject to the above rules, whether the other players have their correct number or not ; but, failing a Nap call, the cards must be redealt should any irregularity be discovered before all the players have declared.

There is one rule at Napoleon that has fallen into disuse, and that relates to playing out of turn. It is so common for persons to play valueless or losing cards out of turn without remark, that many people forget that the fortunes of a hand may often be influenced by the premature exposure of the winning card or a trump. A person who, out of his turn, plays a card that obviously influences the game should be subjected to the same penalty as if he had revoked.

SEVEN-CARD NAP :

A most excellent variation of ordinary Nap, and is played on exactly the same lines except that each player is dealt seven instead of five cards. There is no exchange of cards and no peep.

The players may call anything from three up to " the lot "—*i.e.* seven tricks ; but nap is still five tricks and is paid double, six tricks paid three times, and " the lot " four times. *Misère* is played at seven-card nap and ranks as next highest bid to nap (5 tricks) and is paid double.

In writers' opinions this is quite the best form of nap —indeed few players having once played it, revert to the five-card game.

SPOIL FIVE

THIS game, though little known in this country, is a most excellent round game. As will be seen, it is at once a game of individual effort on the part of each player and yet a combination of all against the individual. Herein lies its charm, and although the values of the cards are peculiar and perhaps complicated, as also are the rules, yet the game is well worthy of the serious consideration of card lovers, especially of those who prefer games of skill—for there is more skill in the play of the cards at Spoil Five than at any other round game.

The values of the cards are as follows :—

> Five of trumps.
> Knave of trumps.
> Ace of hearts.

IN RED SUITS WHEN NOT TRUMPS :

King, queen, knave, 10, 9, 8, 7, 6, 5, 4, 3, 2, ace—but the ace of hearts always is the third best card in the pack irrespective of what suit is trump.

IN BLACK SUITS WHEN NOT TRUMPS :

King, queen, knave, ace, 2, 3, 4, 5, 6, 7, 8, 9, 10.
This is stated concisely as " highest in black, lowest in red."

IN RED SUITS WHEN TRUMPS :

Five, knave, ace of hearts, ace of trumps, king, queen, 10, 9, 8, 7, 6, 5, 4, 2.

IN BLACK SUITS WHEN TRUMPS :

Five, knave, ace of hearts, ace of trumps, king, queen, 2, 3, 4, 5, 6, 7, 8, 9, 10.

So it will be seen that when the suit is not trump the ace of diamonds is the worst card in the pack ; when the suit is trump it is fourth best card.

When hearts are trumps, there is, practically speaking, no ace of trumps ; and whether trumps or not the deuce of clubs or spades is better than all plain cards in their respective suits.

The dealer having been selected by any method, he gives each player five cards, beginning with the player on his left. The cards must be dealt in twos and threes, or *vice-versa*, as at Écarté. Each player puts up a pre-arranged amount to form a pool; the pool usually is limited to a certain maximum, which once reached there is no further subscription, though each dealer is required to tit-up to the pool. The deal passes after each hand in the usual way to the left.

The entire object of the game is to win three tricks out of the five, but each player in trying to win three tricks himself must be ultra careful that his own attempt may not result in some other player winning them. The game must be played unselfishly—that is, more attention must be paid to stopping other players' success than in going for it oneself. When nobody wins three tricks it is a " spoil " ; the deal passes.

The rules are as peculiar as the values of the cards.

The Trump :

After each player has received five cards, the next card is turned up to decide the trump suit.

Robbing :

If an ace is turned up, the dealer can rob ; *i.e.*, he discards a worthless card from his hand, and substitutes for it the ace of trumps. The dealer must *rob before* the eldest hand leads. If an ace is not turned up, any player holding it must rob—*i.e.*, discard a worthless card and take in the turn-up. The player need not declare his intention to rob until it becomes his turn to play, but he must rob *before he actually plays* his first card.

After robbing the dealer may use the turn-up card to trump the first trick, or he may use it to follow to a trump led by the eldest hand, but no other player has this privilege.

The card put out in robbing must not be looked at.

The Play :

The cards are played one at a time, as at any other round game, the highest card played winning the trick.

The winner of the trick has next lead, and so on until the hand is played out or until three tricks are won by the same player.

When a trump is led, players must follow suit except with special cards presently to be mentioned.

To other leads players may trump or follow suit as they think fit, but a player holding no trumps must follow suit ; a player need not head a trick unless he likes.

A player winning three tricks in one hand takes the pool. If no one wins three tricks, the game is said to be spoiled.

RENEGING :

The five of trumps, knave of trumps and ace of hearts are exempt from following suit to an inferior trump led. This is called reneging.

The five of trumps can renege to any trump led. No trump can renege to the five.

The knave of trumps can renege to any trump except the five. But no trump can renege to the knave except the five. Similarly the ace of hearts, which counts as a trump, can renege to any trump led except the five and knave. But when hearts are trumps the five and knave can renege when ace of hearts is led. To ace of hearts, when hearts are not trumps, a trump must be played, but a player holding no trump need not play a heart.

A typical hand at Spoil Five. Four players, A, B, C, D. A deals and turns up nine spades. B leads.

Spades—5.
Hearts—king.
Clubs—9, 8.
Diamonds—6.
C

Spades—knave, 2, 3.　　　　　　　Spades—ace (9).
Hearts—　　　　B　　　D　　Diamonds—
Clubs—king, knave.　　　　　　Clubs—queen, 6 (5).
Diamonds—　　　　　　　　　　Hearts—queen.

A
Spades—
Hearts—ace.
Clubs—3, 4.
Diamonds—7, 8.

Trick 1.—B led knave of spades. C plays 6 diamonds (reneging the 5 of trumps). D robs (discarding 5 clubs and taking in the turn-up, 9 spades, which he now plays). A must play ace of hearts.

1 trick to B.

Trick 2.—B leads king clubs. C plays 8 clubs. D trumps with ace. A plays club.

1 trick to D.

Trick 3.—D leads queen of hearts. A plays club, B trump, C plays king of hearts.

2 tricks to B. .

Trick 4.—B plays knave of clubs, C plays 9 clubs, D plays queen of clubs and wins the trick ; C wins last trick with five of trumps, so it is a spoil.

Notes.—B correctly went for game on his hand. When he found D robbing, he cannot go on with trumps, but hopes to force out the ace with his clubs. C reneges his 5 of trumps—there is no particular object in playing it to the knave.

Trick 2.—D correctly reneges clubs and ruffs the king with his ace of trumps. He now holds the best club and second best heart, so has a chance of game himself.

Trick 3.—B of course trumps queen of hearts and hopes that his knave of diamonds will extract any remaining trump or win the trick, making his game. C of course does not waste his five in over ruffing.

Trick 4.—C's position is unpleasant. B has already won two tricks, and the knave of clubs may be good—it looks so. However, luckily for the table, he passes it, and D wins the trick.

JINKING :

A jink is where a player plays to win all five tricks, the winner being paid the original amount subscribed to the pool by each player in addition to taking the pool.

Any player having won three tricks may declare a jink, but should he fail, he wins nothing at all on the hand. Jinking, therefore, is a very risky business, and it requires considerable judgment at Spoil Five to know when to play for a jink, and when not.

Laws of Spoil Five :

1. The cards must be dealt to each player two at a time, and then three at a time, or *vice-versa*.
2. If a card is faced in the pack there must be a fresh deal by the same dealer, except if the faced card happens to be the trump card.
3. It is a misdeal and the deal passes

     i. If the dealer deals without having the pack cut.

     ii. If the dealer re-shuffles the pack after it has been cut.

     iii. If the dealer deal incorrectly ; that is gives two cards where he should give three, or misses a hand, or exposes a card in dealing, or gives too many or too few cards to any player.

[The deal is a great advantage at Spoil Five, since dealer plays last, and often can win the first trick very cheaply ; the penalty for the misdeal in some places is considered too severe, and the dealer having misdealt may be allowed to deal again by paying into the pool a pre-arranged amount.]

4. If any player has too many or too few cards and the error is not discovered until the hand is partly or wholly played out, it is still a misdeal. (See also Law 8.)
5. Each player is entitled to a deal, *i.e.*, the game must not be abandoned except at the conclusion of a round, unless there is a spoil in the last deal of a round, when the deal continues in order until a game is won.
6. If a player deals out of turn he may be stopped at any time prior to the turning up of the trump card. If not stopped the deal holds good, and the rotation of dealing proceeds to the dealer's left as though he had dealt in turn.

Robbing :

7. If a player neglects to declare his power of robbing before he plays to the first trick, he loses the right of robbing and forfeits his hand—that is, he cannot win the pool in that hand, but he may play to try and spoil it.

PLAYING :

    8. If a player robs without the ace or leads or plays out of turn, or leads without waiting till the trick has been completed, or exposes a card, or omits to play to a trick, or revokes or reneges when not entitled to, or plays with too many or too few cards, he forfeits the pool—that is he cannot win the game that hand, *and he cannot play again for that pool.*

[*Note.*—This is called hanging the hand, and is equivalent to loss of the game. The penalty is severe, but is made so purposely, since faults under Law 8 may be attended by serious consequences to other players. In fact an unscrupulous player could prevent another player from winning the pool at any time by, say, dropping one of his cards under the table and declaring a misdeal. Or say A, B, C and D are sitting in this order round the table, and B has won two tricks. A leads and B beats him, when D, playing out of turn before C, fails to win the trick. This would be a clear intimation to C that he must win the trick if he can, which plainly would be an unfair combination against B. The penalty of simply calling the exposed card, or of forfeiture of the pool on that hand might be no punishment at all. For instance D, in the example given, might have no chance of the game himself. The same applies to reneging when not entitled. The defaulting player might have no chance himself, but by reneging might spoil it for someone else.]

    9. If the pack be found to be incorrect, the deal in which it is discovered becomes void. All preceding deals stand good.

BACCARAT

BACCARAT is a game of chance, and as such is the most popular of all card games. Although from a bare description it may sound stupid and uninteresting, it needs but a single experiment in actual play to prove its charm and fascination—that is of course from a gambling point of view.

At Baccarat Banque—or simply Baccarat—the banker plays a single hand against two hands of his opponents in the following way. The banker takes his place midway down one of the sides of an oval table, the croupier facing him with the waste basket between. On either side of the banker are the punters, twenty such constituting a full table. Any other persons desiring to take part remain standing. The cards rank in value according to their pips—the ace counting one, ten and court cards ten each. From three to six packs of cards are used, shuffled and cut in the usual manner, and these are placed face downwards in a heap in front of the banker. The banker may not handle this heap nor any part of it, but slides one card off the top and passes it to his right, the next card to his left, and the next to himself. Then one again to his right, one to the left, and one to himself. He now looks at his own two cards, and if the sum of the pips come to eight or nine, he turns his cards up and declares a natural. In counting the pips that form the point, tens are disregarded—thus a queen and a two (12) make a point of *two*—and a seven and an eight (15) make a point of five—and two court cards (20) make *o* or baccarat. If the banker's point is not eight or nine, he must declare that he " gives," and the punter on his right looks at his two cards, and if his point is an eight or nine he turns them up announcing his natural. If he has not an eight or nine he may ask for a card, and the banker gives him one, but only one, which he turns face upwards. The left hand punter now goes through the same proceeding, and then the banker himself, if it suits him, may draw one card, but only one. Now the banker wins from or loses to each punter according to whose point is nearer to nine, equality neither winning nor losing. As an example : The banker finds his cards to be a ten and an ace, making his point one, so he must " give." His right hand opponent finds a five and a three. He turns his cards up and announces eight, and *must win*. The left hand opponent finds a nine and a four, his points being three ; he " takes " and the banker gives him an eight, making his point but 1 (9+4+8). But he does not announce his point yet. The banker must now expose his cards, and having but a point of 1, takes a card, and gives himself an 8, making his point 9. So he wins from his left opponent, but loses to his right, although his point is the better one, for the natural beats any point made by the addition of the drawn card. Consequently if the banker himself holds a natural 8 or 9 he does not give a card, since he must win unless of course his opponents also hold naturals, when the higher natural wins. The hands are swept away into the deadwood, and another coup is begun. This is the whole play at the game and there are no variations of any kind. The rules of play, and especially of staking constitute the most important part of the game and these must be rigidly adhered to.

The bank is put up for auction, and goes to the highest bidder. In some places local rules are made whereby between certain hours the bank may be bought for a fixed sum. A list of names of players who so desire to buy a bank is kept, and the bank goes in rotation to these players. The banker must put up in front of him the amount he has paid for the bank, and each side has the right to stake up to the full amount, one half for the right hand lot of punters, the other for the left. The banker may allow an uneven tableau if he likes—that is, say he has £100 in his bank, he may accept bets of £75 on one side and only £25 on the other—but at the same time he has the right to object, and can demand that the higher side be reduced to £25. Whatever money the banker wins he must add to the amount in front of him, and the punters are at liberty to stake up to this full amount. The banker, however, may withdraw from the bank at any time (after the first coup), but if he does so he sacrifices his position as banker, and may not bid for the next bank.

The banker, if he breaks, can refresh his bank as often as he chooses, but he must refresh it with the same amount as he originally paid for it.

The bank automatically finishes when the cards finish. For the last coup there must be at least ten cards left in the deck, that is nine cards and the bottom one, which may not be used.

The rules for the punters are the more important.

The player for the time holding the cards is *playing for all the money staked on his side, and is therefore responsible for playing strictly according to the rules. If he deviates from them he is liable to make good all losses incurred through his error.*

No punter, however, can be compelled to play the cards for his side, and can pass the privilege on to the next player.

Only players *seated at the table* may play the cards.

The punters immediately to the right and to the left of the banker play the first hand, and they continue to do so until they lose a coup, when the player immediately on the right or left of the loser, as the case may be, plays the next hand, and he also continues to play until he loses a coup, when the next player takes the cards, and so on round the table. The player for the time being holding the cards has the right to stake the full amount available in the bank. If he bets the whole none of the other punters on his side can stake, but any balance left in the bank after he has staked can be bet by the player on his right or left, as the case may be, and any balance then left over is open to the next player, and so on round the table. Any balance remaining over in the bank after the *seated* players have made their stakes may be bet by the onlookers. Should the stakes of the punters exceed the amount in the bank, the banker is not liable. The players are paid in rotation round the table, beginning with him who for the time being is holding the cards for his side, and when the funds of the bank are exhausted, the remaining punters pick up their stakes. The converse of this also holds good, e.g., suppose there was but £100 in the bank and £110 staked, the banker could only receive £100, the balance of £10 being taken up by the punter.

For the *first* coup only any player may call banco—*i.e.*, the entire amount in the bank—the first claim belonging to the player immediately on the banker's right, the next to the player on his left, and so on alternately in regular order. Failing any seated player calling banco, one of the onlookers may do so. Banco may only be called once during a bank, and if equality occurs three times running it cannot be continued with. Any punter may *continue* the bank of a retiring banker, but he must put into the bank either the amount originally put in by the retiring banker (in the case of a banker breaking and not wishing himself to refresh), or the amount the banker is retiring with—(the banker must state the amount he is getting away with)—but this amount must not be less than the amount originally put into the bank.

The actual play of the cards is still more important.

The player for the time being holding the cards must not look at them until the banker has declared a natural 8 or 9—or announces that he " gives."

The player must immediately on seeing his cards declare a *natural* 8 or 9 if he holds one, and expose his cards. If the natural is not declared, a better point made on a draw wins. (He must on no account declare his 8 or 9 *on a draw* until the dealer declares his point.)

A player holding a point of four or less *must* take a card.

A player holding 6 or more may not draw a card.

Holding a point of 5 it is optional to draw or not. (But the chances of improving a 5 are slightly against the drawer.)

There are advantages both to the banker and the punter at Baccarat.

The banker can never lose more than the amount he has bought the bank for, and as he has a certain percentage in his favour, he may run his bank to any amount. He is never responsible for more money than is bet on one coup, and can immediately reduce his bank to this amount. That is, say he has £1,000 in his bank at a moment when but £100 is staked, he can withdraw the odd £900, and more than the £100 and anything won and added to it, he can refuse to take on subsequent wagers. So in this case he must get away with £900.

The punter of course is only liable for such sums as he

feels inclined to stake on any coup. The odds are slightly against him, yet given a run of luck, he may with a small initial outlay capture all the money in the bank. He may play a system, and punting in small sums against a rich bank, he can make practically certain of winning a little. In his turn he gets the excitement of holding the cards, and although this does not on paper appear as a very heaven-sent form of rapture, it is the position at the table the most looked forward to. And there are occasions, as will be seen, when the banker deliberately allows him to win a coup that he should have lost—and these are undoubtedly exciting moments. The punter can stake on either or both sides of the table—or he can stake *a cheval*—that is he wins only if the banker loses on both sides, and loses only if the banker beats both sides.

The advantage in favour of the banker—said to be about $7\frac{1}{2}\%$—is arrived at from the fact that he always knows the punter's point within certain limits. We have seen that the punter's only optional point is 5—he must draw on four—he must stand on 6—so the banker, by adding the pips of the card he gives to the punter's unseen point of Baccarat (0), 1, 2, 3 or 4, can tell to a certainty that the punter must hold one of five points. With this knowledge he judges whether it is advisable to draw a card himself. Thus suppose the punter ask for a card, and the banker gives an 8. The punter now holds either 8, 9, Baccarat, 1, or 2 ; so if the banker holds a 3 himself he would not draw a card, the odds being 3 to 2 in his favour already, while there are only two cards that can improve his hand, a 5 or a 6 (plainly it is no good to him to advance his point to a 4, a 5, a 6, or a 7), and there are three cards that reduce his point—a 7, 8, or 9. If, on the other hand, his point was 2, he would draw a card, for although at the moment his chances of win and lose are equal, with the *encarte* of 2 thrown in, yet the chances of improving his hand on the draw are in his favour, the 7, 6, 5, 4, 3, 2, 1 being good against the 8, 9 only as bad draws. Again, suppose the punter draws a 5, and the banker hold as good as a five himself, still he must draw, since he knows that the punter holds either 5, 6, 7, 8 or 9, and only hope of not losing is that the punter drew to Baccarat and is now *encarte* at 5.

Even if the banker held a 7, his chances of winning and losing are but even, but in this case he would not draw a card since he is more likely to spoil his hand than to improve it, so he must stand his ground.

The banker has to apply these principles to *each side* of the table—that is to say, there will be occasions when, supposing he is playing against an uneven tableau, he will know that he loses to one side but has the other side beaten for certain, and he will draw or not according to how the stakes lie. For instance, on his right £50 is bet, and this side draws and he gives a ten ; on his left there is but £20, and this side stands. The banker would stand on a 3 even, for although he *must* lose on his left, his chances of picking up the fifty on his right are three or four to one in his favour, making him £30 up on the deal. On an even tableau, too, he would sometimes stand, as when he is certain of winning from one side and losing to the other. He is square, and it would be bad play to chance the draw, which might and probably would result in his losing to both.

It will be seen then that the banker must exercise a certain amount of judgment, but at public gambling tables even this is not necessary—he need only ask the croupier what to do, and he will be told correctly every time.

CHEMIN-DE-FER

CHEMIN-DE-FER differs from Baccarat in two main particulars: (a) the bank passes in rotation round the table, and each banker may make the bank for as much or as little as it suits his pocket—he need not take it at all if he doesn't want to—and (b) the banker deals one hand instead of two to the punters. With these and one or two minor alterations in the *jeux de règles* the games are exactly alike.

The minor points are:—

(1) The bank passes as soon as the banker loses a coup.

(2) The banker can withdraw his bank whenever he chooses. But, as at Baccarat, so long as he remains in the bank he must leave all his winnings, plus the original amount of the bank, on the table.*

(3) When a banker withdraws, the bank can be claimed by any player for the amount in the bank at the time, the player whose next turn it is to become banker having first claim, the second player next, and so on round the table. If nobody claims the bank it is put up for auction and goes to the highest bidder; but the outgoing banker may not bid for the bank he is withdrawing.

(4) In either of above cases the new banker does not lose his turn as ordinary banker, the bank coming back to him automatically in his turn in the ordinary way. No matter who buys the bank, the next natural bank follows in sequence from where the last natural bank left off.

* In some places it is arranged that the banker may " milk the bank " of half his winnings after three wins in succession.

(5) The player making the largest bet holds the cards for the punters.

(6) The banker having but one hand to play against may not use his judgment for the draw. He *must* draw or stand according to what his point is and the card he gives. The croupier will tell him his game, but he may have a card tabulated for his own information, thus :—

Banker Point.	Punter.	Banker Draws or Stands.
0, 1 or 2	Draws any card or stands	Draws
3 or 4	Draws 10, 9 or 8 - -	Stands
	Draws 7, 6, 5, 4, 3, 2, or 1 or stands.	Draws
5	Draws 10, 9, 8, 2, or 1 -	Stands
	Draws 7, 6, 5, 4, or 3, or stands.	Draws
6	Draws 6 or 5 - - -	Draws
	Draws 10, 9, 8, 7, 4, 3, 2 or 1 or stands.	Stands
7	Draws any card or stands	Stands
8 or 9	———	Declares natural

The table at Chemin-de-Fer is, of course, not divided into sides as at Baccarat, all the punters betting on the one hand against the banker.

The banker has not anything like so great an advantage at Chemin as at Baccarat—probably not 2%—but for small stakes the game is more amusing, since the poorest gets his turn at the bank, and as the bank passes fairly quickly as a rule, this turn comes round often enough to make things exciting.   A player however is not allowed to sit and await his turn for the bank without ever punting. In other words, all players must help to keep the game alive ; a dummy punter can be called upon to give up his seat.

VINGT-UN

VINGT-UN derives its name from the fact that each player aims at making, by the cards he holds, " twenty-one." Any number may play. The full pack of fifty-two cards is used. After they have been duly shuffled and cut, the dealer* distributes one card, face downwards, to each of the other players (whom we will call the punters), and one to himself. The punters look at their cards, and each places on, or beside his card, the coin (or counters representing coin) he proposes to stake. A *maximum* and *minimum* stake are fixed beforehand.

The dealer also looks at his card, and, if he thinks fit, says, " I double you," or simply " Double," the effect of his so doing being that he will receive or pay, as the case may be, *double* the stakes offered by the punters. In deciding whether to double or not, he has two points to consider, viz., (1) the fact of himself holding an exceptionally good card, and (2) the absence or rarity of high stakes among the punters, indicating that their cards are not such as they feel safe in backing freely. It must, however, be remembered that the dealer has the important advantage of receiving from ties, also from all players who overdraw. These two points make a considerable percentage in his favour. With an ace, tenth card, nine, or eight, he should *always* double; and the weighty authority of " Cavendish " is in favour of his doubling with a seven, or even a lower card. In these latter cases, however, we think the amount of the stakes should be taken into consideration, as affording some gauge of the probable strength of the enemy.

All court cards at this game count ten; an " ace," eleven or one, at the option of the holder; all other cards according to the number of their pips. Differences of suit are not recognized.

The object of the game is, as we have said, to make twenty-one, and this may be made either by the conjunc-

* The right to deal is decided by any pre-arranged method.

tion of an ace and a court or other tenth card, called a " natural," or by three or more cards, say a five, six and ten ; ace, *five*, seven, eight ; or ace, seven, three.

The ace is, as will readily be perceived, the most valuable card ; not merely from the fact that there are sixteen cards out of the fifty-two that will form a " natural " with it, but from the fact that (counting as eleven or one at pleasure), it gives the holder a double chance of making a winning number.

The stakes having been made, and the dealer having decided whether to " double " or not (in the latter case, silence is a sufficient negative), he deals a second round of cards, still face downwards.

Each player again looks at his cards. If those of the dealer form a " natural," he turns them up, and receives from each player three times the amount of his stake, or, if he has " doubled," six times. (The proportionate increase in the latter case will henceforth be taken for granted.) What cards the other players may hold is, in this case immaterial, save in the event of some one of them holding a second " natural," in which case the dealer receives the stake.*

We will now take the case of the dealer finding that his two cards do *not* constitute a " natural." If there be any such among the punters, the holder turns up his cards, and receives three times the amount of his stake and if the dealer make 21 only twice. To all other players, beginning with the elder hand, the dealer is bound to offer cards. This he does by the interrogative, " Do you stand ? " or " Card ? " The elder hand looks at his cards. If he has sixteen points or more, he will usually decide not to draw, conveying his decision by the word, " Stand," or " Content."† If he has less than sixteen, which is generally accepted as the average limit, he will probably draw a card, intimating his desire to do so, by replying, " Card," " Please," or " Yes." He may now be in three different positions. The card given him (as where,

---

* Sometimes the punter is allowed to draw cards to try and fill his hand to 21. If he does so he only pays the dealer twice his stake.

† Many players habitually stand at fifteen, and if the dealer is a reckless player, with a tendency to overdraw, it may be good policy to stand upon an even smaller figure. " Cavendish " is in favour of standing, as a rule, on fifteen

holding a six and an eight, he has received a ten), may make his total more than twenty-one. In such case he is " over," and he at once hands his stake to the dealer, and throws his cards, face downwards, in the middle of the table.

The dealer then asks the same question of the next player. We will suppose he holds an ace and a two.

This, according to the value put upon the ace, will represent either three or thirteen. Thirteen is not good enough to stand upon, and the player accordingly draws a card. (This third card, and all following, are dealt face upwards.) He receives, say, a second " two," making him fifteen. Not caring to stand on this amount, he draws another card, and receives a " seven," making him twenty-two, or twelve. With twenty-two he would be over, and with twelve he is worse off than when he started. Again he says, " Card," and receives, say, a " three," making him still only fifteen. He draws again, and this time receives, we will suppose, a " five," when he of course " stands."

And so the game proceeds, all who overdraw paying and throwing up their cards forthwith. Last comes the turn of the dealer himself. If his cards are eighteen or up- wards, he will " stand." At seventeen, he should usually stand. At fifteen, or sixteen, it is an open question, to be decided partly by the number of punters who may be still standing (and who, if numerous, will probably have some low hands amongst them), partly by his knowledge of the idiosyncrasies of his opponents, and partly by the nature of the cards which have been " drawn " by the other players. Should he go " over," he pays all, with the exception of those who, having over- drawn, have already paid up their stakes. If otherwise, he pays or receives as the cards of the punter, or his own are nearest to the critical " twenty-one." Should the cards of any punter amount to exactly twenty-one, he will receive double the amount of his stake from the dealer. In like manner, should the dealer's cards make exactly twenty-one points, each of the punters pays double the amount of his stake. In the event of " ties " (twenty-ones included), the punter pays the dealer or should either dealer or punter hold five cards making 21 or less he pays or receives twice his stake. It must, however, be remembered that a natural vingt-un always takes precedence over one made by drawing.

Should a punter, on receiving his second card, find that both are alike, *e.g.*, two aces, two kings, or two queens, he may, if he pleases, go on both. When it becomes his turn to draw, he says, " I go on both," and the dealer then gives him another card, face downwards, on each. The player then draws as he pleases to complete each hand, but must finish the drawing on one, before beginning on the other. Should the third card dealt be the same as the first two, *i.e.*, a third ace, king, or queen, he can go on all three in like manner. Likewise on a fourth, should the first four be alike. Each hand pays or receives on its own merits, as though belonging to an independent punter.

The occurrence of a natural in any hand but the dealer's usually terminates the deal. By way of a sort of grace, however, it does not have this effect in the first round of a deal. Sometimes, by agreement, the deal is made to consist of a given number of rounds ; say, till all the pack is exhausted, or till two packs are exhausted, the two being shuffled together.

In some circles the deal does not pass in rotation, but the holder of a natural (other than in the first round of a deal) becomes thereby entitled to the next deal. The practice, however, is a bad one, for the deal being an advantage, it is but fair that each should enjoy such advantage in turn.

There is no authoritative Code of Laws for Vingt-Un.

BLIND HOOKEY

THE players, of whom there may be any number, cut for deal, the lowest having the preference. The pack is then shuffled by the player on the dealer's right hand, and afterwards, if he so please, by the dealer himself, after which it is cut by the right-hand player. The two halves are then re-united, and the pack is passed to the player on the left of the dealer, who cuts from the top a small quantity of cards (not less than four, nor more than his due proportion of the pack). The pack is then passed to the next player, who cuts a similar portion, and so on round the circle, the cards left belonging to the dealer. No one looks at his cards, but makes his stake on pure speculation ; hence the name " blind " hookey. The dealer then turns up his cards, and shows the bottom one ; the other players do the same. Each player holding a higher card than that of the dealer receives the amount of his stake ; all below or equal pay the dealer. This is repeated until a hand occurs in which the dealer is a loser all round, when the deal is at an end, and the next player deals.

A second method is as under : The cards having been shuffled and cut, the dealer cuts them into three portions. Two of these are for the company, the third for himself. The other players place their stakes on whichever two packets they please, the rejected packet being taken by the dealer.* The stakes having been made, the cards are turned up, and the players receive or pay as the bottom cards of their packets prove to be higher or lower than that of the dealer.

* As a matter of fact, this arrangement is no guarantee whatever against pre-arranged fraud. For the methods employed by card-sharpers at this game, see *Les Filouteries du Jeu* (Cavaillé). Tit. " Les Petits Paquets."

SLIPPERY SAM

SLIPPERY SAM is a variation of and by many considered an improvement on Blind Hookey. The game is simplicity itself.

The dealer having been selected by any of the usual methods, he puts up as many chips as he likes to form a bank. The cards being shuffled and cut, the banker deals three cards face downwards either one two or all three at a time to each of the other players round the table, beginning with the player on his left. The latter looks at his card and bets either the whole or any part of the amount in the bank that among his three cards he holds something to beat the present top card of the pack. Or he may refuse to bet on his cards, when the player on his left looks at his cards and stakes or not as seems advisable. When the player makes his stake the dealer (banker) turns up the top card of the pack and the player (punter) exposes his three cards and receives from or pays into the pool according to whether he has the beating of the banker's card or not. To win the punter's card must be in the same suit as the turned up card—thus if the punter holds ace of hearts, diamonds, and clubs, but the banker turns up the two of spades, the banker would win.

After each bet the cards, including the turned up card, are swept away to the deadwood, and the bet passes to the next player against whom the banker will turn up the next top card, and so on round the table.

The banker must sit in the bank until he has completed three complete deals, when he may withdraw or have one more round but no more. At any time when his bank is exhausted the deal passes to the next player on the left.

The rules of the game are few and simple.

(1) The cards rank as at whist—ace highest, deuce lowest. Only one pack is used.
(2) Each punter when it is his turn may bet the whole or any part of the amount in the bank at that moment.

(3) The punters may not look at their cards until it is their turn to stake.

(4) The banker may not withdraw anything from his bank during the period of his three deals, and if he elects to play a fourth, he must leave all there is in the bank at the end of the third deal.

(5) As soon as the bank is exhausted—even if should that occur on the very first bet, the deal passes.

(6) The bank passes in rotation round the table to the left and each player in his turn must take the bank. (It is usual to place a minimum on the amount the bank can be made for.)

(7) At the end of each deal, *i.e.*, when the player on the dealer's right has bet or passed all the cards are re-shuffled, cut and dealt.

(8) The banker may not hold the stock in his hand. He must place it on the table, and when a bet has been made turn up the top card.

Slippery Sam naturally comes under the heading of gambling games, yet it has the peculiarity, common to no other gambling game that if played on common-sense lines the punter should have the best of it. The punter seeing his cards before he bets is in the position to calculate whether the odds are in his favour or against him.

The average card is an eight. If therefore the punter holds three eights his chance of winning and losing are equal *provided the card turned up belongs to one of the suits he holds.* In other words, he has a whole suit against him and there are therefore 18 cards—the ace, king, queen, knave, 10, 9, of three suits—plus 13 cards, the entire fourth suit, to defeat him—31 in all. In his favour are the 2, 3, 4, 5, 6 and 7 of three suits—18 cards in all. So on three eights the odds against the punter are 31 to 18 and he would be foolish to bet. Another instance —suppose the punter holds A, K, Q of one suit. He has three complete suits against him—39 cards; in his favour 10 cards. So on the hand the odds are practically 4 to 1 against him, and actually ace, king, queen in the same suit is about *twice as bad a hand* as three eights. The game is therefore deceptive and unless the punters understand that what *looks* a good thing as a rule is bad, they are bound to lose, and indeed this is what generally happens.

If the punter holds ace, king in one suit and another ace, the odds are still against him—26 to 23—and he should not bet.

Suppose however he holds three aces, there are but 13 cards on which he loses and thirty-six on which he wins —he must go the whole bank. Holding three tens the punter may be said to have an even chance for his bet (actually 25 to 24 against), so on anything better than this, the punter should stake, on less he should pass. But always remember the odds are against you unless each of the three cards you hold is in a different suit.

The punter also has an advantage over the banker by observing and making a mental note of the cards exposed by the other punters and by the banker's turn up. If he can remember these and knows that so many high cards and so many cards of a suit are out he can wager with safety on much less than average three tens. For instance he has counted all the spades out, and finds three aces, he bets on a certainty.

None the less as a rule the banker wins.

Another way of playing Slippery Sam is when the banker exposes the top card, and then the punter's stake on their own three before looking. This puts the odds very much in favour of the banker if he finds people foolish enough to bet against him. Nor is the game recommended among strangers : the clever fingered gentry will be seen to turn up a two (of diamonds say) and by extraordinary chance not one of the punters holds a diamond among them.

An amusing way to play this form of Slippery Sam however is to have no particular banker, but to form a joint one by each player putting so much into the pool. Then the punter adds to or takes out from the pool what he bets, so to a great extent the punters are staking against their own investments, and no particular player has the advantage. Stakes soon mount up though, and inexperienced players should be cautious. Five or six playing, a tit up of but a penny each to form a pool, soon turns itself into a game of bank notes.

BÉZIQUE

BÉZIQUE is a game for two players. The piquet pack of thirty-two cards is used, but in duplicate, two such packs of like pattern being shuffled together.

The players cut for deal, the *highest* card having the preference. The rank of the cards in cutting (as also in play) is as under : ace, *ten*, king, queen, knave, nine, eight, seven. Eight cards are dealt (by three, two, and three) to each player ; the seventeenth card being turned up by way of trump, and placed between the two players. The remaining cards, known as the "stock," are placed face downwards beside it. Should the turn-up card be a seven, the dealer scores ten.

The non-dealer leads and the dealer plays to such lead any card he pleases. If he play a higher card (according to the scale above given) of the same suit, or a trump, he wins the trick ; but he is not bound to do either, or even to follow suit. Further, he is at liberty to trump, even though holding a card of the suit led. If the two cards played are the same (*e.g.*, two nines of diamonds), the trick belongs to the leader.

The winner of one trick leads to the next, but before doing so he marks any points to which his hand may entitle him, leaving the cards so marked on the table, and draws one from the top of the stock. His opponent draws a card in like manner, and so the game proceeds until the stock is exhausted.

The holder of the seven of trumps is entitled to exchange it for the turn-up card, at the same time scoring ten for it. The holder of the duplicate seven of trumps scores ten for it, but gains no further benefit thereby.

The game is usually 1,000 up, but, as the score proceeds by tens or multiples of ten, this number is pretty quickly reached.

At the earlier stage of the game, the player scores for the cards he holds in his hand ; certain cards or combinations of cards, duly " declared," entitling him to score so many points, as under :—

	POINTS.
For the seven of trumps, turned up by the dealer, or declared by either player	10
For the second seven of trumps . . .	10
For the last (*i.e.*, thirty-second) trick . .	10
For a Common Marriage, *i.e.*, king and queen of any plain suit, declared together . . .	20
For a Royal Marriage, *i.e.*, king and queen of the trump suit, declared together . . .	40
For Single Bézique (queen of spades and knave of diamonds)	40
For Double Bézique—the same combination again declared by same player with fresh cards . . . . (additional)	500
For Four Knaves (of any suits, *e.g.*, two knaves of spades and two of hearts), duly declared .	40
For Four Queens, duly declared . . .	60
For Four Kings, duly declared . . .	80
For Four Aces, duly declared	100
For Sequence of five best trumps—ace, ten, king, queen, knave	250
Brisques—aces or tens in the tricks won by either player, *each**	10

In order to score, the cards composing the given combination must be all at the same time in the hand of the player. A card played to a trick is no longer available (unless a brisque) to score.

A player can only " declare " after winning a trick. Having won a trick, he is at liberty to score any combination he may hold, laying the cards forming it face upwards on the table. If the cards exposed show two combinations he may declare both, but must elect which of them he will score, reserving the other till he again wins a trick. Thus, having king and queen of spades and knave of diamonds on the table, he would say, " I score 40 for Bézique, and 20 to score." When he has again won a trick, having meanwhile retained the needful cards unplayed, he can then score the second combination (Marriage).

A card which has once scored cannot be again used to form part of a combination of *the same kind*, *e.g.*, a queen once used to form a Marriage cannot again

* Some players do not score *brisques* till the close of the hand. The better rule, however, is to score them when the trick is won.

figure in a Marriage, though it may still score as part of a Sequence, or as one of " Four Queens." In like manner, a card which has once figured in " Bézique " cannot be used to form part of a second Bézique, though it may be used to score Double Bézique. Neither can a card which has been declared in a given combination again be declared in a combination of an inferior order ; e.g., if a king and queen have been declared as part of a Sequence, a Marriage cannot afterwards be declared with the same cards—though their having figured in a Marriage would be no bar to their subsequent use as part of a Sequence.

The declared cards, though left face upwards on the table, still form part of the hand, and are played to subsequent tricks at the pleasure of the holder.

When no more cards are left in the stock, the method of play alters. No further declarations can be made, and the only additional score now possible is for the brisques (aces or tens) in the remaining tricks (scored by the winner of the trick), with ten for the last trick, as before stated.

The mode of play as to these last eight tricks is according to Whist rules. Each player must now follow suit, if he can ; if not, he is at liberty to trump.*

HINTS FOR PLAY

In the earlier stage of the game, tricks are of no value save in so far as they contain brisques, or enable the winner to " declare," the scoring of the different combinations being the main object of the game. The player will probably at the outset find that he has in hand *some* of the component parts of two or more combinations ; but as he must furnish a card to each trick, he will be forced to abandon the one or the other. In choosing between them, two points should be considered ; viz., first, the value of the combination, and, secondly, the prospect of making it. As to the last point,

---

* In some circles, when the Whist tricks are reached, the ten reverts to its Whist rank, *i.e.*, below the knave, but the practice is not recommended.

he may derive important information from the cards declared by his opponent. Suppose, for instance, that he holds a queen of spades and two knaves of diamonds. These he would naturally retain at any cost, in the hope of making Double Bézique ; but should his adversary declare a marriage in spades, showing that he holds the remaining queen of that suit, all hope of Double Bézique is clearly at an end. In the case supposed, it would be the policy of the opponent, knowing or suspecting that Double Bézique was aimed at, to keep the queen of spades in his hand as long as he possibly could, even at some considerable sacrifice.

When a brisque is led, the second player should win the trick if he can do so without too great a cost, for, though a brisque only scores ten to the winner, the capture of the trick means a loss of ten to the opposite party, and practically, therefore, makes a difference of twenty to the score.

Unless a brisque be led, or you have something to declare, pass the trick or win it with a brisque. The best cards to throw away are the sevens, eights, nines, and knaves of plain suits (other than the knave of diamonds, which should be retained on the chance of making Bézique).

It is generally better to risk losing an ace than a queen or king, the two latter having the greater chance of scoring.

If you chance to hold three aces at an early stage of the game, with no prospect of a more valuable combination, retain them, in the hope of drawing a fourth. In any other case, make tricks with aces in plain suits whenever you can.

" Sequence " cards should be kept in reserve as long as possible. A duplicate of a sequence card, though valueless for scoring purposes, should still be held up, as the uncertainty respecting it may hamper your opponent.

Even more important than sequence cards are the bézique cards. After scoring Bézique, the declared cards should still be retained until it becomes clear that Double Bézique is unattainable.

At a late period of the game, when the opportunities for declaration are growing limited, it is often wise to declare (say) Double Bézique without previously declaring Single Bézique, or Sequence without previously declaring a Royal Marriage. If you declare the smaller score, and do not again win a trick, you lose the larger score altogether.

When the stock is nearly exhausted, take a trick whenever you can, as you thereby deprive the adversary of the opportunity of scoring his remaining cards. Note at this stage the exposed cards of the adversary, as you will thereby play the last eight tricks to greater advantage.

In the play of the last eight tricks, your main object is to make your brisques, and capture those of the enemy. Reserve, if possible, a good trump wherewith to secure the last trick.

RUBICON BÉZIQUE

" RUBICON " or " Japanese " Bézique is a modification of the ordinary game. In 1887, a code of laws, which we append, was drawn up by a committee of the Portland Club, and Rubicon Bézique may now be regarded as the standard game.

Four packs, of like pattern and shuffled together, are used. The cards rank as at ordinary Bézique; but *nine* instead of eight ·cards are dealt, singly or by threes, to each player. There is no " turn-up," the first " marriage " scored determining the trump suit. If a " sequence " be declared and scored before any marriage, such sequence determines the trump suit.

The scores, ranging from 20 for a " marriage " to 4,500 for a Quadruple Bézique, are set forth in the laws of the game on p. 177. *Carte Blanche, i.e.,* 50 for a hand that does not hold a court card, is scored at the outset of the game, and before the player has drawn. He must prove his title by exhibiting his nine cards, one after another (as rapidly as he pleases), face upwards on the table. Should the first card he draws not be an honour, he may show the card, and again score carte blanche, and so on, as often as this may happen; but carte blanche cannot be scored after the player has once held a court card.

The first marriage scored is necessarily in trumps, unless a sequence has already been declared.

The procedure as to playing and drawing in " Rubicon " is the same as at ordinary Bézique, save that the tricks are left face upwards in a heap between the players until a brisque is played, when the winner of the trick takes them up, and turns them face downwards, near himself. The value of each brisque is ten points, but they are not scored till the close of the game, and in certain events (see *post*) may not be scored at all.

Only one declaration can be scored at a time, and

that only (save in the case of carte blanche) by the winner of a trick ; but if, on the cards being exposed, the player has more than one combination to score, he may score whichever he prefers, at the same time calling attention to his further claim by saying, " And —— to score." A player is not bound to declare any combination, even when exposed upon the table, unless he thinks fit. If he is compelled to play a card of the combination before he has actually scored it, the right to score is at an end.

A card declared in a given combination may not again be declared in an *inferior* combination of the same class —*e.g.*, a king and queen declared in Sequence cannot be afterwards made available to score a Royal Marriage. The same card may, however, be used in conjunction with a new card or cards to form, not merely a combination of the same kind, but the same combination over again.* Thus, if Four Queens have been declared, the player may play one of them, and, when he next wins a trick, add a fifth Queen to the three left on the table, and again score Four Queens.

If a combination, duly scored, is broken up, one or more cards must be substituted, either from the cards upon the table or from the hand of the player, to entitle him to a fresh score. There is an apparent exception to this rule in the fact that, if a player has declared two independent marriages in the same suit, and all four cards are on the table simultaneously, he may make two more declarations of marriage with the same cards. In truth, however, this merely follows the rule. King 1 (already " married " to queen 1) may again be married to queen 2 ; and king 2 (already married to queen 2) to queen 1 in like manner.

A player who has two or more declarations to score may elect which he will score first, the other remaining in abeyance ; *e.g.*, a player having declared Four Kings, including the king of spades, and subsequently declaring Bézique (the king of spades still remaining on the table) would, *ipso facto*, become entitled to score a Marriage, royal or ordinary, as the case might be. We will suppose the former. In such a case, he

---

* It will be observed that this rule is directly contrary to that prevailing at ordinary Bézique.

would say, " I score forty, and forty for marriage to score."
This declaration should be repeated, by way of reminder,
after each trick, till actually scored. If, in the meantime,
the player becomes entitled to score some other combination, he may, on winning a trick, score the latter in preference to the one previously declared, still keeping this in
reserve. The mere fact of having declared a given
combination " to score " does not preserve the right
to score it, if in the meantime the declarant either
plays one of the cards composing it or makes use of
them to score some higher declaration of the same
class.

The last nine tricks are played like the last eight in the
ordinary game ; but the winner of the last trick, instead
of 10, scores 50.

How the Score is Dealt with

The game is completed in one deal, and is won by
the player who scores most points, according to the
foregoing table, exclusive of brisques. These latter
are only taken into account where the scores are
otherwise equal. If, after the addition of the brisques,
the scores are still equal, the game is drawn.

There is one other case in which the brisques are
reckoned. The score of 1000 points is known as the
" Rubicon," and a player not reaching this score is
" rubiconed." In this case, also, each player adds in
his brisques ; and if the score of the loser is thereby brought
up to 1000, he " saves the rubicon."

Assuming that the rubicon is saved, the score of the
loser is deducted from that of the winner, fractions of
a hundred being disregarded in both cases. To the
difference are added 500 points for game, and the total
is the value of the game, the stakes being usually so much
per hundred points. If it happen that the difference
between the two scores is less than 100, it is reckoned
at that figure, making, with the 500 for game, 600. Thus,
if the respective scores are, A, 1510 ; B, 1240 ;
A wins 1500—1200+500=800. If A's score were
1550, and B's 1520, A would win 100+500=
600.

If B is rubiconed, the value of the game is computed

after a different method. The points made by him (still disregarding fractions of a hundred), instead of being subtracted from, are *added* to the score of the winner, who is further entitled to 1000 for the game and 300 for brisques.* Thus, if A has won 1320, and B 620, the value of A's game will be 1300+600+1000 +300=3200.

If the rubiconed player has scored less than 100, that amount (100) is added to the score of the other player, as well as the 1000 for game and 300 for brisques, as before mentioned.

THE LAWS OF RUBICON BÉZIQUE

SHUFFLING

1.—Rubicon Bézique is played with four packs of thirty-two cards, shuffled together.

2.—Each player has a right to shuffle the pack. The dealer has the right of shuffling last.

3.—The pack must not be shuffled below the table, nor in such manner as to expose the faces of the cards.

CUTTING

4.—A cut must consist of at least five cards, and at least five must be left in the lower packet.

5.—The cards rank as follows, both in cutting and in playing : ace (highest), ten, king, queen, knave, nine, eight, seven (lowest).

6.—The player who cuts the higher card has choice of deal, seats and markers. The choice determines both seats and markers during the play.

7.—If, in cutting for deal, a player expose more than one card, he must cut again.

8.—The cut for deal holds good even if the pack be incorrect.

9.—If, in cutting to the dealer, or in re-uniting the separated packets, a card be exposed, or if there be any confusion of the cards, there must be a fresh cut.

---

* Roughly, the value of all the brisques in the four packs. There are actually 32, which at ten each would be 320 ; but as the odd 20 are not reckoned, this reduces the value to 300.

DEALING

10.—The dealer must deal the cards by one at a time, giving the top card to his adversary, the next card to himself, and so on ; or by three at a time, giving the top three cards to his adversary, the next three to himself, and so on ; until each player has nine cards. The undealt cards (called the " stock ") are to be placed face downward, in one packet, in the middle of the table, to the left of the dealer.

11.—If the dealer deal the cards wrongly, he may rectify the error, with the permission of his adversary, prior to either player having taken up any of his cards.

12.—If, after the deal, and before the dealer has played to the first trick, it be discovered that either player has more than nine cards there must be a fresh deal. If it be similarly discovered that either player has less than nine cards, the deal may be completed from the top of the stock by mutual agreement, otherwise there must be a fresh deal.

13.—If the dealer expose a card belonging to his adversary or to the stock, the non-dealer has the option of a fresh deal. If the dealer expose any of his own cards, the deal stands good.

14.—If a faced card be found in the pack before the play of the hand has begun, there must be a fresh deal.

CARTE BLANCHE

15.—If a player have a hand dealt him without king, queen or knave, he may declare carte blanche before playing a card. Carte blanche must be shown by counting the cards, one by one, face upward, on the table.

16.—If, after playing a card, a player who has declared carte blanche draw a card other than king, queen or knave, he is entitled to declare another carte blanche on showing the card drawn to his adversary ; and so on after every card drawn, until he draws a king, queen or knave.

PLAYING

17.—If a player play with more than nine cards he is rubiconed ; but the amount to be added to his adversary's score is not to exceed nine hundred, exclusive of the thirteen hundred for a rubicon game.

18.—If both players play with more than nine cards, the game is null and void.

19.—If a player play with less than nine cards, the error cannot be rectified. He is liable to no penalty ; his adversary wins the last trick.

20.—If both players play with less than nine cards, the deal stands good, and the winner of the last trick scores it.

21.—If one player play with more than nine cards, and the other with less than nine, the deal stands good. The player with more than nine cards is rubiconed (as provided in Law 17), and neither player scores the last trick.

22.—If a faced card be found in the stock after the play of the hand has begun, it must be turned face downward, without altering its place in the stock.

23.—A card led in turn may not be taken up after it has been played to. A card played to a trick may not be taken up after the trick has been turned, or after another card has been drawn from the stock ; but if two or more cards be played together, all but one may be taken up ; and cards accidentally dropped may be taken up.

24.—A card led out of turn must be taken up, unless it has been played to. After it has been played to, it is too late to rectify the error.

25.—A player who wins a trick containing a brisque should at once take up all the played cards on the table, and turn them face downward near himself. If he fail to do so, his adversary is entitled, as soon as he has won a trick, to take up all the played cards on the table. Tricks turned may not be looked at (except as provided in Law 27).

26.—The stock may be counted, face downwards, at any time during the play. A player counting the stock should be careful not to disturb the order of the cards.

27.—A player may not count the brisques in his tricks so long as more than twelve cards remain in the stock.

DRAWING

28.—If the winner of a trick see two cards when drawing from the stock, he must show the top card to his adversary.

29.—If the loser of a trick draw the top card of the stock and see it, he must restore the card drawn in error, and must show the next card to his adversary ; but, if the loser of a trick draw the top card, and the winner draw the next card and see it, it is too late to rectify the error, and the players retain the cards erroneously drawn.

30.—If the loser of a trick, after the winner has drawn, see two cards when drawing from the stock, his adversary has choice of the two cards of the following draw, and is entitled to look at both before choosing. If he choose the second card, he need not show it.

31.—If a player see several cards when drawing from the stock, his adversary has choice of the two cards of the following draw, and then of the cards of the next draw ; and so on, as long as any card which has been seen remains undrawn ; and he is entitled to look at the cards before choosing.

32.—If there be an odd number of cards in the stock, the last card is not drawn.

DECLARING

33.—Declared cards must be placed face upward on the table separate from the tricks, and (except in the case of carte blanche) must remain there until played, or until the stock is exhausted.

34.—If a declared card be played, and a card which restores any scoring combination or combinations be substituted, these combinations may be declared again.

35.—If a player declare more than one marriage in the same suit, he may declare a fresh marriage whenever he plays one of the declared cards, so long as a king and queen remain on the table.

36.—A player who has declared marriage may afterwards add the ace, ten, and knave of the same suit as the marriage, and declare sequence ; or he may declare sequence without first declaring the marriage.

37.—A king or queen, once declared in sequence, cannot be afterwards used to form part of a marriage ; but a player, having declared sequence, may declare marriage with a fresh king and queen of the same suit.

38.—Bézique combinations may be declared separately, and may be afterwards united to form a superior combination ; or single, double, or triple bézique may be added to any already declared combination, to form a superior one ; or, double, triple, or quadruple bézique may be at once declared, without having been previously declared separately. Bézique cards once declared in a superior bézique combination cannot be afterwards used to form part of an inferior one ; but may be used to form part of equal or superior combinations with a substituted card, or with added cards, or with both.

39.—A player who has cards on the table with which he might form a scoring combination, is not bound to declare it.

SCORING

40.—A player declaring—

Carte Blanche .	.	.	.	scores	50
Marriage in trumps .	.	.	.	,,	40
Marriage in plain suits	.	.	.	,,	20
Sequence in trumps .	.	.	.	,,	250
Sequence in plain suits	.	.	.	,,	150
Bézique .	.	.	.	,,	40
Double Bézique	.	.	.	.,	500
Triple Bézique	.	.	.	,,	1500
Quadruple Bézique .	.	.	.	,,	4500
Four Aces	.	.	.	.	,,	100
Four Kings	.	.	.	.	.,	80
Four Queens	.	.	.	.	,,	60
Four Knaves .	.	.	.	.,	40

41.—The first marriage scored makes the trump suit. If no marriage has been scored, the first sequence scored makes the trump suit.

42.—A player can only score a declaration on winning a trick and before drawing, except in the case of carte blanche, which is scored before playing, and independently of winning a trick.

43.—Only one declaration can be scored at a time; but if a player declare a carte blanche which contains four aces, he may also score four aces if he win the trick, notwithstanding that he has already scored carte blanche.

44.—If the winner of a trick have two or more declarations to score, he may choose which he will first score. On winning another trick, he may similarly choose which of the remaining declarations he will score, or he may make and score a fresh declaration, and leave any unscored declarations still to score on winning another trick.

45.—A player who has a declaration to score should repeat after every trick what he has to score. He may score it at any time on winning a trick, and before drawing.

46.—If a player who has a declaration to score play a card of the combination before scoring it, he loses the score.

47.—If a player have a marriage to score, and, on winning a trick, add to the marriage the ace, ten, and knave of the suit, and score sequence, he loses the score for the marriage.

48.—If a player have an inferior bézique combination to score, and, on winning a trick, add to the bézique combination cards which form a superior bézique combination, and score the superior combination, he loses the score for the inferior one.

49.—A player who has a declaration to score is not bound to score it.

50.—If a player erroneously score a declaration which does not constitute a scoring combination, and the error be not discovered before a card of the next trick has been played, the score marked stands good; and so on for all subsequent scores similarly marked before the discovery of the error.

51.—If an error in marking the score be proved, it may be corrected at any time during the game.

52.—No declaration can be scored after the stock is exhausted.

THE LAST NINE TRICKS

53.—The winner of the last trick adds fifty to the score.

54.—The winner of the last trick is bound to score it (except as provided in Law 21).

55.—If, during the play of the last nine tricks, a player fail to follow suit when able, or fail to win the card led when able, on detection of the error, the card erroneously played, and all cards subsequently played, must be taken up and replayed.

COMPUTING THE GAME

56.—The brisques (aces and tens) score ten each to the player having them in his tricks ; but the brisques are only taken into account as provided in Laws 60 and 61.

57.—The winner of the game deducts the score of the loser from his own (excluding fractions of a hundred), and the difference, with five hundred added for the game, is the number of points won. If the difference between the scores be less than a hundred, the winner adds a hundred to the score of five hundred for the game.

58.—If the loser fail to score a thousand, he is rubiconed. The winner, whether his score reach a thousand or not, adds the score of the loser to his own (excluding fractions of a hundred), and the sum, with thirteen hundred added for the game, is the number of points won.

59.—If a player who is rubiconed has scored less than a hundred, the winner adds a hundred to his score, in addition to the score of thirteen hundred for the game.

60.—If the loser of a game fail to score a thousand, but have in his tricks a sufficient number of brisques to bring his total score to a thousand, he is not rubiconed. Each player adds his brisques to his score, and the game is computed as provided in Law 57.

61.—If the scores be so nearly equal that the brisques must be taken into account in order to decide who wins the game, and the loser be not rubiconed, each player adds his brisques to the score, and the game is then computed as provided in Law 57 ; but if the loser be rubiconed, the brisques, though taken into account in order to decide who wins the game, are not added to the scores, and the game is computed as provided in Law 58. In the case of a tie after adding the brisques, the game is null and void.

INCORRECT PACKS

62.—If a pack be discovered to be incorrect, redundant, or imperfect, the deal in which the discovery is made is void. All preceding deals stand good.

63.—If a card or cards which complete the pack be found on the floor, the deal stands good.

CHANGING CARDS

64.—Before the pack is cut to the dealer, a player may call for fresh cards at his own expense. He must call for four fresh packs.

65.—Torn or marked cards must be replaced, or fresh packs called for at the expense of the two players.

BYSTANDERS

66.—If a bystander call attention to any error or oversight, and thereby affects the score, he may be called upon to pay all stakes and bets of the player whose interest he has prejudicially affected.

BOSTON

BOSTON, a four-handed game played with the full pack of fifty-two cards, is the parent of the better known Solo Whist (see p. 60), over which its chief advantage is that it affords greater scope to the gambler, and its chief disadvantage that its scoring is both complex and inconsistent.

The cards are dealt round by four, four, and five to each, and the trump suit is decided by the player facing the dealer cutting a second pack, the card left on the lower half fixing the suit, which is known as *First Preference*. The other suit of the same colour is *Second Preference*, and the remaining suits *Plain* or *Common Suits*, for that deal.

Red and white counters are used, one red counter being equivalent to ten whites ; the value of the white is, of course, a matter of arrangement. Each player puts an agreed number of counters (say, one red) in the pool, the dealer usually paying double.

The cards rank between themselves as at Whist ; but there are no honours, the only factor in the count being the number of tricks taken (or lost, as the case may be). The player proposing the most highly awarded bid must, as at Solo Whist, be allowed to try. The bids rank in the following order, beginning at the lowest :—

Call.	Object of Call.
BOSTON	To win 5 tricks.
SIX TRICKS	To win 6 tricks.
SEVEN TRICKS	To win 7 tricks.
LITTLE MISÈRE	To lose 12 tricks after having discarded a card which is not to be shown.
EIGHT TRICKS	To win 8 tricks.
NINE TRICKS	To win 9 tricks.
GRAND MISÈRE	To lose every trick.
TEN TRICKS	To win 10 tricks.
ELEVEN TRICKS	To win 11 tricks.

Call.	Object of Call.
LITTLE SPREAD (or Little Misère Ouverte)	To lose 12 tricks after having discarded a card—which is not to be shown—the remaining 12 cards being exposed, but not liable to be called.
TWELVE TRICKS	To win 12 tricks.
GRAND SPREAD (or Grand Misère Ouverte)	To lose every trick, the player's cards being exposed, but not liable to be called.
GRAND SLAM	To win all the tricks.

Any of these calls is better than any above it on the list, and it must be remembered that in each call (apart from the Misères, which are played without trumps) a bid in First Preference overrides one in Second Preference (or Colour, as it is also known), and this, again, overrides one in a Plain Suit.

The deal being completed, bidding commences, the elder hand having first say. If he thinks that, with the privilege of making the trump suit what he likes, he could win five tricks, and that any more would be risky, he will declare Boston ; if he has nothing worth calling on, he says, " I pass." We will assume that he declares Boston. The second player has then to consider whether he can do any better ; he may be able to make five tricks in Colour (*i.e.*, with Second Preference as trumps*) ; if so, he says, " I keep." If the third player thinks that he can make five tricks with First Preference as trumps, he says, " I keep over you." The fourth player can then call Six Tricks, or some higher bid, and the bidding goes on until no player will risk more. A player who has once dropped out of the bidding cannot re-enter, except to make one of the Misère calls— and then, of course, only if it is superior to the last call made.

When a player has made a bid, and all the others pass, he may name any suit he likes as trumps ; and if the highest bidder omit to declare which suit he plays he is bound to play in the first suit led.

In the rare event of every player passing, it is usual to play a *Grand*, or *Misère Partout :* all pay into the

---

* Rule 9 says :—When the elder hand makes a bid of five or more tricks, and another player bids the same number, the latter shall be bound to play *in colour*. A third player bidding the same number shall be bound to play *in trump*.

pool, there is no trump, and the object of each player is to take as few tricks as possible.

A player undertaking to make Boston, or a larger number of tricks, and succeeding, receives a specified number of counters (as shown in Table I, below) from each of his opponents. If, on the other hand, he fails —as, for instance, if he has declared to make seven tricks and makes five only—he is said to be " put in for " the number of tricks by which he is short, and pays as shown in Table II.

TABLE I.

Counters payable by each opponent to winner of declaration. The American system is to ignore over-tricks, thus making bidders call up to their hands and saving time, as hands do not have to be played out: the awards for tricks won under this system are shown in the right-hand column.

Number of tricks bid by player.	Number actually taken by him.									Am. Sys.
	5	6	7	8	9	10	11	12	13	
Five	12	12	13	13	14	14	14	15	15	10
Six		15	16	16	17	18	19	20	20	15
Seven			18	20	21	22	23	24	26	20
Eight				23	24	26	28	29	31	25
Nine					32	34	36	39	41	35
Ten						42	45	48	52	45
Eleven..............							63	68	72	65
Twelve								106	114	105
Thirteen									166	170

TABLE II.

Counters payable to each opponent by a player failing in his bid.

Tricks bid by the player.	Number of tricks won by which the player falls short of his declaration.												
	1	2	3	4	5	6	7	8	9	10	11	12	13
Five	11	21	31	41	50								
Six	15	24	35	45	55	66							
Seven	19	29	40	50	60	72	82						
Eight	23	34	46	56	67	78	89	110					
Nine	33	44	57	68	82	92	103	115	127				
Ten	44	56	70	82	94	107	119	132	145	157			
Eleven..............	67	80	95	109	123	138	151	165	180	194	208		
Twelve	113	130	148	165	182	200	217	234	252	270	286	304	
Thirteen	177	198	222	241	262	284	305	326	348	369	390	412	433

The complex and illogical arrangement of these two Tables is a drawback to the game, and a decimal system for Table II has been devised and is in use in many Boston-playing circles. To construct it, substitute for Column I the numbers: 10, 15, 20, 25, 35, 45, 70, 120, and 180; and for the Rows, proceed from these points in tens, the first row reading :—10, 20, 30, 40, 50.

If a Misère is bid, the caller wins from or loses to each adversary as follows, there being no over-tricks :—

Little Misère,	20 counters.
Grand Misère,	40　　,,
Little Spread,	80　　,,
Grand Spread,	160　　,,

In the Misère Partout call the loser is the player who makes the largest number of tricks, and he pays each of the other players ten times the difference between the number of his tricks and theirs. For instance : A wins 5 tricks, Y 3, B 4, and Z 1 ; A loses 70 counters, Y receiving 20, B 10, and Z 40. If two players tie for the greatest number of tricks taken they each pay half of the total losses ; and if three players take four tricks each, they pay the other hand ten.

All the declarations having been made, the elder hand leads for the first trick—no matter whose bid was successful—and play proceeds exactly as in Whist.

If a caller make his bid he not only receives from each of the other players, but also, if his bid were for seven tricks or better (known as a *pool bid*), takes the pool. In some circles the pool is not allowed to exceed a specified limit (say 250 counters), all contributions over this amount being set aside to form a nucleus of a new pool. In a game in which few calls are successful it may happen that there are quite a number of pools in existence at the same time ; any of these that are not worked off by the end of the game are usually divided equally among the players. Misère Partout does not touch the pool.

If a caller fail in his bid he doubles the contents of the pool (paying the limit should there be more than one pool on the table), besides paying out as above. The pool is also added to in the course of play by the dealer putting in ten at each deal, and by any agreed penalties—such as ten for a misdeal, forty for a revoke, and so on ; while in the event of all four players passing each makes a fresh contribution, and the deal passes.

The second round is played with the second pack of cards, and the two packs are now used alternately. Each is thoroughly shuffled at the commencement of the game, *but never afterwards;* in all ubsequent deals the cards are gathered as they lie on the table, and are cut by each player in turn, beginning with the one on the new dealer's left. If the cards were shuffled before each deal the higher declarations would be of very rare occurrence.

There is one more variation from Whist play that must be mentioned, and that is in the matter of revoking. In Boston, if a revoke be made by the highest bidder and the error be discovered before the hand is played out, further play of that hand shall be discontinued. The offender shall be *put in for* one trick, and shall pay a fine of forty to the pool. If the error is not discovered till the hand is played out, and the offender has thereby been already put in for more than one trick, then the payment to the pool shall be the only penalty.

Also, if a revoke is made by any player other than the bidder, each of the remaining players participates in the offence, and each must pay to the bidder the value of his bid, as if won, whether he would actually have been successful or not. The player who was responsible for the revoke must further put forty in the pool.

A variation adopted in some circles is the right accorded to the highest bidder of asking for a partner, or " whister," as he is called. A player accepting has to make three additional tricks, and the hand is played as at Solo Whist, the partners playing from where they happen to sit. If they succeed in making the required total their gains are divided, each receiving from one of the opposite players. In the event of failure the joint losses are usually divided ; but some players prefer to arrange that where the loss is one-sided only, *e.g.*, where the bidder has made his five, or his partner has failed to make his three tricks, or *vice versa*, the whole penalty should be borne by the defaulter.

BOSTON DE FONTAINEBLEAU

BOSTON DE FONTAINEBLEAU, or French Boston as it is sometimes, though improperly, called, has a general resemblance to ordinary Boston, but offers a good many differences in detail, the chief being that the suits rank in a definite order (consequently there is no cutting for trumps), there is an extra call, and the order of the calls is not the same in the two games.

In the English and American form of the game the suits rank as follows :—(1) Diamonds, (2) Hearts, (3) Clubs, (4) Spades (in France, Hearts come first and Diamonds second) ; so that a player undertaking to make six tricks in Diamonds overcalls one who has declared for six in Hearts. The new call is known as *Piccolissimo*, and signifies that the player undertaking it will, after discarding one card (as in Little Misère), make neither more nor less than *one trick*. Honours are, under certain circumstances, added to the score of the winner.

The declarations rank as follows :—

1. Boston (to win five tricks).
2. Six tricks.
3. Little Misère.
4. Seven tricks.
5. Piccolissimo.
6. Eight tricks.
7. Grand Misère.
8. Nine tricks.
9. Little Spread (Little Misére Ouverte).
10. Ten tricks.
11. Grand Spread (Grand Misère Ouverte).
12. Eleven tricks.
13. Twelve tricks.
14. Slam (Grand Boston).
15. Open Slam (with the player's cards exposed).

A highest bidder who has called either No. 1, 2, 4, 6, 8, or 10, has the right of calling for a partner ; and, if accepted, the two players must, as in ordinary Boston, score three more tricks than those originally bid for. The eldest hand always leads for the first trick, irrespective of whose was the highest bid, and play proceeds as in Whist, trumps winning all other suits, except in the case of a Misère or Piccolissimo, when trumps are ignored. The ace, king, queen, and knave of the trump suit are honours, and if the bidding player (or players) hold four they are " four by honours," and if three " two by honours," as at Whist, these counting as additional tricks if (and *only* if) the full score declared has been made.

In the event of all passing, the hand is played out, and the pool goes to the player who wins the smallest number of tricks ; in such a case there is, of course, no trump suit.

The following table shows the number of counters to be paid to a successful bidder, according to the suit in which the hand is played :—

	No trump	The trump being			Extra tricks
		Club or Spade	Heart	Diamond	
Boston, five tricks.........	....	10	20	30	5
Six tricks	....	30	40	50	5
Little misère	75				
Seven tricks	....	50	60	70	5
Piccolissimo	100				
Eight tricks	....	70	80	90	5
Grand misère	150				
Nine tricks	....	90	100	110	5
Little spread	200				
Ten tricks	....	110	120	130	5
Grand spread	250				
Eleven tricks.............	....	130	140	150	5
Twelve tricks	....	150	160	170	5
Slam, thirteen tricks......	....	400	450	500	
Spread slam	....	600	700	800	

A player who is unsuccessful in making his call pays to each of his adversaries the same number of counters as he would have received in the event of success, and not as in the ordinary game ; and another point in which the two differ is that in Boston de Fontainebleau a player having once passed cannot come into the bidding again, even to call a Misère.

HEARTS

HEARTS is a game primarily for four players, played with the full pack of fifty-two cards very much as is Whist, with the following important exceptions :—(1) There are no partners, (2) there is no trump suit, and (3) the object is to avoid taking any trick containing a card of the heart suit.

The deal (except that there is no turn-up for trumps) and play proceed exactly as in Whist, the eldest hand leading and each succeeding player in turn to the left following suit if possible, and when this is not possible naturally taking the opportunity of discarding a heart. The winner of the first trick leads for the second, and so on, until the hand is played out ; the hearts that are in the tricks that each player has won are then counted and settled for, each hand being a game in itself.

The rule with regard to revokes is as in Whist ; the penalties are :—If the revoking player loses he must settle for all the others, if he wins he must put his winnings in the pool.

The usual method of paying is for the holder of the lowest number of hearts to receive from each of the other players one counter (or any previously agreed stake) for each heart card he holds, in the event of a tie the total being divided between them, an odd counter—if any—remaining in the pool for the next deal. Each player usually begins with the same number of counters, and the sitting comes to an end either when one player has lost all his stock, or when any player has won an agreed number of counters.

Another favourite way of settling is by the *Sweepstake* method : each player pays one counter into the pool for each heart taken ; any player having taken no heart wins the whole thirteen, and if two are in this position it is divided, the odd counter being left for the next pool. If all players have taken hearts, or if one has taken the lot, the pool remains, and forms a *Jack*, which can be won only by a single player in a subsequent deal taking no hearts, each of the others having taken at least one. These Jack pools are, of course, increased by thirteen counters every deal until some player takes it off.

HEARTSETTE

HEARTSETTE is played in the same way as Hearts, with the addition of a " Widow," and an arrangement by which the game can be adapted for any number of players from three to six.

When three or four players are taking part the deuce of spades is taken out ; the full pack is used when there are five or six. When there are three players sixteen cards are dealt to each ; when there are four, twelve ; when five, ten ; and when six, eight, one at a time. The remaining cards are left face downwards on the table, and form the " Widow," which must be gathered up and added to the hand of the player who takes the first trick immediately that trick is complete, he alone being allowed to see what it contains. The game then proceeds as in Hearts; payments are made to the pool for all hearts taken in, and the pool is then won, divided, or left to form a Jack.

The chief difference between the two games is that in Heartsette the other players do not know whether the winner of the first trick is loaded or not, and only he knows how many or what hearts are to be played.

CATCH THE TEN OR SCOTCH WHIST

CATCH THE TEN is so called because one of the chief objects of the game is to *catch the ten* of trumps and have it in one's hand at the final count.

A pack of thirty-six cards is used, the twos, threes, fours, and fives being rejected, the remainder ranking (as at Whist) ace, king, down to the six, with the exception of the trump suit for the time being, in which the order is J, A, K, Q, 10, 9, 8, 7, 6.

Any number from two to eight may play, and, as it is necessary that each player has the same number of cards, when there are eight players all the sixes are removed from the pack, and when there are five or seven the six of spades is removed. In some circles this last is not done, and the same effect is produced by the thirty-fifth card being turned up for trump and the thirty-sixth being discarded, after being shown round.

If the party consist of two, three, five, or seven, each plays on his own account. Four play in partnership, as at Whist; six may either play three against three, A, C, and E, against B, D, and F, or in three couples, each pair, A and D, B and E, and C and F, playing against the two others. Eight may either play four against four, or in four independent partnerships, each pair against the other three pairs. Partners and adversaries sit alternately, as at Whist.

The method of dealing varies with the number of players taking part. When there are only two the dealer gives six cards, one at a time, to each, then six more, in a separate heap, and then—again in a separate heap—six more, the last being turned up for trumps. Thus, each player has three separate hands, which are played independently. When three play the cards are dealt in much the same manner, two separate hands of six being given to each. With any other number of players the cards are dealt in rotation from left to right, as usual, due allowance being made, as above, for an odd number of cards when there are five or seven taking a hand.

If the dealer omit to have the pack cut before dealing, if he expose any of his adversaries' cards (unless already faced in the pack), or if he give too few or too many to any player, it is a misdeal, and the deal passes. When stakes are played for, they are for so much a game; there are no rubbers. In partnership games losers pay the winning opponent on the right; and it should be settled before play commences who pays for revokes, the revoking player or his side.

The object of the players is to secure the tricks containing certain cards which have a special scoring value, and the first side (or player) to score forty-one points wins. The scoring cards are :—

Knave of trumps counts 11 points.
Ten	,,	,,	10 ,,
Ace	,,	,,	4 ,,
King	,,	,,	3 ,,
Queen	,,	,.	2 ,,

Any court card in trumps can " catch the ten," but the knave is the best, so cannot go to any player but he to whom it is dealt.

Scores are also made for " cards." At the end of each hand players count the number of cards taken in tricks, and score one point for each held above the number originally dealt to them. Thus, if four be playing they would each have nine cards to start with ; if the players on one side take seven tricks (twenty-eight cards) they would score ten for " cards," as they have ten more than they began with, and this is added to anything they may have won in trumps or in " catching the ten."

The play of the hand follows the rule of ordinary Whist ; but the special object in the play is to " catch " or save the ten, as it makes a difference of 20 to the score. It is not necessary to keep the tricks separate, as at Whist, but one player should gather for his side. When two or three play the hands must be played in the order in which they were dealt, and the trump card must be left on the table until the dealer takes up the last hand.

One player should keep the score—which is made up at the end of each hand—on a sheet of paper.

GERMAN WHIST

GERMAN WHIST is a somewhat old-fashioned substitute for Whist when only two players are available ; but as it is quite a good game, and it is still occasionally played, some account of it will not be out of place in a modern " Hoyle."

The full pack is used, and, after it is cut as in Whist, the dealer gives his opponent and himself thirteen cards, one at a time, turning up the twenty-seventh for the trump suit, and laying it on the top of the remainder (the *talon*), which is left face downwards.

The non dealer begins by leading any card he fancies, and the dealer must follow suit if he can. The winner of the trick adds the trump card to his hand, and the loser takes the top card of the talon—but without showing it. The next card on the talon is then turned up ; a new trick is played in the usual way, the winner takes the turned-up card and his adversary the one under it, as before, again turning up the next.

So the game proceeds, the winner of each trick getting a new card which is known to his opponent, the loser getting one that is known only to himself ; until, the talon being exhausted, each player should be able accurately to name the thirteen cards held by the other, and the game resolves itself into a problem in " double dummy."

German Whist is usually played for so much a point, the player winning the majority of the twenty-six tricks receiving for all in excess of those won by his opponent. Each game is complete in one hand.

RUMMY

RUMMY is one of the most popular card games, for, while it calls for a certain amount of facility in elementary maths and care in watching points, it is very easily learnt and imposes no undue mental strain; it is, therefore, as much a favourite with "teen-agers" as it is, in its more highly specialized and gambling forms, with the more mature. Counters are a necessity, but whether one attaches a money value to them or not is entirely a matter for the party to decide, and so is the size of the party— for almost any number can take a hand.

There are no national or international Laws governing Rummy (which is an off-shoot, or perhaps progenitor, of the Coon-can family) consequently details of play vary from place to place and time to time; but the general idea is the same everywhere.

Take a pack of cards, complete with Joker, or if there should be more than five players, two packs, and shuffle the whole well together. Cut for deal, and then deal seven cards to each player, one at a time in the usual way, with one extra card face upwards in the middle of the table; to the right of this place the remainder of the pack (or packs) face downwards as "stock." Now the player on dealer's left, having examined his cards, turns the top card of the stock and looks at it without letting the others see it; he may then exchange either this or the exposed card for any card in his hand, his discard (or the top card of stock if not wanted) being placed on top of or in place of the card first exposed. He is not obliged to take either; if he "stands pat" the card from stock goes on top of the exposed card. This over, the next player has his choice in the same way, then the next and the next and so on, until eventually one player stops the round by laying his hand face upwards, whereupon all the other players do the same and the counting takes place.

The object of each player is to reduce the counting-

value of his hand to zero, or as near zero as he can, and
it is at his next turn after he decides that he has reached
this point that one lays down his cards. To acquire a
zero score the player must, by means of the drawing,
convert his holding so far as possible into " sets " or
" sequences," a " set " being any three or more cards of
the same denomination, as three twos, four Queens, etc.,
and a " sequence " a run of three or more of the same
suit, as 5, 6, and 7 of Clubs, 9 to Queen of Hearts, etc. ;
an Ace, for sequence purposes, counts either high (Q, K, A)
or low (A, 2, 3), unless it is otherwise agreed at the start ;
and the Joker, of course, has for the time just any value
the holder chooses to give it. In a hand, for instance,
containing a sequence of three with four " odd " un-
attached cards, if the Joker is drawn one of the odd cards
is discarded and the holding is converted into a sequence
of four, with three odds ; but if among the original four
odds there happens to be a pair one of the other odds is
discarded and the Joker joined to the pair, the hand then
containing a sequence, a set, and only one odd ; and
this is of great importance because of the following rule.

No hand can be laid down if its scoring-value is higher
than 6, and it is only the odd cards that are counted :
for sets and sequences nothing is scored, and for odd
cards their pip-value, Aces being counted as 1 and
court-cards as 10 each.

As we have seen, once a player has laid down his hand
the others follow suit, and that deal is at an end : the
individual scores are entered on a sheet provided for the
purpose ; all except the player with the lowest score pay
1 counter into the pool—which has already been started
by a contribution of 2 from everybody ; and the next
player in rotation deals afresh. The game is usually
played for 100 up, and as a player reaches or exceeds the
100 he drops out : at the finish two only are left in, and
these divide the pool, two-thirds going to the lower and
one-third to the higher scorer—unless they chance to be
level pegging in which case they share it equally.

The skill of the game is shown in the exchanging of
cards for your hand, in noticing and making deductions
from your opponents' discards, and in keeping track of
the scores. It is especially in the final stages of a game
that care and judgment are necessary : when your score

is at 96, let us say, you would not pass if you held a set of three, a sequence of three, and an odd 4 of a suit, for this would put you out ; you would cross your fingers and hang on till luck brought you a Joker, a card that would convert one of your threes into a four, a lower card—or until you were obliged to lay your hand on the table and " take your medicine." Similarly, if your score is 98 you could go down on a hand like the above only if the odd card were an Ace (bringing you to 99), and then on the next round only a " full house "—in which there is no odd card—would save you. Your solution of such problems will depend very much upon the state of the other players' scores ; to stay in will, of course, cost you another counter in the pool, but, on the other hand, the more quickly you go down the more your opponents will have to pay up and the fuller the pool will grow.

This is a simple form of the game which, as already mentioned, has many variations. Here is one that, as " Pay Me," was a great favourite with the troops in the off-times during the second World War—perhaps because it is even simpler, as score-sheets are not wanted.

PAY ME

THE preliminaries and the dealing of the seven cards are conducted in exactly the same way as in the game described above but the eighth card, instead of being immediately placed face up, the dealer deals to himself and discards from the eight cards face up, as before ; further, he is not allowed the option of taking the top card from the stock. Another difference is perhaps due to the fact the Jokers were often among the missing in Army packs, so the card to take its place was decided for each hand thus : the dealer passed the shuffled pack to the player on his right to cut, and all cards of the denomination next lower to the cut became Jokers—for that hand only ; thus, if a seven were cut all the sixes were Jokers, and if an Ace all Kings. If the real Joker happened to be present that counted as well, so in a 1-pack game there would be five Jokers and in a 2-pack, 10 ! Ace counts low, except when acting as a Joker.

The object of the game is also the same, namely, the building up of sets and sequences. After the dealer has discarded the card of least use to him and laid it face upwards next to the stock the others follow in rotation and may take either the exposed card or the top card of stock in the same manner as in ordinary Rummy. When any player has a full hand of sets or sequences, or a combination of both, with no odds, he, *at his next turn*, that is, when the draw comes round to him again, lays them face upwards on the table and, with a call of " Pay me ! ", claims the pool.

In a rather more advanced form of this game dealing, drawing, etc., are conducted as before but any set or sequence held or formed in a player's hand is laid down at once, before the floating eighth card is discarded. In this variation any player who has laid down at least one set or sequence may get rid of his cards by " building up " on any exposed set when his turn comes round ; if, for instance, there is a 6, 7, 8 of Hearts exposed and he has the 5 or 9 (or both) of Hearts he can add it (or them) to the sequence ; also, if he has a card that can take the place of a Joker in an exposed set or sequence he may take the Joker and put his own in its place—a very valuable privilege. When one player has got rid of all his cards the hand is over and the score is totted up ; cards left in a holding are counted as before—pip-value, 10 for any court-card, and 1 for each Ace.

Players start with 201 points ; as each hand finishes individual scores are deducted, cumulatively, from this, and the winner is the last player left with any points.

COON-CAN

In an earlier chapter we have dealt with " Colonel, ' a form of two-handed Coon-can, and here we propose to describe the game as usually played by three, four, or five players.

The name is Spanish (*con quien*, with whom), and the game comes originally from Mexico, where it is still played with the Spanish pack of forty cards, the eights, nines, and tens of our ordinary packs being omitted. In the United States (where the game here described is known as " Double-pack Rum ") and in England certain modifications have taken place, and it is played with two full packs, including the two Jokers, shuffled together and used as one.

In cutting for the deal, the highest deals ; king counts high, joker low, and ace next lowest to the joker. In the play ace may be high or low, as desired, and the jokers, of course, take any denomination the holder wishes.

Ten cards are dealt to each player, one at a time, and the next card is turned up and laid beside the " talon " (the cards left after dealing) to start the discard pile.

The object of the game is to get rid of all the cards dealt to one ; this is done by laying out (in turn) sequences of three or more in suit, or three or more cards of the same denomination.

The player to the left of the dealer has first " say," and after him the other players on his left in rotation. He is under no obligation to lay out anything, but he *must* take in one card, either from the face-up discard pile or from the face-down talon, just as he fancies. He may then lay out in front of him, face upwards, three or more cards of the same denomination or any sequence of three or more cards of the same suit. The ace may be used in an ace-deuce-three or a queen-king-ace run, but it cannot be used in a " round the corner " straight (king-ace-deuce). Should he be unable to discard any combination, or should he prefer not to, he *must* discard a single card, face up, on the stack to replace the one he has drawn, unless he is in the fortunate position of being able to lay down all his cards. Once having discarded a single he is not allowed to lay out any combinations or get rid of any cards until his turn comes round again.

As play proceeds each player has the right, between drawing and discarding, of " fattening " any combination already on the table, that is, he may add to a sequence, or to threes or fours, etc., and he may do as much of this as his cards will allow. Thus, there is a 5, 6, 7 of clubs on the table, and a group of three knaves ; if the player whose turn it is holds the 3, 4, 8 of clubs and a knave, he can discard the lot—making the sequence in clubs 3, 4, 5, 6, 7, 8, and the knaves a group of four instead of three.

If the joker is played as part of a sequence it must take the position of the card it represents ; and if it stands at an open end of a sequence any player may move it to the other end if he can take advantage of this. Thus, if there is a sequence in hearts of the 5, 6, and joker, a player holding the 7 of hearts can, if it is his turn, take the joker to the other end (making it represent the 4) and play his 7 in its place ; or, if he holds the 3 and not the 7, he can still move the joker and play his 3, making the sequence 3, joker (4), 5, 6. A joker in an internal position in a sequence cannot be moved at all, and nor can a joker that has been once moved. For this latter reason it is usual to place a joker that has been moved *crossways*, to signify that it is now a fixture.

As soon as any player has got rid of all his cards the game is over, and that player is declared the winner. The others, beginning at the left of the winner, expose the cards they have left and pay for them according to their pip value, the jokers counting fifteen, aces eleven, court cards ten each, and all the rest their face values. The winner of the game takes all the counters paid out, and the deal passes to the left.

In the unusual event of no one winning the game before the pack is exhausted the drawing is made from the discard pile only, each player laying out a different card from that taken in. If that does not finish the game, pips are counted and the value put into a pool, which is taken by the winner of the next hand.

CASSINO

CASSINO is a good old " family " game, and can be played by two, three, or four players, for counters, small stakes, or just for the score. The full pack of fifty-two cards is used, scores may be kept on a sheet of paper or on a cribbage board, and each hand is a game in itself, being settled for immediately. When four play, two usually play against two, the partners sitting opposite each other, as at Whist; otherwise the play is " all against all."

The dealer deals, by two at a time, four cards to his adversary, or to each player in the case of there being more than two, then to the table (for the " lay-out "), and lastly to himself. The remainder of the pack is left face downwards at his left, the lay-out is turned face up, and the play begins. This deal constitutes the first hand, and when it is played out the same dealer deals four cards round again as before, and so on till all are played, the only difference being that there is no lay-out after the first hand.

The object of the game is to capture certain cards and combinations of cards that count towards game. These are as follows :—

			Points.
Great Cassino (ten of diamonds)	.	. .	2
Little Cassino (deuce of spades)	.	. .	1
The majority of *cards* taken in	.	. .	3
The majority of *spades* taken in	.	. .	1
An ace of any suit . . .	.	. .	1
A sweep of all the cards on the table .	.	1	

and this may be done in four different ways as under :—

1. PAIRING.—A card played from the hand will take any card or cards of like value on the table: *e.g.*, there are one or perhaps two sevens on the table, and the player whose turn it is has a seven in his hand; he may play this, face upward, and then gather it in again with the other seven (or sevens).

2. COMBINING.—This is an extension of the principle of pairing. If a player holds a card (not being a court card) of the pip value of a group or groups on the table, it will take them. Thus, we have a 3, 4, 5, and 6 on the table; the player whose turn it is holds a 9; he can combine the 3 and the 6, and the 4 and 5, making two nines, and take the lot with his 9. He does this by first combining the cards, at the same time calling attention to the fact that each group makes nine, playing his card face upwards, and finally gathering in and turning down all five cards.

3. BUILDING.—This signifies the playing of a card from the hand to one on the table, so as to make an aggregate equal to a larger card in the hand, with a view to capturing the two on the next opportunity of playing. Thus, there is a 5 on the table, and the player has an 8 and a 3 in his hand; he may play the 3 on the 5 (at the same time saying " Eight "), with a view to take both with the 8 when it is next his turn to play. His calling " Eight " notifies the other players that those two cards cannot be separated; but it is quite in order for any player following him who happens to hold an 8 to take them himself, and it is also in order for any following player to " raise " the " build " by playing another card to it, in which case it can only be taken by a card of the total value. Thus, in the present instance, a player may add an ace to the group of 5 and 3, saying " Nine "; if the original " builder " happen to have a 9 he can still take it, but he cannot do so with his 8. A player cannot raise his own build, and, of course, no player can raise any build unless he hold in his own hand at the time a card the pip value of which is equal to the new aggregate. In America, and in many circles in England, the rule that a player may not raise his own build is not observed, the idea being that there is no reason why a player should be denied a privilege that is freely granted to his opponent.

A player need not at once take a given card, combination, or build, but can, instead, " call " it. This he does by placing his equivalent card on the other (or others) on the table, and "calling" the value, in anticipation of taking the lot with some other card in his hand at his next turn. Thus, there are a 3 and a 5 on the table, and the player has two 8's in his hand. Obviously, he can take with either of them, but if he does so he will only take in *three* cards (his own 8, and the 3 and 5), whereas if he waits he has a good chance of taking in *four*. So he plays one of his 8's on the combination, and says " Eights " (not " Eight ") ; and at his next turn—unless he is forestalled—he takes all three cards with his second 8, making four in all, similarly if a 2, 3, 4, and 6 be on the table, and he has a 5 and 10 in his hand, he may combine the 4 and 6, making ten, and play his 5 on the 2 and 3 (making another), and call "Tens." If a following player happen to have a 10 he will have "called" to no purpose ; but the cards thus called lose for the time their individual value, and nothing but a 10 can take them.

It must be borne in mind that no combination of cards once announced, and left on the table, can be changed, except by the addition of a card *from hand;* and it should also be remembered that any player who has made a build is obliged either to win it, when it is his next turn, or to win something else, or to make another build. In the four-handed game with partners, partners may take in one another's builds, or may make builds which can be won by the card declared in the partner's hand. For instance : a player has built a 9 ; if his partner has the opportunity of building another 9 he may do so, although he does not hold a 9 in his hand ; the 9 already built by his partner is sufficient. Also, if a player has built a 7, say, that has been taken in by an opponent, and is still holding the 7 he was building for, his partner may build for the declared 7.

Every now and then it will happen that a player is able to clear the board of all the exposed cards. This is the " Sweep," and counts one to such player, but it is only the majority of sweeps that are actually scored. The winning card (called the " sweep card ") is kept face upwards until an opposing player makes another sweep, when the two cancel each other and the card is turned down again.

When a player cannot pair, combine, or build, he

must play a card, and his best policy is to play a small one (but not an ace or Little Cassino), because as other players in similar circumstances will probably discard small cards these may be combined and won with the larger ones in the player's hand. This is known as " trailing "—because one is trailing along waiting for opportunities.

In the last round all the cards remaining on the table are taken by the winner of the last trick ; but this does not count as a Sweep, unless it would have been one in any event.

As has been said, the game is complete in a single deal ; the usual way of settling is to pay for all scores at the end of the game ; another way is to play eleven points up, deducting the lower score from the higher at the end of each deal. In this method if one side reaches eleven before the other reaches six it is a " lurch," and counts as a double game.

VARIETIES OF CASSINO

BESIDE the foregoing there are four principal varieties of Cassino, and the differences between each and their parent are slight. They are as follows :—

1. TWENTY-ONE POINT CASSINO.
2. ROYAL CASSINO.
3. ROYAL DRAW CASSINO.
4. SPADE CASSINO.

1. TWENTY-ONE POINT CASSINO.—There is no difference here except the method of scoring. Twenty-one points is the game, and the usual way is for each player to take mental count of the number of cards, spades, and other points he has made, and then claim game as soon as he reaches 21. The count is then made ; and if it be found that he has *not* reached 21, his opponent wins, no matter what his score may be. If, on the other hand, he *is* 21, it is his game, even though his adversary has scored more. If neither claims to be " out," and it is found that both *are* " out," the game must be continued to 32 points ; and so on, adding 11 points to the score to be reached until one player claims to have won the game.

2. ROYAL CASSINO.—This is played in exactly the same way as the ordinary game, except that the court cards come into action. This gives the game a more scientific turn, for the court cards can now be used in combining and building, whereas in " straight " Cassino they can only be employed in making pairs.

Aces count one or fourteen, at the option of the player ; kings count thirteen, queens twelve, knaves eleven ; hence a 7 and a 4 can be taken with a knave, a 7, 4, and 2 with a king, and so on.

3. ROYAL DRAW CASSINO.—The only difference between this and the foregoing is that no more cards are dealt after the first round, but each player, after

playing his card, draws the top card from the pack, thus restoring the number of his cards to four. When the pack is exhausted the hands are played out, and the count made in the usual way. If a player misses his draw he cannot correct the mistake until his next turn, when he must draw two cards.

4. SPADE CASSINO.—This variety (which may be played either as Royal or "straight" Cassino) has the additional interest that each card in Spades counts one point for game, the jack counting two. Sixty-one points go to game; points are scored on a cribbage board as soon as made, and all that remains to be counted at the end of play are the cards.

It should be remembered that the ace and deuce (Little Cassino) already count one each, so in Spade Cassino they count two.

BRAG

BRAG is one of the oldest English card-games, and is especially interesting as it is the ancestor of the modern Poker and the descendant of the ancient Primero, that game that was being played by Henry VIII. and the Duke of Suffolk when the Bishop of Winchester broke away from them at one o'clock in the morning of a certain day famous in English history (Shakespeare's *Henry VIII.*, v. 1.).

It has two varieties, Single and Three-stake Brag, both played with the full pack. The ace of diamonds, knave of clubs, and nine of diamonds are known as " braggers," and have a special value, ranking as does the Joker, or Mistigris, at Poker, *i.e.*, they are allowed to stand for any other card at the pleasure of the holder. The other cards rank as at Whist.

In *Single-stake Brag* the dealer starts the game by putting up any stake up to the agreed limit, and then deals three cards singly to each player. Each in turn (beginning with the age), must then, after looking at his cards, put up at least as much as the ante, or drop out of that round. He may put up more (" raise it ") ; and in any case each player coming in must pay into the pool as much as the highest individual stake, or forfeit anything he may already have paid and abandon his hand. If no one will " see " the ante, the dealer receives one white counter from each of the others, and the deal passes to the left. Should any player bet an amount that no other player will meet, he takes the pool without showing his hand. Should a call be made all the hands must be shown, and the best brag hand wins.

The order of value in brag hands is as follows :—

1. Three aces *natural* (*i.e.* in which no bragger is employed).
2. Three aces made by the assistance of a bragger.
3. Three kings, or other smaller cards in due order, the higher being preferred to the lower, and as between threes of equal value, *naturals* being preferred to those made with the help of a bragger.

4   Pairs, from aces downwards, in like manner, with the same preference of *naturals*.
5. In default of any pair, or better, the hand holding the best single card : the ace of diamonds ranking first, and after it any other ace, and so on.

As between the holders of absolutely equal cards, the elder hand has the preference.

In *Three-stake Brag* there are three separate stakes made at the outset by each player, the winning of each being determined in a different manner. Three cards are dealt round to each, but the third is dealt face upwards, and the best card so dealt entitles the holder to the first stake. The order of priority is as above mentioned.

The second stake goes to the holder of the best brag hand, the game being played out just as in Single Brag.

The third stake belongs to the player whose cards when counted are nearest thirty-one, aces counting as eleven, and court cards as ten each. Any player whose cards fall short of that number is entitled—in his proper turn—to receive a card or cards from the pack, in the hope of amending his " point " ; but if he over-draws he is out of the game. This drawing to " fill up " is not in vogue in all circles, but it is just here where judgment is necessary, for all the hands are exposed, and each player knows exactly what he is " up against."

SLOBBERHANNES

SLOBBERHANNES does not seem to be so well known as its merits deserve—perhaps its name is against it ! —but it is really quite an excellent game for the family circle, and can be played with equal enjoyment either for counters or for small stakes.

It is a four-handed game, played with a pack from which the twos, threes, fours, fives, and sixes have been removed. The cards rank as at Whist—ace high, seven low—and there are no trumps and no partnerships. The players cut, not for *deal*, but for *lead*, the highest having the preference and the player on his right dealing. Dealing and playing is as at Whist, and the object of the game is to avoid taking either the first or last trick, or the queen of clubs. The player who wins any of these loses one point, and if he wins all three of them he loses another. The penalty for a revoke is also the loss of a point.

The lead is a great advantage, for the player is pretty sure to hold one safe losing card, which he will lead accordingly. The general policy of the other three players will be to follow suit with the lowest card possible, subject to the proviso that if he sees that he is bound to win the trick, he should in such case do so with his *highest* card, to avoid the possibility of being compelled to win a damaging trick with it at a later stage. The second and following tricks may be won with impunity, so long as the queen of clubs does not figure in them, and players will therefore avail themselves of these to get rid of their high cards.

But the main interest of the game lies in the general struggle not to be left with the queen of clubs, and it will be seen at once that the ace and king of clubs are very dangerous cards to hold—until the queen is safely out of the way ; these three are, therefore, discarded at the first opportunity. The best card of any suit of which there are only a few remaining is a very bad lead, as, being certain of winning, it gives the opponents a safe opportunity for discarding.

The reversal of the ordinary condition of play may cause a few blunders at the outset, but a player who knows anything of Whist will soon master the pitfalls of Slobberhannes, and will find himself very well repaid for doing so.

POPE JOAN

THIS popular old round game is now rarely met with. It is played with a pack of fifty-two cards, from which the eight of diamonds (for a reason which will presently appear) has been removed, and often with a special board, consisting of a circular tray revolving round a centre pillar, and divided into eight compartments, as shown in the illustration, respectively marked Pope (the nine of diamonds), Matrimony, Intrigue, Ace,

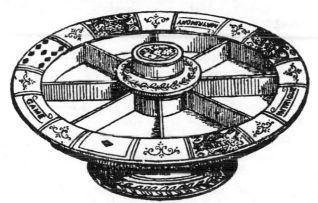

Pope Joan Board.

King, Queen, Knave, and Game. "Matrimony" signifies the combination in the same hand of the king and queen of the trump suit; "Intrigue" that of knave and queen. This elaborate "board" is, however, not a *sine qua non;* the game will give equal amusement with a home-made "lay-out" after the manner of that described in "Matrimony."

Each player has an equal number of counters bearing an agreed value, and the first dealer has the privilege of "dressing" the board, *i.e.,* of distributing between the various divisions fifteen counters from his own store, as under : Six to Pope, two to Matrimony, two to Intrigue, and one each to Ace, King, Queen, Knave and Game.

The cards are dealt round one by one, but with an extra hand, this last towards the centre of the table, facing the dealer. The last card of the pack is turned up to decide the trump suit. Should the turn-up be Pope (nine of diamonds), or an ace, king, queen or knave, the dealer is entitled to all the counters in the corresponding compartment of the board.

The player to the left of the dealer leads any card he pleases, at the same time naming it. We will suppose it is the three of diamonds. The player who chances to hold the four thereupon plays and names it ; then the persons holding the five, six and seven play them in a like manner. In any other suit it would be possible to continue with the eight, but the eight of diamonds, as we have stated, is removed from the pack. This makes the seven what is called a "stop" *i.e.,* the run of that particular lead can be continued no further, and the player of the seven is entitled to lead again. But besides the permanent removal of the eight of diamonds, it will be remembered that a certain number of cards were dealt as an extra hand. We will suppose that these were the two, five and nine of spades, the six and ten of hearts, the knave of diamonds, and the king of clubs. The cards immediately preceding them (viz., the ace, four and eight of spades, the five and nine of hearts, the ten of diamonds, and the queen of clubs) thus become " stops " also.*
As play proceeds other cards also will become " stops," by reason of the cards next following them having been already played. Thus, in the case supposed, of the three of diamonds being led, the two of diamonds thenceforth becomes a stop, and the holder should note the fact for his subsequent guidance. All kings are necessarily stops, as being the highest cards of their respective suits.

Whenever, in the course of play, the ace, king, queen or knave of the trump suit appears, the holder is entitled to the counters in the corresponding compartment of

* By some players the dealer is allowed the privilege of looking at the extra cards (sometimes, but incorrectly, themselves spoken of as " the stops "). and to act as a kind of referee as to whether a given card is a stop or otherwise but the practice is not recommended.

the board. Should knave and queen, or queen and king of trumps fall from *the same hand*, the holder is entitled to the proceeds of Intrigue or Matrimony, as the case may be. Any one playing " Pope " is entitled to all the counters in the corresponding division. Unless actually played, the above cards have no value, save that the holding of Pope (unplayed) exempts the possessor from paying for any surplus cards as hereinafter mentioned.

The game proceeds as above described until some one of the players is " out," *i.e.*, has got rid of all his cards. By so doing he becomes entitled to all the counters in the " Game " compartment of the board, and to receive in addition from each of the other players one counter for each card such player may have left in hand, save that the holder of Pope is exempt from payment. If Pope is played, the exemption ceases.

The skill of the player will be shown in his keenness to note, on the one hand, which of the cards are or become " stops," and on the other, what cards cannot be led to, and which, therefore, it is expedient to get rid of as soon as possible. At the outset, the only *known* cards which cannot be led to are the four aces, Pope (the removal of the eight of diamonds being purposely designed to place the nine in that position), and the card next higher than the turn-up (the next lower being a " stop "). But the list increases as the game goes on. If the nine of hearts is declared to be a stop by reason of the ten being in the surplus hand, it is clear that the knave cannot be led to, and must itself be led in order to get rid of it.

Sequences are valuable, inasmuch as they enable the player to get rid of two, three or more cards simultaneously. Nearly, but not quite, as useful are alternate sequences, as seven, nine, knave. The lowest should, of course, be led. Whether the card proves to be a " stop " or not, the leader can still continue the sequence, subject to the contingency of some other player going " out " with one of the intermediate cards. A sequence or alternate sequence terminating with king forms a very strong lead. Next to these, and to known stops, the lower of two pretty

close cards of the same suit (as three and six, three and
seven, or four and eight) should be led ; especially if the
higher is known or believed to be a " stop." After these
the lowest card of the longest suit, especially if an
ace.

" Pope," as we have seen, can only be played when
the holder has the lead ; and it is usually well, therefore,
to play it at the first opportunity, first, however,
playing out any known stops.

The unclaimed counters in each compartment are
left to accumulate. In the case of Matrimony and
Intrigue, a whole evening may occasionally pass without
the necessary combinations of cards being played from
the same hand, and these compartments therefore
frequently become very rich. The counters in " Pope,"
or one or more of the Ace, King, Queen, and Knave
compartments may in like manner be unclaimed
during several rounds. The best method of disposing
of any such unclaimed counters at the close of
the game is to deal a final round face upwards
(without the surplus hand) ; the holders of Pope, and
of the ace, king, queen and knave of the diamond suit
(which in this case is regarded as the trump suit) being
entitled to the counters in the corresponding compartments. The holder of the queen takes, in addition,
half the amount in Matrimony and in Intrigue, the
remaining halves going to the holders of the king and
knave respectively.

NEWMARKET

NEWMARKET (known in the United States also as "Boodle" and "Stops") is a derivative of "Pope Joan," and simpler, inasmuch as there is no use for the elaborate "board" that is usually considered necessary for that game. Its place is taken by a "lay-out" of an ace of spades, king of hearts, queen of clubs, and knave of diamonds from a spare pack : these are placed in a square in the centre of the table, each a little apart from its neighbour.

Each player stakes an agreed number of counters (preferably four, or a multiple of four), and the dealer, double that number ; these may be divided between the four cards in the "lay-out" in any manner the player pleases. The cards are then dealt one by one, with an extra hand (as at Pope Joan) to create a corresponding number of stops. There is no trump suit.

The player on the dealer's left leads ; he may lead from any suit, but he *must* lead the lowest card he holds in that suit (ace counting lowest), and he names it as he plays it. The holder of the next highest card of the same suit plays and names it, and so on till a " stop " is reached, when the player of the stop leads to the next round. When one of the players is " out," *i.e.*, has played all his cards, he receives from the others one counter for each card left in their respective hands, and the game is over.

Whenever in the course of a game a card corresponding to a card in the " lay-out " is played, the player receives all the counters on that card.

The general method of play, and the division of any unclaimed stakes, are the same as described in Pope Joan.

SPINADO

SPINADO (or *Spin*) is a variant of Newmarket, and is thus of the Pope Joan family, than which game it is decidedly less complicated; no board is wanted, and there are only three pools, viz., Matrimony, Intrigue, and Game, or "First Out." The dealer contributes a dozen counters to the first mentioned, and half a dozen to each of the other two; the remaining players each contribute three counters only, and these are placed in the Game division. *Matrimony* is formed by the king and queen of diamonds, and *Intrigue* by the queen and knave, and the ace of diamonds is known as " Spinado," or more frequently " Spin."

The four twos and the eight of diamonds are removed from the pack and the cards are dealt with an extra hand, as at Pope Joan, only in this case there is no turn-up. The player to the left of the dealer leads, and the holders of the next highest cards play them in succession till a " stop" is reached, when the last player leads for the fresh round. At any time that the holder of Spinado is able to play he may play it (naming it) with his own card, and when he does so it makes the card with which he plays it a stop. Thus, if the six of spades be led and he holds the seven, if it is to his advantage to do so he will play it and his ace of diamonds together, at the same time crying, " Seven and Spin!"; he then receives three counters from each of the others, and the lead passes into his hand. It may very well happen that it is not to his advantage to play Spin with his first card; thus, suppose the ten of clubs led, and the holder of Spinado has knave and king. It would be bad policy to play Spin with the knave, for if knave prove to be a stop there was no need to do so, and if any other player follow with the queen, the king, which is a natural stop, lies over him. A skilled player would therefore play up to this point without declaring Spin; then play

216

out any known stops, and finally some card which he does *not* know to be a stop together with Spin, thereby still retaining the lead.   By this means he would in all probability be "First Out," and would become entitled to the counters in that division of the pool, as also a counter for each card left from all the other players.

On the other hand, it is not safe to keep back Spin too long ; for a player holding it at the final count has to pay double for each card he is left with.

The holder of the king of diamonds receives two counters from each player : if he play both king and queen he takes the *Matrimony* pool in addition.   Anyone playing queen and knave of diamonds receives the counters in the *Intrigue* pool ; and if the same player hold (and play) all three cards he receives the counters in both pools.   The player of a king, other than of diamonds, receives one counter from each of the other players.

"First Out," besides taking the counters in that pool, is exempt from contributing to the pool for the next turn —unless he chance to be the dealer.

FAN TAN

FAN TAN, the simplest game of the " Pope Joan," or
" Stops " family, is somewhat unfortunately named,
as it is apt to be confused with *Chinese Fan Tan*, an
illegal gambling game that now and then achieves an
unenviable notoriety by being dragged into the police
courts.   The game with which we are now dealing is
perfectly innocuous, and is well suited to the family
circle.   Its old name was " Play or Pay," and there
seems to be no reason why this should not be re-
assumed.

The full pack of fifty-two cards is used, and any number
of players can take part, though the game goes
best with six or seven.   The cards rank from ace
(low) to king ; each player is provided with an equal
number of counters at the start, and his object is to be
the first to get rid of the cards dealt him.   All put an
agreed number of counters in the pool, and the cards
are then dealt out, one at a time, there being nothing
to worry about if one or two players have more than
the others.

Play begins by the eldest hand placing a 7 face up
in the middle of the table ; if he has no 7 he pays one
counter into the pool, and it is the next player's turn.
As soon as a 7 has appeared the next cards to be played
are a 6 or an 8 of the same suit, or a 7 of another suit.
If a 6 or an 8 is played, the 6 comes on the left and the
8 on the right of the 7 : if another 7, it is placed immediately below the first seven to start another row.   The
game then goes on by bringing out the remaining 7's,
and building down on the left to the aces and up on the
right to the kings.

Any player who has to miss his turn pays one counter
to the pool : should he fail to play when possible, he
pays three ; and if, at such a time, he is holding a 7 he
forfeits in addition five counters each to the holders of
the 6 and 8 of that suit.   The first player getting rid

of all his cards wins the pool, and receives from each of the other players one counter for every card he holds.

In another form of Fan Tan an entire suit is played out before another is started. *Any* card is led, and players must follow only in ascending sequence, the ace, two, etc., following the king. Whoever plays the last card of a suit starts another suit with any card he pleases. Penalties, and the destination of the pool, are as in the previous variety.

QUINZE

QUINZE is a sort of Vingt-Un (see p. 157) with a difference. It is usually played as a two-handed game, and the object is to make, not twenty-one, but fifteen (Fr. *quinze*).

The players cut for deal, the lowest having the preference, ace counting low. In play ace counts as one, court cards as ten, and the others according to their pip value.

The stake having been agreed upon, the dealer deals one card to his adversary and one to himself. The former has the option either to stand on that card or to draw one or more additional cards in the hope of making fifteen, or near that number. The dealer then examines his card, and either stands or draws in like manner.

The cards are then shown, and the player who has made fifteen (or the nearest smaller number) is the winner. Should either overdraw, he pays : should both overdraw, the stakes are doubled for the next deal.

THIRTY-ONE

THIRTY-ONE is another member of the same family as Quinze, but, though it is quite a simple family game, there is rather more in it than there is in Quinze.

The full pack is used, and the cards rank as at Whist. The agreed stakes having been put in the pool, each player (and any number can play) receives three cards, and three over are placed face upwards in the middle of the table. The players, beginning with the elder hand, draw one card each from this in turn, leaving a discard face up in its place.

The primary object of the game is to hold three cards of the same suit, the pip value of which will amount to thirty-one—the ace counting eleven, court cards ten each, and the others the number of their pips. Obviously, the desired number can be made only by an ace and two ten-cards. Next in value to thirty-one is three-of-a-kind, and among these the higher have the preference (three aces beating three kings, and so on); three-of-a-kind counts thirty and a half, and therefore overrides thirty or any smaller number. In default of thirty-one or three-of-a-kind the highest total in any one suit wins.

The discarding process continues either till one of the party makes thirty-one—in which case he shows his cards and claims the pool—or until some player is "content," which he signifies by knocking on the table. Each of the other players has then the right to exchange one more card, after which the hands are shown, and the highest wins and takes the pool.

FIVE HUNDRED

THIS game, largely played in the United States and Canada, is not so well known in England as it deserves to be. It is primarily for three players, and this is a great merit, for good three-handed games are rare.

"Five Hundred" has been characterised as a "patchwork" or "mosaic" game ; but such expressions do not do it justice, for though it borrows from Euchre, Loo, Nap, and Auction, the result is a new and harmonious whole, producing the effect of novelty without taxing the brain to assimilate unfamiliar methods. Many players, indeed, prefer it to Auction, for it is without the patent defects of the latter —the interminable length of the rubber, the undefined limits of loss, and the supersession of skill by "bluff."

In the following description the typical form of the game is assumed, in which three players take part, each being opposed to both the others. The pack used is the piquet pack of thirty-two cards (cards below the seven being omitted) *plus* the Joker—thirty-three cards in all.

Those who are not Euchre-players must begin by familiarising themselves with the functions of the Joker, and with the peculiar rank and attributes of the Right and Left Bower.

When there are trumps, the Joker is the master trump ; then follows the knave of trumps (the "Right Bower ") ; then the other knave of the same colour (the "Left Bower ") ; after which come the ace, king, queen, ten, nine, eight, seven of trumps, in descending order. The trump suit thus consists of *ten* cards ; the plain suit of the same colour consists of *seven* only ; the other two plain suits consist of eight each. The knaves of the latter two suits take their ordinary Whist and Bridge rank, between the queen and the ten.

When there are no trumps, all the cards, except the Joker, rank as in Whist or Bridge. The Joker remains the master card of the pack ; if it is led, the leader names the suit which he elects it to represent, and the other players must follow suit accordingly.

In cutting for deal, the Joker is the lowest card, and an ace the next higher. After which come the seven, etc., upwards to the king.

After shuffling and cutting, the dealer distributes three rounds of three cards each to the three players, followed by one round of one card each. The remaining three cards are laid face downwards on the table, and constitute the "widow."

The bidding then begins. The eldest hand has the first right to declare how many tricks (not fewer than six) he will contract to win. At the same time, he must either name a trump suit or declare No-trumps. The eldest hand is not bound to bid, but may pass. Each successive player, in the usual Bridge order, may either overbid, or may also pass. A player who has once "passed" cannot subsequently bid. With this exception, the bidding and overbidding continue, until every one is content. If no player bids, the cards are played No-trumps, and in this case the "widow" remains unappropriated, the eldest hand has the first lead, and each player scores ten points for each trick that he may make.

When the bidding, if any, is completed, the player who bid the highest—thenceforward known as "the bidder"—has the first lead.

The bidder, before playing, takes the "widow" into his own hand, and then discards any three cards out of the thirteen. These rejected cards are to be laid face downwards on the table, and may not be inspected by anyone. There are penalties for discarding too many or too few cards, and for illegally looking at the discard.

The value of any bid depends, as in Auction, on the number of tricks contracted for in conjunction with the value of the trump suit. There is more than one schedule of values, but that in most frequent use in England, the " Avondale," is as follows :—

Bids.	6 Tricks	7 Tricks	8 Tricks	9 Tricks	10 Tricks
In Spades	40	140	240	340	440
In Clubs	60	160	260	360	460
In Diamonds ...	80	180	280	380	480
In Hearts	100	200	300	400	500
In No-trumps ...	120	220	320	420	520

The scale is uniform, and easy to remember. The numbers increase downwards by 20 at a time, and horizontally by 100 at a time. It will be noticed that no two bids are numerically equal.

There are certain restrictions on the power of the Joker in the case of No-trumps. The leader of it cannot nominate it to be a suit in which he has previously renounced ; and if he plays it (not being the leader) to the lead of a suit in which he has previously renounced, it has no winning value.

When there are trumps, the Joker and both Bowers form part of the trump suit in the order of precedence already explained.

If the bidder fulfils his contract, or makes any greater number of tricks fewer than ten, he scores the number of points set out in the above table, *but no more*. If he wins all the ten tricks, he scores a *minimum* of 250 ; but if his bids be worth more than 250, he scores nothing extra. Should he fail in his contract, the value of his bid is set down in his *minus* column, and has to be deducted from his past or future *plus* score. In every case, each opponent of the bidder scores ten points for every trick that he wins.

The winner of the game is he who first scores 500 points (hence the title of the game). If two players score more than 500 each in the same deal, one of them being the bidder, the latter is the winner. If neither is the bidder, he who first makes the trick that brings his score over 500 is the winner.

Each player keeps his score in three columns, one for *plus* points (headed " Won "), and one for *minus* points (headed " Lost "), and the third for the net total.

REVOKES.

The American rule is as follows :—

" Upon the revoke being claimed and proved, the hands shall be immediately abandoned. If it is an adversary of the bidder who has revoked, the bidder scores the full amount of his bid, while the side in error scores nothing."

Professor Hoffmann's rule is as follows :—

" If the bidder be the offender, he shall be set back the amount of his bid [i.e., the amount shall be scored in his *minus* column], each of the opponents scoring as usual for any trick or tricks he may have made, including any which, but for the revoke, would have fallen to him.

" If one of the opponents be the offender, the cards of the trick in which the revoke occurred, and of any subsequent trick, shall be taken back by their respective holders, and the hand played anew from that point. The bidder and the opponent not in fault shall each score according to the result of the play, but the offender can score nothing for that hand, and shall further be set back 100 points."

If a player finds that he holds the Joker, two knaves of the same colour, and any two other cards of the same suit as one of the knaves, he has four tricks certain, by declaring the three-suit trumps, unless all the other five trumps be in the same hand. Should he hold two more tricks in the side suits, he will be quite justified in bidding six.

The chances of getting another trump, by taking in the " widow," are an important element in arriving at sound decisions. The odds evidently vary with the number of trumps already held by the player. The following figures should be carefully borne in mind :—

If a player holds four trumps, it is 8 to 5 on his finding one more at least in the " widow."

If he holds five trumps, the odds are only 7 to 6 in favour.

If he has six, he must not reckon on getting another, the odds being 6 to 5 *against*.

QUINTO

THIS game, the invention of Professor Hoffmann, contains several new and interesting elements, and, carefully avoiding the fatal error of excessive complexity, is compounded of skill and chance in very happy proportions.

It is a game of two against two, as Whist. The pack, however, contains an extra card (five " crowns "— —known as " Quint Royal "), whose place can be supplied by the " Joker," which all ordinary packs now contain. The score can be kept on a Bridge score-block (ignoring the horizontal division), or on an ordinary cribbage-board.

After settling partners and deal in the usual way, the cards are shuffled and cut, and the dealer then lays aside the five top cards, face downwards, to form what is known as the " cachette." The remaining forty-eight cards are dealt out as at Whist, so that each hand contains twelve cards ; but no trump card is turned up.

The players in rotation, commencing with the eldest hand, have then the option of once doubling the value of each trick, and of once re-doubling an opponent's double. The option passes round the table once only, and does not affect the value of the " quints," as defined below.

The normal value of each trick, reckoned irrespective of its contents, and counting to the side which wins it, is five points. Each side scores the number of tricks that it actually wins. If A B win 11 tricks, and Y Z 2, A B score 55, and Y Z 10. These values may, however, be doubled or quadrupled before the play begins, as previously explained. The winners of the twelfth trick take the " cachette," which itself counts as an extra trick. Thus the winning of the twelfth trick bears a double value.

So far as regards " trick " scoring. The " honours " are known as " Quints," and are (1) the five of any suit, a fifth " honour " being the " Joker " or " Quint Royal " ; (2) an ace and four, or a deuce and trey, of the same suit, falling to the same trick. " Quints " count not to the side to which they are originally dealt, but to the side that wins the trick containing them. They are marked as they occur in course of play, according to the following scale :—Quint Royal, 25 ; Quint in Hearts, 20 ; in Diamonds, 15 ; in Clubs, 10 ; in Spades, 5. The contents of the " cachette " (if of any value) are similarly scored by the side that takes it.

The play of Quint Royal is peculiar. It has no trick-taking value at all, and can be scored by the holder only if he can throw it on a trick won by his partner. This he is always allowed to do, whether he holds one of the suit led or not.

With the preceding exception, every player, having one of the suit led, must follow. If he has not, he may trump or over-trump. No selection is made of any particular suit for trumps, but for trumping purposes the suits ascend in power, in Bridge order, from spades to hearts. Thus any spade may be trumped by the deuce of clubs, which may be over-trumped by any other club or by the deuce of diamonds —and so on up to the one card, the ace of hearts, which is a winner against all the rest.

Game is 250 up. A distinction between quints and tricks is that the former are marked up as they occur in course of play, and that, as soon as the scoring of them brings either side up to or beyond 250, that game is at an end, and the rest of the hand is abandoned. The value of the " cachette " may make the winners of it game ; if so, the tricks are not counted. If neither side is 250 up after counting all quints, the value of the tricks won is added in. Should such addition bring both parties beyond 250, the higher of the two totals wins. Those who first win two games win the rubber, and score 100 points extra therefor.

There is another method of scoring—by " single," " double," and " treble " games—but the former way has been preferred wherever the writer has seen the game played.

Before Quint Royal has been played, a player who does not hold it should be always on the alert to give his partner the chance of making it. The original leader, therefore (not holding Quint Royal himself), is always expected to start with the ace of spades, if he has it. If not, with the ace of clubs. The ace of hearts is certainly, and the ace of diamonds probably, too valuable to be led out in this way.

The establishment of a black suit is obviously a hopeless task, for both red suits cannot be got out of the way. Hearts, however, may sometimes be extracted for the benefit of a good long suit of diamonds.

DUMMY (OR THREE-HANDED) QUINTO

In the case of three players only, one plays a Dummy hand in combination with his own. This being a very decided advantage, the Dummy-player is handicapped 25, that number of points being scored to his opponents' credit before the game begins. Rubbers are not played, each game being settled for separately, and the three players take Dummy in rotation, game by game. The partner of Dummy always takes first deal of each game. When either of Dummy's opponents deals, the Dummy-player must look first at the hand from which he has to lead, and must double or re-double from his knowledge of that one hand only.

PELMANISM

PELMANISM is a very simple game indeed, and, as its name implies, is a splendid exercise for the memory, besides a source of amusement to the players—of whom there may be any number.

A full pack of cards is spread either circle-wise or in rows face downwards on the table. Player No. 1 raises two cards, looks at them, and shows them to the others ; if they happen to form a pair, he removes them from the lay-out and secures a trick ; if they are not a pair, he replaces them, being careful to see that they are put back in their original positions.

The next player now takes a card, looks at it, and shows it round, as before. If this will form a pair with either of the two cards that have been replaced he may take that card, secure the trick and draw again ; should he make a mistake, and raise a wrong card, he replaces both—again in the positions they formerly occupied—and it is the next player's turn to draw : should the second player, however, have been successful, he draws again, and if the card does not pair with one already shown he draws another to see if he can make a pair " on his own "— a rule, be it noted, that applies equally to his first draw. If it makes a pair, he goes on again ; if it does not the draw passes to player No. 3, and all repeat the process till the last pair is removed, when the player holding the greatest number of pairs is declared the winner.

It will be seen that the call upon the visual memory increases as the game goes on ; and it is surprising how, after a few turns, both one's memory and one's enjoyment grow keener.

We may add that the Pelman Institute for the Scientific Development of Mind Memory is in no way responsible for the game, and that, to the best of our belief, the rules have never before appeared in print.

COMMERCE

COMMERCE is a very old-fashioned English card-game, and is, perhaps, one of the most primitive of the Poker family. There are a number of varieties; all are played with the full pack of fifty-two cards, and all are very simple. The usual method of play in England at the present day is as follows :—

A pool is formed by an agreed contribution, then three cards are dealt face downwards to each player (of whom there can be almost any number), and three more face upwards, as a " Widow." Dealer has first " say," and before looking at his own cards he can exchange the lot for the " Widow "; should he prefer not to do so the " say " passes to the elder hand, who may exchange one of his cards for one of those face up on the table. The discarded card is left face up with the other two, and the next player has a similar option, and so on round and round the table, subject to the qualification that a player who has once passed cannot change a card in any subsequent round. This continues till two of the players are satisfied with their hands, which they signify either by saying, " Content," or by knocking on the table. The object is to obtain either (1) threes, (2) a sequence, or (3) the point, in this order.

(1) Three aces will beat three kings; three kings, three queens; and so on down to three twos, which will beat—

(2) A Sequence, *i.e.*, three cards of the same suit in order of rank, as ace, king, queen, or queen, knave, ten, etc., down to three, two, ace—a higher sequence taking a lower, and the ace being capable of being placed either high or low. Any sequence will beat—

(3) The Point, which is the greatest number of pips on two or three cards of the same suit; ace counting 11, and the court cards 10 each. If a tie occurs in the Point, a point made with three cards will

beat one made with two—the odd card counts for nothing. If the number of cards is also a tie, the elder hand, or the dealer—if he is one of the parties concerned—is declared the winner.

Two other scores, *flush* and *pair* are sometimes introduced, the former signifying three cards of the same suit, the latter two of the same denomination. If two flushes are out, that with the highest cards takes the other ; if two pairs are equal, the player holding the higher third card is the winner.

In another variety Commerce is played without a " Widow " ; here the hands are improved by *trade* or *barter*, at the holder's pleasure. If the player *trade*, he gives his discard and one counter to the dealer, and receives a card in exchange, face down, from the top of the pack. The dealer keeps the counter, and the discard remains on the table. If he decide to *barter*, he offers his discard to the player on his left, who, without seeing the card, can accept or refuse as he likes. Should he accept, he must give one of his own in exchange (which *must* be accepted), and then can trade or barter himself ; should he refuse, he knocks on the table to signify that he will stand by the cards he has. The trading and bartering goes on until some player knocks, when the game is over and the hands are shown, the best hand winning the pool.

MATRIMONY

MATRIMONY is another old-fashioned family card game, and still affords many a pleasant evening for the young people. It is played with the full pack of fifty-two cards, and everyone taking part is provided at the outset with an equal number of counters. The only "apparatus" necessary is a good-sized strip of paper or cardboard on which are marked the words:—

MATRIMONY	INTRIGUE	CONFEDERACY	PAIR	BEST

This is called the "lay-out." Any king and queen is *Matrimony*, queen and jack *Intrigue*, king and jack *Confederacy;* any two cards of the same denomination form a *Pair*, and the ace of diamonds is always *Best*.

The dealer takes any number of counters he fancies from his supply, and distributes them just as he chooses over the various divisions of the lay-out—all having at least two—and then each player takes a number of counters, one less than the dealer's, and distributes them as he pleases.

The cards are next cut, and the dealer gives one to each player, face down ; and then another, face up. If the ace of diamonds should be one of the face cards, the player to whom it has fallen takes all the counters on the lay-out, and the cards are gathered, shuffled, and dealt again by the next player on the left, he beginning a fresh pool in the same way as before. If the ace of diamonds does not turn up each player in turn, starting with the hand on the dealer's left, exposes his down card. The first who turns up *Matrimony* takes all the counters on that division of the lay-out, and, in the same way, the first to discover *Intrigue, Confederacy*, or a *Pair*, takes all on that particular division. Apart from the face cards, the ace of diamonds is of no value except as one of a pair, and the pool for it remains until the card is dealt face up. Any of the pools that are not won remain until the following deal—or until they are won—and may be added to in the ordinary way.

OLD MAID

WE make no apology for including this very simple round game in the modern " Hoyle " : for it has happened more than once at children's gatherings that an adult has suggested, " Let's have a game at Old Maid ! " only to find that he has quite forgotten how it should be played, and the youngsters never knew !

The Queen of Hearts is taken out of a full pack of cards, which is then dealt, one card at a time, to all who wish to try their luck. Each player then sorts his—or, more usually, her—hand, and puts all the pairs (two threes, two knaves, etc.) face downwards on the table without showing them to anyone. This discarding being complete, the dealer takes his remaining cards, spreads them fanwise in his hand, and offers them to his left hand neighbour, who is obliged to take one at random. If this pairs with anything already in his hand the two are discarded ; if not, the newcomer is retained ; and, in any case, the cards are spread and offered to the next player on the left, who is bound to take one, as before.

So the game goes round, until one player is left, holding a solitary card. This, of course, turns out to be the odd queen, and is popularly held to signify that its owner will be—at any rate for some time to come—an Old Maid, or Old Bachelor, as the case may be !

ALL-FOURS

ALL-FOURS, known in America as OLD SLEDGE, or SEVEN UP, is usually played by two players, with the full pack of fifty-two cards, which rank in play as at Whist, the ace being the highest, and the two the lowest. The game is seven points.

There are four different items which count towards the score, whence the name *All-Fours*. Such items are as follows :—

High.—The highest trump out, scoring one to the original holder.

Low.—The lowest trump out, scoring one to the original holder.

Jack.—The knave of trumps, scoring one to the dealer, if turned up; if otherwise, to the winner of the trick to which it falls.

Game.—Scoring one to the ultimate holder of the more valuable cards in the tricks won by him, according to the following scale :—

For each ten (trump or otherwise). • • •	10
For each ace ,, • • • •	4
For each king ,, • • • •	3
For each queen ,, • • • •	2
For each knave , • • • •	1

N.B.—In the case of the players being equal in this particular, or of neither party holding any card which counts towards Game, the elder hand scores the point.

METHOD OF PLAYING

The players cut for deal, the highest card having the preference.* The dealer gives six cards to each, turning up the thirteenth as trump. If the elder hand is dissatisfied with his cards, he may say, " I beg," in which case the dealer is bound either to allow him

* This is the old-fashioned rule but at the present day the Whist rule of " lowest card deals " is frequently followed.

235

(by the phrase, "Take one") to score one point, or to give each player three more cards from the pack, turning up that next following by way of fresh trump card. If this should be of the same suit as the original trump, the dealer is bound to give three more cards to each, again turning up the seventh, until a new suit does actually turn up. If the turn-up card be a knave, the dealer scores one, this taking precedence of any other score. If, by reason of the elder hand "begging," there is a further deal, and the dealer a second time turns up a knave, he again scores one. The elder hand leads any card he pleases. His antagonist must follow suit or trump, his right to do the latter not being affected by his holding cards of the suit led. If, however, having a card of the suit led, he neither follows suit nor trumps, he becomes liable to the penalty of a revoke.

The player of the highest card of the suit led, or a trump, wins the trick, which is turned down as at Whist, and so on throughout the six tricks. In scoring, the order of precedence is (1) High, (2) Low, (3) Jack, (4) Game; subject, as we have seen, to the contingency of Jack having been the turn-up card, the point for this being scored before the hand is played.

The play is mainly directed to capturing the Jack, and such cards as may score towards Game.

Some players score a point whenever the adversary does not follow suit or trump. Some, again, make it the rule that each player must count his score without looking at his tricks, under penalty of losing one or more points, as may be agreed, in the event of a miscalculation.

FOUR-HANDED ALL-FOURS

The players cut to decide who shall be partners; the two highest playing against the two lowest, and facing each other, as at Whist. The right to the first deal is decided by the cut, the highest dealing. Afterwards each player deals in rotation.

The dealer and the elder hand alone look at their cards in the first instance, the option of begging resting with the latter. The other two players must not take up their cards till the dealer has decided whether he will " give one " or " run the cards " for a new trump.

The players play in succession as at Whist, four cards constituting a trick. In other respects, the play is the same as in the two-handed game.

SPECULATION

SPECULATION is a popular game in the family circle, and is played with the full pack by any number of persons, each of whom is provided with a like number of counters. A pool is formed by each contributing the same amount, the dealer paying double.

Three cards are dealt to each player, and the next card turned up for the trump suit ; this extra card belongs to the dealer, and should it prove to be an ace, that round is over and the dealer takes the pool.

The object of the players is to hold the best trump among the cards dealt. If the turn-up—not being an ace—is a fairly high card, it becomes an object of " speculation " : the dealer enquires, " Who buys ? " and names his price—so many counters— and the purchaser, if any, takes the card after paying for it and places it face upwards on the top of his hand. No player may look at his hand until the time comes, and anyone transgressing this rule is fined so many counters for each card looked at, these being added to the pool.

Play begins by the elder hand turning up his top card ; if it is not a trump the next player turns up his, and so on in rotation until a higher trump than the turn-up card is reached. This in turn becomes an object of speculation, and the owner, whether by purchase or otherwise, of the highest trump exposed for the time being is exempt from turning up any further card until his has been beaten.

The essence of the game is sale and purchase, and cards may be auctioned and sold to the highest bidder. Not merely may an *exposed* card be sold, but *any* card, or even *a whole hand*. The purchaser may not look at them, but adds them to those he already holds, exposing one at a time as his turn comes round. It will be readily understood that an unknown card is of much less value than one which is a probable winner.

and prices rule accordingly. The price of the highest exposed card naturally increases towards the close of the hand, when there are but few cards remaining to be turned. When there are only two or three left, it is often worth while for the holder of the exposed card to purchase them unseen—to avoid the risk of one of them destroying the value of his own. Of course the turning up of the ace of trumps ends the hand, and a new deal starts.

There are one or two optional additions to the game, which can be adopted if it is not sufficiently exciting as it stands. In some circles, for instance, anyone turning up a 5 or a jack pays one or more counters (as may be agreed) to the pool. In others, again, the game is played with an extra hand, which is not touched till all the rest have been exposed. Should this prove to hold a higher trump than the apparent winner, the pool is left, there being, therefore, a double pool for the next round.

RANTER GO ROUND

RANTER GO ROUND is an old Cornish game, and though it is not often seen there is no reason why it should not be, for it is a capital round game for children, and causes no end of fun and amusement.

The full pack is used, any number of players can take a hand, and each starts with three counters, or "lives," which, of course, may represent an agreed sum. One card is dealt to each player, and the object of the game is to avoid holding the lowest card (quite irrespective of suit), ace counting low.

Each looks at his card and the player on the dealer's left, if not pleased with what he has been given, passes it face downwards to his left-hand neighbour, saying, "Change." The latter is bound, however good his own card may be, to make the exchange—*unless he chance to hold a king*, in which case he replies, "King," and retains it. We will suppose, however, that he has to make the exchange: if he, too, is dissatisfied with the card he has received, he passes it on in like manner, and so the card circulates, until it is stopped by a king or one of the recipients gives a worse card in exchange, in which case he is safe for that round, and has no motive for a further change. He, therefore, "stands," and the player next in order then changes or not with *his* left-hand neighbour as he pleases. Any player giving in exchange an ace, a 2, or a 3, is bound to announce the fact If such a card has been given in response to a request for exchange, it naturally remains with the recipient and the other players, therefore, will be safe in standing on cards of any higher denomination, however low in themselves. Thus, if an ace has been declared the holder of a deuce (or higher) will have no inducement to exchange. If, however, the card be one offered in exchange by an elder to a younger hand, it will probably circulate till it reaches the dealer. If he, too, desire to change it, he does so by cutting the pack and taking the uppermost card of the cut. The cards are now turned up, and the holder of the lowest loses a life, with this qualification—that if the dealer, cutting as just mentioned, turn up a king, he is the victim, even though there may be an ace among the exposed cards.

When a player has lost all three of his lives he is " out," and the game continues between the survivors, the last " out " taking the pool. Of course, as the lives decrease in number they increase in value, and an additional interest is imparted to the game by allowing the selling of lives at any agreed price between buyer and seller. No one, however, should be permitted to purchase while he has still a life in hand.

POKER PATIENCE

THIS game consists of laying out twenty-five cards face upwards on the table, in five rows of five cards each. A full Whist pack of fifty-two cards is shuffled and cut, and the cards are dealt by the player, one by one, in order from the top.

Each card, after the first, must be laid down, as it is dealt, next to one already on the table, either vertically, horizontally, or diagonally. That is to say, it must be placed immediately above, or below ; to the right, or to the left ; or corner to corner. The resultant oblong is considered as comprising ten Poker hands (of five cards each), five hands being reckoned horizontally (which we will call the rows) and five vertically (which we will call the columns). The object is to lay out the cards so that the aggregate total score of the ten Poker hands shall be as large as possible. The score-table is as follows (for definition of terms, see our chapter on Poker) :—

Straight flush	30	Threes	6
Fours	16	Flush	5
Straight	12	Two pair	3
Full	10	One pair	1

(It will be noticed that the relative values differ from those in Poker proper.)

The game may be played by two or more players, each against all. Each player is provided with a separate pack. One is appointed dealer ; his pack is shuffled and cut in the ordinary way. The packs of the other players should, for convenience, be sorted out previously into suits. As a card is dealt, the dealer names it aloud ; each of the other players then selects the same card from his own pack. Every one uses his own judgment as to the laying-out of the cards ; and when the twenty-five are all played, and the *tableaux* are complete, the total scored by each player is added up, and the losers pay the winners on an agreed scale.

Supposing five players have scored as follows :—

A, 87 ; B, 81 ; C, 78 ; D, 78 ; E, 65. A is paid 6, 9, 9, 22 points by B, C, D, E respectively. B is paid 3, 3, 16 points by C, D, E respectively. C and D are each paid 13 points by E. Thus A, B, C, D win 46, 16, 1, 1 points respectively , and E loses 64.

Or we may proceed by adding all the scores together (making 389), multiplying each player's score by five (the number of players), and paying for the *differences*, above or below the total. If we multiply each player's total, as given above, by five, we get A, 435 ; B, 405 ; C and D, 390 ; E, 325. The differences (by excess or defect) between these and 389 give the same result as before.

Serpent Poker Patience

This is a " problem " variety of the above game introduced by Ernest Bergholt. In the preceding game the cards are dealt " blind "—that is to say, when we lay down any given card we are in ignorance of those that are to follow.

In " Serpent Poker Patience," the twenty-five cards are dealt, in fixed order, *face upwards*, and are all known to the player before he begins to lay them out. This is a pastime for one player only.

If there were no limitation of the rule for laying out the cards, the analysis would be too complicated to be practicable ; hence the added restriction, which forbids the *corner to corner* contact, and enjoins that each card must be laid *vertically or horizontally* next to the one *last* played. We have, in fact, to make a " rook's path " on a chess-board of twenty-five squares, beginning and ending where we please.

While analysis is thus simplified, there still remains considerable scope for variation in the total score obtained. The art of play often consists in the sacrifice of valuable combinations in order to obtain others which, in the aggregate, will count a higher number of points ; and curious results may thus be sometimes exhibited. I give the following by way of illustration : it is not difficult.

The twenty-five cards are dealt in the order specified :—

D.6, S.5, C.Q, D.Q, H.Q. H.10, C.10, H.6, C.3, H.J,
H. ace, H.5, H.8, H.K, S.Q, H.4, C.2, D.2, H.7, S.J,
S.3, H.3, D.3, S.6, H.2.

*What is the highest score that can be made by laying
out the above cards in serpentine order ?*

A few trials will suggest the following arrangement,
with two straight flushes, intersecting in the ace of hearts,
whereby a total of 78 may be secured :—

H.8	H.5	C.3	H.6	C.10
H.K	H.A	H.J	H.Q	H.10
S.Q	H.4	C.2	D.Q	C.Q
S.6	H.2	D.2	H.7	S.5
D.3	H.3	S.3	S.J	D.6

The rows count a straight flush (30), threes (6), a pair
(1), threes (6) ; the columns count a straight flush (30), two
pairs (3), pair (1), pair (1). Total, 78.

But the correct solution is as follows (abandoning one
of the straight flushes) :—

H.8	H.5	C.3	H.6	C.10
H.K	H.A	H.J	H.Q	H.10
S.Q	S.J	S.3	D.Q	C.Q
H.4	H.7	H.3	D.6	S.5
C.2	D.2	D.3	S.6	H.2

The rows count a straight flush (30), threes (6), a
straight (12), threes (6). The columns count fours (16),
full hand (10), pair (1). Total, 81.

PATIENCE GAMES

PATIENCE, or " Solitaire," as it is more often called in the United States, is the name given to a large number of games usually intended to be played by a single player. The reason for its American name is obvious ; the English name was given to the series because in many of the games *patience* is the virtue most necessary for successful play.

The underlying idea in all Patience games is to arrange the cards of a well-shuffled pack (or, more usually, two packs) in a definite order, the dictates of certain rules—which vary with the individual game— being obeyed ; and the games themselves progress from the very simplest, in which not skill but merely the " run of the cards," decides the issue, to really intricate games, in which opportunities for the exercise of judgment and skill are ever present. Space forbids us to mention in detail more than a few of the two hundred or more Patience games that are played ; and we therefore start with one or two that serve to while away the time in sickness or weariness and finish up with some which require all one's concentration and powers of observation. And, first, we will explain some of the terms that are constantly cropping up in Patience.

The arrangement of cards on the table before play commences is known as the *lay-out*, and cards left " in hand " as the *stock*, or *talon*. A *waste-heap*, or *rubbish-heap*, is in many games formed in course of play by the accumulation of cards which, by the rules of the particular game, it is at the moment impossible to play either on the main or auxiliary sequence ; and when—as in some games is allowed—these are gathered together and re-played, they become part of the stock. The top card of the waste-heap is always available for any use that can be made of it.

A *sequence* is, of course, a run of cards in numerical

order; an *ascending sequence* is one progressing from a lower card to a higher (Ace to King), a *descending sequence* one progressing from a higher card to a lower (King to Ace). A *main sequence* is the final arrangement of the cards, *i.e.*, the order in which the player aims at ultimately getting them. In many games provisional formations of sequences—from which the main sequence is to be " packed "—take place; these are known as *auxiliary sequences*, and either of these may be, according to the rules of the particular game, ascending or descending. The card which forms the starting-point of a sequence is a *foundation card*, and the sequences are said to be *built up*, or *packed*, on these.

When the player reaches a point at which he can make no further progress he is said to be *chockered*, or *blocked;* in many cases this is the finish of the game; but in others some form of indulgence by which the player is given another chance is allowed. This is known as a *grace*. There is no final authority for Patience, as there is for Cricket or Billiards, for instance, so the number and kind of graces that one can take in different games is largely a matter of individual judgment. In " The Sultan," for instance, some players will go three times through the stock, while others will consider themselves defeated unless the King is surrounded by his eight Queens by the close of the second turn.

The simpler Patience games are usually played with a single pack of fifty-two cards, though in some the thirty-two card pack (twos to sixes being omitted) is used; nowadays, however, the two-pack games are more popular. They have their disadvantages, as two packs are awkward to handle and their display takes a good deal of table-space; but, on the other hand, eight cards of each denomination give a much greater variety than four, and the formation of eight simultaneous sequences makes a livelier and more interesting game.

One word of advice : before starting any game at Patience make sure that the cards are *well shuffled;* ordinary shuffling, which would serve well enough at any round game, will not do here, for at the close of each game the cards—or most of them—are arranged in sequences, and if one is not very particular these will, of course, be repeated at the next " lay-out." About the best way to ensure the breaking up of the sequences is to gather the cards together haphazard, shuffle them lightly, and then deal them out face downwards in the following way : first, three : then three more on top of these, adding a fourth ; then four on top of these, adding a fifth ; and so on, adding a packet each time until you have seven on the table ; then go on dealing on the seven heaps, but in the reverse direction, *i.e.*, from right to left, till all are dealt out, when the packs are picked up in any order and again lightly shuffled.

ROLL-CALL

THERE could hardly be a simpler game than Roll-Call; and if any apology for including it should be needed it must be that it has its uses in teaching children the signification of the cards.

The pack is dealt face upwards to a waste-heap, the dealer counting out as he does so, *one, two, three, four, five, six, seven, eight, nine, ten, knave, queen, king, one, two, three*—and so on. Whenever the card turned up corresponds with the number called it is thrown aside.

When the pack is worked through the cards are picked up, without disturbing the order, and the operation is repeated, beginning at the number next to that at which the previous deal finished. This goes on either until all the cards have been thrown out—in which case the game is won ; or until the cards keep on coming up in the same order—in which case the game is lost.

THE TRAVELLERS

THIS is another simple game ; only one pack is used ; and it is dealt out in three rows of four packets, four cards in each packet. This will leave four cards over, and they are the " Travellers."

The object is to arrange all the denominations together in the packets, the four aces coming in the first of the top row, the twos in the second, threes in the third, and so on, to the Queens in the twelfth and last. To do this take the top card of the " travellers' " packet (which has been laid face down on the table) and place it under the packet to which it belongs, e.g., if it happens to be a three it goes at the bottom of the third pack, if the Knave at the bottom of the eleventh, and so on. The top card of the packet to which the addition has been made is then removed and sent, in the same way, to its own packet, and this process is continued until a King turns up at the top of a packet. There is no place for Kings in " Travellers," and consequently this has to be discarded, and the next card from the " travellers' " packet taken, and started off in the same way as the last. If a King is drawn from the four " over " cards this cannot " travel " at all and is at once discarded.

With any luck, by the time the last card has finished travelling the player will find that all his packets are complete ; but, especially when there are one or two Kings in the travellers' packet to start with, or one or two at the top of one of the packets in the lay-out, it is quite easy to fail.

THE DEMON

(From Bergholt's " New Book of Patience Games.")

THE DEMON, an old but excellent game, is decidedly more difficult than either of the last two, and is probably about the best of single-pack Patience games.

Deal thirteen cards from the top of the pack, and place them to the left of the board, squared together and face upward, one card being thus visible. The next four cards are dealt in a row, face upward, a little further to the right. The fifth card of the pack is then placed, face upward, vertically above the first of the row of four.

This fifth card will be the foundation of a packet to be built upon, upward and in suit. As the other three cards of the same denomination come out they are also made the foundations of three similar packets. In the diagram below the first foundation card is the five of diamonds. The packet of thirteen cards is called the " stock," the four cards laid out in a row are to be the heads of four columns, and these columns are to be built upon in downward sequence, with cards alternately red and black. The remaining cards, kept in hand, are called the " reserve." For purposes of building. either upon the foundation packets or upon the columns, the top card of " stock " is always available. If this card, or any of the four " column " cards, had been a five, it would have been put out at once for another foundation, and the vacancy in the row would have been supplied from " stock " Since, in the case of our diagram, there is no other five visible, we proceed to deal from the reserve, always taking *three* cards at a time, and turning them in a squared packet face upward. Should it be possible to build with the faced card of the three, then the second card may be used, and if this also will build, then the third and last.

If the faced card of the three cannot be built with, three more cards must be taken from reserve and treated in the same way, and so on until the whole of the " reserve " cards have been gone through. Should there be only two cards at the end of the reserve, you are allowed to build with *either* of them

In the diagram shown, the game goes as follows :—

The first three cards from " reserve " show the 10 of hearts. Nothing can be done with this, so three more cards are taken, showing the 6 of diamonds. This is placed on the 5 of diamonds (our first foundation card), showing the card beneath it to be the 10 of clubs, with which again nothing can be done. The next three cards from reserve show the ace of spades, which is placed on the two of hearts ; the card beneath is the 7 of spades, placed on the 8 of hearts. The king of hearts is taken from " stock " and laid on the ace of spades. The 7 of diamonds is now exposed in " stock," and is built on the 6 of diamonds, exposing in "stock " the 2 of spades. The next three cards from " reserve " show the 5 of hearts, which is put out for a second " foundation," exposing ace of clubs, which is useless. The next three cards show the queen of clubs, which is laid on king of hearts, exposing 7 of hearts, which is laid on 8 of spades, exposing 5 of clubs, which is put out as a third " foundation." The remainder of the " reserve," dealt in threes, supplies no available card.

We now take up the " reserve " from the table, *not disturbing the order of the cards*, and begin to deal again, in threes, from the top as before, and in a short time we arrive at the second diagram below :—

THE DEMON (just started):

FOUNDATION CARD :

STOCK :   THE COLUMNS :

THE DEMON (in progress):

FOUNDATION CARDS :

STOCK   THE COLUMNS :

The 6 of hearts has just come up, and has been placed on the 5. Now the 7 of hearts, in the third column, can be moved on to the 6. In laying out the "columns," let the cards overlap (although in the diagram, for typographical reasons, they are not so shown).

A sequence may always be moved from one column to another. Thus, if the first column should be extended to a black 9, the 8 and 7 in second column may be moved on to it. The 2 of spades in "stock" could then be moved into the vacancy, exposing a fresh card. It is very desirable to reduce the "stock" as quickly as possible.

The process of dealing by threes from "reserve" is continued until it is found to yield no further result.

When you are thus blocked, only one grace is permitted. You may move one top card from a foundation packet and place it (if it will fit in) either at head or at foot of a column. Should this device not set the game going again, you have failed. It is not a game that often comes out. If it succeeds, all the cards will have been transferred to the foundation packets.

THE WINDMILL

THIS is one of the most effective Patience games, and though there are many that are more difficult there are few that require more careful watching if one is to bring it to a successful conclusion. It is played with two packs, but these are not shuffled together.

Begin by placing an ace from pack number one in the centre of the table; then lay two cards (separately) above, below, and on each side of this, producing a figure roughly representing the sails of a windmill; if there is a deuce at the end of one of the "sails" this is at once placed on the ace; if there is also a three—or one becomes exposed by the removal of the deuce—this is similarly placed, and the blanks refilled from the pack. Now deal the remainder of pack number one to a waste-heap, one card at a time, taking care to build as occasion offers, and as the Kings turn up they are placed between the sails, as in the illustration.

The lay-out is now complete. The object of the game is to build fifty-two cards on to the central ace—four sequences of ace to King—and to build *down* on the Kings, so that in the final result we have a pack of fifty-two cards in the centre surmounted by a King, and, surrounding it, four packs of thirteen cards surmounted by aces, the sails, meanwhile, having disappeared.

In this game suits are entirely ignored, the value of each card alone determining its position. The central pack must be started during the dealing of pack number one, but it must not be carried beyond the first Queen until this is exhausted; only exposed cards or the top card of the rubbish heap may be taken for building, but at any time if there is a card or cards on one of the King packets that can be placed on the central packet, this may be done, unless there is also a card available on a sail; the King himself cannot be moved.

By the time the first pack is exhausted the central heap will be surmounted by the Queen, if the player has had any luck, and each of the Kings will have some cards on it; for reasons that will appear in play, it is not advisable to complete these auxiliary packs too early, for when once an ace has been placed on top of one of them it cannot be removed. Pack number two is dealt out to the rubbish-heap just as pack number one, and as soon as a King turns up it must be placed on the Queen in the centre, the next ace coming on top of this, and so on. It should be noted that though cards may be moved from the Kings' sails to the centre, the reverse process is not allowed, a card once placed on the centre cannot be moved. There is no obligation to place a card, and it may often be found advisable not to do so.

In all but the very strictest circles it is allowable to turn the waste-heap once; if by then the five packets are not completed the game has failed.

THE FLOWER GARDEN

(With one Whist pack.)

THIS is one of the best and most interesting games, and is widely popular. Lay out six groups of six cards each, spreading each group fanwise, so that the faces of the cards may be visible. These are the *flower* beds. The remaining sixteen cards are kept in the hand, and are called the *bouquet*. They may be conveniently sorted into suits, as is shown in the diagram below.

The object is to get out the four aces as foundations, and to build upon these, in suit, up to their respective kings. *Any* card may be taken from the *bouquet;* but only the " exposed " card of each flower bed (*i.e.*, the outer card of the fan) is available. When straight-forward building on to the ace-packets cannot be done for want of available material, the cards must be skilfully manipulated by building on the exposed cards of the flower beds in *downward* sequence, *regardless of suit.* Exposed sequences (*i.e.*, sequences which terminate in an exposed card) may be shifted bodily, when-ever they fit ; and cards from the *bouquet* may at any time be put out to help in forming any sequence that will carry the game forward. Whenever all the cards of one of the flower beds have been cleared, and a vacancy thus made, you can either fill the space from the *bouquet*, or can transfer into it an exposed card or sequence from another flower bed. There is much scope in this game for thought and ingenuity, which is what makes it so fascinating. The rules will be best understood by playing attentively through the sub-joined. (See diagram, p. 257.)

At first sight this deal looks a very difficult, if not an impossible one, as all the four aces are buried. A little thought, however, will show that it can be successfully worked out, one method being as follows. Cards taken from the *bouquet* are distinguished by an asterisk (*).

EXAMPLE.

THE FLOWER BEDS:

THE BOUQUET:

Put the knave of clubs on queen of clubs. Put 6 of spades on the 7 of spades, then 5 of spades on the 6. Put 8 of hearts on 9 of clubs, and *ace of diamonds will go out* for our first foundation.

Put 7 of hearts on the 8, and the 6 on the 7, making a *space*, into which transfer queen and knave of clubs. The 2 of diamonds goes out on the ace. Put 5*, 4*, 3*, of clubs on 6 of hearts. Put 2 of spades on 3 of clubs. Put 4 of diamonds on 5 of spades. The 3 of diamonds goes out, followed by the 4. Put the 7, 6, 5 of spades on 8 of spades, and *ace of hearts goes out* for our second foundation.

Put 4 of spades on 5 of spades, knave of diamonds on queen of diamonds, 10 of clubs on knave of diamonds, 9* of diamonds on 10 of clubs, and 8, 7, 6, 5, 4 of spades on 9 of diamonds. The *ace of clubs goes out* for our third foundation. The 2* of clubs goes on the ace. Move the sequence from queen of diamonds to 4 of spades on to the king of diamonds, and the *ace of spades goes out*.

Now build up spades to the 8, using the 3* in the *bouquet*. Build up clubs to the 5. Move the 9 of clubs four-card sequence on to the ten of diamonds Transfer queen of hearts into the vacant space. The 6 of clubs goes out. Put 8 of diamonds on to 9. The 2 of hearts, 5 of diamonds, 6 of diamonds go out. Then 7* of diamonds, followed by the 8 and 9. Move the six-card knave-of-hearts sequence on to the queen of hearts. The 3 of hearts goes out : then 7* of clubs, followed by 8 of clubs, and we put into the vacancy the 10 of spades and 9 of hearts. The 4* and 5 of hearts are built on the 3, and the rest of the cards run out quite easily.

THE SULTAN

THE SULTAN is played with two full packs of cards shuffled
together; the eight kings and the ace of hearts
are taken out, and arranged on the table as follows :—
a king of hearts in the centre, with a king of diamonds
on each side of it; above the heart the ace of hearts,
and above the two diamonds the two kings of clubs;
below the first king of hearts the other king of the same
suit, and on either side of this a king of spades. This
done, the first eight cards of the combined packs are
dealt face upwards, four on each side of these, crossways, but in vertical lines; these latter are known as
the " Divan." The lay-out is now complete and the
game can start, the object being to build on the kings
and the ace in ascending sequence, so that at the end
the central king—which remains uncovered throughout
the game—is surrounded by the eight suits, on top of
each of which is a queen. On the kings you start building
with the aces of the same suit, and on the ace of hearts
with the two.

First see whether the Divan contains any cards that
can be played on to the foundations; if it does, play
them, and at once fill their places from the pack;
continue this until there is nothing that can be played,
then turn up the remaining cards one by one to a waste-
heap, taking care to play any playable card at once to
its proper position and filling up from stock any gap
in the Divan as soon as a member of it has been put into
its correct place.

You are permitted to deal twice through the stock
(some players make it three times); and if after
this any cards remain unplaced in their respective
sequences, the game is lost.

MISS MILLIGAN

(With two Whist packs.)

(From Bergholt's " New Book of Patience Games.")

THIS is an old-established favourite, though not at all an easy one to bring to a conclusion. Deal out eight cards, face upwards, in a row. Put out any aces to form the foundations of packets to be built upon upward in suit. Cards on the board are to be built upon each other downward in alternate colours. If none of the first eight will so build, deal out eight more, and so on continually, forming eight columns, until " stock " is exhausted. In building on the board or on the ace-packets, only " exposed " cards can be moved on to " exposed " cards (an " exposed " card being the lowest of a column or the top of an ace-packet), but a sequence at the foot of a column may be moved bodily, if it will fit. The game will be made clear by an

EXAMPLE :

Suppose the first eight cards dealt are 6 of clubs, 5 of diamonds, king of hearts, ace of diamonds, 3 of clubs, 7 of clubs, 2 of clubs, 3 of hearts. The ace of diamonds is put out for a foundation. This leaves a vacancy in the fourth place. Put the 5 of diamonds on the 6 of clubs. Put the 2 of clubs on the 3 of hearts. Since no more packing can here be done, we must deal out eight more cards in order into the eight places. If a card or cards be already there, the new card is dealt underneath : if there be a vacancy, the new card fills it. Suppose the next eight cards to be 3 of diamonds, king of clubs, 4 of hearts, 6 of hearts, 10 of hearts, 2 of diamonds, 4 of clubs, 6 of spades. Put out the 2 and 3 of diamonds on the ace. Put the 4 of clubs on the 5 of diamonds. Put the 6 of hearts on the 7 of clubs. Being again at a standstill we deal eight cards more—say, the 8 of spades, 6 of spades,

6 of clubs, 10 of spades, 4 of diamonds, knave of
spades, queen of spades, knave of spades. No packing
can here be done, and we must deal again—say, knave
of clubs, knave of diamonds, ace of clubs, 9 of hearts,
4 of clubs, 3 of spades, 3 of hearts, 9 of hearts. The
ace of clubs is put out for a second foundation. Pack

MISS MILLIGAN PATIENCE (*in progress*).

FOUNDATION PACKETS:

THE COLUMNS:

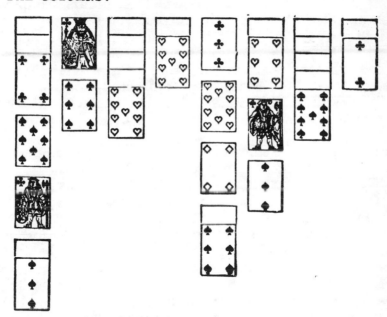

the 9 of hearts on the 10 of spades standing immediately above. Deal again—4 of hearts, 7 of clubs, 8
of clubs, 10 of spades, 2 of clubs, king of clubs, 9 of clubs,
3 of clubs. Put out 2 of clubs on the ace ; 3 of
clubs on the 2 ; 4 of clubs on the 3. Pack the 9 of hearts
on 10 of spades, and the 8 of clubs on 9 of hearts.
Deal again—ace of hearts, queen of hearts, 2 of
hearts, 5 of clubs, 7 of diamonds, 10 of hearts, 9
of spades, 3 of spades. Put out the ace of hearts, and

upon this the 2 of hearts. Pack 3 of spades on 4 of hearts ; 10 of hearts on knave of spades ; 9 of spades on 10 of hearts ; queen of hearts on king of clubs. Move the knave of spades sequence (at foot of the eighth column) on to the queen of hearts. Build up in succession (on the club foundation packet) the 5, 6, 7, 8, 9 of clubs. Put out 3 of hearts on the 2 ; then the 4 of hearts (at foot of third column) on the 3. Put queen of spades on king of hearts ; knave of diamonds on queen of spades ; 10 of spades and 9 of hearts on the knave of diamonds ; 6 of spades on 7 of diamonds. Move the king sequence (at foot of sixth column) into the vacancy of the seventh column. The cards are now as diagrammed on p. 261.

Eight more cards must now be dealt, and so on until " stock " is exhausted. When this occurs, and you still find youself unable to proceed, you have the special privilege (peculiar to " Miss Milligan") of " waiving " a card. That is to say, you may take up from the board the lowest card of any column, and if this will set anything above it free, and enable you to proceed, you may do so before restoring the " waived " card to its place. You may continue in this way to " waive " cards, one at a time, as long as you find it useful. If, even with this help, you find that you cannot complete the eight foundation-packets, each up to its proper king, the game has failed.

There is a variety of this game known as " Giant " Patience. In this *any* card or sequence may be lifted from the foot of a column into a vacancy whence a column has been cleared. In " Miss Milligan " only a king or a king sequence may be so lifted. Instead of the special privilege of " waiving," you are allowed to " worry back," that is, to return the top card of a foundation-packet to the foot of any column, if it will fit there according to the rule for packing. This will often set the game going again when it is " blocked." In other respects " Giant " is identical with " Miss Milligan."

MILTON

(With two Whist packs.)

(From Bergholt's " New Book of Patience Games.")

THIS game is founded upon simple principles, but is very fascinating, although by no means easy to conduct to a successful conclusion.

Deal out eight cards in a row, face upward. If any two of these cards are of the same suit, and next to each other in order, the higher of the two is brought down and placed in a second line (the line of packets) immediately under the index line. The vacant space in the index line is then filled up by dealing another card from stock.

Suppose the line of index cards, as first laid out, to be as follows :—

MILTON PATIENCE (*commencing*).

INDEX CARDS :

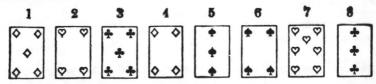

The 5 of diamonds is removed to a second line under the 4 of diamonds, and the 4 of spades to the same second line under the 3 of spades. We must now deal a fresh card (say, 5 of diamonds) into vacancy one, and another card (say, 9 of diamonds) into vacancy six.

We now continue dealing from stock. Cards that will build upward, according to suit, on the second line are placed there ; if they will not build, they are laid aside, face upward, on to a waste heap, the topmost (exposed) card of which is also at any time available for building.

As soon as one of the index cards can be built on to a second row packet, it is brought down and placed thereon, and all the cards in the second row that are vertically under the index card are taken down simultaneously, and built upon the same packet. Vacancies thus made must be at once filled up, *either* from stock, *or* by taking the topmost card of the waste heap.

In the preceding example, suppose our next card from stock is the king of clubs ; there is no place for this, so it is put aside as waste. The next card dealt is the 6 of clubs, which goes in second row under the 5 of clubs in column 3. Deal the knave of diamonds, which goes on waste heap. Deal the 7 of clubs, which is packed on the 6. Deal the 10 of hearts, which goes to waste. Deal the 8 of clubs, packed on the 7. Deal the 8 of spades to waste. Deal the 6 of diamonds, which goes in second row, column 1.

If we can deal the 8, 9, 10 of hearts successively into the second line packet, column 7, and if we then deal the 5 and 6 of hearts into second line, column 2, we must bring down the 7 of hearts (index card) on to the 6 of hearts, and place on the 7 of hearts the packet, 8, 9, 10 of hearts. The vacancy in place seven must then be filled in the manner described above.

No index card can be brought down in its own column, but only into one of the other seven columns.

Whenever aces are dealt they are treated, in the first instance, exactly the same as other cards, being built on to any packet that has got as far as its *first* king. But the *second* king of any packet stops all further progress, and the *second* ace of the suit can therefore only go into a vacancy among the index cards, or on to the waste heap. It is usual to make a break in a packet as soon as the first ace is reached, so that we may not inadvertently build a second ace on to the same packet. After one ace of a suit has been built through, avoid putting the remaining *deuce* of the same suit into the index row, because there will never be another ace for it to come down upon. For a similar reason, get the second *ace* of each suit into the row of index cards (where it will finally have to

remain), whenever you can manage it. The choice
allowed you between " stock " and " waste," when
dealing out, will be your help in so trying to avoid a
block. As is shown in the example played below, you
may be able to avoid blocking, even if you are forced to
put a deuce into the index row, but the cards will have
to fall very luckily, so that the deuce can come down
under its own second ace in another part of the index
row.

The eventual result which you aim at is to leave all
four aces of different suits in the index row, the corresponding packets in the second row being each built up
to its second king.

The waste heap may be turned and re-dealt *twice*,
so that the game will succeed or fail (more frequently
the latter) at the end of the third round.

As it is towards the latter part of this game, when
the difficulties increase, that the procedure is not easy
to make clear except by setting out full details, we will
suppose that the first round has been already played
through, and that the aspect of the board is as
follows :—

THE INDEX CARDS :

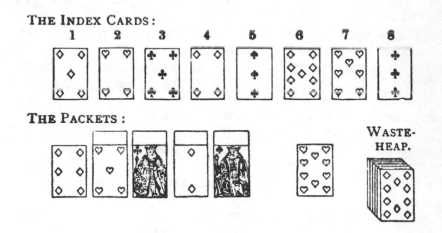

THE PACKETS :

WASTE-
HEAP.

One ace of each suit has been incorporated into packets
2, 3, 4, 5. Packet 2, for example, consists of the 5, 6,
7, 8, 9, 10, J, Q, K, A, 2, 3, 4, 5 of hearts, the packet
being separated into two portions, so as to make it clear
to the player's eye that one ace of the suit has already

been used. Packet 1 consists of *one* card only ; packet
7 of *three* cards only (the 8, 9, 10 of hearts). The waste
heap, which we are now about to turn and re-deal
for the first time, consists of the following twenty-
three cards (in order from the exposed card at the
top) :

$\Diamond$ 10, $\clubsuit$ 4, $\Diamond$ Q, $\Diamond$ 3, $\Diamond$ 3, $\Diamond$ J, $\spadesuit$ A, $\Diamond$ 7, $\Diamond$ 8,

$\Diamond$ K, $\heartsuit$ J, $\Diamond$ 4, $\clubsuit$ A, $\heartsuit$ 2, $\Diamond$ A, $\heartsuit$ 6, $\heartsuit$ Q, $\Diamond$ 2,

$\heartsuit$ K, $\heartsuit$ A, $\clubsuit$ 2, $\heartsuit$ 3, $\spadesuit$ 2.

If the reader will arrange the board and the waste heap
according to the above directions, he will be able to
play through the rest of the game without the slightest
difficulty.

The waste heap having been turned face downward,
the uppermost card will be the 2 of spades, and this is
therefore the first card dealt. Neither this nor the
next six cards are playable on the board, and are therefore
laid aside in order face upward, the topmost (exposed)
card of the heap being the queen of hearts.

The next card dealt is the 6 of hearts, which goes on
packet 2. Bring down from column 7 the 7 of hearts,
accompanied by its packet, and put all the four cards
on the 6 in packet 2. The next card dealt ($\Diamond$ A) goes
into space seven thus vacated. Three more cards go
on the waste heap, then $\heartsuit$ J is put on packet 2. Two
more cards go to waste, then $\Diamond$ 7 goes on packet 1.
Play on this the $\Diamond$ 8, which is the top card of waste
heap, and on the 8 play the 9 in column 6. The next
card dealt ($\spadesuit$ A) goes into the sixth space thus vacated,
the next card into waste. The 3 of diamonds goes on
packet 4, the next two cards into waste. The 4 of clubs
is put on packet 8 ; the 5 of clubs from column 3 and
the whole of the corresponding packet are then put
upon the 4. The 10 of diamonds goes on packet 1,
and the top card of the waste heap ($\Diamond$ Q) is put into space
three.

The board is now as follows :—

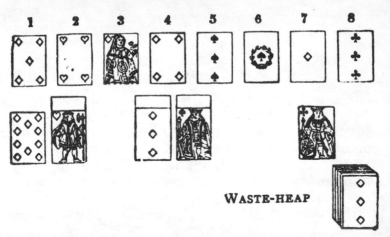

WASTE-HEAP

and we have to turn our waste heap for the second and last time.

The top card is ♠ 2, which goes under the ace : on it are brought down the 3 of spades from column 5 and the whole of the spade packet in the same column, thus completing the double suit of spades. The 3 of hearts goes into space 5 ; bring down into same column the hearts from column 2. The 2 of clubs must be put into space two, there being no card in waste to serve as alternative. Bring down the clubs from column 8.

The ace of hearts is dealt into vacancy 8 ; the king of hearts into waste ; the 2 of diamonds goes into column 7 ; the queen of hearts into column 5 ; on her is played the king from the waste heap. The 2 of hearts goes into column 8 ; all the rest of the hearts come down from column 5, and the double suit of hearts is completed. The ace of clubs goes into vacancy 5 ; all the other clubs come down from column 2, and our third suit is complete. The remaining four cards run out quite easily, and the game is won (see diagram below).

MILTON PATIENCE (*completed*).

LANSQUENET

LANSQUENET is a banking game of considerable antiquity, but of pure chance, there being no skill in the play. It is said to have been popular in the Middle Ages among the German mercenaries, or *lanzknechts* (Fr. *lansquenets*), hence its name.

It is played with the full pack of fifty-two cards; after they have been shuffled the dealer lays the two top cards face upwards on the table as " hand cards "; he then deals a card for himself, and next one for the players, both face up, the last being known as the *réjouissance* card. If either of these is of the same denomination as either of the hand cards, it must be put with them and another card dealt in its place, because all bets must be made on single cards.

The players—of whom there may be any number—then make their stakes, and the banker, having covered them, proceeds to turn up cards from the pack, one at a time. If he draws the same denomination as the players' card he wins all the bets on it; if he draws his own denomination he loses all bets upon the other card; if he draws a card that matches neither of these nor one of the hand cards, it is placed on the table and the players can bet on it.

As soon as the players' card is matched, the banker withdraws both cards, but he cannot withdraw his own. All cards matching the hand cards must be placed with them.

In another form of the game the rule is that, when a card appears matching the *réjouissance* card, the dealer takes all that is staked upon it, and in like manner with any other card on which stakes have been laid. But so soon as a card appears matching his own card, he is bound to pay all outstanding stakes, and the deal comes to an end, subject to the qualification that should both of the hand cards be paired before his own, he is entitled to a second deal.

MONTE BANK

" MONTE " is another banking game, and, as will readily be seen, has affinities with Lansquenet.

The Spanish pack of forty cards (the 10's, 9's, and 8's being omitted) is used, and any number of players may take part. One is selected for banker, and he must expose on the table all that he proposes risking on the game, so that the " punters " may see what is to be won.

The cards having been shuffled and cut, the banker holds the pack face down and draws two cards from the bottom, placing them face up on the table ; this is the " bottom lay-out." He then takes two from the top of the pack for the " top lay-out."

The punters can now bet on either lay-out up to the limit of the bank ; and, when this is complete, the remainder of the pack is turned face up, and the face card becomes the " gate." If there is a card of the same suit as the " gate " in either of the lay-outs, the banker pays all bets on that lay-out, while he wins the bets on any lay-out if it does not contain a card of the same suit. Thus, he may win or lose from either or both on the same " gate."

All bets are settled, the pack is turned down again, the gate and lay-outs are thrown aside, and a new show started, as before. This process is continued until the pack is exhausted.

FARO

FARO (so called from *Faro*, or *Pharaon*, the name of one of the kings in the old French pack of cards), belongs to the Lansquenet and Monte Bank family, but it is rarely met with in the domestic circle, partly because of the apparatus required, but chiefly, it may be said, because the game has for long been in pretty bad odour through the large sums of money that may be lost at it and through the almost unlimited opportunities that are afforded to (and often taken by) an unscrupulous banker to " fleece the lambs." It is a pity ; because Faro, when honestly played, is one of the best of all the banking games.

The apparatus necessary is, firstly, a long, oblong table covered with green cloth and having all round it, at a distance of about 8 inches from the edge, a raised beading to divide the money (or, more usually, counters) placed before each player as his stake on a particular event. In the centre of the table is the " lay-out," *i.e.*, a complete suit of spades enamelled, in two rows, on green cloth. The ace is nearer the banker on his left, and that row ends with the six ; the seven turns the corner, and the second row starts with the eight (opposite the six) and finishes with the king (opposite the ace).

Besides this there is a specially constructed box (described below) for holding the pack, and usually a " case-keeper," which is a suit of thirteen cards with four buttons running on a steel rod opposite each of them. The *raison d'être* of this is to let the punters know how many cards of each denomination are still to come from the box, and what cards are left in for the last turn, a button being slipped along the rod as each card comes. Each punter also has a card, as mentioned below, on which—if he is wise—he keeps track of the cards played.

In some circles specially printed cards are also provided for the convenience of punters staking on several cards at the same time—but these are neither necessary nor general.

The banker is seated midway down one side of the table, the croupier or croupiers facing him. The ordinary pack of fifty-two cards is used, and the game turns on the card staked upon pairing with one or other of the cards dealt to the dealer and the players alternately. Difference of suit is ignored.

The players make their stakes by placing them upon or near one or more cards of the lay-out (or on one of those special cards, already alluded to, that are some-times provided); when placed midway between two cards a counter is considered to be staked upon those two cards; when placed midway between four, on all four of them, and so on, according to certain rules, which vary locally.

The cards, after being shuffled and cut, are placed face upwards in a box of such size as just to contain them conveniently, and having the top cut away so that, while the pack is still held, the face of the top card for the time being is plainly visible. In dealing, such card is pushed out through a narrow slit at the side or end of the box, and there is a spring beneath the pack forcing the cards upwards, so that, to the very last, they are kept pressed against the top of the box.

The first card, having been seen, does not count. The banker pushes it out and throws it aside, bringing into view the next card, which is, we will suppose, a queen. This card is for himself, and he forthwith takes possession of all stakes placed upon the queen. The next card, which we will suppose to be a nine, is for the players, and the banker accordingly pays all who have staked on that number. The other players neither lose nor win in this " turn "—a deal of two cards constituting a turn—and the punters now make their stakes anew, or leave them to abide the result of the next *coup*, which is dealt with in like manner.

So far the chances are equal between the banker and the punters, but the banker's advantage lies in the fact that should the two cards of a given turn be alike, he takes half the stakes upon them. This is known as a " split." To avoid such a contingency befalling their own stakes, wary players are accustomed to keep their eyes on the " case-keeper " (*see above*) and take note of the cards which appear, refraining from making a stake (or making only very low ones) until, a given card having already appeared three times, there is no possibility of its appearing in duplicate. Such a card—the last of any denomination remaining in the box—is known as a *case*, or *case-card*, and of course it is not considered " the thing " for a player to wait for cases before making a bet.

It is obvious that the nature of the cards that have already appeared must considerably influence the probabilities as to the remainder. Thus, if three cards of a given value have been dealt, and none at all of another, the latter is four times as likely to be dealt as the former in any future turn. If a card has already appeared four times it is useless to stake on it any longer, and so on. To enable the punters to keep an accurate record each is usually provided with a printed card as under :—

Ace —	Ace — 01
2 —	2 — 11
3 —	3 — X
4 —	4 — 00
5 —	5 — 110
6 —	6 — 00
7 —	7 — 0001
8 —	8 —
9 —	9 — 01
10 —	10 — X1
J. —	J. —
Q. —	Q. — 0
K. —	K. — 111
FIG. 1.	FIG. 2.

It will be seen that the first letters or figures of the column answer to the thirteen cards of a suit, from the ace downwards. When handed to the player the rest is blank, as Fig. 1 ; but, as each card appears, he puts a mark against it, say a 1 if it wins and a 0 if it loses, while x denotes a " split," so that, by the time the deal is half over, the card assumes somewhat the appearance shown in Fig. 2. According to the various indications of Fig. 2, we gather that twenty-six cards have been dealt (x, of course, standing for two cards). Among these, two aces have appeared, the first having lost, the second won ; two deuces, both of which won ; two threes, appearing together and so constituting a " split " ; two fours, both of which were on the losing side ; and so on. Four sevens have been dealt, and there is consequently none left of this denomination. On the other hand, we have had no eight, and the knaves are in the same position ; and there are four cards, viz., the five, nine, ten and king, each of which has appeared three times, and as to which, therefore, there is now no possibility of a " split."

Should a punter wish to bet *against* a particular card or cards, he does so by *coppering, i.e.*, putting a copper coin or counter on the top of his stake. If the card thus " coppered " turn up for the bank, he wins.

A player winning may desire to follow his luck by letting his stake run on. This may be done in various ways. He may wish to hazard only his winnings, reserving his original stake. In such case, he acquaints the banker of the fact in some way recognized by local custom and leaves his money on the table, the banker at the same time withholding the winnings that he has just made. Should the punter's card again win, he receives twice his original stake ; should it lose, he receives nothing, but his original stake remains untouched. Should the punter win, the same thing may be repeated a second and third time, and so on, the player receiving proportionately, but still saving his original stake if he loses.

A more speculative player may desire to venture not only the money just won, but his original stake also. In such a case he plays what is called a *paroli* (the former call is known as a *paix, double paix, treble paix*, etc., as the case may be) ; this is indicated to the banker, whose payment, as before, is suspended until the player again wins or loses. Should he win, he receives *three times* his original stake : should he lose, his stake is swept away by the croupier. In the former case, should he desire to continue, but on this occasion to save his stake, he plays a *paix-paroli*, and if he win this time receives *six times* his original stake. Under the same circumstances, should he elect to risk his original stake in addition, he plays a *double paroli*, also known as a *Sept et la va*, because if he wins he receives *seven times* his stake. So he can go on ; the next step is *Quinze et la va*, receiving—if it wins— *fifteen times* the original stake ; then *Trente et la va*, receiving *thirty-one times;* then *Soixante et la va*, receiving *sixty-three times* the original stake ; then—but here we think we had better stop !

The player thus pursuing a *paix* or *paroli* is not compelled to bet throughout on the same card (which would in many cases be impossible), but is entitled to alter the card bet upon as often as he pleases.

At the last turn, when there are only three cards left in the box, if they are all different, the punters have the right of *calling the turn*, *i.e.*, naming in what order they think the cards will come. They must come in one of six ways, and the banker pays four for one if the punter can " call the turn."

If two of the three cards are of the same denomination, it is termed a *cat-hop;* this can come in only three ways, and the banker pays two for one.

In the rare event of there being three cards of the same denomination left, the call is by colour, and is paid two for one. Suppose there are two reds and one black ; these must come in one of three orders, viz. :— black, red, red ; red, black, red ; or red, red, black. The bets are placed on the dealer's right for black first, on his left for red and black, and in front of him for two reds.

There are a few other special terms in Faro that we have not yet mentioned. The top card of the pack —the first to be removed by the dealer—is known as *Soda*, and the last card in the box as *Hoc*. When a punter bets one card to lose and another to win, and he loses both bets on the same turn, he is said to be *whipsawed;* and a bet placed—or left—on a card of which none remains in the box, is termed a *sleeper*, and becomes the property of the first player who is wide-awake enough to take it.

A *heeled bet* is one in which the counters of the stake are placed diagonally across from one card to another, signifying that the punter is playing both cards to win.

PART II

GAMES OF CHANCE AND RACE GAMES

THERE are a good many race-games on the market, varying in apparatus, in details, and in method of play, but all having this in common—that winning and losing is a matter of pure chance.

In those with which we here deal, skill—in the card-player's sense of the word, at any rate—has no place whatever : all that is necessary, once one has use of the apparatus and has mastered the elementary rules, is a cool head, some knowledge of odds and of the mathematics of the Turf, a sufficient amount of capital, and an unlimited capacity for hope.

ROULETTE

AS PLAYED AT MONTE CARLO

BY MAJOR BROWNING.

THE Roulette table, which is covered with a green padded cloth, is divided into two portions, the Roulette, or Wheel as it is commonly called, being let into the centre of the table between these two portions.

The figure is an illustration of one half of the table, the other half being marked in an exactly similar manner. It will be seen that the cloth is divided into three long columns of figures, marked from 1 to 36. At the bottom end of these columns there are three spaces, representing all the numbers in the first, second, and third column respectively. There are three similar spaces both on the right and on the left, marked 12D, 12M, 12P, indicating the third

(*Dernière*), the second (*Milieu*), and first (*Première*) twelve (*Douzaine*) numbers.

On either side of the column of figures are further spaces to mark the *Rouge* (or Red numbers) ; *Impair* (or odd numbers) ; *Manque* (all numbers from 1 to 18 inclusive) on the one side ; and the *Noir* (or Black numbers) ; *Pair* (or even numbers) ; and *Passe* (all

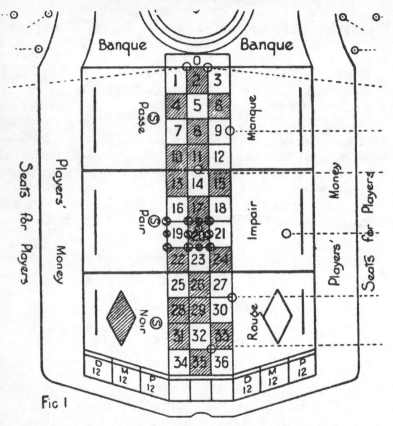

Fig 1

numbers from 19 to 36 inclusive) on the other side ; at the top of all is the space reserved for zero. In our diagrams the shaded divisions represent *Noir* (black), those left blank *Rouge* (red).

The Roulette, or Wheel, itself consists of a narrow circular ledge (A.A.) fixed in the table, and sloping inwards. Within this ledge is a brass cylinder (C.C.), suspended on a pin at its centre, and capable of being made to revolve by means of a cross-head or handle (H.H.).

The outer edge of the brass cylinder is divided into thirty-seven small compartments, numbered in irregular order from 1 to 36, and coloured alternately Red and Black; the 37th compartment being zero.

The game is played in the following manner. A croupier—styled the *Tourneur*—calls out, "*Messieurs, faites vos jeux*," when the players place their stakes on that portion of the cloth which indicates the chance they wish to play upon. The *tourneur* then says, "*Les jeux sont fait*," and throws a small ivory ball round the

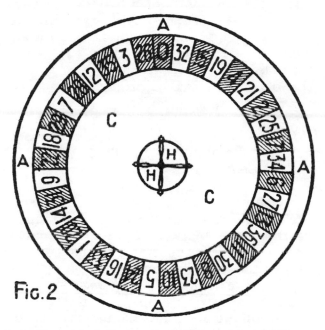

Fig. 2

inclined ledge (A.A.) in one direction and turns the cylinder in the opposite direction. When the ball is coming to rest the croupier calls out, "*Rien ne va plus*," after which no further stakes can be made. As the ball comes to rest it gradually slips down the ledge, and finally lodges in one of the compartments in the cylinder. The number of this compartment is the winning number, and upon its colour, figure, etc., depend the results played for. It is announced by the *tourneur* in this way, "*Onze, noir, impair, et manque*," which means that number 11, the Black, the uneven, and the *manque* (numbers 1 to 18) win. The losing stakes are first raked into the Bank, then the winnings are paid out, after which the *tourneur* again says, " *Messieurs, faites vos jeux,*" and the game proceeds as before.

The different methods of staking at Roulette are very numerous. Besides the three even chances : Red, Black ; *Pair, Impair; Passe, Manque;* one single number may be backed. This is called staking *en plein.* Or two numbers may be coupled (*à cheval*) ; or three numbers (*transversale pleine*) ; or four numbers (*carré*) ; or six numbers (*transversale simple,* or *sixaine*). In addition, the first, second, or third dozen of numbers (*Douzaine Première, Milieu, Dernière*), and the first, second, or third column of each of twelve numbers may be staked upon. The odds offered by the Bank against backing a single number *en plein* is 35 to 1, and the odds against the other chances in proportion : thus against either of two numbers appearing 17 to 1 is paid ; against either of three numbers, 11 to 1 ; against either of four, 8 to 1, and so on ; while obviously against each dozen, or column, 2 to 1 is paid ; the Red, Black ; *Pair, Impair; Passe, Manque,* being even-money chances.

A player wishing to stake on any of the even chances, or the dozens, or the columns, places his money on the portion of the cloth marked out for that chance. To back a single number, the stake is placed where that number is painted on the cloth ; to back both of two numbers, the stake is placed *à cheval*—that is, on the line between these two numbers. To stake on three numbers with one coin, the amount is placed on the border-line of the outside number of three numbers. Four numbers are backed when the coin is so placed that it touches all four numbers, and six numbers are combined in one bet by placing the stake on the outside of the line dividing these six numbers. Zero may also be staked upon by placing the coin in the zero area ; also zero, 1, 2, 3 (*quatre premières*), by putting the stake on the outside of the line dividing zero from 1, 2, 3 ; or zero coupled with 1 and 2 ; or 2 and 3 in a similar manner. In the first illustration an example is given of staking in all these various ways. It will be noticed that consecutive numbers on the table only can be staked upon in combination, not consecutive numbers on the

Wheel. Thus, to combine the three *voisins*, or adjacent numbers, 0, 26, 32, on the Wheel, three separate stakes would be required.

Any two dozens may be combined, or any two columns, by placing the stake on the line between the two ; and the player, when successful, receives one-half of the amount risked. Also any two even chances, such as *Rouge* and *Impair*, whose position is adjacent on the cloth, may be combined with one stake by placing the coin on the dividing line between the two ; the player is paid even money when both events turn up, and he only loses when neither event appears. But to bet on both *Passe* and *Noir* or *Rouge* and *Manque* at the same time, two separate stakes would be required.

The maximum stake allowed on the even chances is 6,000 francs (at par, £240)—on a single number 180 francs is the highest possible stake ; the maximum stakes on the other chances are in proportion—thus 3,000 francs on a dozen or column, and 720 francs on a *carré* of four numbers. In each case the minimum stake is 5 francs, except when two dozens or two columns are combined with one stake, when at least 10 francs must be risked.

Each table is presided over by two *chefs-de-partie*, who sit on elevated chairs on either side of the Wheel. There are four croupiers, who sit at the *Banque* (one being the tourneur), whose duty it is to pay out the winners and rake in the losings. In addition, there is a croupier sitting at either end of the table, who looks after the interests both of the players and of the Bank generally.

There being thirty-seven compartments in the Wheel, and as the odds of 35 to 1 only are paid on the winning number, it follows that on all stakes on numbers, or combination of numbers, the Bank has one chance in thirty-seven, or a percentage of under 3 per cent. (2.7) in its favour.

The percentage in favour of the Bank on all monies staked on the even chances, however, is only one-half of this amount. On the appearance of zero, all the money at stake is swept into the Bank, with the exception of that on zero itself—which is paid at the same rate as any other number—and the amounts on the even chances—*Rouge, Pair, Manque*, etc.: these stakes are placed on the lines on the outside of the table, and are then said to be " in prison."

On the next coupe, if these stakes happen to be on the winning chance, they are allowed to be withdrawn by the player. The reader will notice that this is theoretically exactly the same thing as if the punter halved his stake with the Banker, and this he is allowed to do if he so choose. *Partager* is the term used for halving the stake with the Bank. (The Bank's advantage over the player on the even chances at zero is therefore halved, being reduced to one-seventy-fourth). Should two zeros appear consecutively the stakes are placed still further over these lines, they are now doubly in prison, and have to be doubly released therefrom before the player gets his own money back.

Thus it will be seen that, theoretically, once in every thirty-seven spins the Bank wins *half* of all money staked on the even chances; on which chances, consequently, the Bank may be said to have a percentage of rather over $1\frac{1}{4}$ per cent. (1.35) in its favour. This difference in the percentage in favour of the Bank is either unknown to, or totally disregarded by, the great majority of punters at Monte Carlo; but the player, by judicious methods of staking can, to a great extent, defeat the Bank's higher percentage. An examination of the table will show that the following are Red numbers, viz.: 1, 3, 5, 7, 9, 12, 14, 16, 18, 19, 21, 23, 25, 27, 30, 32, 34, and 36. The *Impair* contains ten Red numbers, and but eight Black ones. The first column includes six; the second column four; and the third column eight Red numbers. Thus a player staking on Black and *Impair* has no less than twenty-eight numbers in his favour, on eight of which he wins both his stakes, and on twenty he neither wins nor loses. Or a punter staking on the third column and Black is guarded by twenty-six numbers, on four of which (the four Black numbers in column 3) he receives $1\frac{1}{2}$ times his stakes, on eight (the eight Red numbers in column 3) he receives $\frac{1}{2}$ times his stakes, and on the remainder he neither wins nor loses. Similar wagers can of course be made by combining Red and *Pair*, or the first column and Red, and so on. Now a player wishing to stake on a great many numbers (which is a very frequent occurrence, and is popularly known as " plastering the table "), instead of placing his money on the various *transversales*, *carrés*, and *en pleins*, by which method he loses all his money if zero appears, should rather stake the equivalent amount on Black and *Impair*, or Red and *Pair*, which, as explained, covers twenty-eight numbers. By this method he loses only one-half of his money if zero appears. Nothing is more usual than to see a player stake *à cheval* on two dozens. A more idiotic method of gambling cannot be conceived. The equivalent amounts (supposing the *douze* P and the *douze* M are selected) should be staked on *Manque*, and the *transversale* of 19 to 24. Now if zero appears half the stake on *Manque* is saved, but in the former case the entire stake would be lost !

Many similar instances of good and bad staking could be quoted, but the average player at Monte Carlo considers the percentage against him to be so insignificant that it is scarcely worthy of his notice. However, as its *insignificance* represents a gain of many hundreds of thousands of pounds sterling per annum to the Administration, it should be worthy of a passing thought at any rate !

Nearly every player at Monte Carlo has a system of some sort, generally played on the even chances. There are, however, systems for playing on numbers, dozens, etc., but these for the most part are of the most fantastic and insane order. The writer has actually known a player whose system was to back thirty-five out of the thirty-six numbers, on the principle that, having but two numbers against him, he would be very unlucky not to win one unit per coup !

Hundreds of people play on one particular number after the appearance of some other particular number, and are confident in themselves that, for example, 3 always turns up after 25 ; or 10 after 0. A very favourite stake is zero *et les quatre premiers*—that is, zero *en plein*, and zero coupled with 1, 2, 3. Another very general stake is *les voisins de zéro*—or zero and the numbers on either side of it on the Wheel. This is a simple bet to make by putting one coin *à cheval* between o and 3, one between 32 and 35, and one each on 26 and 15. The underlying idea of these zero bets is that the Bank cheats; that it wants zero to turn up; and that the *tourneur* is skilful enough to throw zero when he wishes. A more ridiculous assumption could not be made—in the first place, because the *tourneur* cannot throw the ball even to a particular section of the Wheel, much less into zero itself; and in the second place, because the gambling could not possibly be carried out in a more straightforward manner than it is by the Administration at Monte Carlo. If the *tourneur* could throw the ball into any compartment he chose, he could, through his friends, ruin the Bank whenever he wished.

A systematic method of staking is always advisable for play—be it never so weird and fantastic—as it keeps the player within certain limits, and prevents him from losing his head, and making wild plunges to retrieve all his losses by one lucky spin of the Wheel.

The more business-like systems are played on the even chances. Many are exceedingly ingenious, and on paper would appear certain to " break the Bank at Monte Carlo ! " Their underlying principle is to play a martingale—that is, after each loss to increase the stake in various proportions until all previous losses have been recouped, and a profit is shown. The commonest and simplest to play is the " *Montant et démontant*," which consists in increasing the stake after a loss by one unit per coup until the player is one unit to the good. Thus if the first stake be lost, the next stake would be two units, which is also lost, as is the next one of three units. The player would now have lost six units in all. His next stake becomes four, which, supposing it to be won, would leave him a net loser of two units. The stake would now be dropped to three units; for the object is to be but one unit to the good. Should this stake win, the game would be started all over again with one unit. On the other hand, if the three had been lost, the next stake would be four, and so on. There are many other systems. The general principle of them all is exactly the same; the calculations and paper results being nothing more

nor less than an ingenious method of juggling with
figures.

The Fitzroy system aims at winning one unit per
coup played. For the working of this system it is
necessary to keep a column in which *imaginary* losses
are written down : the player assuming that he loses
one unit more and wins one unit less than he actually
does. The stakes are increased by unity as in the *Montant
et démontant* system, with the exception of the second
stake, which (after a loss) is three instead of two
units, until the *imaginary* losses column comes out
clear. Here is an example of ten coups played on the
Fitzroy system :—

Stake.	W or L	Net + or −	Imagy. Loss	Stake.	W or L	Net + or −	Imagy. Loss.
I	L.1	−1	−2	6	W.6	−3	−9
3	L.3	−4	−6	7	W.7	+4	−3
4	W.4	0	−3	4	L.4	0	−8
4	L.4	−4	−8	5	W.5	+5	−4
5	L.5	−9	−14	5	W.5	+10	±0

Showing ten units won for ten coups played, the imaginary
loss column now reading ±0.

Another very ingenious scheme is that known as the
" *Labouchère*." To play this so many figures are written
down that their total equals the " *grand coup*,"
(see p. 294, footnote) that is being played for. Ten
is the customary coup, and the figures 1, 2, 3, 4 are
written down on a piece of paper. The method of play
is to stake the sum of the extreme figures, and if a win
is scored, these two figures are erased ; while if a loss
is incurred the amount of the stake is written down
at the end of the row of figures, and the next stake is
the sum of the new extremes. When all the figures
have been erased the coup is made, and the player either
begins a fresh game or retires from the table. Here
is an example : 1, 2, 3, 4 : first stake 5, which
is lost. The row now reads 1, 2, 3, 4, 5 ; and the next
stake (6) is won, the row reading 1, 2, 3, 4, 5 ; the
next stake (2+4) is lost, when we have 1, 2, 3, 4, 5, 6.

The next stake is 8, which is won, and we read 1̶, 2̶, 3, 4, 5̶, 6̶; the next stake being 7, which is won, the 4 and 3 are erased, when it will be found that the net profit is 10 units.

Example of a bad run at a *Labouchere*. The *grand coup* is 10; so the starting figures are 1, 2, 3, 4. The player is supposed to stake on Red throughout. The dot shows which colour wins.

The Figures.	The Stake.	R.	B.	Net + or −
1̶	1+4	5 .		+5
2̶	2+3	5	.	±0
3̶	2+5	7	.	−7
4̶	2+7	9 .		+2
5̶	3+5	8	.	−6
7̶	3+8	11 .		+5
8̶	5	5	.	±0
5̶	5+5	10	.	−10
10̶	5+10	15	.	−25
15̶	5+15	20	.	−45
20̶	5+20	25	.	−70
25̶	5+25	30 .		−40
25̶	5+20	25 .		−15
35	10+15	25	.	−40
	10+25	35	.	−75
	10+35	45 .		−30
40̶	15+25	40	.	−70
55	15+40	55	.	−125
70̶	15+55	70	.	−195
	15+70	85 .		−110
80	25+55	80	.	−190
105̶	25+80	105	.	−295
	25+105	130 .		−165
120	40+80	120	.	−285
160	40+120	160	.	−445
200̶	40+160	200	.	−645
	40+200	240 .		−405
215	55+160	215	.	−620
270	55+215	270	.	−890

Showing 29 coups, of which the player wins 9, with a net loss of 890 units. The next stake would have to be 55+270 (325), *i.e.*, if the game had been played with a one louis unit, a heavier stake than is allowed at Roulette.

Systems are very amusing and profitable to play, provided nothing abnormal occurs. But something abnormal *will* occur sooner or later, and the amounts staked and lost become colossal, and finally the maximum is reached: no higher wager can be made, so the system fails. The flaw in all systems is that the losses on an unfavourable run are out of all proportion to the gains on a favourable one. A *Labouchere* runs into hundreds in no time, and is in fact one of the most treacherous systems to play for this reason. Let the reader dissect the play of a *Labouchere* on such a run as that on p. 286, which is a far from uncommon one.

This tableau, in which the player only wins 9 out of 29 coups—or, say, one in three—may be said to be far out of proportion, as the player is " entitled " to win as many coups as he loses (leaving zero out of the question). Let it be noted at this point that zero does not affect a system played on the even chances in any degree whatsoever. Any system worthy of the name must withstand zero. It is the Bank's limit, and the limit alone, that proves the downfall of all systems. To resume. Of course a player " ought " to win two coups out of four, and so he will as a rule, and systems are devised so that a player may be a winner, even if he loses three and four times as many coups as he wins. A glance at those figures not yet erased in the example quoted will show that had the punter not been debarred from staking, owing to the Bank's limit, with three successive wins, he would have got all his money back and been ten points to the good on the whole transaction, and still have only won twelve times against the Bank's twenty. What no system, played with a Martingale, has yet been able to accomplish, is to prevent the stakes becoming colossal when the series of losses turn up in some particular sequence or disposition.

The best method to keep the stakes within reasonable limits, and to guard against arriving at the Bank's maximum on an adverse run, is to employ a varying unit. Thus after a net loss of so many single units, operations are re-started with a double unit ; if an equal number of double units are lost, the play is re-started with a triple unit, and so on : the same unit being employed until all previous losses have been retrieved, and a gain of one " single " unit made.

A *Montant et démontant* system can be played very easily in this manner, by increasing the unit employed after each complete loss of ten units—*e.g.*, after a loss of 10 single units the system is started afresh with a double unit ; when 10 double units have been lost, or a net loss of 30, the system is started afresh with a 3 unit stake, and so on.

This system may be varied by changing the unit after successive losses of 10, 20, 30, 40, etc., and by staking sufficient to show a net win of the amount of the unit employed. Thus when playing with a double unit, to try and win 2 ; or if playing with a unit of 5, to try and win 5 units net.

Every system has its Waterloo—it will succeed for days, possibly weeks, and small gains be made ; but finally the occasion must and will arrive when all previous profits and the system player's capital will be swamped.

Here is an example of a *Montant et démontant* played in the usual method, and played with an increasing unit after each net loss of 10 units. The player is supposed to stake on the Red throughout ; and the dot indicates which colour wins.

Ordinary Method.			A varying Unit employed.			Remarks.
R.	B.	Net + or −	R.	B.	Net + or −	
1.	.	—1	1	.	—1	
2	.	—3	2	.	—3	
3	.	—6	3	.	—6	
4	.	—10	4	.	—10	Having lost 10 single units, the system is re-started with a double unit.
5	.	—15	2	.	—12	
6	.	—21	4	.	—16	
7.	.	—14	6.		—10	
8		—22	8	.	—18	
9.	.	—13	10.		—3	
10	.	—23	9	.	—17	As the object is to be +1, 9 is a sufficiently high stake.
11		—34	11	.	—28	
	.					
12		—46	2	.	—30	As not more than 30 may be lost while employing a double unit, 2 is the highest stake allowed.
13	.	—59	3	.	—33	
14.		—45	6.		—27	
15.		—30	9.		—18	
16.		—14	12.		—6	
15	.	—29	7	.	—13	As explained before.
16.		—13	10.		—3	
14.		+1	4.		+1	As explained before.

Had the player lost 60 units, he would have restarted the system and played 4, 8, 12, etc. ; and if this play showed a net loss of 100 units, 5, 10, 15, etc., would have been staked, and continued with until either the net loss was 150, or the net gain 1 unit, in which case the player would begin all over again with a single unit.

Another style of play is to bet on the prospect of the colour, or even chances, running in a particular way. Some people play for an intermittence of colour, consequently always stake on the opposite colour to that which turned up last. Others play for the run, and so always stake on the colour that last appeared. A very popular wager is to stake on the " *Avant dernier,*" or on the colour that turned up the last time but one. By this means there is only one combination of events by which the player loses, and this is if the colours go two of one kind, followed by two of the other ; but the weak point about it is that the player may miss his first stake and his last one, although the series goes in his favour. Yet another common method of staking is to play " the card "—that is, to play in expectation of previous events repeating themselves. Thus if the previous throws have given three Blacks, followed by three Reds, the expectation is if three Blacks immediately occur, that three Reds will also occur.* Such theories, of course, have absolutely no scientific basis, and, in the opinion of the writer, are only vexatious and a cause of trouble to the player, who should *invariably stake on the chance that is most convenient to where he is sitting*. He has an equal chance of winning, and by this means will save himself the trouble of reaching across the table, both to place his stake and to retrieve his winnings.

There may be, however, some reason in playing for a run on one colour or chance, but *not staking* until after this colour or chance has appeared. By this means the player, if he plays flat stakes, is square on all runs of two, wins one on all runs of three, two on all runs of four, and so on. He loses one unit on every *intermittence*, but against this he loses nothing at all on all runs of the opposite colour or chance.

* This is a more common method of play at " Trente et Quarante."

Had this method of staking been followed in the example given on p. 286, it will be seen that the player would have won 2 units on Red and 4 units on Black, and the highest stake necessary on any coup would have been 3 units ; and had it been adopted in the example given on p. 284, only 70 units would have been lost on the Red side, and the highest stake risked 16 ; while on the Black, 41 units would have been won, with 9 as the highest stake.

Some people consider it advisable, when playing a system, to play on both sides of the table at once. The calculations for both Red and Black are kept, and the differences staked on the Red or Black as the case may be. The writer has actually seen a player stake the full requisite amount demanded by his system on both Red and Black *at the same time*. This of course gives the same net result as staking the difference on one colour, provided zero does not turn up. If it does, however, the player loses one-half of two large stakes in the one case, instead of only one-half of a small stake in the other case.

The alleged advantage of playing a system on both sides of the table at the same time is that double as much can be won with the same capital that is required for playing on one side only. Indeed, slightly less capital is required, for obviously the player must be winning something on one side to go against his loss on the other. The objection, of course, to this dual system of play is that there is a double chance of striking an adverse run, which neutralizes its advantages.

While on the subject of where to stake one's money, the reader, if a novice at Monte Carlo, is recommended to hand the amount of his wager to one of the croupiers to place on the table for him. This will ensure both the money being placed exactly as the punter desires, and the receipt of any winnings, without disputes on the part of other players. Unless one's French accent is above reproach, it is advisable to talk English to the croupiers.

TRENTE ET QUARANTE

By Major Browning.

TRENTE ET QUARANTE, also called ' Rouge et Noir,"
is played with six packs of cards on a table marked as
in the illustration, which represents one-half of the
table, the other half being exactly similar. There are
but four chances—*Rouge, Noir, Couleur*, and *Inverse*,
which are played on in the following manner. The six
packs of cards, having been well shuffled, are cut, and
so many cards dealt out face upwards in a row until the
sum of the pips (Aces, Kings, Queens, Knaves, and
Tens counting ten each, and the Ace one) *exceeds* 30.
Then a second row is dealt out in a similar manner,
below the first one, until the number of the pips in this
second row also *exceeds* 30. The top row is called
" Black," the second or underneath row " Red," and
the Red or Blacks win according to which row contains
the fewer number of pips—*e.g.*, whichever row of cards
adds up nearest to 30.

The number to which each row adds up is called
" the point," and it will be plain that the best point
possible is 31, and the worst point possible 40. It is
customary, when calling out the " point " of Black
and Red to drop the " thirty " and say simply 2 and 6.
which would mean that the point of Black amounts to
32, and the point of Red 36, in which case the Black
or top row would win. The Black " point " is always
called out first.

The other chance, the *Couleur* and *Inverse*, is
decided by the colour of the *first* card turned up. If
the colour of this card corresponds with the colour of
the winning row, then *Couleur* wins ; if it is of the
opposite colour, then *Inverse* wins. Thus suppose the
top or Black row of cards amounts to 35, and the *first*
card in this row is a Black card, and the Red row amounts
to 36, then Black and *Couleur* would win ; had the
first card in the Black row been a Red card, then *Inverse*
would have won, being of the opposite colour to the
winning row (Black).

The players wishing to back any particular chance place their stakes on that portion of the table reserved for Black, Red, *Couleur*, or *Inverse*, as shown in the

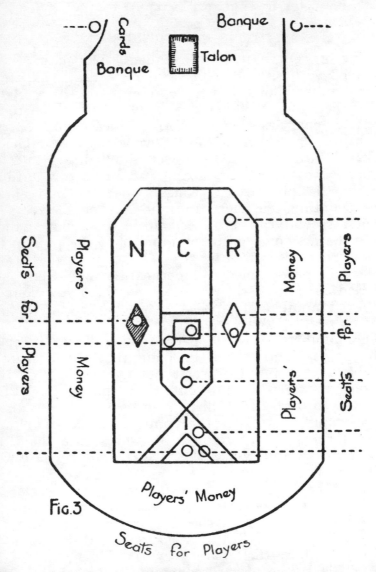

Fig. 3

illustration (Fig. 3). There are two *chefs-de-parties* employed to supervise the game, and four croupiers to receive the losing stakes and pay the winning ones, one of the croupiers also being the *tailleur*, or dealer of the cards. The *tailleur* calls the game by saying,

" *Messieurs, faites vos jeux,*" when the players stake on the different chances. He then says, " *Les jeux sont faits. Rien ne va plus,*" after which no further stakes may be made. He then deals out the cards, and when both rows are complete he calls the result thus, " *Deux, six, Rouge perd et Couleur gagne,*" or " *Rouge perd et Couleur,*" as the case may be, meaning that the point of Black is 32 and that of Red 36, so that Black and the colour win : or Black wins and the colour loses. It should be noted that the *tailleur* never mentions the words " Black " or " *Inverse,*" but always says that *Red* wins or *Red* loses, and that *the colour* wins or *the colour* loses. On the conclusion of each coup both rows of cards are swept into a small basket called the *talon,* which is let into the centre of the table, and the game begins again. When the six packs of cards are exhausted, the *tailleur* says, " *Monsieur, les cartes passent,*" when all the cards are collected out of the *talons,* re-shuffled and cut, and a fresh deal is started.

All four chances—Red, Black, *Couleur,* and *Inverse* —are of course even chances, and are paid as such by the Bank : but should the total (or point) of both rows of cards be exactly 31 each, the same procedure occurs as upon the appearance of the zero at Roulette—that is to say, the stakes are put *en prison;* then another deal is made, and those stakes which are on the winning chances are allowed to be withdrawn by the players. Or, as at Roulette, the stakes, at the players' option, may be halved with the Banker in the first instance.

Saving 31, all other identical points made by the Red and Black cause that deal to be null and void, the player being at liberty to remove his stake or otherwise, as he chooses. The condition of affairs (both rows coming to 31 each) which corresponds to the Roulette zero is called a " *Refait,*" and is announced, as are all other identities of the points, by the word " *après.*" Thus suppose the Black row counts up to 38, and the Red row to the same figure, the *tailleur* announces " *Huit, huit après.*" If it happens to be a *Refait,* he says, " *Un, un après,*" and the stakes are put into prison.

The *Refait* is *said* to occur once in 38 deals on the average : and if this were true, the Bank would have a slightly less advantage at Trente et Quarante than it has at Roulette. To arrive at the mathematical odds in favour of the Bank would involve an exceedingly complicated calculation, and it is doubtful if they have ever been exactly computed.* At a glance it would seem that the odds against both rows being 31 each is 81 to 1 ; there being 10 possible points for each row, the chances against any named point appearing would seem to be 9 to 1, in which case, of course, the chances against *both* points being identical would be 9×9, or 81 to 1. But as the point of 31 can be formed in 10 ways—for the last card may be of any value, while the point of 32 can only be formed in 9 ways—for now the last card cannot be an ace , and to form a point of 33 the last card can be neither an ace nor a deuce, and so on with every point up to 40, which can only be formed in one way—viz., when the last card is a 10—it is obvious that 31 is the easiest possible point to arrive at.

In actual play, however, the punter may insure against the *Refait* by paying a premium of 1 per cent. on his stake (at a minimum cost of five francs) ; thus it is safe to assume that for all practical purposes the percentage in favour of the Bank is exactly 2 per cent.†
Thus it would seem that once in 38 is an under-estimate of the appearance of a *Refait*.

The maximum and minimum stakes allowed at Trente et Quarante are 12,000 francs and 20 francs respectively. Much heavier amounts are to be seen at stake at this game than at Roulette. This probably arises from two facts : because the games are generally carried out in a quieter manner and the coups are more quickly played than is the case at Roulette, and because there is unquestionably a prevailing idea amongst the gamblers at Monte Carlo that the Bank's advantage is not so

---

* A German mathematician is said to have calculated the percentage in favour of the Banks to be 1.28 per cent., which is slightly more advantageous to the player than is zero at Roulette (1.35).

† It must be remembered that as the player is at liberty to withdraw half his stake when there is a *Refait*, he is really paying a premium of 1 per cent. to insure only *half* his stake.

great at Trente et Quarante as it is at Roulette. The
latter consideration is probably wrong : and, as far
as the writer's experience goes, it is a very paying business
to insure the stake at Trente et Quarante. If this really
is so, it follows that the percentage in favour of the
Bank is over 2 per cent., or something like 1 per cent. *more*
than it is at Roulette.

Any system that is applicable to the even chances
at the Roulette table can of course be played at Trente
et Quarante ; but for some reason or other it is unusual
to see any system properly worked at this game, possibly
because too large a capital would be required.

The almost universal method of play is to follow the
tableau—that is, to follow the pattern of the card on
which the game is marked. If there have been two
Reds followed by two Blacks, ninety-nine people out
of a hundred will stake on Red, in the expectation of
two Reds now appearing, while if there is a run of one
colour, thousands of francs will be seen on that colour,
and not a single 20-franc piece on the other. Sometimes the colours do run in the most inexplicable manner
at Trente et Quarante. The writer has played at a
table where there were seventeen consecutive Blacks,
then one Red, to be followed by sixteen consecutive
Blacks. When such runs occur, the Banks of course
lose heavily, and are constantly broken. To break
the Bank in the true sense of the word is of course an
impossibility. When a Bank gets into low water the
chef-de-partie sends for some more money, which is
" *Ajouter à la banque*," and to this extent only is it possible
to " break the Bank at Monte Carlo."

The method of play on the even chances that will
now be explained is based on the three following
assumptions :—

First. That every system at present played is
successful only for a certain time, when an adverse run,
long enough to defeat the progression adopted, is almost
certain to occur, whereby the Bank reaps a rich
harvest.

Secondly. That only on rare occasions does the
system show the desired profit, without the player
having been at some period of the game a very heavy
loser.

Thirdly. That the failure of systems is not due to zero, but to the Bank's maximum.*

These conditions are *assumed*, though in the first two cases they undoubtedly are realities, and within the experience of every system player.

Now as regards maxim No. 1, it may be taken for granted that for all practical purposes the system player makes his *grand coup†* on not more than (say) twenty occasions, and on the twenty-first he meets such an adverse run that he loses his entire profits plus his entire capital ; or say, for argument, he had already spent his profits and so loses only his entire capital. The proportion of the coup played for to the capital employed is generally some 2½ per cent. ; consequently after twenty good days' play, and one bad one, a system player is a loser of 50 per cent. of his money—and this is a very low estimate.

Now supposing a player had played stake for stake on the opposite chance to that played on by the system player, it is obvious that he would have lost on twenty days, and won on the twenty-first sufficient to recoup all his previous losses, with 50 per cent. profit.

The mathematician will say " No " to this—" the Bank will have reaped its zero percentage from each spin of the Wheel during the progress of the play." But why ? A, who is playing the system, stakes 10 louis on Red ; B (who is playing against him) stakes 10 louis on Black, and zero crops up. They are both put in prison, and A comes out safely, so B is now 10 louis worse off than A. But in a short time A and B again both stake 10 louis, and zero appears. But this time B comes out safely, in which case A must write this down as a losing coup, and his next stake will be say, for example, 15. To meet this B has only to add 5

---

* If there were no limit everyone could win at Monte Carlo, by the simple method of doubling up after each loss. Hence *sans* maximum, zero does not prevent the Bank from losing.

† Most system players try to win a percentage of their capital per diem. Having done so, they retire from the table. By *grand coup* is meant this amount of daily winnings. There is no reason why a player should not play his system *ad infinitum.* He, however, instinctively knows the grave risk he is running by continuing his game, and is generally very pleased to retire after having made a certain daily profit.

louis to the 10 he has just retrieved out of prison—so
his profit and loss account due to zero is exactly
square, as far as it affects his transactions with A.
And surely during the course of a game A and B
will both get out of prison the same number of
times. (And A does not fear zero—he only fears reaching
the maximum—consequently B does fear zero : he
but awaits the time when *his* stake gets to the
maximum.)

Is it not desirable to be B ? He requires no capital—
or very little—and yet is in a position to win all that
A is eventually going to lose—as he most certainly *must*
lose. To play on this method is exceedingly simple.
All that has to be done is to take *any* system, and play
it in reverse order to what it is designed to be played
in. The effect of this is, in a word, to compel the Bank
to play this system in its correct order against the punter.
The writer has always employed a *Labouchere* to play
on this method, and it is the simplest one by which to
explain the procedure.

A reference to p. 283 will show that the *Labouchere*
system is played by writing down so many figures, so
that their sum amounts to the *grand coup*—or stake
being played for—and that it is usual to write down
the figures 1, 2, 3, 4 : so that the *grand coup* is 10 units.
To play this sytem in the usual manner it is generally
assumed that a capital of 400 or 500 units is required.
By reversing matters in play the first important advantage
gained to the player is that he needs but a capital of
10 units, and his *grand coup* becomes 400 or 500 units.
Very well. The figures 1, 2, 3, 4, are written down,
and the first stake is the sum of the extreme figures
—5. This sum is lost : but now the 5 is not written
down after the 4, but the 1 *and the* 4 *are erased*. The
next stake is again 5 (2+3), and is again lost, the 2 and
3 are erased and the player retires. Suppose this second
stake of 5 had been won, then instead of erasing
the 2 and 3, the figure 5 would be written down
on the paper, so the row would read ̶1̶, 2, 3, ̶4̶. 5,
and the next stake would be (5+2) 7. Should this
be lost the 5 and 2 are erased, the next stake being
3. Suppose it is won, this figure is written down,
and the row now reads ̶1̶, ̶2̶, 3, ̶4̶. ̶5̶. 3, and the

next stake is 3+3 (6), and so on. But the moment all figures are erased, the player will have lost 10 units and must retire. This he will have to do a great many times, but finally such a run as the following will occur. The Red is staked on throughout—the dot indicating which colour wins :—

Figures.	Stake.	R.	B	+ or −
1	1+4	5	.	−5
2	2+3	5 .		0
3	2+5	7 .		+7
4	2+7	9 .		+16
5	2+9	11 .		+27
7	2+11	13	.	+14
9	3+9	12	.	+2
11	5+7	12 .		+14
12	5+12	17 .		+31
17	5+17	22 .		+53
22	5+22	27 .		+80
27	5+27	32	.	+48
	7+22	29	.	+19
28	12+17	29 .		+48
41	12+29	41 .		+89
	12+41	53	.	+36
46	17+29	46 .		+82
	17+46	63	.	+19
29	29	29 .		+48
58	29+29	58 .		+106
87	29+58	87 .		+193
	29+87	116	.	+77
87	29+58	87 .		+164
	29+87	116	.	+48
58	58	58 .		+106
116	58+58	116 .		+222
174	58+116	174 .		+396
232	58+174	232 .		+628
290	58+232	290 .		+918

This shows a run of 29 coups, of which the player wins 20 and loses 9. He is 918 units to the good, and his next stake would be 348 !*

Assuming a player had been working a *Labouchere* on this run in the usual manner, on Black with a capital of 500 units, he would have to retire after the 27th coup through lack of capital ; and assuming him to have been playing with a 20-franc unit, he would have had to retire from Roulette on the 28th coup, and from

* In the series shown on p. 284, had a player been fortunate enough to have played a " *Labouchere* reversed " on Black, he would have won 890 units.

Trente et Quarante after a few more coups if the bad sequence continued, no matter how large his capital had been.

It has been stated that the Bank beats the system player only on account of its limit. This is not quite true; it has also one more great advantage over the player, and this is the fact of its being a machine, while the punter is human; and although a player will stake his all to retrieve his previous losses, he will not—nature will not allow him to—risk his winnings to win still more.

This is a psychological fact that cannot be explained. It must be to the knowledge of most people who have visited Monte Carlo, that a player will stake as much as 500 francs to retrieve a loss of a single 5-franc piece. Yet the same player, having turned a 5-franc piece into as little as 50 francs, will refuse to adventure another stake, and retire from the gaming table. When the player is having his bad run, the Bank cannot help playing their winnings to the maximum stake—they *must* do so; but the player on his good run is not compelled to play up his winnings, and really cannot be expected to do so. Theoretically he should, and I firmly believe there is a lot of money awaiting the player who has the patience to wait for such a run—which must come to him, equally as it must and does, we know, come to the Bank—and then play on and on until he is prohibited by the Bank from staking any higher. To play a system upside-down, or in reverse order, requires great patience and equanimity, until the favourable run occurs, when indomitable pluck and perseverance are the necessary qualifications.

The writer feels bound to take the reader into his confidence so far as to acknowledge that he himself has never had such pluck, but has always retired on winning between 200 and 300 units. But he has always watched the future run of the table, and on no less than five occasions would have reached the maximum stake and won over 1,000 units. He has, however, always had the patience, and lost his *petit coup* time after time with perfect equanimity, and only wishes he had had the other qualifications as well.

Referring for one moment to the assumed fact No. 2

on which this method is based—that a player more
often than not is in deep water before bringing off his
grand coup; which he must be, owing to the losses being
so disproportionate in magnitude to the gains—it might
be a good plan to discover what the average highest
loss of a system player is before the system shows
a profit, and then to play the same system in reverse
or upside-down order, making this figure the *grand
coup.* Playing in this manner, a visitor will have
a cheap and enjoyable visit to Monte Carlo, and may
be assured of one of the most exciting little periods of
his career when this favourable run of luck does come his
way.

One final word of advice to all system players. Play
on the chance that is most convenient to your seat at
the table. It is as likely to win as any other. Never
get flurried with your system or calculations. It is not
at all necessary to stake on every coup. You are just
as likely to win if you postpone staking until the day
after to-morrow, or next year, as if you stake on the
very next spin of the Wheel—the Rooms are open for
twelve hours per diem, which should allow ample time
for the number of coups you wish to play.

There may or not be such a thing as " luck." There
can, however, be no harm in giving its existence the
benefit of the doubt. If on some particular occasions
you find you cannot do right, *assume* you are out of
luck, and stop playing. Do not consider either that
you owe a grudge to the Bank, because you have lost,
or that it is absolutely necessary to retrieve your fortune
then and there ! Postpone playing until the following
day, or week, or year, when you may be in " good luck,"
and can easily recoup yourself.

Always bear the clever gambler's great maxim well in
mind : " Cut your losses—play up your gains ! "

The writer's only object has been to try and explain
how the games of chance are played at Monte Carlo, and
to point out that the player is at a disadvantage on each
occasion that he stakes, though that disadvantage may
be increased or reduced by bad or good staking. It now
remains for the reader to decide whether the pleasure he
derives from gambling is likely to recompense him for his
probable losses.

PETITS-CHEVAUX

PETITS-CHEVAUX, one of the most popular and exciting of the race-games, is best known to the Englishman through visits to Dieppe, Ostend, and other continental watering-places, where it continues to flourish at the expense of the tourist. The tourist, of course, is well aware of this ; and, unless his losses have been *too* great, does not grudge paying for the pleasure he derives from watching the " little horses " in their perpetual circling round the flag, and for the excitement and exhilaration of waiting to learn the fate of his francs.

The apparatus necessary is a round table, covered with green cloth, on which the race takes place, and some (usually four) oblong tables radiating from this, each of which is marked in a way presently to be explained. In the centre of the first-mentioned table is a flag, and round this nine horses race in concentric rings, the ring nearest the flag-staff being about eighteen inches in diameter, and the outermost some five feet, or even more. These circles are really slits in the table ; and through each slit comes a rod that carries at the top end a miniature horse and jockey and is connected beneath the table with a simple piece of machinery by means of which the steward, or " starter," sets all the horses in motion at the same time. The winning-post stands at the outer edge of the circle, and from its base comes a line—usually an electro-plated rod let into the green cloth—to the centre, thus cutting across the track of every horse. A thin cord is attached to the central flag-staff, and when there is any question as to a horse's nose being over the line this is stretched across to the winning-post, and the matter is decided. The cord is also used in cases of apparent dead-heats.

Each jockey carries his number (1 on the outer circle to 9 on the inner) ; and, moreover, each has his distinctive colour. No. 1, on the outside, wears a red jacket and rides a white horse; No. 2 wears blue, and his horse is brown; No. 3 has a yellow jacket with blue sleeves, and a cream-coloured mount; No. 4 wears a white jacket with a blue cap, and rides a brown; the jockey on No. 5—an important horse, as will presently appear—has a red jacket and a white mount; No. 6's jacket is spotted with blue and white, and his horse is brown; the horse at No. 7 is dark grey and carries a jockey in red; the jockey on No. 8, a light brown, is dressed in blue and red; and No. 9 wears green and is mounted on a light bay.

The four tables surrounding the " course " are marked out as shown in the plan herewith; and a study of it is important for an understanding of the game and for an appreciation of the whys and wherefores of when to play and what to back.

It will be noticed that each number has a separate division to itself, that on the two sides, or *bandes*, as they are technically called, are groups of two odd and two even numbers (2, 4, 7, 9, and 1, 3, 6, 8), and that also there are divisions for an even group (2, 4, 6, 8), and for an odd (1, 7, 3, 9). Stakes may be laid on (a) any horse to win, (b) either of the *bandes*, or (c) either of the odd or even groups. As will be seen, No. 5 does not appear in any of the groups; and it is just here that the advantage of the bank comes in; for, should No. 5 win, the bank takes all money staked on the groups and pays out only to the lucky punters who put their money on this horse as a " single."

The stakes are paid as follows :—for all money on an individual horse, seven to one; that is, a punter having one franc on a winner receives his franc back with seven others; the *bandes*, and odds or evens, give you single, that is, your stake back and the same again. One franc is the lowest stake accepted at the tables in most continental Petits-Chevaux saloons, and five francs the highest on any individual horse; but, as there are four tables, the punter who has a particular fancy can put a louis on it by backing it to the limit at each table.

The actual play is simplicity itself. The official in charge of the race—the " starter "—adjusts the handle by which the machinery is actuated and gets all the horses into line. Meanwhile, the bets are being made; at each table there are two croupiers, one who sees that the stakes are placed according to the intentions

THE TABLE

CROUPIER

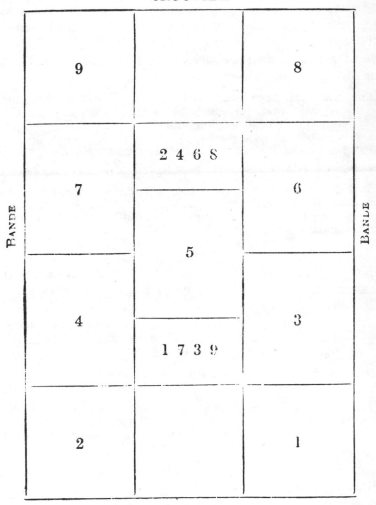

of the punters, the other takes or pays the money lost or won. The starter now, by one or two sharp turns of the handle, sets the horses flying round together, releases a clutch—thereby allowing them to revolve independently of each other, and " They're off ! " No stake may be laid after the horses have gone round once, though here the croupier is, as a rule, allowed to exercise his discretion. At the finish, the master of the ceremony calls out the number of the winner, the stakes are paid on the spot, the course is cleared for the next race, and so on, *da capo*. Each race occupies about three minutes ; so that with bad luck and putting the limit, five francs, on a horse to win outright each time, you can easily get rid of a considerable amount in the course of a morning's amusement. Now for some ways of playing Petits-Chevaux : and first, bear in mind these three simple maxims :—

1. Find out the favourite of the day—for every day, curious as it may seem, there *is* a horse that comes in winner more frequently than any other—and stick to it.
2. Don't follow losing horses.
3. Keep a card of the winning numbers, and note any group which are running in succession for that day. It is remarkable how often it happens that a given winner, No. 7, for instance, is followed in the next race by a definite horse as winner, and this by another. The careful player will take a note of such things, and if he punts carefully ought to make a lot of money.

Some players make a rule of taking a number and keeping to it. They put their stake on it each time, and **then** put on double on one of the odd or even chances as a sort of hedge (on odd if the horse backed to win is even, and *vice versa*). If both come off they do very well ; if only the horse wins they have nothing to grumble about ; if the odd or even wins they make a single stake ; and if neither comes home they " get the knock " and begin again. Another plan is to take a horse and put a single stake on it ; if it loses to double this, and again double if a loss, then begin again with a single stake, and so on. This often pays in the long run.

Another excellent plan, but one which requires a certain amount of capital and patience, is the following. Seven times running put a franc on the day's favourite —or any other horse you fancy—whether it wins or not ; then do the same with two francs, then with three and four and five, going seven times with each. This, if you happen to have lighted on a good horse, is most paying ; and the total loss if your horse does not win once in the thirty-five times is 105 francs. It would be only very occasionally that such a thing would happen ; and, in any case, you get a lot of play for your money, and if you keep it up daily the chances are in favour of it paying. The same system can be carried out by going some less number than seven, your risk of loss and also of gain being proportionately reduced. For instance, if you go three times on each and your horse never wins, your total loss is only forty-five francs.

One other thing : remember that to Petits-Chevaux the old saying, " Nothing venture, nothing have," applies with even more force than to most games !

SANDOWN

In England SANDOWN is probably the favourite of the race-games, for it is not only the most long-established, but also, in the domestic circle and among young people, a good deal of fun—not to mention instruction in " odds " and practice in keeping cool and collected in face of losses—can be got out of it when the game is played merely with counters. In such circumstances it is best if all the " punters " start with the same number, say 100 counters, representing £5.

Sandown was invented somewhere about the early 'nineties of last century, and is the copyright of Messrs. F. H. Ayres, Ltd., the well-known games manufacturers of Aldersgate Street, in the City of London. The apparatus consists of a circular disc enclosed in a solid frame and surmounted by a sheet of glass having a hole in the centre through which comes and electro-plated handle. By means of the latter the banker—or " book-maker," as he is usually called—spins the disc, which revolves freely on a central pivot.

The disc is segmented in the following proportions, and in each segment is a well drawn representation of a racer with a jockey " up " :—One thirty-seventh of the entire area is allotted to " Bolter," two thirty-sevenths to " Mr. Pickwick," three to " Maid Marian," four to " Peeping Tom," six to " Waverley," nine to " Dorothy," and twelve thirty-sevenths to " Esmeralda." On the stationary circle in which the disc revolves is the winning-post, and the winning horse is that which occupies that division of which *any part* is opposite to the winning-post line when the disc comes to a stop. In the rare event of one of the lines of division exactly coinciding with that of the winning-post it is a dead-heat, and the winner receives half only of what he would have been entitled to as an absolute winner.

Now for the odds.   Of the seven divisions, that occupied by Bolter (one thirty-seventh only of the entire disc) is in favour of the table, and cannot be backed without the consent of the bookmaker ; the chances of the other horses are therefore calculated as if there were only thirty-six divisions. Of these no less than twelve——one-third of the whole—are occupied by Esmeralda ; she is therefore " favourite," and runs at two to one against ; Dorothy takes nine divisions, starting at three to one against ; and so on with the others, as shown in the following table :—

Against	" Esmeralda "	2 to 1
,,	" Dorothy "	3 to 1
,,	" Waverley "	5 to 1
,,	" Peeping Tom "	8 to 1
,,	" Maid Marian "	11 to 1
,,	" Mr. Pickwick "	17 to 1
,,	" Bolter "	35 to 1

These odds are mathematically correct, but it is worth noting that in many clubs where Sandown is played the odds on the last four in the list are frequently reduced, and Bolter (when played) is limited to 20 to 1 against.

Even chances can be played by backing Esmeralda and Waverley (coupled) against " The Field," as these two occupy together eighteen divisions out of the thirty-six ; and, in the same way, " The Field " can be backed against Esmeralda and Waverley coupled.

The player taking the bank is called the bookmaker ; he need not lay the odds against any horse oftener than he chooses, and it is optional with him to refuse to allow any stakes larger than those agreed upon at the commencement of the game. It is usual to arrange a limit, but of course punters can back as many horses as they like.

A green cloth marked out with divisions for each horse, for " Evens " and for " The Field " is often used with the game, and on this the players deposit their stakes, in the desired division, at the start of each game. The cloth, however, is not necessary, as tickets, with the name of the horse and the odds printed thereon are supplied with the apparatus, and the punter receives from the bookmaker a ticket for each horse he wishes to back and places his stake upon it. The tickets are returned to the bookmaker after each race, he paying on the winners and receiving from the losers.

When all the money has been put on the bookmaker spins the disc, and the horses are " Off ! " Each must pass the winning post at least six times before they come to a stop, otherwise it is a false start and does not count ; but a hard spin is quite unnecessary, for no one wants to be kept waiting five minutes—or even more— before he is " put out of his agony."

The hints for play given above under " Petits-Chevaux " will, *mutatis mutandis*, serve for Sandown ; but the absence of any backing on the odd and even groups and on the *bandes* in the latter, makes a difference. Also, in Sandown there would seem to be less chance of making paying forecasts by taking note of consecutive runs ; we have tried many times to find repeated consecutive runs, and always without success, and have come to the conclusion that about the best way for a punter to leave the disc " in pocket " is always to back a stationary figure on an even chance, and at the same time to follow one of the higher priced horses with bets increasing one point at a time—win or lose— in series of, say, sevens ; the same system, in fact, as the last that we mention in the case of " Petits-Chevaux."

MINORU

MINORU, the last of the race-games with which we propose to deal, was so named in honour of King Edward VII.'s famous horse that won the Derby and the Two Thousand Guineas in 1909, and though it is one of the youngest of the race-games in point of years it is one of the most popular—and for excellent reasons.

It is played with five miniature horses that actually race along a course. The course is an oblong piece of green cloth marked out into five longitudinal strips, or tracks, which, in turn, are divided into an unequal number of compartments, three, four, five, or six, as the case may be. At one end of each strip is the starting-place, and at the other the winning-post; and it is owing to the fact that each track is differently divided that the horses start at different odds, thus assimilating the game to the actual conditions of the betting-ring.

At the beginning of the game, the horses are placed at their respective starting points, and the " Book-maker " deals from a well-shuffled pack of cards one card on each of the spaces behind the tracks. The horse to which the highest card has been dealt moves one space up its course : then five more cards are dealt, and the horse obtaining the highest is similarly moved : and so on, until one or other of the horses reaches the winning-post and is declared winner.

The aces count highest ; if two or more cards tie for highest in the same round they are to be counted in Bridge order, *i.e.*, first, Hearts, second, Diamonds, third, Clubs, and fourth, Spades ; so if, say, the ten of diamonds and the ten of spades are dealt in the same round, and these are the highest in that round, the horse to whom the ten of diamonds falls is the one to move. The five cards dealt in each deal are put on one side before the next deal is commenced, and when the pack is exhausted it is used over again, after having been thoroughly shuffled.

Two horses, " Minoru " and " St. Amant " (St. Amant, one of Lord Rothschild's horses, was winner of the Derby and the Two Thousand five years before Minoru), have each the lowest number of spaces to cover before reaching the winning-post ; there is therefore more chance of their winning, and if one of them does the Bank pays only twice the stake. " Game Chick," the winner of the Champagne Stakes at Doncaster in 1901, comes next at five to one : " Miss McGiggle " runs at seven to one : and " Gou-Gou," with six spaces, is ten to one. In addition to backing on the horses, counters may be placed in either of the spaces (Red and Blue) marked " Even Chances " : if either of the horses under the colour staked upon gets home first, the Bank pays out an amount equal to the stake. Any number of horses, or both the colours as well, may be backed at the same time, but there is usually a limit (six to ten counters) placed on any one bet ; and, as in all race-games, the Banker may, at his discretion, refuse to take any bet. No stakes can be made or withdrawn after the race has once commenced.

An additional interest can be imported into " Minoru " by including a " Joker " in the pack of cards. If this is done, as soon as it turns up " Gou-Gou " has the move, no matter to which horse it falls or what cards the remaining horses have dealt to them. With this very substantial advantage, of course " Gou-Gou " cannot be allowed to run at ten to one, and her odds are consequently reduced to six to one.

In a development of this popular race-game we have the advantage of being able to indulge in place-betting, i.e., betting on the first three. This is known as the " Double Event Minoru," and there are eight—instead of five— horses, the cloth being divided into eight longitudinal strips. Four of these strips are marked with the suits, and the other four with " Kings," " Aces," " Knaves," and " Queens " respectively. At the head of the cloth— beyond the winning-post—are shown the odds allowed to each horse both for a win and for a place.

The horses being at the start and the money down, the

banker takes a well-shuffled pack and, after it has been cut, deals out one card at a time, the horse (or horses) indicated as each card is exposed moving one place. When a court-card (*i.e.*, King, Queen, or Knave) is turned two horses move, one for the value and one for the suit ; but note that in the case of the Knaves it is only the " one-eyed " Knaves (Hearts and Spades) that affect the horse on the Knave track ; at the turn of the Knave of Diamonds or Clubs, therefore, it is only the horse on the suit track that will move.

The race proceeds until three horses have reached the winning-post, and should the pack of cards be exhausted before this is accomplished—an unlikely eventuality—the cards are gathered up, well shuffled, and re-dealt as before until the race is over.

There are many good points in favour of " Minoru " as a Race-Game ; it is most exciting to see the actual horses moving along the tracks to their goal, but beyond this there is the fact that there is something going on all the time. To watch the spinning disc at " Roulette " and similar games has a very great fascination for many, but the waiting—especially when one happens to be having a run of bad luck—is apt to be tedious. Now in " Minoru " there is none of this waiting ; for, except when the stakes are being laid and the counters being raked in and paid out, the deal is going on, and is being intently watched, all the time. Each race is short and rapid, and there are many close and exciting finishes. The varying odds give ample scope for " hedging " and for the invention of " systems " ; but it is unnecessary to enter further into these, for what we have said on the point in treating of " Petits-Chevaux " and " Sandown " is equally applicable to " Minoru," due allowance being made for minor differences in the games.

It only remains to add that in most circles the " Banker," or " Bookmaker," retains his position for four races, when the Bank passes to the player on his left, and so on round the table ; and, further, that, " Minoru " is the patent and property of Messrs John Jaques & Co., the well-known sports and games manu-facturers of Thornton Heath, Surrey.

PART III

BILLIARDS—AND ITS RELATIONS

BILLIARDS

THE origin of this noble game, one of the finest games of skill ever devised by the wit of man, is—like so many other origins—wrapt in mystery : but it goes back for a number of centuries, and seems to have been developed from an outdoor game of the croquet family, the invariable green cloth of the table representing the turf of the village green.

It was introduced into England from Spain some time in the late sixteenth century, and is classed by Edmund Spenser in his *Mother Hubberd's Tale* (1591) with mumming and masking and with such " thriftles games " as dice, cards, and " shuttlecocks." Shakespeare's reference to it in *Antony and Cleopatra* (II., v.) is well known . but his making the swarthy Queen say, " Let's to billiards ! " is as anachronistic as the remark of Cassius in *Julius Cæsar* (II., i.)—" The clock hath stricken three "—for neither billiards nor striking clocks were known in the days of ancient Rome.

Since the early eighteenth century the game has undergone many modifications, and until comparatively recent times was subject to no definite code of rules. Even to-day it is played under widely differing conditions in the United States, on the continent of Europe, and in England . but in the latter country all the Championships, both professional and amateur, and practically all games—especially those played in clubs and in public rooms—are governed by the rules codified and published by the Billiards Association and Control Council.

It was not until 1885 that billiards had any controlling body or recognized code of rules ; but in that year the Billiard Association was formed and the epoch that has culminated in raising the game from the somewhat ignoble obscurity that it then occupied to its present position as one of the great national sports was inaugurated.

One of the earliest activities of the Association was the copyrighting of a code of rules ; these speedily received universal recognition—so far, at least, as English billiards is concerned—and thus imparted to the game that unity and cohesion in which it had hitherto been sadly deficient. Other most important functions which it fulfilled were the promotion and management of the Amateur and Professional Championships, and the issuing of " standard templates " for determining the size of the pocket openings on tables of standard dimensions. These latter have been adopted by all billiard-table makers, and a certificate for a record break is granted only if it was made on a table which had previously been tested with these templates and passed as of " standard pattern."

From 1885 to 1908 the Billiard Association continued to exercise undisputed control as the sole governing body of the game ; but in the latter year the Billiards Control Club was established in opposition to the older body, and issued a code of rules varying in many essential details from those which had hitherto been recognized. The professionals seceded *en masse* from the Association, and consequently all the professional matches and the professional Championships were played under B.C.C. rules ; but the large majority of amateurs continued to play under the B.A. code, and great confusion naturally was the result. It was ultimately agreed by both bodies, however, that the continued existence of this dual control, with its two codes of rules, was inimical to the best interests of the game, and the amalgamation of the Billiard Association with the Billiards Control Club, under the title of the Billiards Association and Control Council, which took place in 1919, has happily restored that unity of management which is essential to the efficient government of any game : and to-day the Council stands in the same relationship to Billiards as does the M.C.C. to Cricket.

The best introduction to an account of Billiards as played to-day will be a brief explanation of the implements of the game and the terms used in connection with it.

The bed of a full-sized table (see Fig. I) is 12 feet long, and 6 feet $1\frac{1}{2}$ inches wide ; it is fitted with six pockets, one at each corner and one at each side midway between these, the mouth of each measuring $3\frac{3}{4}$ inches across the fall of the bed. Its height from the floor to the top of the cushion rail is from 2 feet $9\frac{1}{2}$ inches to 2 feet $10\frac{1}{2}$ inches, and the cushions must not project more than 2 inches or less than $1\frac{1}{2}$ inches over the bed. The Spot, or Billiard Spot, S, is $12\frac{3}{4}$ inches from the centre of the top cushion, opposite to the baulk. The Pyramid Spot, P, is placed at the intersection of two lines drawn from the two middle pockets to the opposite top pockets   The Centre Spot, M, is exactly between the middle pockets. The " Baulk " is the space behind a line drawn across the table, 29 inches from the face of the bottom cushion, and parallel to it. The " Half-circle," or " D," is 23 inches in diameter, its centre, K, coinciding with the centre of the baulk-line.

The game is played with three balls of equal size and weight, one *red*, one *white*, and one *spot-white*. The diameter of a ball must not be less than $2\frac{1}{16}$ inches, nor more than $2\frac{3}{32}$ inches.

The choice of balls and order of play is, unless mutually agreed upon, determined by "stringing" (*i.e.*, playing from baulk up the table, so as to strike the top cushion). The striker whose ball stops nearest the lower cushion may take which ball he likes, and play, or direct his opponent to play, as he may deem expedient.

The red ball is, at the opening of every game, placed on the spot, and must be replaced after being pocketed or forced off the table, except that, if it should be pocketed *twice in succession in one break* from the spot (or from the pyramid spot), it shall be placed on the centre spot, or on the pyramid spot if that is occupied, and if both happen to be occupied then replaced on the spot. If from the new position it is again pocketed, then it is placed on the spot.

When any player plays from baulk, he must place his

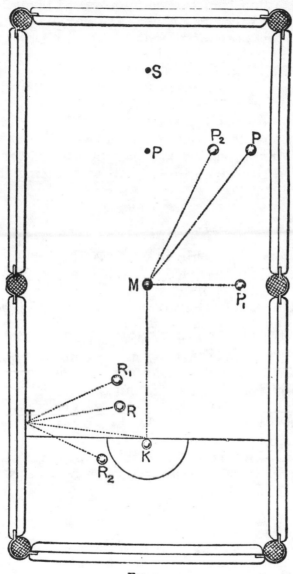

FIG. 1.

ball within the half-circle, or on the line that contains it.

Whoever *breaks the balls* (*i.e.*, leads off) must play out of baulk ; he may give a miss if he likes, and he may leave his ball in baulk, but to do so he must strike a cushion out of baulk. No player who is in hand is allowed to strike any ball in baulk, or on the baulk-line, unless his ball has first struck a cushion out of baulk. Should, however, a ball be out of baulk, the player in hand may strike any part of that ball without his own ball necessarily going out of baulk.

The player continues to play until he ceases to score, when his opponent follows. During the course of a break the cue-ball must cross the baulk-line at least once in each 200 points—Rule 10 (b).

The various strokes are as under :—

1.—A *winning hazard* is made by the player causing his own ball to hit an object ball and forcing the latter into a pocket.

2.—A *losing hazard* is made by the player causing his own ball to hit an object ball and forcing his own ball into a pocket. Consecutive hazards are limited to 25.

3.—A *cannon* is made by causing the player's ball to strike the two object balls. When a losing hazard is combined with a cannon and the two object balls have been struck simultaneously, the hazard shall be scored as if the white had been struck first.

A *ball to ball cannon* is one that is made without striking a cushion either before striking the first object ball or between striking the two. Consecutive ball-to-ball cannons are limited to thirty-five and a break in which this number has been reached without an intervening score can only be continued after an indirect cannon or a hazard.

4.—A *coup* is made by forcing the player's own ball into a pocket without striking another ball.

A *miss* counts one, a *coup* three, to the opposite player. The following rule (Rule 12), setting a limit to successive misses, is important :—

A player may not make two misses in successive turns unless he or the opponent scores after the first miss. Any miss given when the striker is in hand, and there is no ball out of baulk, does not count as one of the two misses which constitute a foul stroke.

The scores are counted as follows :—

A.—A two stroke is made by pocketing an opponent's ball—*i.e.*, a winning hazard ; or by pocketing the striker's ball off his opponent's—*i.e.*, a losing hazard ; or by making a cannon.

B.—A three stroke is made by pocketing the red ball —*i.e.*, a red winning hazard ; or by pocketing the striker's ball off the red—*i.e.*, a red losing hazard.

C.—A four stroke may be made by pocketing the white and spot-white balls ; or by making a cannon and pocketing an opponent's ball ; or by making a cannon and pocketing the striker's ball, the opponent's ball having been first hit, or both that and the red having been hit simultaneously.

D.—A five stroke may be made by scoring a cannon and pocketing the red ball ; or by a cannon and pocketing the striker's ball, after having struck the red ball first ; or by pocketing the red ball and the opponent's ball without cannoning, or by making a losing hazard off the white and pocketing the red ball.

E.—A six stroke is made by the red ball being struck first, and the striker's and the red ball pocketed ; or by a cannon off an opponent's ball on to the red and pocketing the two white balls.

F.—A seven stroke is made by striking an opponent's ball first, pocketing it, making a cannon, and pocketing the red also ; or by making a cannon and pocketing the red and an opponent's ball ; or by playing at an opponent's ball first and pocketing all the balls without making a cannon ; or by playing at the red first, cannoning, and pocketing your own and the opponent's ball.

G.—An eight stroke is made by striking the red ball first, pocketing it, making a cannon, and pocketing the striker's ball ; or by hitting the red first and pocketing all the balls without making a cannon.

H.—A nine stroke is made by striking an opponent's ball first, making a cannon, and pocketing all the balls.

I.—A ten stroke is made by striking the red ball first, making a cannon, and pocketing all the balls.

Reverting to the terms used in the game, the CUE is the stick with which the player strikes the ball. It varies in length from 4 feet 6 inches to 5 feet, and in weight from about $13\frac{1}{2}$ ozs. to 18 ozs. The thick end or butt has a diameter of about $1\frac{1}{2}$ inches. The small end varies from $\frac{1}{2}$ to $\frac{1}{4}$ inch in diameter. The tip is formed of two pieces of leather glued together ; in play this is frequently rubbed with a piece of chalk to ensure getting a " grip " on the ball.

One of the most important points for the beginner, as well as for the more experienced player, is the selection of a thoroughly good and reliable cue. Strangely enough, this matter generally receives very little attention, the neophyte being content to take the first that comes to hand. What is even worse, he will change about from day to day—or from hour to hour— using cues of different shapes, weight, and balance ; and is then surprised that he does not make the progress that he expected.

THE REST.—The real " rest," that is, the support on which the cue is raised in order to strike the ball, is the left hand. This, however, is more generally termed the " bridge " ; what is known as the " rest," or " jigger," is a metal cross fixed at right angles to a handle about the same length as the cue, in order to enable a player to strike a ball when it is too far away to allow him to use his hand as a bridge. Special rests, and cues of extra length, are made to meet exceptional positions of the balls.

IN HAND.—A ball is said to be in hand when it is off the table, and the player has to play from the half-circle or D.

BREAKING THE BALLS.—Whoever plays, being in hand, when the red ball is on the spot and the other ball also is in hand, is said to break the balls.

IN BAULK.—A ball is said to be in baulk when it is between the baulk-line and the bottom cushion.

BREAK.—The series of scores terminating with the stroke in which the player fails to score is called a break.

SCREW AND SCREW-BACK.—This is putting a rotatory motion on a ball, causing it to spin on a horizontal axis backwards. Screw is put on by striking the ball *below the centre*.

FOLLOWING STROKE.—This is putting a rotatory motion on a ball, causing it to spin on a horizontal axis forwards instead of backwards. This stroke is made by striking the ball high up *above the centre*. It is useful in playing a cannon or a losing hazard when the two balls—or the ball and the pocket, as the case may be—are *nearly* in a direct line with the cue-ball. When the stroke is played with considerable force, the cue-ball seeming to stop almost " dead " before running on, it is known as a *stun follow through*.

SIDE.—This is a rotatory motion put on a ball, making it spin on a perpendicular axis.

In each of the foregoing cases the ball is made to take, after striking another ball, or a cushion, a direction different from that which it would take did no such rotatory motion exist.

In order that the learner may the better understand the meaning of screw, screw-back, following stroke, and side, we will illustrate them by means of a diagram.

In Fig. 1 we will suppose the red ball to be placed on the middle spot in the table, M. The player places his own ball in the centre spot in the baulk-line, K, and aims his ball, first of all, so as to strike the object ball with the ordinary HALF-BALL STROKE—that is, the centre of his ball advances towards the extreme edge of the object ball.

In Fig. 2, O is the object ball ; S, the striker's ball. In order to play the half-ball stroke, it is necessary that the player should aim so that the centre of his ball is running directly towards the point E, the extreme edge of the horizontal diameter of the object ball. Of course, as the diagram shows, he will not strike the ball at this point, but as S_2, in the point C. When the object ball is thus struck, the striker's ball, supposing there is no screw on the ball, will take the direction indicated as S_2. This angle is called the NATURAL ANGLE ; about this natural angle we shall have to say more by-and-by. Suppose the stroke played thus. After playing, the ball will follow the line M P (Fig. 1). Now suppose some strong screw had been put on the ball by hitting it low down. The ball, owing to the *hit*, and to its after-contact with M, would follow the line M P ; but, owing to the backward rotatory motion given to it by the screwing stroke, it has a tendency to run back towards K, the point from which it started. Under the influence of these two forces, the ball takes the middle course, M P_1. In other words, the striker, although he hits the object ball a half-ball stroke, screws into the middle pocket.

Now suppose, instead of hitting the ball *below* the centre, he hits it high up above the *centre*, so as to make the ball rotate forwards. After the balls have come in contact, the rotatory motion forwards has a tendency to make the striker's ball run onwards towards the top cushion and away from K, the point

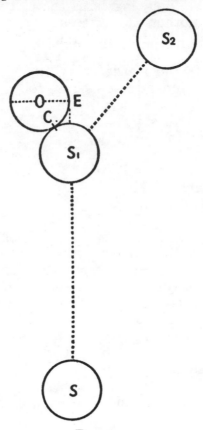

FIG. 2.

from which it started ; but the contact with the object ball would—did no rotatory motion exist—cause it to follow the direction of the line M P. Under the influence of these two forces the ball again takes a middle course, and follows the line M P.

If the player hit M *full*, that is, in its nearest point, and put screw on, his own ball would, after striking M,

stop and run back towards K, fast or not according to
the amount of rotatory motion he imparted to his own
ball when he struck it. If, on the other hand, he hit
his own ball high up and above the centre—the following
stroke—his ball, after striking M, would *follow on* in the
direction of the spots, P and S.

In putting on *side*, the ball is caused to rotate on a
perpendicular axis. For instance (*vide* Fig. 1), suppose
the player places his ball on the centre spot in baulk, K,
and hits the cushion in the point T without putting on any
side, then the ball would rebound in the direction of T R,
just as the angles of incidence and reflection are equal.
Suppose, however, the player strikes his ball on the right-
hand side, causing it to rotate on a perpendicular axis.
When the ball touches the cushion at T, this rotation,
owing to the friction between the ball and the cushion,
causes the ball to take the direction shown in the diagram
by the line T R_1. If, on the other hand, the player
hits his ball on the left-hand side, the ball will
rebound in the contrary direction shown by the line
T R_2. This latter stroke is what every player has to
make when he wishes to give a miss in baulk. Side
has but little effect till the ball touches a cushion or
another ball.

FLUKE —When a player plays for one thing, misses
it, and gets another, the stroke is called a fluke. Thus,
if a man plays for a cannon, misses, and runs into a pocket
off the other ball instead, it is a fluke. If, however, he
plays for the cannon and *makes* it, and *then* his ball runs
into a pocket, it is not regarded as a fluke, although he
gets what he did not play for.

A JENNY is a losing hazard into one of the middle
pockets off a ball near to one of the lower side cushions.
A LONG JENNY is a losing hazard off a ball similarly
placed in one of the top pockets.

SPOT STROKE.—A stroke by which a player pockets
the red ball from the billiard spot, at the same time
bringing his own ball into position to pocket the red
again, when the latter is replaced on the billiard spot.
This may not be done more than twice in succession,
that is, without another score intervening. A game
in which this rule is observed, and nowadays that means
every game, is termed SPOT-BARRED.

THE MASSÉ SHOT.—A very effective shot from the spectators' point of view, and very useful when one has to make a cannon in which the two object balls are in a line with the striker's ball, all being close together and no cushion being conveniently available. The cue is held with the tip coming down on the ball, the butt pointed towards the ceiling at an angle of about 70 degrees, the direction being towards the extreme edge, left or right as the case requires, of the first object ball. The cue ball is struck with a " pinching " stroke at a point about a quarter from the top and at the spot that, were it not for the direction of the cue, the ball would be pinched off at a right-angle to the line to the object balls. The cue-direction, however, pulls the ball round, making it follow a line midway between these ; and if the ball has been properly struck this retrograde motion will gradually overcome that imparted by the " pinch," and the ball will come round in a curve towards the first object ball, contact with which will rob it of all but the forward motion, and it will roll on and make the cannon. The stroke needs a considerable amount of practice ; do not hit hard, and see that your cue is well chalked ; and be careful not to cut the cloth.

TO GET ON THE SPOT. When a player gets his own ball into an easy position for playing the spot stroke, he is said to get " on the spot."

KISS.—When the balls come into contact a second time they are said to kiss.

NURSERY CANNONS.—A series of cannons made when all three balls are very close together. As stated above, no more than twenty-five *consecutive* ball-to-ball cannons may be made.

SAFETY.—When any one plays with the object of leaving the balls in such a position that it is next to impossible for his opponent to score by his next stroke, he is said to play for safety.

TWIST.—Another name for screw.

STAB.—A stroke made to leave one's own ball on the spot occupied by the object ball.

LINE BALL.—A ball whose centre is exactly on the baulk-line ; such a ball is, of course, not playable from baulk.

FOUL.—A stroke which infringes any rule of the game.

OBJECT BALL.—The ball upon which the striker's own ball impinges.

JAMMED.—When the two object balls touch in the jaws of a pocket, and each touches a different cushion at the same time.

Reverting to the subject of the half-ball stroke, it is of the greatest importance that all beginners should understand how much depends upon their being able to hit the object ball in the way shown in Fig. 2. Their success will depend upon the mastery of this stroke.

First of all, the beginner must learn to hit his own ball freely. We would recommend him to take his first practice-lesson by learning simply how to hit a ball hard—*i.e.*, have only one ball to play with. After he has gained a certain amount of what is called freedom of cue, he must next learn to aim at the object ball, so that he always hits it in what we have described as the half-stroke. To ascertain whether he has required sufficient " freedom of cue," let him see how many times he can send his own ball up and down the table.

It is important to learn to strike your own ball hard *without putting on side.* Place your ball on the spot in the middle of the baulk-line ; now play straight up at the top cushion *hard*, sending it directly over all the other spots. If you hit your ball fairly in the centre, it will come back straight ; if you don't you will have put on side, and you can tell how much by the angle at which the ball rebounds from the top cushion. Commence learning, therefore, by hitting your own ball hard enough to send it four or five times up and down the table without side. This is not so easy as many persons would think.

Having learnt to hit his own ball fairly in the centre, the beginner must next learn to hit the object ball a half-ball stroke : and for this purpose it is a very good exercise, at the commencement, to place the red ball on the spot, S (*vide* Fig. 3), and the striker's ball in position A, that is, just in front of the middle pocket, an inch or two along an imaginary line drawn from the centre of the middle pocket to the edge of the object ball placed on the spot.

The losing hazard off the red into the right-hand top pocket ought now to be a certainty, it being a simple half-ball stroke. After making the hazard, the red ball should, after striking the top cushion, rebound in a line right down the centre of the table (as shown by the dotted line W W).

By watching the direction of the red ball after striking, the beginner will be able to see if he has struck the ball correctly. If he hits it too fine, the red ball will come down the table on the left of the centre line, W W. Should he strike the red ball too full, the red will come down the table on the right-hand side of the line W W.

When the beginner has practised this stroke till he can make a certainty of it, he may begin to practise what may be called "forcing hazards." For this purpose he can gradually place his own ball lower and lower down the table, as shown in Fig. 3. Suppose, for instance, he places his own ball at B. There is still an easy losing hazard off the red into the top corner pocket, the only difference being that the stroke must be played *harder*. When the ball was placed at A, the losing hazard could be made by simply "dropping" on the ball. In fact, it could be played so slowly, that the red ball, after striking the top cushion, would not rebound more than a foot down the table. As, however, the striker's ball is placed lower and lower down the table in the positions shown by B and C, so the stroke must be played harder and harder.

Another perfect half-ball stroke that can be played either slowly or fast, is shown by the two lines, in Fig. 3, drawn from S to the two top pockets. Suppose a ball to be placed in the centre of either top pocket, or a few inches along the line drawn from the pocket to the spot. Then it is a simple half-ball stroke to go in off the red into the other top pocket.

Place the white ball an inch or two away from the top pocket along the line drawn, and place the red ball on the spot. Then drop on to the ball quietly. The hazard is easy, and, supposing you play from, say, the left-hand top pocket, you will not only make the losing hazard, but you will leave the red ball in a

position for another easy hazard into the middle pocket.
Your own ball, the white for the next stroke will be in
baulk · the red ball will, if you play the stroke correctly,

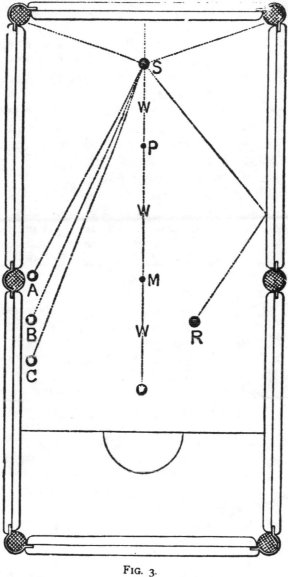

FIG. 3.

travel along the dotted line shown in the diagram, and
stop somewhere about R, thus leaving an easy hazard
next time into the right-hand middle pocket.

Having thus practised the half-ball stroke with slow strength and fast strength, the next point to be considered is losing hazards into the top pockets from baulk. These losing hazards may be called the very backbone of the game.

The chief difficulty experienced by a beginner will be to know where to spot his ball in baulk. This will only come with practice. The eye will gradually accustom itself to the angle. A good player can tell at a glance whether or not a stroke is easy. We would recommend anyone learning the game to make one or two spots on the table as follows. First place a card or thin piece of wood upright against the top cushion, and then measure down the table 3 ft. 9½ in., A (Fig. 4). Make a little cross on the cloth, and there place the red ball. Next place the white ball on the centre spot in baulk (K). Now there is an easy losing hazard, if the stroke be played with the ordinary half-ball stroke, into either top pocket off the red ball.

This stroke is capital practice for the beginner, as it gets his eye used to the angle which we have called the " natural " angle.

The advantage of playing the natural angle is that, supposing you fail to hit the ball *exactly* as you intended, a very slight error in aiming does not alter materially the direction of your own ball after it has come into contact with the object ball.

Suppose, now, the beginner has succeeded in going into first one top pocket and then the other several times, let him place the red on M, the centre spot (Fig. 4), and his own ball in baulk on the proper spot to go into say, the left hand top pocket off M. The proper spot is B in the diagram, but then where is B? B *ought* to be seven and a half inches from K, the centre spot in baulk Similarly if the player wished to go into the right-hand pocket off the red ball at M, he would have to spot his own ball seven and a half inches to the right of K.

As a rule, beginners all make the same mistake. They will, as a rule, spot their ball too near to K, and, of course, the further they are out in their reckoning, the more they have to learn. It would be as well, however, to let a beginner play the stroke. Suppose, for instance, that instead of spotting his ball at B, seven and a half inches to the left of K, he spots his ball only five inches to the left of K. Let him play his

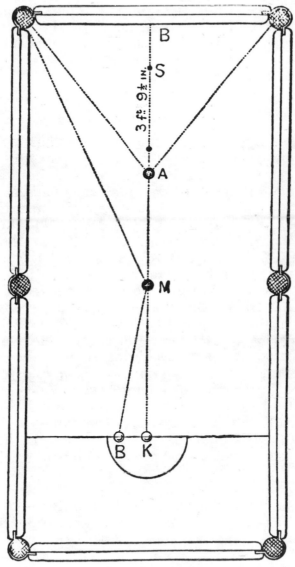

FIG. 4

stroke, and instead of going into the left-hand top pocket, his ball will strike the left-hand upper cushion several inches below the pocket. Now let him measure

the correct seven and a half inches, and, although **he**
will think he is going to miss the stroke, to his own surprise
he will make it. It is very good practice to **go**
in off a ball placed on the middle spot M, first **into**
one top pocket, and then into another, being careful
always to watch the direction taken by the red ball **after**
the stroke, with an eye to playing the right strength **to**
leave an easy losing hazard next time.

We next come to—

Middle-Pocket Hazards.

We will suppose that the beginner has now **fairly**
learned how to play losing hazards in the top pockets,
and also how to spot his ball for the natural angle.
In playing losing hazards into the middle pockets,
it is quite as important that this angle, and this only,
should be used. In Fig. 5 we give two illustrations
of simple hazards into the middle pockets. The hazards
themselves are, comparatively speaking, easy ; but the
chief point to be borne in mind is position—that is,
having made the hazard, how can we leave the red
ball so that there shall be another easy hazard next
time? The endeavour should be to keep the red ball
in the centre of the table as much as possible. As a rule,
the game is to play to bring down the red ball
over the middle pocket again. Now, in Fig. 5, suppose
the player at H tries to go into the right-hand middle
pocket off a ball at D, the proper play would be to strike
the red ball so that it goes up the table, and, following the dotted lines, returns to D_1. If the player
hits the red a trifle too fine the red ball would travel
to the left of this dotted line, and a losing hazard would
be left off the red into one of the top pockets. If, however, in playing the stroke, the player hits his ball a trifle
too full, the red ball would then probably travel along the
dotted line terminating in D_2, and there would be little
chance of scoring next time.

A similar stroke is shown in the left-hand middle
pocket. The striker spots his ball at B, and goes
into the middle pocket off a ball at A. The endeavour
should be to send the red ball up the table in the
direction shown by the dotted line A C.

It the red is sent up the table to the left of this line, unless very accurate strength is played, there will be probably no score left next time. If, however, the

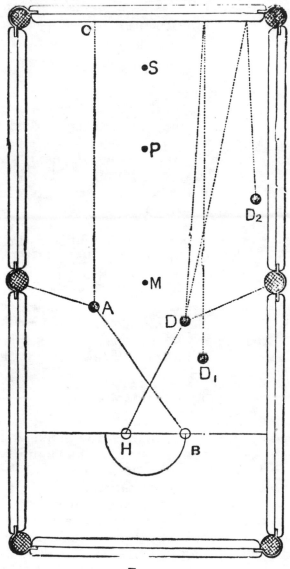

FIG. 5.

player is careful not to hit the ball at A too full, the ball will travel rather to the right of the line A C, and then, being in the middle of the table, if the strength is insufficient to bring the ball over the *middle* pocket, there will still be a losing hazard left into one of the top pockets. This is the chief point to be considered in making losing hazards into the middle pockets, and naturally introduces that all-important subject for consideration in learning to play Billiards, viz. :—

POSITION.

There are thousands of men who have played Billiards all their lives, but are still very poor players, because in learning to play they never studied position. They play simply for the stroke, and never give a thought to what will happen in the next stroke. If you watch a first-class player make a break, you will probably see him make a long series of very easy strokes, any one of which you yourself could have made with the greatest ease. The one difference, in fact, between your play and his would have been this— that you would make the easy stroke, and fail to leave another easy stroke next time, whereas he would *not* fail ; hence *his* break—a series of easy strokes · hence *your* break—one easy stroke, and a breakdown.

Space will not allow us to give a long series of diagrams, explaining the various ways of playing for position, but we will indicate a few general principles. First—

LOSING HAZARDS.

In playing for any losing hazard, it should be remembered that the position of the striker's own ball after the stroke is fixed—it will be " in hand." Hence, he has only to consider the position of the object ball, which we will suppose to be the red. Now, the object of the player is to leave an easy stroke next time. As a rule, the red ball must be hit in a certain spot to ensure the hazard, the only exception being when it is close to the pocket, and the player's ball close to the red. In this latter case it is often the best plan just to graze the red so as hardly to move it, and—supposing, of course, it is not one of the bottom pockets—to leave the red ball over the pocket where it is. If, however, you are some way off the red ball, you will have to hit it in one place in order to make certain of the hazard. Consequently position will simply depend upon *strength*. It is as well to remember that if a ball is left anywhere near the middle of the table, there is always a hazard left next time.

No player can leave a ball on a certain spot *exactly*. The greatest expert cannot do more than leave it " there or thereabouts." In fact, very often in playing a losing hazard, all we have to do is not so much to play where to leave the red, but *where not* to leave the red. Sometimes it may be the best play to try to leave it close to the white, so that the next stroke will be an easy cannon. As a rule, however, the best play is to leave the red over a pocket, so that you can go in off it again next time. The best " all-round " breaks are made by a series of losing hazards with occasional cannons. It is in playing cannons that the chief difficulty arises in getting position, but before we discuss cannons, a few words about—

WINNING HAZARDS.

It is evident that after playing a winning hazard the position of the object ball is known—viz., as a rule, on the spot. Should the player put in the white, his only excuse must be either at the next shot, or after making such scores off the red as he can see are " on," to make a baulk : for his opponent, next time he plays, can spot his ball anywhere he likes in the D, and if the other balls are out of baulk, he is almost certain to score. Consequently, the only winning hazards worth discussing are red winning hazards. In making a winning hazard, the player, as a rule, should try to get near the spot himself, so as to play for the spot, or else play to leave his own ball where there would be an easy losing hazard off the spot next time. In Fig. 6 we give two illustrations. Suppose, first of all, the red is over the right-hand middle pocket at H, and the player is in hand ; the proper play would be to put the ball in the pocket, and then run up the table towards L, getting into position for the spot, but the ordinary amateur, if when he gets this position, can only make one hazard and then breaks down, had better not play for the spot at all. In the position given in the diagram, it would be better play to put the red ball in the pocket, and try and leave your own ball at H₁, then

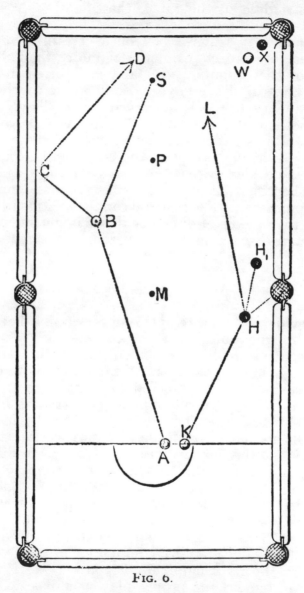

FIG. 6.

there is a certain losing hazard next time off the red into the left-hand top pocket.

Again, suppose the balls are left in the position W

(the white ball), and X (the red ball), many beginners would play for the six stroke, but success would leave the red ball on the spot, and the striker in hand. The proper play is to put the red ball in the pocket and leave your own in the jaws, thus leaving an in off the red into the opposite top pocket, a stroke in which it is always easy to leave the red over the middle pocket for the following stroke.

However, as we have said, the chief difficulty in getting good position is when playing—

CANNONS.

Here the player has to consider the position of all three balls at the end of the stroke. There are two ways of getting position in playing a cannon. We can leave the red over a pocket, or play to bring the balls together. It is obvious that when all the balls are close together, it is almost a certainty that there is an easy score left : but *see* the MASSÉ SHOT above.

Suppose, in Fig. 6, the red ball is on the spot S, the white ball at B, and the player in hand. There is, of course, a cannon " on," but how ought he to play it so as to leave an easy score next time ?

The game here is to leave the balls together at the end of the stroke. The striker spots his ball at A, so as to strike B the ordinary half-ball stroke. The stroke should be played slowly, so that the white ball rebounds off the left-hand upper side cushion at C, and travels towards D. The player's own ball hits the red gently, and all three balls are left close together near the top of the table, one of the best positions possible.

In playing to leave the red over a pocket a good deal depends upon whether you play off the red or off the white. For instance, in Fig. 7, suppose the striker in hand, and the two other balls stationed at A and R. If A is the red ball, the stroke is played one way, and if A is the white ball it is played another way. If A is the red you should play to make the cannon with just sufficient strength to double the red across the table, and leave it in position A_1, over the middle pocket. If R was the red ball, you ought to play with just sufficient strength, and also sufficiently accurately, to hit the red ball full and leave it in position R_1, over the left-hand top pocket.

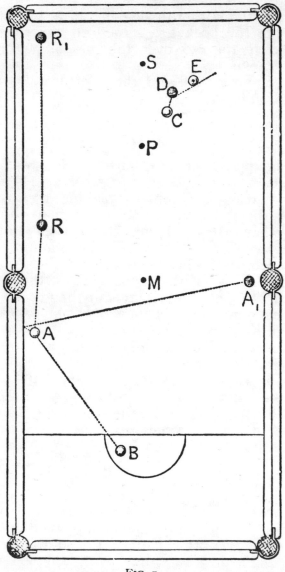

FIG. 7.

Another important point in playing cannons is to play what is called " outside " the balls when they are close together. Suppose, in Fig. 7, the balls are

in the position shown in C, D, and E.   C is the player's
ball.   If he hits D and makes the cannon hitting E full,
he separates the balls, but if he plays so as just to touch
D and E, hitting them on the extreme edge, he keeps them
together.

Although in actual play the " spot stroke " is
" barred," it affords excellent practice to the beginner,
and we will therefore, in conclusion, give a brief
explanation of it.   It is in fact, as we have already seen,
a series of spot hazards, but we must give the
warning that though nothing looks more simple,
nothing really is more difficult.   The simplest position for
the spot stroke is when the striker's ball is in a direct
line with the red and the pocket (Fig. 8).   Of course,
the proper play is to screw back and bring your own
ball into the place from which it started.   Were this a
" certainty," and were the stroke allowed, the striker
would go on scoring for ever ; but sooner or later his
ball will come back slightly nearer the top cushion, or
rather more away from it.   In the first of these cases
(Fig. 9), the best plan is to follow through the red ball.
This can be done simply by a following stroke.   A is
the striker's ball ; B the position of the striker's ball
after the stroke.   When the balls are nearly, but not quite
straight, this is done by means of a stab shot.   In
the second supposed case the striker's ball is at A
(Fig. 10).   The play now is to drop on to the red with
sufficient strength to put it in, and get position at B
off the top cushion.   Sometimes a little side is necessary.

In position 4 (Fig. 11) the striker's ball A is nearly,
but not quite, in a line with the red ball and the pocket.
When this is the case, the play is to run through the red
and get position off the two cushions.   You must hit
your ball very high and with a great deal of freedom of
cue.   It is a stroke in which a beginner would probably
fail.

It is as well to know within what limits the spot stroke
can be played.   Suppose we draw a line X Y (Fig.
12), through the spot S, parallel with the top cushion.
If the striker's ball is within this line or nearer to
the top cushion, it is no use cutting in the red
gently, as position would be lost.   The only plan to

recover position is to play all round the table. Suppose the striker's ball is at A, he cuts the red

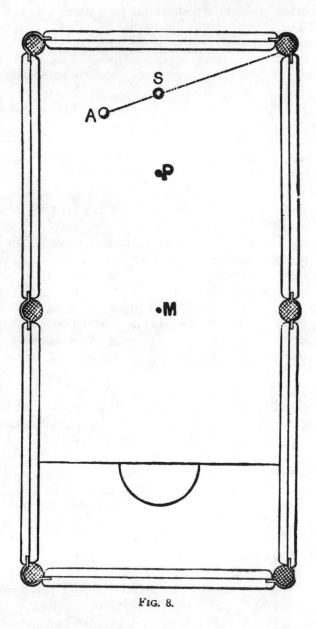

FIG. 8.

into the right-hand top pocket and recovers position by going right round the table till his ball stops at B.

This is a difficult stroke, but is often played for and obtained.

The Rules of the Billiards Association and Control

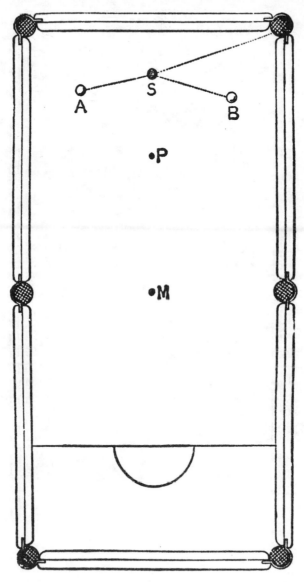

FIG. 9.

Council, by which the English game is now governed, were issued in 1920 and are, as has been said above, the copyright of the Council. They are based on the old Rimington-Wilson Code, and have particularly in view the reduction of safety misses to a minimum and the imposition of one definite penalty for each and

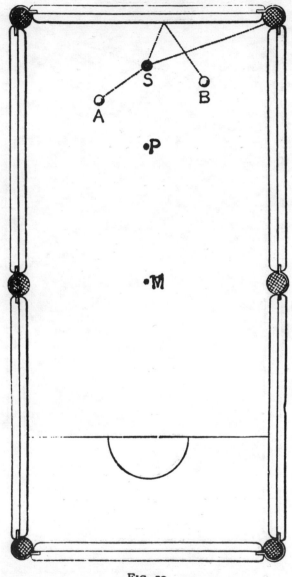

FIG. 10.

every kind of foul stroke or illegitimate miss. Special stress is laid on the following provisions :—

A player may not make two misses in successive innings,

unless he or the opponent scores after the first miss, or a double baulk intervenes. (*Rule* 12.)

When striker's ball remains touching another ball,

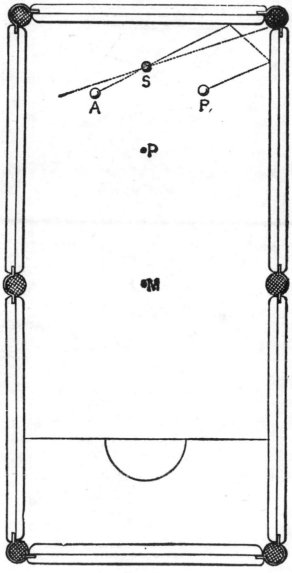

FIG. 11.

red ball shall be spotted, and non-striker's ball, if on the table, shall be placed on the centre spot; striker shall play from the D: if non-striker's ball is in hand, red shall be spotted, and striker shall play from the D as before. (*Rule* 13.)

Consecutive ball-to-ball cannons are limited to 25;

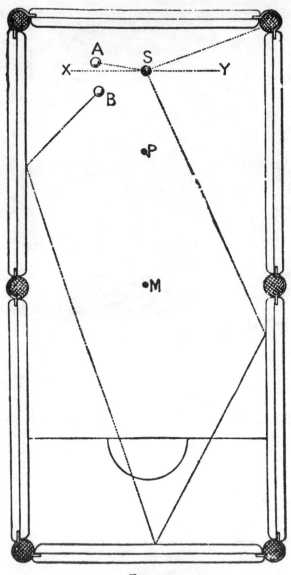

FIG. 12.

on the completion of this number the break shall only be continued by the intervention of a hazard or indirect cannon. (*Rule* 10.)

This rule put an end to the enormous breaks made with the famous " anchor-cannon " shot, in which the player got the balls jammed in a corner pocket and then went on tapping them with his own till he got tired. Reece once pulled up a break of 499,135 *unfinished* by means of this !

PENALTIES.

If, after contact with another ball, striker's or any other ball is forced off the table, the non-striker shall add two points to his score. (*Rule* 18.)

For a foul stroke the striker loses his turn and cannot score for that stroke : his opponent may go on from where the balls are left (red being spotted if off the table), or, at his discretion, he may have the red spotted, the white placed on the centre spot, and play from hand. (*Rule* 18.)

For refusing to continue the game when called upon by the referee or marker to do so, or for conduct which, in the opinion of the referee or marker, is wilfully or persistently unfair, a player shall lose the game. (*Rule* 18.)

POOL

POOL is the most sociable game for the billiard table, as any number of players can take part in it ; and, though it is a game in which only losing hazards count, the most successful player is not necessarily he who can " pot " with the deadliest accuracy, but he who combines potting with effectively playing for position. A man *must* know how to leave himself for the succeeding shot, and *must* know how and when to play for safety ; otherwise, in spite of accurate potting, he will never be more than an average player. This remark applies with equal force to " Snooker," and the other games of the Pool family.

There are several varieties of Pool ; that which we here describe is the only one recognized by the Billiards Association and Control Council, and in most circles has supplanted all the others. Each player has a ball of a different colour, which he uses throughout the game as his cue-ball, and buys three " lives " to start with, the money so collected forming a pool which, in the case of three players or less, goes to the survivor. When there are more than three players, and two only are left with an equal number of lives, they divide the pool ; if they have an unequal number the game goes on until they become equal, when they divide, or until one player loses all his lives, when the pool goes to the survivor. The pool is known as the *major stakes*, the forfeits for fouls, etc.—always a third of the sum contributed by each player to the pool—as the *minor stakes*.

The order of play is usually settled by as many balls as players being shaken out of the " pool bottle " by the marker, each taking one in turn before seeing it ; they then play in the following order, and keep to this order throughout the game —White places his ball on the spot ; the Red plays at white, Yellow at red, Green at yellow, Brown at green, Blue at brown, Pink at blue, Spot-white at pink, Spot-red at spot-white, and so on till all have come in when White plays at the ball of the last player and is in turn played on again by Red.

The object of the game is to pocket the ball played on (and, of course, to avoid being pocketed oneself), and when this is done, when—in other words—the striker has "taken a life" from the owner of the pocketed ball, striker continues to play on the nearest ball as long as he can take a life and does not make a foul, till all the other balls are off the table; he then places his own on the spot as at the commencement of the game, and the next player plays from hand. Balls pocketed remain in hand until it is the turn of the owner to play, when he plays from hand; baulk is no protection at any time; the next in turn plays when the striker fails to score or makes a foul; and the winner is the player who remains longest in the game.

A life is lost, and the loser loses his turn and pays the agreed forfeit, when the owner's ball is lawfully pocketed, and also in the following cases of "fouls": When the striker pockets his own ball, forces it (or any other ball) off the table, or touches it (or any other) before it has finished rolling: when he misses the ball he is lawfully "on," or strikes another with his own before hitting this; when he strikes two balls simultaneously; and when he plays out of turn. or with a wrong ball.

A player who loses a life in any way pays the player upon whose ball he was—or ought to have been—playing, unless the loss is incurred by playing out of turn or with the wrong ball, in either of which cases he pays the preceding player. If he misses his ball and in the same stroke pockets another he loses a life, his ball is removed from the table, and both balls remain in hand until it becomes the turn of their owners to play. If the striker pockets the ball he is on, and in the same stroke loses a life, the player whose ball is pocketed is not penalized in any way, but his ball remains in hand until it is his turn to play. Not more than one life is lost for any number of fouls in the same stroke, and the first foul determines the receiver of the forfeit.

If at the beginning of a stroke the striker's ball is touching the ball he is on, he must remove his ball and play from hand ; and if, *in similar circumstances*, his ball is touching some other ball, such ball must be removed from the table until the stroke is played : but, if *after scoring* the cue-ball is touching another when it has come to rest, the striker must play away from such ball without moving it and may pocket any other ball, but shall incur no penalty from a miss.

The rule governing the removal from the table of balls that interfere with the striker's freedom of action, and the replacement of such balls, is of such importance that we give it *in extenso :—*

12.—BALLS UP. The striker is, in all cases, entitled to a stroke clear of a ball which is not *on*, directly in a straight line to any point of the ball he is *on* (if in hand, from the centre of the baulk line). The Referee shall take up any ball that interferes with such stroke or the reasonable use of the striker's hands or rest. The Referee shall replace all balls so removed after the stroke. Should the striker's ball, after a score, come to rest and occupy the position of a ball *up*, the striker plays on the ball then nearest. If there is no other ball on the table, he must spot his ball, and the next player continues from where his ball is replaced by the Referee, or from hand. Should any ball come to rest and occupy a position from which a ball is *up*, the Referee shall take all such balls up, and replace the balls in the order of their turn, as the position becomes unoccupied, and where this is not feasible, must direct the striker to play from hand.

If the striker is prevented from playing direct at the ball he is on by being *angled*, he can have any ball removed for the purpose of taking his stroke off the cushion, but his own ball must not be touched.

We now come to *starring*, a method by which a player who has lost his three lives can buy more. In a pool of six players, or less, only one star is allowed, and the first player to lose his three lives is entitled to purchase it by paying into the pool the value of three lives · for this he receives as many lives as remain to the player with the lowest number. He must decide whether or not he will take it before the next stroke is played : if he refuses, it is at the option of the second to lose three lives : if he, too, refuses, the third, and so on until only two players are left, when the privilege ceases. When there are seven or more in the pool two stars are allowed, and the taker of the second—who may already have taken the first—pays double.

If two or more balls are pocketed by the same stroke, including the ball played at, and the owners of each have only one life left and a star is available, the option of starring belongs to the owner of the ball first struck ; if he refuses, and more than one remain, they must toss up for it—which is also done by the owners of balls pocketed simultaneously when the ball played at was not pocketed.

Any number of balls may be pocketed by the same stroke, provided that the first ball struck by the striker's ball is that that he was lawfully *on*.

If the cue-ball is still on the table after the striker has lost a life, it shall be removed and remain in hand until the striker's next turn, the next player playing on the nearest ball. If at any time there is a question as to the distances of balls it is settled by the Referee ; he measures from the player's ball to the others, except when player is in hand, in which case the measurement is made from the centre of the baulk line. If the distances are equal the owners of the balls must toss up.

A player, or his ball, is said to be *dead* when he has lost all his lives.

For the rest. Pool is governed by the same general rules as Billiards : *i.e.*, the " push-stroke " is barred, the ball must not be struck more than once in the same stroke, and must be struck only with the tip of the cue, one of striker's feet must be touching the floor at the moment of striking, etc.

PYRAMIDS

THIS game is usually played by two persons,* with sixteen balls—one white, and fifteen red. The latter are arranged in the form of a solid triangle, with its apex on the Pyramid spot (P in Fig. 1, p. 313), and its base towards the top cushion and lying parallel thereto.

At the commencement of the game, one player leads off from the half-circle, and plays at any one of the red balls. Should he pocket one or more balls, he scores one for each red ball pocketed. He continues playing till he fails to score.

If a player gives a miss, or pockets the white ball, a point is taken off his score, and he must replace one of the red balls he has previously pocketed on the Pyramid spot, if unoccupied, or, if that be occupied, as near to it as possible in a line directly behind it. If he has not previously pocketed a ball, he *owes* one, and must pay it by replacing the first ball that he pockets later on.

After a miss, the opponent follows on from where the white ball stopped : but after a pocketing of the white ball, the opponent follows on from the half-circle. In playing at a red ball, baulk is no obstacle.

If a striker pockets the white ball, and at the same time pockets one or more of the red balls, he gains nothing by the stroke, but one is deducted from his score : the red balls pocketed must be spotted on the table, as well as one of the striker's red balls previously pocketed. The opponent follows on from the half-circle.

When the red balls have all been pocketed but one, the player making the last score continues playing with the white ball, and his opponent uses the other. If a striker now make a miss, or pocket the ball he is playing with, the opponent adds one to his score, and the game is over.

* Four, or any convenient even number, can play, sides being arranged.

SHELL OUT

THIS is a form of Pyramids in which more than two persons play, and each is for himself and against all the others.

When a striker pockets a red ball he receives from each of the other players a stake previously agreed on. No ball* is ever replaced on the table after a miss, or after pocketing the white. Should any player miss or pocket the white, he pays for each of the other players as well as for himself whenever the next red ball is pocketed. When only one red ball is left in play, each player continues playing with the white. Pocketing the red is now paid double all round; and if a striker miss, or pocket the white, he pays double all round.

The order of play is drawn for at the beginning of each game.

* Except, of course, the white.

SNOOKER, or SNOOKER'S POOL

THIS popular version of Pool is really a combination of Pool and Pyramids : it is a game solely of winning hazards, and the remarks at the opening of our Pool section, when we tried to impress upon the reader that accurate " potting " is by no means sufficient of itself to make a first-class pool player, applies with at least equal force to the game at present under consideration. At the same time, we would warn bad hazard strikers to think twice before joining in Snooker, even for small stakes, with better players than themselves for, with the high values of the pool balls, large scores can be run up by an expert, and those players who own the lowest scores at the end of the game may find themselves mulcted for quite a considerable sum, especially when playing " all against all."

Snooker is played on the ordinary billiard table by two or more persons, either as sides, or independently, with the fifteen red balls, six pool balls, and the white—the latter being used by each player in turn as the cue-ball. The fifteen " reds " are placed on the table by means of the triangle in the same position as at Pyramids, *i.e.*, with the apex on the Pyramid spot and the base parallel to and nearest the top cushion ; and the scoring value of each is one.

The following are the six pool balls, or " colours," as they are usually called their order in the list should be noted, and they have the scoring value shown :—

Yellow	.	.	scoring value		.	.	2
Green	.	.	,,	,,	.	.	3
Brown	.	.	,,	,,	.	.	4
Blue	.	.	,,	,,	.	.	5
Pink	.	.	,,	,,	.	.	6
Black	.	.	,,	,,	.	.	7

At the beginning of the game Yellow is placed on the right-hand corner of the D, Green on the left, and Brown

346

in the middle of the baulk line · Blue is placed on the centre spot, Pink touching the apex of the triangle of reds, and Black on the billiard spot. After the red balls have been moved, when Pink has to be respotted it is placed on the pyramid spot.

The order of play—which must be kept to throughout the game—having been decided, the first player takes the white and plays from hand at red : he *must* strike a red, and if he fails to do so he plays again (from hand) until he is successful, no penalty being exacted for such initial misses. Each player is bound to play at a red ball first, and having pocketed it (or another red or reds) he is " on " any pool ball he likes · if he lawfully pockets this he scores the value of the ball, and is again on the red, and so on. While any red balls remain on the table the colours, after having been pocketed, are replaced on their respective spots* before the next stroke is made (reds are never respotted) · but after all the red balls have been taken, the players play at the colours in the order as given above, until every ball has been lawfully pocketed, or the last black has been " given away," when the game is at an end. The player who takes the last red can, with his next stroke, play at any colour : if he pockets it the colour is respotted, and the striker is then on the yellow : from this point no ball is respotted, unless it is forced off the table or pocketed unlawfully. If at any time the cue-ball is forced off the table or pocketed, the next player plays from hand : otherwise, when the striker fails to score, the next player plays from where the cue-ball comes to rest. Baulk is no protection at any time. There is no obligation upon the striker to nominate the ball he is on unless he is requested to do so by a player : but he may do so unasked, for his own protection.

Snooker is played under slightly differing rules— especially as regards penalties for " fouls "—in different

---

* If the spot on which a colour should be replaced is occupied it must be placed on the first of the following spots that happen to be vacant, viz., the billiard spot, pyramid spot, centre spot, middle of baulk line, left corner of D, right corner of D. If there is *no* spot available, then the ball is placed as near its own spot as possible, between it and the top cushion.

localities : but as there is a code of rules authorized by the Billiards Association and Control Council it is just as well that these should be observed. Many of the minor points here to be given (all taken from the above-mentioned code) do not seem to be sufficiently well known ; and we would urge snooker players and club secretaries to take particular note of them, and, further, to obtain a copy of the Rules, which it is impossible for us to give here in their entirety, from the Council.

In addition to the usual foul strokes (such as touching the ball more than once, forcing a ball off the table, playing when both feet are off the floor, before the balls have come to a rest or have been spotted, striking otherwise than with the tip of the cue, playing out of turn or with the wrong ball, etc.), the following are the fouls special to Snooker and similar games —Making a miss or a losing hazard : causing the cue-ball to strike or pocket a ball the player is not "on" · and striking more than one ball (other than reds) simultaneously. After making a foul of any kind the striker (a) cannot score, (b) loses his turn, (c) loses the right of leaving a " snooker," and (d) forfeits certain points.

With regard to (c). A player is said to be " snookered " when a ball he is not " on " is in a direct line between the cue-ball (or, if in hand, between the centre of the baulk line) and any point of the ball he is " on." Now, if after a foul stroke the next player is snookered with regard to all the reds or to the colour he is " on," he may then nominate any ball and play on it. If he pockets it (or has to " give away " on it) it shall score as though it were the ball that striker would have been " on " but for the " snooker " : if a red is still on the table he continues his turn on any colour (provided that he has scored), but if all the reds are gone, on the colour in regard to which he has been snookered.

These are the forfeits payable for the various foul strokes : points forfeited must be added to the opponent's score, all opponents benefiting should there be a number playing " all against all."

Foul Stroke	Penalty.
For causing the cue-ball to strike a red when on a colour.	7 points (*not* the value of the ball striker was '' on.'')
For playing with other than the cue-ball.	7 points.
For a miss (including running a coup, or forcing the cue-ball off the table).	The value of the ball striker was on, or 4 points, *whichever is the higher*.
For striking a colour when on a red or anoth r colour.	Th value of the ball struck, or the ball he was on, *whichever is the higher*.
For pocketing any colour that is not on, or for forcing any ball off the table.	The value of the ball so treated.
For forcing the cue-ball off the table after impact, or for a losing hazard.	The value of the ball struck, or of the ball striker was on, *whichever is the higher*.
For pocketing more than one ball (other than reds) by the same stroke, or for striking more than one ball (other than reds) simultaneously.	The value of the highest-scoring ball so pocketed or struck.
For other fouls.	4 points; the value of the ball fouled or pocketed : or the value of the ball striker was on, *whichever is the higher*.

As at billiards, the push-stroke is barred, and the first impact of the cue-ball governs all strokes ; if the cue-ball be touching another it must be played away from it without moving it, otherwise it is counted a push-stroke ; and if, in these circumstances, the cue-ball strike and lawfully pocket a ball that is '' on,'' such ball shall be scored, while if in thus playing away from a ball that is '' on '' the striker makes a miss or hits some ball not '' on '' he shall incur no penalty.

A cue-ball that is angled must be played from where it lies ; unless it is angled after a foul, when it is played from hand.

The game is ended by the first score made or forfeit given when only the black ball remains on the table ; unless the scores are then equal, when the black is spotted, and the players toss up for choice of playing at it from hand. The next score or forfeit ends the game. The winner is not necessarily he who takes the last black, but the player, or side, making the highest score.

At Snooker the great thing is to get on the colours, especially those of high value, as often as possible : hence one must learn to play for position. Safety play is also frequently essential : and hazards should be played for with sufficient strength to avoid leaving a ball over the pocket for the benefit of the succeeding player.

VOLUNTEER SNOOKER

VOLUNTEER SNOOKER is an interesting variety of Snooker, and is played in the same manner and with the balls spotted in the same positions as the ordinary game, the main difference lying in the fact that whereas in Snooker pocketing the colours must alternate with pocketing the reds until the latter are all off the table, and thereafter follow in a settled order, in Volunteer Snooker the player has greater freedom and incurs greater penalties in cases of non-success.

So long as there is a red ball on the table, at the commencement of his turn the striker must first pocket a red, and his next stroke must be on a colour. In subsequent strokes he is at liberty to " volunteer " for any ball (other than one red in succession to another) : if he does not avail himself of this privilege and strikes alternately reds and colours in the same stroke, as in the ordinary game (or, when there is no red remaining, the colours in their snooker order), such balls shall be *free;* but if he " volunteers," *i.e.,* ignores the reds or takes the colours (reds being off the table) out of the usual order, such balls are *penalty balls.*

Bearing this in mind, the following extract from Rule 5 of the code authorized by the Billiards Association and Control Council will fully explain the mode of procedure :—

. . . . If the striker fail to pocket a *penalty ball* the stroke shall be foul ; if the *penalty ball* is pocketed without further contravention of these Rules, the foul shall be condoned, and the value scored, provided that, if any pool ball be pocketed from the same spot three times in succession in the same turn, it shall remain off the table till after the next stroke, for which any ball nominated by the striker shall be *free*. Each pool ball pocketed or forced off the table must otherwise be respotted before the next stroke, until finally pocketed under these Rules. If the striker fail to score, the next player shall play from where the cue-ball came to rest. If the cue-ball is pocketed or forced off the table, the next player shall play from hand. The game is thus continued until all the reds are off the table. If the player who lawfully pockets the last red pocket any pool ball by the next stroke of his turn, this ball is respotted. After this stroke (or all reds off the table) the lowest valued pool ball then remaining, if lawfully pocketed, must not be respotted.

In all other respects, including the scoring and the rules that cover snookering after a foul and regulate the stroke when the cue-ball is touching another, there is no difference between Volunteer Snooker and the parent game.

BAGATELLE

BAGATELLE is played with nine ivory or composition balls on an oblong table or board from 6 to 10 feet long, and about one-fourth of this in width, as shown in Fig. 14. At that end of the board which in use is farthest from the player are sunk nine hemispherical holes or cups, one as a centre, with the others in a circle

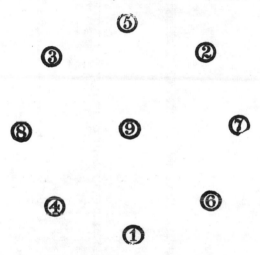

FIG. 13.—Arrangement of the Holes.

round it. Each hole bears a number, as shown in Fig. 13.

Of the nine balls one is black, four are white, and four are red. Whatever the diameter of the balls, that of the cups must exactly correspond with it. The sides of the board are furnished with a continuous cushion, such cushion at the upper end forming a semi-circle, concentric with the circle made by the cups. The upper edge of each side of the board is pierced with a double row of small holes, sixty in each row, arranged in groups of five. The score is marked by inserting ivory pegs in these holes, each player using one side of the board. To score the number obtained, the player removes his hinder peg for the time being, and places it the re uired number of holes in front of the foremost peg.

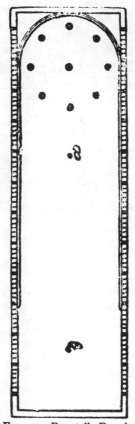 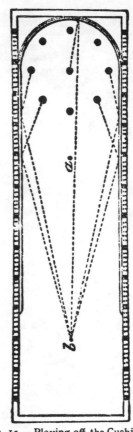

FIG. 14.—Bagatelle Board.   FIG. 15.—Playing off the Cushion.

The balls are propelled, at the option of the player, either with a cue (Fig. 16), like a small billiard cue, or with the mace (Fig. 17), which consists of an oblong "shoe," or block of wood, slightly curved, attached to a long thin tapering handle.

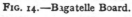

FIG. 16. –The Cue.

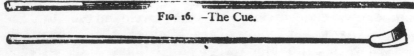

FIG. 16.—The Mace.

The cue is used as at Billiards. The mace is handled in a different manner. The shoe at its foot is placed in actual contact with the ball, the handle pointing over the right shoulder of the player, grasped about one-third from the top, between the thumb and second and third fingers of the right hand. The ball is then pushed forward in the desired direction. At best the mace is but a clumsy implement, and would never be used by anyone who had acquired even the most elementary skill in handling the cue.

At starting, the black ball is placed on the spot marked *a* (Fig. 14). The player, taking the remaining balls, places one of them on the spot marked *b*, and impels it in the direction of the black ball. If he hits this latter, the stroke is good, and he plays another ball, continuing till the whole eight have been played. If, however, the first ball played miss the black, it is removed from the table (whether it fall into a hole or not), and is lost to the player for that turn, as also any succeeding ball until the black ball is hit, after which the obligation to strike it ceases. If any ball is so struck as to be driven back towards the player more than half-way down the board, it is in like manner removed. After the black ball is once struck, the player is no longer obliged to place his own ball on the spot *b*, but may place it at any point behind such spot. He continues till the whole of the eight balls have been played.

The object of the player is to " hole " as many of his balls as possible, preferably in the cups bearing the higher numbers. The black ball counts double, and a good player will, therefore, endeavour to get this into the centre hole. This, however, is somewhat difficult, for, if struck directly towards the 9, it must pass over the 1, and is very likely to hole itself therein. It is, therefore, safer play to strike it lightly on the right side, and so drive it towards the 8, into which it may probably be coaxed by a subsequent ball. When the black ball has found a resting-place, the efforts of the player are directed to place his remaining balls to the best advantage. The approved methods of play for doing this, as to holes 4, 6, 7, 8, 9, are indicated by the dotted lines in Fig. 3, the ball being so struck as to go " off the cushion " into the desired hole. The best mode of playing a given ball will, however, be greatly governed by the positions occupied by preceding balls.

It frequently happens that a number of balls lie at distances less than their own diameter from the semi-circular cushion at top. In such case, a ball sent slowly round the cushion will strike them all in succession, and, driving them towards the centre, may hole one or more of them. If, on the other hand, the balls in question are *more* than their own diameter from the cushion, the ball sent in pursuit of them will run harmlessly round, and very probably be lost by over-passing the half-way line. Or, again, the balls may be lying close under the cushion, and the impact of the ball in play may simply drive them further round.

It frequently happens that a ball lies just on the brink of a hole, and that a discreet touch in the right place will cause it to drop therein. For such strokes as these the instructions given for securing winning hazards at Billiards may be studied with advantage.

The game is usually 120 points—*i.e.*, up and down the board. This number, is, however, not absolute, the player who first reaches it continuing to play until the whole of his eight balls are exhausted, and scoring the whole number obtained. If he be the second player, the game is then at an end, but if he was the first to play, the second player is entitled to play his eight balls also, and the player attaining the larger total is the winner.

If, when the game is won, the loser has not turned the corner—*i.e.*, begun to score on the downward journey, the game is a " double," and if there was any stake, the loser pays double accordingly.

Where four persons take part, two play as partners against the two others, one of each side playing alternately the whole of the eight balls.

There are a number of other games played on the bagatelle table ; space will not permit of our dealing with all of them, and we therefore select the two most popular, viz., the *Sans Égal* game and the *Cannon* game.

"SANS ÉGAL" BAGATELLE

THIS game is played by two persons, one taking the four white, and the other the four red balls. The black ball is placed as in the ordinary game, and the players each play one ball alternately. Each ball played must strike the black until the black is holed ; if it fails to do so it is not removed from the board, but the player forfeits five points, and does not count the score made by that ball should it drop into a hole. The player who holes the black scores the value of the hole, and that of each hole occupied by his own, whether holed by himself or by his opponent.

The highest scorer with his four balls wins, unless it had been agreed that the game should be for a definite number of points, usually 25 or 31.

THE "CANNON" GAME

THIS is played by two players, with three balls only, one taking a white, and the other a red ball. Having decided who is to begin, the non-striker's ball is placed mid-way between the 5 and 9 holes, and the black ball on the usual spot. The player then strikes at the black, endeavouring to make a cannon on to his adversary's ball. If he succeed he scores two for the cannon, the number of the holes (if any) into which his own or his opponent's ball has fallen, and double the number of any hole into which the black has fallen. In such case, also, he plays again, and continues to do so until he ceases to score. If, on the other hand, he fail to make the cannon, he scores nothing, and if at the same time his own or the black ball is holed it is replaced on its proper spot, either ball not holed remaining in the position which it happens to occupy. The adversary removes his own ball to the further end of the board, and plays in his turn, and so on till the agreed limit of the game, which may be any number "up," is reached.

PART IV

BOARD GAMES

CHESS

THE game of Chess is a battle between two armies, numerically equal, of which the two players are the generals. The battlefield is a square board divided into sixty-four equal alternate white and black squares, and is so placed that each player has a white square in the corner at his right.

THE MEN

The forces consist of thirty-two " men ", each side having eight Pieces and eight Pawns, of a light and dark (" white " and " black ") colour to distinguish the opposing forces from each other.

WHITE'S FORCES			BLACK'S FORCES
♔	One King = K		♚
♕	One Queen = Q		♛
♖ ♖	Two Castles, or Rooks = R		♜ ♜
♗ ♗	Two Bishops = B		♝ ♝
♘ ♘	Two Knights = Kt		♞ ♞
	Eight Pawns = P		
♙ ♙ ♙ ♙ ♟ ♟ ♟ ♟			
♙ ♙ ♙ ♙ ♟ ♟ ♟ ♟			

At the commencement the men are placed as shown in Fig. 1 (note that the White King occupies a black square, and the Black King a white square) ; no square is ever occupied by more than one man at the same time.

The horizontal rows of squares are called " ranks ", and the vertical rows " files ". The " diagonals " are series of adjacent squares of the same colour extending from corner to corner and from any edge of the board to any adjacent edge. There are 8 ranks, 8 files, and 26 diagonals.

MOVEMENTS AND POWERS OF THE MEN

A piece or pawn can take any adverse piece or pawn, according to the laws governing its movements. The King alone, as will presently be seen, is inviolable. If the King is attacked, the fact must be notified by the warning " Check ", and if he cannot escape from the attack he is " Checkmate ", and the game is at an end.

Taking, or " capturing ", is effected by removing the captured man and replacing it, on the same square, by the piece or pawn making the capture.

1. THE KING.—The King, as the name denotes, is the most important piece on the board, inasmuch as the object of the game is to capture the King. It is, however, never actually " taken ", the game ending whenever (the opposing player having the move) the King remains liable to capture. The King may move from the square upon which it stands to any adjoining square not " commanded " by his opponent nor occupied by a man of its own colour. If any adjoining square is occupied by an undefended man of the opposite colour, the King may take such man.

Black.[1]

White.[1]

FIG. 1.—The Men in Position.

"Castling", a special privilege of the King, is explained at pp. 367-68.

2. THE ROOK.—The Rook (or Castle) moves upon ranks and files only (i.e. in a horizontal or vertical direction), to any square not occupied by any man of its own colour. If the line on which it operates is closed by a man of the opposite colour, it can take such man.

[1] Note that in all Diagrams White plays from the bottom, upwards, and Black from the top, downwards.

3. THE BISHOP.—Bishops move and take upon diagonals only : the King's Bishop upon the diagonals of its own colour, the Queen's Bishop on those of the opposite colour ; stopping short, however, at a square before one occupied by any man, or capturing one of the opposite colour.

4. THE QUEEN.—The Queen combines the power of Rook and Bishop, i.e. it may move and take horizontally or vertically like a Rook, or upon diagonals like a Bishop. It is, therefore, the most powerful piece on the board, because not only has it the power of Rook and Bishop, but it has also the privilege to move like either Bishop, according to the colour of the diagonal it may for the time being stand upon.

5. THE KNIGHT.—The movement of the Knight is more complicated. One move of the Knight combines two King's moves : one square straight, and one square diagonally to any but a square adjoining its starting-point. Unlike any of the other men, it appears to leap over any piece or pawn of its own or the opposite colour intervening between its starting-point and the square to which it moves.

Thus, in Fig. 2, the White Knight may move to KB2, KKt5, Q6, QB5, or QB3, but not to Q2, that square being occupied by a piece of its own colour.[1] It may take the Black Pawn at KKt3, or the Black Knight at KB6. It will be noticed that with every move the Knight changes the colour of its square, viz. from white to black, and *vice versa ;* also that, having moved, the squares that it attacks are all of the same colour as that from which it has come.

FIG. 2.—The Knight's Move.

6. THE PAWN.—The Pawn, in spite of its limited power of movement, plays a most important rôle amongst the forces. The Pawns are the rank and file of the army. The Pawn is, so to speak,

[1] For the meaning of these letters and figures, see Chess Notation (p. 363).

the *tirailleur;* it engages the enemy, advances into the opponent's camp, and clears the road for the officers who follow in its wake to the attack ; the Pawn is mostly the first victim, and in the large majority of cases decides the game. Like the private soldier, who " carries the marshal's baton in his knapsack ", the Pawn may be promoted to the highest rank. If it reaches the eighth rank, it must be converted, according to the choice of the player or the state of the game, into a Bishop, Knight, Rook, or Queen, irrespective of whether or not the player has still his full complement of pieces ; it cannot remain a Pawn, or merely disappear from the board.

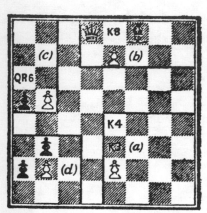

FIG. 3.—The Pawn's Moves.

The Pawn may only move one square at a time, straight forward on the file on which it stands, with the option of moving *two* squares at first starting. Thus in Fig. 3, section *a*, the Pawn at K2 may move either to K3 or at once to K4. But the Pawn *takes* on diagonals only ; thus, in section *b* of the same figure, the Pawn at K7, having the move, can take either the Black Bishop at KB8 or the Queen at Q8, and in either case it must be converted, as already explained, and acts immediately in its new capacity.

The Pawn cannot move backwards, nor—except when taking—sideways. Thus any adverse man standing on the adjacent squares to a Pawn (other than forward diagonals) cannot be taken. Pawns placed as shown in section *c* or *d* of Fig. 3 could not take each other.

The Pawn may also take " *en passant* " (P × Pe.*p*.), which means that if a Pawn moves two squares at starting and in doing so " passes " a Pawn which could have taken it had it moved only one square, such adverse Pawn has the option of taking it as if it had moved one square only ; but the taking *en passant* must form the next move of the adversary. Thus in section *c* of the diagram, supposing the Black Pawn to have just moved from QR2 to QR4,

it may be taken by the White Pawn at QKt5; the White
Pawn standing, after the move, at his QR6 ; Black's 8th
and White's 9th moves in our recorded game, p. 365, will
make the procedure perfectly clear.

NOTATION

There are two chief systems of naming the squares
(" notation ") for the purpose of recording games, viz. the
" Descriptive " (or " English "), which is commonly used
throughout the British Empire, the U.S.A., Spain, and
Argentina, and the " Algebraic " (or " German "), current
in the U.S.S.R., most of Europe, and almost everywhere
else. In Fig. 4 we illustrate, diagrammatically, both
systems, the Descriptive at the bottom of each square,
and the Algebraic in the centre of each square.   In this
article we use only the Descriptive, so we will take that
first ; but the student will increasingly find it necessary
to familiarize himself with the Algebraic (explained below)
as well.

As will be seen from the diagram, each square is named
from the piece that originally occupied the square at the
end of its file ; e.g. the square upon which the King stands
is called "Ksq.", or "K1", and all the squares are numbered
vertically on the whole file from 1 to 8, and so on upon
each file.   Taking Black and White King and Queen as
the centre pieces, all the pieces on the King's side are called
the King's pieces, i.e. King's Bishop (KB), King's Knight
(KKt), King's Rook (KR) ; and those on the Queen's
side the Queen's pieces, i.e. Queen's Bishop (QB), Queen's
Knight (QKt), Queen's Rook (QR).   It follows from this
that—as is seen in Fig. 4—Black and White have different
names for the same square ; thus White's Ksq. is Black's K8
whilst Black's Ksq. is White's K8 ; and so on with all
the other squares.

In the Algebraic system the files (vertical rows) are
lettered a, b, c, . . . h, starting at the bottom left-hand
corner (White's QRsq.), and the ranks (horizontal rows)
numbered 1, 2, 3, . . . 8, starting at the same square ;
each square has one identification only, so that the fourth
square on the White King's file (K4), for instance, is always
" e4 ", and Black's King's square " e8 ".   The use of the
two systems is made clear by a few moves of an opening

recorded in both on the opposite page. It will be noticed that a minimum of space (and type) is used in recording a move ; in the Descriptive, it is not specified which R, B, or Kt moves to the named square unless either could make the move ; e.g. in our French Defence, below, although on White's 4th either B could go to Kt5, " B—Kt5 " is sufficient to indicate the QB, for had the KB made the move the recording would necessarily have read " B—Kt5ch." ; but at White's 12th " KR—K1 " must be used, because it was open to QR to make the identical move. Compression goes even further in the Algebraic system ; it has no symbol for Pawns, and when a P makes a capture only the file from which it moves is named (e.g. Black's 12th) ; no man captured is named, the square to which the capturer is moved being sufficient indication ; the dash (" moves to ") is usually, as here, omitted ; and a moving or capturing piece about which ambiguity is possible is identified by the file on which it stands (e.g. White's 12th), not by its original square.

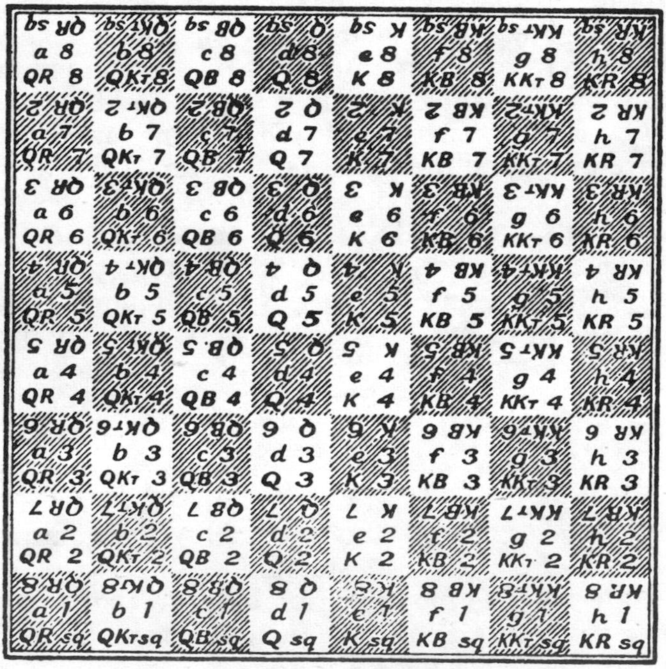

FIG. 4.—Guide to Notation.

METHOD OF RECORDING

The above abbreviations are always used in recording games, positions, problems, etc., in English (though " N " or " S "—the German *Springer*, Knight—sometimes replace " Kt " to avoid confusion with " K ", for King), and to them we must add the following : ch.=check (shown in the Algebraic by *) ; dis. ch.=discovered check ; *e.p.=en passant* ; Castles, Castles K, or O—O=Castles on the King's side, and Castles (*if only the Queen's side is available*), Castles Q, or O—O—O=Castles on the Queen's side. — means " moves to " (P—K4=P moves to K4) ; to take is noted " takes " or, more usually, by × ; (!) indicates a good move ; (?) a bad or indifferent move. At the end of a recording + indicates the better game, — the inferior game, = an even game, ± White has a slight advantage, and ∓Black has a slight advantage. = is also the symbol for " is exchanged for " ; thus : P—K8=Kt signifies that the Pawn moves to K8 and is exchanged for a Knight.

To familiarize himself with both systems the student is recommended to study, *with the board*, the following example, a " French Defence " (see p. 406) recorded in the Descriptive and Algebraic notations.

	DESCRIPTIVE			ALGEBRAIC	
	White	Black		White	Black
1.	P—K4	P—K3	1.	e4	e6
2.	P—Q4	P—Q4	2.	d4	d5
3.	Kt—QB3	Kt—KB3	3.	Ktc3	Ktf6
4.	B—Kt5	B—K2	4.	Bg5	Be7
5.	P—K5	KKt—Q2	5.	e5	Ktfd7
6.	B×B	Q×B	6.	B×e7	Q×e7
7.	Q—Kt4	Castles	7.	Qg4	O—O
8.	B—Q3	P—KB4	8.	Bd3	f5
9.	P×P*o.p.*	Q×P	9.	e5×f6*e.p.*	Q×f6
10.	Kt—B3	P—B4	10.	Ktf3	c5
11.[1]	Castles Q	P—KR3	11.[1]	O—O—O	h6
12.	KR—K1	P×P	12.	Rhe1	c×d4
13.	R×P	Kt—Kt3(!)	13.	R×e6	Ktb6(!)
14.	R×Q	B×Q	14.	R×f6	B×g4
15.	R×Rch	K×R ∓	15.	R×f8*	K×f8 ∓

The so-called " Fractional " notation is merely a variation of the Descriptive, White's move being recorded above and Black's below a line—e.g. :

[1] The position at 11. Castles Q . . . is shown in Fig. 6.

$$\text{I.} \frac{\text{P—K4}}{\text{P—K4}}; \quad \text{2.} \frac{\text{Kt—KB3}}{\text{Kt—QB3}}; \quad \text{3.} \frac{\text{B—Kt5}}{\text{P—QR3}}, \text{ etc.}$$

The moves may be set out in columns or in lines, according to individual choice. A single move of Black is recorded thus : 1. . . . P—K4 ; 16. . . . KB × Kt, the dots standing in lieu of White's preceding move.

Having mastered the notation, the student should next familiarize himself with the—

TECHNICAL TERMS

CHECK AND CHECKMATE.—The whole object of the game is the capture of the opponent's King, though, as we have said, the King is never actually taken, the game coming to an end when the next move, if made, would result in his capture. If the King is attacked, the attack must be accompanied by the warning " Check ". A check may be met in three different ways. The player may either interpose one of his own men[1] between the King and the attacking piece ; he may move it out of the range of the attacking piece ; or he may take the attacking piece with the King or with any of his forces which may be available for that purpose. If he cannot resort to either of these three defences, he is checkmated, or "mated", and the game is lost.

" Discovered " check is given when, by moving a piece, another piece is unmasked which attacks the adversary's King (see Fig. 5B), and " double " check when a piece on making a move not only checks the King but unmasks a piece that also gives check ; in this case, of course, release from check cannot be obtained by interposition, nor by capture of one of the checking pieces, as will be seen in Fig. 5B, when . . . Kt—B7db.ch.

DRAWN GAME.—Beside the decisive issue of checkmate, there is another, and very frequent, termination of a game—viz. the " drawn game ", or " draw ".

A draw ensues : 1. If neither side can give checkmate.

2. If both sides remain with King only, or with a single Bishop, or single Knight only in addition.

3. If both players repeat the same series of moves three times, thereby tacitly admitting that they are not

[1] This is not possible in case of a check with a Knight or Pawn.

strong enough to give checkmate, or that they do not intend to venture upon another line of play.

4. If either player can prove that in the course of 50 moves (by each) no Pawn has been moved and no capture made.

5. Through "perpetual check"; for instance, if a player, having otherwise a lost game, can save it by constantly forcing the opponent to move his King by repeated checks. In Fig. 5A Black is threatened with checkmate by Q—R8, or Q—Kt7. But, it being Black's move, he would play Kt—Kt6ch.; White *must* play K—R2; Black returns to his old position again, checking and as there is nothing to prevent his repeating these two moves *ad infinitum*, the game is drawn.

FIG. 5.—A: Perpetual check; B: Discovered check (KtB5), and Double check (KtB7); C: Stalemate.

6. In case of a "stalemate"—i.e. when the player whose turn it is to move cannot make a legal move. For instance, in Fig. 5C, Black (having the move) would be "stalemate", as his King (his only piece) cannot move without placing itself in check, the white Pawn guarding the squares KR8, KB8, and the King guarding the Pawn, KR7, and KB7.

7. By mutual agreement.

CASTLING.—Once in the game the King has the privi-

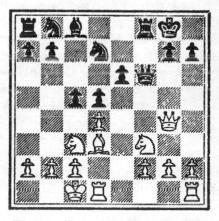

FIG. 6.—French Defence (p. 365), after 11 Castles Q: showing the position of K and R after Castling—Black on K-side, White on Q-side.

lege of making a double move in conjunction with either Rook; this is called "Castling". In castling on the King's side, the K is moved to KKtsq. and the R is placed next to it on KBsq. ; in castling on the Queen's side, the K is moved to QBsq., and the QR placed next to it upon Qsq. (Fig. 6).

Castling is permitted only in the following conditions :

1.   That no piece of its own or the opponent's colour be between the King and the Rook with which the King is to be castled.

2.   That neither the King nor the Rook with which it is to castle has yet moved.

3.   The King cannot castle if in check, nor into check ; neither can he cross a square which is commanded by any of the opponent's pieces.

Additional Technical Terms

ATTACK.—The attempt to capture, or force to an inferior position, any adverse piece or Pawn, or to check or checkmate the King ; also the concentrated offensive action of several pieces. As a rule the player who has the first move has the " attack ", and the second player the " defence ".

CLOSE GAME.—See pp. 372, 406.

COMBINATION.—The plan made by either side to obtain an advantage. The opponent will try to counteract it, therefore its subtlety is the best standard by which the strength of a player may be judged.

CENTRE.—The central position of the board, i.e. K4 and Q4 of each side ; the squares immediately adjacent to these are known as the " Outer Centre ", and the K's and Q's Pawns as the " Centre Pawns ".

COMMAND.—A piece commands a square, or a rank, file or diagonal, if it can take any adverse piece in its range.

DEVELOP.—To move a piece from its original position is to develop it or to bring it into play. The quicker the development the more advantageous it is ; and a player who is able to concentrate upon a given point a greater number of pieces than his opponent is enabled to develop for its defence, must obtain an advantage.

DOUBLED PAWN.—Two Pawns of the same colour on the same file. A "doubled Pawn", though very occasionally advantageous, is usually weaker than two Pawns on the same rank, because they are incapable of mutual self-defence.

EN PRISE.—A piece or Pawn is *en prise* if left either

undefended or insufficiently so. If a man is put *en prise* designedly, to obtain some advantage or to recover it later, it is paradoxically called a " sacrifice " ; of course, temporarily, till the goal of the combination is attained, it *is* a sacrifice.

END-GAME.—See pp. 371, 413-21.

EXCHANGE.—The giving up of a piece or Pawn for another of equal value. " Winning the exchange " is gaining a Rook for a minor piece (B or Kt) ; " losing the exchange " is losing a Rook for a minor piece.

FALSE MOVE.—An illegal move, one made contrary to the laws of the game.

FORCED MOVE.—The move made when the player has only one at his disposal.

FORK.—A simultaneous attack by one man on two.

GAMBIT.[1]—An opening in which material, usually a Pawn, is sacrificed by the first player for the sake of an earlier or stronger attack or a quicker development. A Pawn so sacrificed is called the " Gambit-Pawn ". A " counter-gambit " is a similar sacrifice by second player, with a similar object.—See also under " King's Gambits ", p. 400.

ISOLATED PAWN.—A Pawn not having a Pawn of its own colour on an adjacent file.

J'ADOUBE.—A call (" I adjust ") made by a player to inform his opponent, *before* touching a man of his own or his adversary's, that the man is only to be set properly on its square, not played.

LOSING A MOVE.—As a rule, the pieces should be so developed that they attack directly or indirectly an adverse piece. This " gains time ", as the opponent is obliged to make a defensive move, thus allowing first player to bring another piece into play. It is clear, therefore, that if a useless or indifferent move be made, a move (time) is lost.

MAN.—A comprehensive term embracing every unit— King, Pieces, and Pawns.

MIDDLE-GAME.—That part of the game between the close of the Opening and the commencement of the End-Game (see further p. 371).

OPENING.—See p. 372.

[1] From Italian *Gambetto*, a tripping up.

PIECE.—Any man, King and Pawns excepted. The Queen and Rook (either of which can give mate without assistance except from the King) are Major Pieces, the Bishop and Knight Minor Pieces.

PIN.—A piece is " pinned " if it is attacked by an adverse piece in such a way that, by moving the attacked piece a more valuable piece would be " unmasked " and put *en prise*, and especially if such piece is unable to move because it guards the King from check.

VALUE OF THE PIECES

The approximate value of the pieces, as they stand at the beginning of a game, is estimated to be as follows : Taking the Pawn as unit, the value of the Knight is $3·05$; of the Bishop, $3·05$; of the Rook, $5·48$; and of the Queen, $9·94$. Other authorities give B and Kt 3 each, R $4\frac{1}{2}$ (or 5), and Q 9, and make the King in the End-Game worth 4. Obviously the value of piece or Pawn changes as the game advances ; there are, however, general principles which hold good in a large majority of cases. For instance, two Bishops are more serviceable than two Knights in the End-Game ;[1] Bishop and Knight are also preferable to two Knights.

GENERAL OBSERVATIONS

A good system for the student is to practise one Opening only, attack and defence alternately, till it is thoroughly well mastered, before going on to other Openings. He should not get into the habit of playing with one colour only, or he will find himself at a disadvantage when he has to take the other. He must not make a move without carefully weighing the possible replies, and must *never* touch a man till he has finally decided to move it. If he finds *a good move*, let him still look for *a better one*. When his opponent makes a move, he must try to discover its object, whether it is immediately menacing or only indirectly so. In the first case, a suitable defence must be found ; in the latter, he may profit by the respite to bring a piece into play.

[1] In the End-Game with two Bishops checkmate can be forced, whilst with two Knights only checkmate cannot be given except through a slip on the part of the defence (see p. 419).

The first principle is to develop the pieces quickly, and never to commence an attack with insufficient forces. The Opening correctly played is frequently half the battle won.

Avoid useless checks. Avoid useless exchanges. Bear in mind that it is disadvantageous to be left with two Knights only, as mate cannot be given with them. If the player has the better game, he should avoid remaining with a Bishop of different colour from a like piece of his opponent, as Bishops of different colour frequently lead to a draw.

The student should further accustom himself to strict adherence to the laws of the game ; never to take back a move ; never to touch a man until he has determined where to move it ; and to move his pieces unostentatiously : a " poker face " is almost as useful at Chess as it is at poker !

Having now given the elementary instructions necessary for the playing of Chess we will proceed with the theory underlying the game, which consists essentially of three phases : the Opening, the Middle-Game, and the End-Game.

THE OPENING is merely the development of the pieces, and the more rapidly and judiciously this is effected the better ; from a mistake in the opening—assuming both players to be of equal strength—it is difficult to recover. The Openings, therefore, should be studied carefully.

THE MIDDLE-GAME is entirely a matter of practice, and its proper management can only be acquired by study and experience : Openings can be learnt by heart and reproduced by memory ; End-Games may often be won by mathematics ; but "the Middle-Game in chess is chess itself "[1], for here both players are thrown upon their own resources, and it is here that the superiority of a player asserts itself.

THE END-GAME is also a study in itself, and one which will repay the most careful attention ; certain positions occur frequently in end-play and have been systematically, even mathematically, arranged ; these may be committed to memory, but the larger number depend (like the Middle-Game) upon ingenuity and individual skill (see pp. 413-21).

[1] *The Middle-Game in Chess*, E. Znosko-Borovsky, George Bell & Sons. A work strongly recommended to the student.

THE OPENINGS

The Openings are divided into three main groups, viz.
(1) the *Open Game*, in which both sides play 1. P—K4 ;
(2) the Semi-open Game, in which White plays P—K4
and Black replies with a different move (e.g. P—QB4,
P—K3, P—QB3, etc.) ; and the *Close Game*, in which
White's first move is any other than 1. P—K4 (usually
P—Q4). The *Open Games* will be first dealt with ; but
it must be remembered that these divisions are not to be
regarded as absolutely rigid ; by a mere change in the order
of the first few moves the apparent original grouping may
be changed ; and certain forms of the Giuoco Piano and
Ruy Lopez, for instance, are Close, not Open, games.
In the Open Game there is an immediate clash in the centre,
while in the Closed many moves are frequently played before
any clash is possible (cf. Figs. 21 and 22, p. 406).

The first opening we describe is the Giuoco Piano (Italian
for the " plain game "), so called because it is a quiet,
strategical development of the forces ; it is presented
just as if it were being explained to a beginner by a tutor
during its actual play.

THE GIUOCO PIANO

WHITE	BLACK
1. P—K4	. . .

This move allows most scope for the development of
two pieces, Q and KB ; P—Q4 also allows this, but it
gives less scope to the Queen ; both moves are good,
because the P—for the moment—dominates the centre
by commanding two important centre squares.

. . .	P—K4

The same observations apply to Black's first move.

2. Kt—KB3	. . .

The aim of the player being a quick development of
his forces, it is advisable to bring each piece into play
by attacking an adverse piece or Pawn immediately, if
possible. The Kt here attacks Black's KP.

. . .	Kt—QB3

This move not only defends the attacked KP, but
at the same time brings a piece into play, and thus establishes an equilibrium in the development. 2. . . . Q—K2,
or 2. . . . Q—B3, would be unfavourable, because the

former move would prevent the development of the KB, and the latter the *sortie* of the Knight, besides exposing the Queen to attack. As a general rule the defence of pieces of less value with pieces of greater value should be avoided as much as possible. Black could also play here 2. . . . P—Q3, which changes the opening to " Philidor's Defence ", or 2. . . . Kt—KB3 (" Petroff's Defence "), attacking White's KP. These will be treated later on.

   3. B—B4   . . .

Clearing the King's side for castling, and posting the Bishop ready for attacking the present weakest point in Black's position, viz. his KBP, weakest because defended by the King only.

   . . .   B—B4

No immediate danger being apprehended, Black brings a piece into play. These three completed moves constitute the Giuoco Piano opening, whatever the moves that follow.

   4. P—Q3   P—Q3
   5. B—K3   B—Kt3

Better than 5. . . . B × B ; because White would be left (after 6. P × B, Kt—R4) with two Kts against B and Kt, and would obtain an " open Bishop's file ", doubling his Rooks upon it after castling ; while the " double pawn ", in most positions a weakness, may well be a strength in the centre.

   6. QKt—Q2   . . .

The object being to play this Knight to KBsq., and then to Kt3. This could also be done if White had played 6. Kt—B3, then Kt—K2, and Kt—Kt3. The manœuvre in the text is generally adopted, because if 6. Kt—B3, Black could " pin " it with 6. . . . B—R4.

   . . .   Kt—B3

   7. P—B3   . . .

Intending to advance the QP, and thus prepare the formation of a strong centre.

   . . .   B—Q2

Threatening to attack and exchange White's KB, by playing upon his next move, if feasible, 8. . . . Kt—QR4. He could not have done so before, because of White's reply, 8. B—Kt5ch., forcing the Knight back to B3, or leaving it at R4 out of play.

8. B—Kt3   . . .

White, who does not want to exchange his Bishop
for Knight, retires it, so that he may play, should Black
attack it with 8. . . . Kt—R4, 9. B—B2.

        . . .   Q—K2

In the Giuoco Piano it is not advisable for either player
to castle early, and Black wisely makes a waiting move.
He is now able to castle on either side, according to circumstances.

        9. Q—K2   P—KR3

This move is strictly defensive ; Black could equally,
and with better effect, have improved his Queen's Knight's
position by 9. . . . Kt—Qsq., and then to K3.

        10. Kt—Bsq.   B—K3
        11. B—R4[1]   B—Q2
        12. Kt—Kt3   P—Kt3

FIG. 7.—11. B—R4.

Black is up against a
superior player, and his
defence is somewhat timid.
He had previously intended
to exchange his QKt against
White's B, and now when
White "pins" the Knight
with 11. B—R4, he retires
the B, so as to avoid a
doubled Pawn. Now he has
to prevent White's Kt from
moving to B5, attacking the
Queen, but in doing so he
weakens his King's position
for the purpose of castling
on the King's side. *The student should bear in mind that
these Pawns are strongest in their original position.*

        13. B—B2   . . .

The Bishop is better placed now at B2. At R4 it was,
owing to the changed position, less useful. At its new
post it strengthens the centre.

        . . .   P—Q4

Black anticipates White's possible P—Q4 by himself
advancing.

    [1] See Fig. 7 and cf. Fig. 10 showing the same stage in another
variation of the Giuoco Piano.

14. Castles KR   P × P
15. P × P   Kt—Qsq.

Black is now executing
the manœuvre suggested at
his ninth move—but it is not
good at this stage. The
position is now as shown in
Fig. 8.

16. QR—Qsq. . . .

It is always good to occupy
an open file with a Rook.

. . .   K—Bsq.

Black cannot play 16. . . .
Kt—K3, because he would
thereby leave his KP *en
prise ;* he cannot castle,
because then his KRP would
be *en prise ;* and if he were

FIG. 8.—Position after Black's
15th move.

to return with the Kt to B3, he would have lost a move.
Therefore he has nothing better than to move his King
into safety to Bsq., and then to Kt2.

17. Q—Q2 (?)   K—Kt2

Black, as defender, has improved his position.

18. P—KR3   . . .

To prevent Black from playing 18. . . . B × B ; Q × B,
Kt—Kt5, attacking the Queen.

. . .   Kt—B3
19. Kt—R4   QR—Qsq.

Occupying the " open file ", defending the Bishop,
and freeing his KKt, which was the Bishop's sole defence.

20. B × B   RP × B

When there is a choice it is usually better to take with
the RP, for it gives an additional " open file " for the entry
of the Rook, and also because, other things being equal,
capturing towards the centre adds to its strength.

21. Q—K2   . . .

White has now lost the attack, and is virtually on the
defensive. He is obliged to move his Queen, because
Black threatens 21. . . . B × P, discovering an attack upon
the Queen with his Rook.

. . .   B—K3
22. R × R   R × R

23. B—Kt3   K—R2

A good move, because White threatens, in case Black should exchange Bishops, to win the Queen with either Kt—B5ch., P × Kt ; Kt × Pch. ; K moves ; Kt × Q.

24. B × B   Q × B

White, having failed in his attack, exchanges pieces, so as to simplify the position and bring about an End-Game that may enable him to draw.

25. P—R3   Q—Q3

Doubly occupying the " open file ", and so preventing White from moving 26. R—Qsq., and forcing his Rook off the "file", or an exchange of Rooks. But he would have done better to play 25. . . . Q—Q2, as White's next move will show.

26. Q—B3   Q—K3

Black has lost a move by not playing 25. . . . Q—Q2, for now he cannot move his Queen away from the protection of the Knight, and the Knight he cannot move, because his KBP would then remain *en prise*. If he moved 26. . . . K—Kt2, defending Kt and P, White would win his Queen by playing either Kt—B5ch., etc., as pointed out after Black's 23rd move ; it is, consequently, a " forced " move.

27. Q—K3   . . .

To prevent Black from playing 27. . . . R—Q7, which would obviously be a powerful move, as it would attack White's Pawns on the Queen's side.

         . . .   Q—B5

28. Kt (R4)—B5   . . .

White sacrifices a piece on the chance of Black not seeing the right defence. In which case the subtle threat is :

         . . .   P × Kt

29. Kt × P   KKt—Ktsq.
Defending the threatened RP.

30. Q—Kt3   . . .

And wins, as the mate with Q—Kt7 cannot be prevented.

FIG. 9.—Position after White's 28th move.

. . .   P × Kt

Black would have done better not to take the Knight, but to play 28. . . . KKt—Ktsq. After the capture, Black has no further chance of winning.

    29. Kt × P   Kt—Ksq. !

As pointed out above, if Black had made what seems to be the obvious move, viz. defended the RP with 29. . . . KKt—Ktsq., White would win with 30. Q—Kt3 and mate to follow at Kt7 with the Q.

    30. Q × Pch.   K—Ktsq.
    31. Q—Kt5ch.   K—R2

and the game is drawn by White giving "perpetual check". That is the utmost he can hope, being a piece down.

As in the case of all the Openings the Giuoco Piano has many branches, depending upon the choice of move following its conclusion. In the game just given White's 4. P—Q3 constitutes the "Pianissimo", or "very quiet", variation ; others arise from 4. Castles, and many from 4. P—B3 which, when followed by 5. P—Q4, gives a much more aggressive game ; for instance :

1. $\dfrac{\text{P—K4}}{\text{P—K4}}$; 2. $\dfrac{\text{Kt—KB3}}{\text{Kt—QB3}}$; 3. $\dfrac{\text{B—B4}}{\text{B—B4}}$; 4. $\dfrac{\text{P—B3}}{\text{Kt—B3}}$; 5. $\dfrac{\text{P—Q4}}{\text{P × P}}$;

6. $\dfrac{\text{P × P}}{\text{B—Kt5ch.}}$; 7. $\dfrac{\text{Kt—B3}}{\quad}$; this move prepares the

ground for the lively "Möller Attack" (9. P—Q5) ; 7. B—Q2 is less enterprising, and allows Black to neutralize.

7. $\dfrac{\quad}{\text{Kt × KP}}$; 8. $\dfrac{\text{Castles}}{\text{B × Kt}}$; 9. $\dfrac{\text{P—Q5}}{\text{B—B3}}$; 10. $\dfrac{\text{R—Ksq.}}{\text{Kt—K2}}$;

11. $\dfrac{\text{R × Kt}}{\quad}$ (see Fig. 10, and compare with Fig. 7 showing

another Pianissimo at the same stage of the game). Now, whether Black play 11. . . . Castles, or 11. . . . P—Q3 he is exposed to a dangerous attack, which he could have avoided by Kt × Kt (instead of B × Kt) at his 8th move ;

thus : 8. $\dfrac{\quad}{\text{Kt × Kt}}$; 9. $\dfrac{\text{P × Kt}}{\text{B × P}}$; 10. $\dfrac{\text{Q—Kt3}}{\text{P—Q4}}$; 11. $\dfrac{\text{B × P}}{\text{Castles}}$.

FIG. 10.—11. R × Kt.

For other variations the student should consult one of the books devoted to the Openings ; but we must mention the Max Lange Attack at this point for, though it may arise by transposition from the Scotch Gambit, Petroff's Defence, Two Knights' Defence, Centre Gambit, and others, it is in fact a complicated off-shoot of the Giuoco Piano and is nowadays often treated as a separate Opening.

THE MAX LANGE ATTACK

After the first three moves (see above) the game continues:

4. $\dfrac{\text{Castles}}{\text{Kt—B3}}$; 5. $\dfrac{\text{P—Q4}}{\text{P} \times \text{P}^{1}}$; 6. $\dfrac{\text{P—K5}}{\text{P—Q4}}$; 7. $\dfrac{\text{P} \times \text{Kt}}{\text{P} \times \text{B}}$;

8. $\dfrac{\text{R—Ksq.ch.}}{\text{B—K3}}$; 9. $\dfrac{\text{Kt—Kt5}}{\text{Q—Q4}}$; 10. $\dfrac{\text{Kt—QB3}}{\text{Q—B4}}$; 11. $\dfrac{\text{QKt—K4}}{}$;

and whether Black play 11. . . . O—O—O, or 11. . . . B—KB sq. (Rubinstein's Defence) White has a violent attack. Black can avoid the dangers of the Max Lange by playing P—Q3 as his fourth move, followed (after White's 5. P—B3) by 5. . . . B—KKt5.

THE EVANS GAMBIT

The Evans Gambit, another lively variation of the " Giuoco ", first brought to notice by a Captain W. D. Evans, R.N., in the late 1820's, is constituted by White's attack on Black's KB at his fourth move.

In our example (p. 377) of the more aggressive form White plays 4. P—B3, followed by 5. P—Q4 in order to force Black to exchange his KP, thus gaining an advantage by having his own KP stationed on the 4th rank with Black's QP on his 2nd, and so having more space in which to manœuvre. In the Evans Gambit Accepted—for it may be " Declined " (see p. 382) White succeeds in speeding

---

[1] If 5. . . . B × P, then 6. Kt × B, Kt × Kt ; 7. P—B4, P—Q3 ; 8. P × P, P × P ; 9. B—KKt5, etc.

up the process by again attacking the B and gaining a complete move by 6. P—Q4 before Black has been able to bring out his KKt. As he has given up a Pawn he must however, press home the attack with the utmost energy, for Black will win in the End-Game if he is able to hold the position.

The following game, a " classic " played in the 1860's by Anderssen against Dufresne and known as the " Evergreen", is a good illustration of the possibilities of the attack.

	WHITE	BLACK
1.	P—K4	P—K4
2.	Kt—KB3	Kt—QB3
3.	B—B4	B—B4
4.	P—QKt4	B × P
5.	P—B3	B—R4
6.	P—Q4	P × P
7.	Castles	P—Q6

a move often played in such a position. White would have welcomed a further capture by . . . P × P ; or, alternatively, would have completed the occupation of the centre by playing P × P, himself ; . . . P—Q6 temporarily upsets his plans, nor is it a wasted move as sooner or later White will have to capture this advanced Pawn—though Black must make sure that he does not improve his position in doing so.

8. Q—Kt3	. . .

Wisely deferring the capture until a more opportune moment.

. . .	Q—B3

Here . . . Kt—R3 would not protect the KBP because of B × Kt.

9.	P—K5	Q—Kt3
10.	R—Ksq.	KKt—K2
11.	B—R3	P—Kt4

returning the Pawn in the hope of obtaining some counter play by developing his QR and QKt.

12.	Q × P	R—QKtsq.
13.	Q—R4	B—Kt3
14.	QKt—Q2	B—Kt2
15.	Kt—K4	Q—B4

This allows White to capture the advanced Pawn with an attack on the Queen (see note to move 7).

16. B×P   QR4
17. Kt—B6ch. !   . . .

Grand play, opening the KKt file by force.

. . .   P×Kt
18. P×P   R—Ktsq.

FIG. 11.—After 18. . . . R—Ktsq.

The position is most dramatic ! Black has succeeded in engineering an attack on White's K's position (see Fig. 11) with two Bs on the long diagonals supported by KR and Q. Black threatens ... Q×Kt; with mate to follow. But— White holds the centre and could simply and logically cut across Black's plans by playing B—K4, with immediate threats. White's next move, however, if less logical, is the beginning of a combination of wondrous beauty.

19. QR—Qsq.   Q×Kt

Black should have played ... R—Kt5, after which it is doubtful whether White could do more than draw ; but the lure of " mate in one " was too strong for him !

20. R×Ktch.   Kt×R
21. Q×Pch.   K×Q
22. B—B5db.ch.   K—Ksq.
23. B—Q7ch.   K—B(or Q)sq.
24. B×Kt mate.

This ending is a monument to human ingenuity, and exhaustive analysis has proved that the combination inaugurated by Anderssen with his 19th move wins whatever Black may do. The position in the diagram would repay careful study.

The following are some of the recognized lines of attack and defence in the " Evans ".

Repeat the first six moves on both sides, and now, if Black after White has castled plays 7. . . . B—Kt3 followed by 8. P×P, P—Q3 we arrive at what is known as the " Normal Position ". This gives White the choice of three continuations, viz. (i) P—Q5, (ii) Kt—B3, and (iii) B—Kt2, this last leading to play rather too involved for the beginner.

(i) 9. $\dfrac{\text{P—Q5}}{\text{Kt—R4}}$ (especially in the "Evans" Black's QKt is liable to be driven to QR4, and, of course, White will keep him there, inactive, as long as he conveniently can);

10. $\dfrac{\text{B—Kt2}}{\text{Kt—K2 !}}$; 11. $\dfrac{\text{B—Q3}}{\text{Castles}}$.

12. $\dfrac{\text{Kt—B3}}{\text{Kt—Kt3}}$; 13. $\dfrac{\text{Kt—K2}}{\text{P—QB4}}$,

resulting in the position shown in Fig. 12 and leading to a game in which the odds should be slightly in favour of Black.

FIG. 12.—13. . . . . P—QB4.

(ii) After the same first eight moves—9. $\dfrac{\text{Kt—B3}}{\text{Kt—R4}}$;

10. $\dfrac{\text{B—KKt5}}{\text{P—KB3}}$; 11. $\dfrac{\text{B—K3}}{\text{Kt—K2}}$; 12. $\dfrac{\text{P—KR3}}{\text{B—Q2}}$; 13. $\dfrac{\text{B—Kt3}}{\text{Kt} \times \text{B}}$;

14. $\dfrac{\text{Q} \times \text{Kt}}{\text{Q—Bsq.}}$; 15. $\dfrac{\text{P—QR4}}{\text{B—K3}}$, and White should win.

The "Compromised Defence", so called because Black's undeveloped position somewhat imperils his game in spite of his three Pawns to the good, arises when, after White's 7. Castles, Black replies 7. . . . . P × P; play may proceed :

8. $\dfrac{\text{Q—Kt3}}{\text{Q—B3}}$; 9. $\dfrac{\text{P—K5}}{\text{Q—Kt3}}$; 10. $\dfrac{\text{Kt} \times \text{P}}{\text{KKt—K2}}$; 11. $\dfrac{\text{B—R3}}{\text{B} \times \text{Kt}}$;

12. $\dfrac{\text{Q} \times \text{B}}{\text{Castles}}$; 13. $\dfrac{\text{QR—Qsq.}}{\text{R—Ksq.}}$ and White, though still with a minority of two Pawns, has a strong attack. The game might also have gone (after Black's 8th)—

9. $\dfrac{\text{B—Kt5}[1]}{\text{Q—Kt3}}$; 10. $\dfrac{\text{Kt} \times \text{P}}{\text{B} \times \text{Kt}}$; 11. $\dfrac{\text{Q} \times \text{B}}{\text{P—B3}[2]}$; 12. $\dfrac{\text{B—B4}}{\text{P—Q3}}$

—and White still has the better game.

[1] Inferior to 9. P—K5.
[2] The best move. 11. . . . . Kt—B3 would be inferior.

Further, Black has also the option, on his 5th move, of retiring his Bishop to K2, Q3 (neither of which is to be recommended as White has little difficulty in maintaining the superiority of his position), or to his B4. This last has little advantage, as Black can readily reach the " Normal Position " by transposition of moves, as in :

$$5. \frac{}{\text{B—B4}}; \quad 6. \frac{\text{P—Q4}}{\text{P} \times \text{P}}; \quad 7. \frac{\text{P} \times \text{P}}{\text{B—Kt3}}; \quad 8. \frac{\text{Castles}}{\text{P—Q3}}; \quad \text{etc.}$$

But, as has been said, the Gambit may be declined, and, as it is exceedingly complicated both for the attack and the defence, perhaps it is safer for Black to do so. It is done by playing 4. . . . B—Kt3, and the opening then reverts to a Giuoco Piano, White having (theoretically speaking) compromised his pawns on the Queen's side by having advanced them prematurely. which advance may prove a weakness in the ending.

THE EVANS GAMBIT DECLINED

After

$$1. \frac{\text{P—K4}}{\text{P—K4}}; \quad 2. \frac{\text{Kt—KB3}}{\text{Kt—QB3}}; \quad 3. \frac{\text{B—B4}}{\text{B—B4}}; \quad 4. \frac{\text{P—QKt4}}{\text{B—Kt3}};$$

there are three main continuations open to White. He may play : 5. B—Kt2, the most natural move—counter-attacking the centre before incurring further commitments on the wing ; 5. P—QR4, weakening the Q-side still more ; or 5. P—Kt5, seeking to liquidate the position of his advanced Pawn, a hazardous procedure.

FIRST VARIATION

The first four moves as above.

$$5. \frac{\text{B—Kt2}}{\text{P—Q3}}; \quad 6. \frac{\text{P—QR4}}{\text{P—QR3}}; \quad 7. \frac{\text{P—Kt5}}{\text{P} \times \text{P}}; \quad 8. \frac{\text{P} \times \text{P}}{\text{R} \times \text{R}};$$

$$9. \frac{\text{B} \times \text{R}}{\text{Kt—Q5}}; \quad 10. \frac{\text{B} \times \text{Kt}}{\text{P} \times \text{B}} \quad \text{— with equal chances.}$$

SECOND VARIATION

The first four moves as above.

$$5. \frac{\text{P—QR4}}{\text{P—QR3}}; \quad 6. \frac{\text{Castles}}{\text{P—Q3}}; \quad 7. \frac{\text{P—R5}}{\text{B—R2}}; \quad 8. \frac{\text{P—Kt5}}{\text{P} \times \text{P}};$$

$$9. \frac{\text{B} \times \text{P}}{\text{Kt—K2}}; \quad 10. \frac{\text{P—Q4}}{}; \quad \text{and White has made no headway.}$$

THIRD VARIATION

The first four moves as above.

5. $\dfrac{\text{P—Kt5}}{\text{Kt—R4}}$;   6. $\dfrac{\text{Kt} \times \text{P}}{\text{Kt—R3}}$;   7. $\dfrac{\text{P—Q4}}{\text{P—Q3}}$;   8. $\dfrac{\text{B} \times \text{Kt}}{}$.

Now Black has the choice of capturing the Kt or the QB, the former being preferable on the whole.

8. $\dfrac{}{\text{P} \times \text{Kt}}$;   9. $\dfrac{\text{B} \times \text{P}}{\text{R—KKt1}}$;   10. $\dfrac{\text{B} \times \text{Pch.}}{\text{K} \times \text{B}}$;   11. $\dfrac{\text{B} \times \text{P}}{}$

and Black will withstand the attack and have the advantage. If, on the other hand, White captures the Bishop

8. $\dfrac{}{\text{P} \times \text{B}}$;   9. $\dfrac{\text{B} \times \text{Pch.}}{\text{K—K2}}$;   10. $\dfrac{\text{Q—B3}}{\text{B} \times \text{P}}$;   11. $\dfrac{\text{Kt—B3}}{\text{P—B3}}$,

the chances are equal.

Black can avoid all the various attacks arising from the Giuoco Piano and Evans Gambit by playing on his third move, . . . Kt—B3, and thus adopting what is known as—

THE TWO KNIGHTS' DEFENCE

1. $\dfrac{\text{P—K4}}{\text{P—K4}}$;   2. $\dfrac{\text{Kt—KB3}}{\text{Kt—QB3}}$;   3. $\dfrac{\text{B—B4}}{\text{Kt—B3}}$.

White has various replies to this opening, of which we have space to mention five, and to give examples of two. (i) Kt—Kt5 ; (ii) P—Q4 ; (iii) Kt—B3 ; (iv) Castles ; (v) P—Q3. The last two are safe but unenterprising variations of the " Giuoco ", but as they give Black a wider choice of continuation—in that he can develop his KB at K2, B4, or Kt5 according to circumstances, and play his QP to Q3 or Q4—they are best avoided. 4. Kt—B3, also, is not easy to manage without giving Black the advantage.

(1) 4. Kt—Kt5. This attack, though in advance of White's development and therefore premature, has dangers, but not such as make it impossible for Black to equalize. After the first three moves (above) proceed :

    4. Kt—Kt5   P—Q4
    5. P × P   Kt—QR4

This move of Black's disposes of both the White pieces which have undertaken so early an attack. 5. . . . Kt × P, in place of it, is very hazardous ; as, for instance : 6. Kt × BP, K × Kt ; 7. Q—B3ch., K-K3 ; 8. Kt—B3, etc. —and Black's position is soon hopeless.

    6. P—Q3   . . .

If 6. B—Kt5ch.; then, . . . P—B3; 7. P×P, P×P; 8. B—K2, P—KR3; 9. Kt—KB3, P—K5; 10. Kt—K5, Q—B2; 11. P—Q4, B—Q3; 12. P—KB4, P×P, *e.p.*; 13. Kt×P (B3), Castles, or Kt—Kt5—and Black has a nice open game.

. . .	P—KR3
7. Kt—KB3	P—K5
8. Q—K2	Kt×B
9. P×Kt	B—QB4
10. KKt—Q2	Castles
11. Kt—Kt3	B—Kt5
12. Q—B1	. . .

Black has the initiative, and this humiliating retreat of White's Q is the result.

. . .

FIG. 13.—12. . . . B—Kt5ch.

B—Kt5ch.

Now White cannot very well play 13. B—Q2, because of . . . B×Bch.; 14. QKt×B, R—K1: followed by . . . P—K6; while if he tries 13. Kt—B3 the game could continue: $13.\dfrac{\overline{\quad\quad}}{\text{P—QKt4}}$;

$14.\dfrac{\text{PKR3}}{\text{B—KR4}}$; $15.\dfrac{\text{P—Kt4}}{\text{B—Kt3}}$;

$16.\dfrac{\text{B—Q2}}{\text{B×Kt}}$; $17.\dfrac{\text{B×B}}{\text{P×P}}$; $18.\dfrac{\text{Q×P}}{\text{Q×P}}$;

$19.\dfrac{\text{Q×Q}}{\text{Kt×Q}}$ and Black has at least maintained equality, whereas the alternative, 13. P—B3, seriously weakens White's Q3, as now appears:

13. P—B3	B—K2
14. P—KR3	B—R4
15. P—Kt4	B—Kt3

The B is well posted here, as White obviously will have to Castle on the Q-side. This in itself is a disadvantage, as, when both players have castled on opposite wings, the Q-side offers a more vulnerable target. Here, moreover, Black has completed his development and is ready for the attack.

16. B—K3	Kt—Q2
17. QKt—Q2	Kt—K4
18. Castles	P—Kt4

Opening new lines of attack on the King's position.

    19. P×P   Kt—Q6ch.

A serious consequence of the weakness of White's Q3, brought about by 13. P—B3.

    20. K—Ktsq.   Q×P

    21. K—Rsq.   . . .

getting out of the line of the B —

    . . .   Q×P

    22. P—KB4   P—QR4

    23. R—QKtsq.   P—KB4

    24. Kt—Q4   Q—R5

    25. Kt×BP   R×Kt

Superior development nearly always provides opportunities of finding a short cut to victory by brilliant sacrifices.

FIG. 14.—24. . . . Q—R5.

    26. P×R   Kt—Kt5

Threatening a smothered mate at B7, and also Q×P mate.

    27. P×Kt   P×P

    28. P—R3   B—B3

    29. K—R2   Q×Pch.

    30. P×Q   R×P

                       mate.

(2) 4. P—Q4 is an aggressive continuation to the Two Knights' Defence, designed to maintain White's position in the centre ; but it means sacrifices, and requires great care on both sides, as is exemplified in the following play :

1. $\dfrac{\text{P—K4}}{\text{P—K4}}$;   2. $\dfrac{\text{Kt—KB3}}{\text{Kt—QB3}}$;   3. $\dfrac{\text{B—B4}}{\text{Kt—B3}}$;   4. $\dfrac{\text{P—Q4}}{\text{P×P}}$;

5. $\dfrac{\text{Castles}}{\text{Kt×P}^{1}}$;   6. $\dfrac{\text{R—Ksq.}}{\text{P—Q4}}$;   7. $\dfrac{\text{B×P}}{\text{Q×B}}$;   8. $\dfrac{\text{Kt—B3}}{\text{Q—Q1}}$;

9. $\dfrac{\text{R×Ktch.}}{\text{B—K2}}$;   10. $\dfrac{\text{Kt×P}}{\text{P—B4}}$;   11. $\dfrac{\text{R—B4}}{\text{Castles}}$;   12. $\dfrac{\text{Kt×Kt}}{\text{Q×Qch.}}$;

13. $\dfrac{\text{Kt×Q}}{\text{P×Kt}}$;   14. $\dfrac{\text{R—B4}}{\text{R—Ksq.}}$;   15. $\dfrac{\text{B—B4}}{\text{B—R3}}$;   16. $\dfrac{\text{R×P}}{\text{B—Kt2}}$

[1] If here Black had played, 5. . . . B—B4, he would have, by transposition of moves, let himself in for the dangers of the Max Lange Attack (see p. 378).

and the games are even (if 17. R × P, Black wins by . . .
B—Q3, threatening mate).

THE RUY LOPEZ

This Opening, invented by the Spaniard, Ruy Lopez,
in the sixteenth century, is still regarded as the strongest
of the K-side Openings, largely because its attack on the
centre is indirect, and an indirect attack—if sound in
principle—is always difficult to meet. Instead of developing the Bishop at QB4 with the intention of an attack
upon Black's weakest point—viz. KBP, White plays
3. B—Kt5, threatening to win Black's KP by exchanging
its only support, the Kt, for White's KB. But Black
need not, as yet, defend his KP ; he can counter-attack by
3. . . . Kt—B3, or make other replies which will be mentioned
later. It has, however, become the usual practice to play
. . . P—QR3, so that, after 4. B—R4, Black can, if he so
chooses, eliminate the awkward pin by . . . P—QKt4.

After 3. . . . P—QR3 ; 4. B—R4, Kt—KB3 ; 5. Castles,
Black must decide whether to adopt a purely defensive
attitude by protecting his KP or to play an aggressive
game by himself playing Kt × P.

In the former case, Black must play . . . P—Q3 ; and if
White increases the pressure by P—Q4, Black's liberating
move . . . P—Q4 is postponed indefinitely.

This move is available where Black adopts the continuation . . . Kt × P ; but in that case . . . P—QKt4
will have to be played and the QBP is in danger of remaining
backward while the loose formation of Black's Q-side
Pawns militates against an otherwise promising Defence.

The following most instructive game was played between
the masters Alexander Alekhine (White) and Reuben Fine
(Black) in 1937.

WHITE	BLACK
1. P—K4	P—K4
2. Kt—KB3	Kt—QB3
3. B—Kt5	P—QR3

As we have seen, the Opening is completed with White's 3rd
move ; Black's 3rd constitutes the "Morphy Defence" (see p. 390) ;
3. . . . Kt—B3 (the "Berlin Defence"—turning it into a "close"
game—see p. 372) attacking the KP at once, was formerly the
usual continuation.

4. B—R4 . . .

Here White has the option of playing 4. B × Kt (the
" Exchange " variation) ; this has the merit of making
Black's 3. . . . . P—QR3 a wasted move ; but as this
should usually lead to a draw it is but seldom played.

. . .   Kt—B3

5. Castles   . . .

At Black's 4th he can also play P—Q3, freeing his QB
and giving his KP additional protection ; White has many
replies, e.g. 5. P—B3 ; P—B4 (guarding his Q5) ; B × Kt
(not particularly favourable) ; Castles ; and Kt—B3. Of
these P—B3 is probably the best, leading to : 5. . . . B—Q2 ;
6. P—Q4, P—KKt3! ; 7. Castles, B—Kt2 ; or to 5. . . . Kt—B3
6. P—Q4, B—Q2 ; 7. Castles, B—K2 ; 8. R—Ksq.,
Castles ; in both these variations Black attains a fairly
equalizing position. By White's text-move (Castles) he
leaves his KP unprotected and continues his development.
If Black captures the P, White has an open file on which to
to attack.

. . .   B—K2

6. R—K1   . . .

Now that Black has a B on the K file, the capture of the
White KP would be less risky, and so White supports
it with his last move. The student should note that the
original threat in the Ruy Lopez, the capture of Black's
KP after B × Kt, has become a reality and it becomes
essential to eliminate the attack on the QKt.

. . .   P—QKt4

7. B—Kt3   P—Q3
8. P—B3   . . .

The object of this move
is twofold : White wishes
to provide a safe retreat
for his KB, his main
attacking piece, which
Black could otherwise
exchange for his Kt (. . .
Kt—QR4), and to prepare
for P—Q4. He cannot
play 8. P—Q4 at once, as he
would then lose material by:

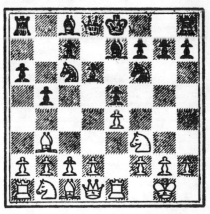

FIG. 15.—7. . . . . P—Q3.

8. P—Q4, Kt × QP ; 9. Kt × Kt, P × Kt ; 10. Q × P,
P—B4 ; and Black wins the B by . . . P—B5.

       . . .   Kt—QR4

Black must make way for his QBP to advance, in order to contest the centre.

    9. B—B2   P—B4
   10. P—Q4   Q—B2

FIG. 16.—10. . . . Q—B2.

A difficult position for both sides. If White now play 11. P—Q5, he blocks the centre and ends that fluidity so essential to his strategy in this Opening. His only chance then is a K-side attack, whilst Black, with . . . B—Q2 ; and . . . P—Kt5, will attempt a counter-demonstration on the Q-side.

   11. QKt—Q2   . . .

strengthening the centre. The further progress of this Kt will be via KB1—K3 or KKt3, or, upon occasion, direct to QB4.

Other playable continuations are : 11. P—KR3 (preventing Black's . . . B—Kt5. Black can continue with 11. . . . B—Q2 ; 12. QKt—Q2, R—QB1), or : 11. P—QR4, an attempt to break up the Q-side which Black can answer with 11. . . . R—R2 (the alternative, R—QKtsq., though often tried, has not been very successful).

       . . .   Castles

Here Black could have played : (i) 11. . . . Kt—B3 (the more usual move), or (ii) B—Kt5, White replying with (i) 12. P—QR4, or (ii) P—Q5, neither alternative leading to an easy game for Black ; or (iii) 11. . . . BP×P, with a chance of equalizing through—12. P×P, Kt—B3 ; 13. P×P, P×P ; 14. Kt—Bsq., B—Kt5 ; 15. B—K3, R—Qsq.

   12. Kt—Bsq.   B—Kt5
   13. Kt—K3 !   B × Kt
   14. Q × B !   . . .

White's offered sacrifice of a Pawn on his 13th is justified by his hold on the centre and by the fact that Black's QKt is out of play and would need three valuable moves

to return for the defence of the K-side ; by his 14th
he preserves his Pawn formatior unbroken.

		BP × P
15.	Kt—B5	P × P
16.	Q × P !	. . .

The point of this subtle combination : as Black cannot
exchange Queens because White, before recapturing, plays
Kt × Bch., winning a piece, Black must move or protect
his Queen and White gains a move for the attack on Black's
KKt2.

		KR—Bsq.
17.	Q—KKt3	B—Bsq.
18.	B—Q3	Kt—B3
19.	B—Kt5	Kt—Ksq.
20.	QR—Bsq.	Q—Kt2

With every move Black has to ward off troublesome
threats, for White has the initiative.

21.	P—QR3	P—Kt3
22.	Kt—R6ch.	B × Kt
23.	B × B	Kt—Q5
24.	QR—Qsq.	. . .

The defender, when hard pressed, should nearly always
try to exchange as many pieces as possible to relieve the
pressure. The attacker, on the other hand, should, as
here, avoid exchanges. It looks, however, as if this R
ought to have gone to Qsq. in the first place.

		P—Kt5
25.	P—B4	P × BP
26.	Q × P	P × P
27.	P × P	R—B6
28.	Q—B2	. . .

Black is attempting a counter-demonstration on the
Q-side ; White wisely takes no notice. In a complicated
attacking position the ability accurately to time attacking
and defensive moves, and patience, are of inestimable value.

		Kt—K3

Return of the wanderer.

29.	P—QR4	QR—Bsq.
30.	R—KBsq.	KR—B2

Either R could have moved to B2, but the text-move
is the better ; the QR, had it moved to B2 for the protection of KB2, would have had the additional task of covering

his companion, and *a piece needed for the protection of an essential point cannot safely be relied on for other tasks.*

31. R—Ktsq.	Q—B3
32. P—R5	. . .

If Black attempts to win this Pawn or to exchange Queens by 32. . . . Q—B4; White plays 33. B—K3, Q×P; 34. B—Kt6, winning the exchange.

. . .	Kt—B4

To prevent the loss of the QRP after 33. R—Kt6, but it allows, if anything, a worse evil, as now the KB can participate in the direct attack.

33. B—QB4	Q—Q2

There is no good move.

34. Q—R2	Kt×P

If . . . Kt—K3; 35. B×Kt, Q×B; 36. Q×Q, P×Q; 37. R—B8 mate.

35. R×P	Q×R
36. B×Qch.	R×B
37. Q—K6	Resigns

He cannot avoid the loss of at least a piece.

The following is, perhaps, the most enterprising and lively defence to the Ruy Lopez:

1. P—K4	P—K4
2. Kt—KB3	Kt—QB3
3. B—Kt5	P—QR3
4. B—R4	Kt—B3
5. Castles	Kt×P

This is the " Morphy Defence "; and here Black tries to assume the initiative. White would gain nothing by 6. R—Ksq., Kt—B4; 7. B×Kt, QP×B; 8. P—Q4, Kt—K3; 9. Kt×P, B—K2; 10. P—QB3, Castles.

6. P—Q4	. . .

White, having lost a centre Pawn, must replace it by another. Merely winning it back would be insufficient; the text-move is the only method because for Black now to capture the QP would be highly hazardous, for it would be followed by 7. R—Ksq., and Black would have to play a difficult defensive game for, at least, many moves.

. . .	P—QKt4
7. B—Kt3	P—Q4
8. P×P	B—K3

9. P—B3   . . .

The sequence of moves is very important: Black has now secured his KKt (. . . P—Q4) ; and his QP (. . . B—K3) so is free to play . . . Kt—QR4, attacking White's KB ; hence White provides a flight square.

. . .   **B—K2**

Black could have played . . . B—QB4 ; but it is not advantageous, for it would not only block the later advance of his QBP, but would, also, not be in

FIG. 17.—9. P—B3.

accord with his strategy, which is to attack White's Q-side (weakened by the loss of a Pawn), just as it is White's strategy to attack Black's K-side (weakened in a like manner).

10. QKt—Q2   Castles

White cannot proceed with his plan until he has driven away Black's advanced Kt ; nor can Black proceed with his before his K has been removed to safety.

11. Q—K2   **Kt—B4**
12. Kt—Q4   . . .

12. B—B2 would have allowed . . . P—Q5, with good prospects for Black.

. . .   **Kt × B**

13. QKt × Kt   . . .

keeping the vital QB5 under fire.

. . .   **Q—Q2**
14. Kt × Kt   **Q × Kt**

Again Black's QBP is blocked !

15. B—K3   . . .

Always directing his forces on the same fateful square.

. . .   **B—KB4**
16. KR—Qsq.   **KR—Qsq.**

If now White play 17. Kt—R5 (taking away a piece from his control of QB5), Q—KKt3 ; 18. Kt—Kt7, threatening to establish itself at QB5 and preventing permanently the advance of Black's QBP, at the same time attacking the Black Rook, Black follows with 18. . . . P—Q5 (attacking the Bishop) followed by 19. . . . B—K5, attacking the Knight, threatening mate, and winning.

    17. P—B3   B—KBsq.

sheltering an unprotected piece before continuing operations.

    18. Q—KB2   P—QR4

The battle for Black's QB4 seems now won by White, but Black has re-grouped his forces for further efforts, and this game—played between Botwinnik and Euwe, both of whom were later World Champions—was eventually drawn at Black's (Euwe's) 49th move.

The Morphy Defence (3. . . . P—QR3) need not, however, result in the retreat of the Bishop; White may prefer the perfectly sound " Exchange Variation ", viz. 4. B × Kt, QP × B (better than . . . KtP × B) ; but he must not follow by capturing the KP, for Black would regain it at once by 5. . . . Q—Q5, with an excellent position. So the game may proceed : 5. Kt—B3, P—B3 ; then 6. P—Q3, B—Q3 ; 7. B—K3, Kt—K2 ; 8. Q—Q2, P—QB4 ; 9. Kt—K2, Kt—B3 :—or 6. P—Q4, P × P ; 7. Q × P, Q × Q ; 8. Kt × Q, B—Q2 ; 9. B—K3, Castles—and in either case Black has equalized.

The Ruy Lopez is one of the most prolific in variations of all the Openings, but space will only allow us to mention —without giving extended examples—a few of the more important.

Black on his 3rd move may, as has been said, counter-attack by 3. . . . Kt—B3 (the " Berlin Defence ") ; White's best reply is 4. Castles, disregarding the capture of his own KP, which he will soon recover after R—Ksq. or Q—K2, with pressure on the open K-file. The defence usually results in a cramped game for Black, and has practically fallen into disuse. The same may be said of the " Steinitz Defence ", 3. . . . P—Q3, for many years after 1876, when introduced by the great Steinitz, immensely popular ; 4. P—Q4 should afford White a slight advantage (e.g. : 4. . . . B—Q2 ; 5. Kt—B3, Kt—B3 ; 6. B × Kt, B × B ; 7. Q—Q3). The " Steinitz Defence Deferred ", however (1. P—Kt4, P—Kt4 ; 2. Kt—KB3, Kt—QB3 ; 3. B—B5, P—QR3 ; 4. B—B4, P—Q3) is frequently played by masters and others. White has many replies, the most important being : 5. P—Q3, preparing the way for P—Q4 and the development of the QKt by way of Q2 and KB1 either on K3 or KKt3. The " Classical Defence ", 3. . . . B—B4, is strong in that it gives White no immediate advantage, and seems to be best met by 4. P—B3, followed (after 4. . . . KKt—K2 or P—B4) by 5. P—Q4, or (after 4. . . . B—Kt3) by 5. P—Q4 or Castles. " Bird's Defence ", 3. . . . Kt—Q5, is another that has had a revival, especially in the U.S.S.R. The continuation : 4. Kt × Kt, P × Kt ; 5. Castles, Kt—K2 ; 6. P—Q3, P—QB3 ; 7. B—QB4, P—Q4 ; 8. P × P, leads to an interesting game with the odds on White. Other defences, such as the " Fianchetto " (3. . . . P—KKt3, leading to 4. P—Q4, Kt × P ; 5. Kt × Kt, P × Kt ; 6. Q × P, etc.), and the " Schliemann ", a counter-gambit offered by 3. . . . P—B4 (best met by 4. Kt—B3) are rarely seen and are not recommended.

The remaining Openings, though not less important, we shall be compelled to deal with more briefly. It must be remembered that it is only the first three or four moves (or even less) on either side which constitute a given Opening ; the best moves in continuation on either side that have, in many cases, been ascertained by careful analysis are known as " book " moves.

PHILIDOR'S DEFENCE

This, the defence of Black's King's Pawn by 2. . . . P—Q3 after 1. P—K4, P—K4 ; 2. Kt—KB3, is one of the oldest of the Openings and, although it is theoretically unsound— for Black unnecessarily and without compensation blocks his own pieces—still occurs from time to time, even in Tournament play.

WHITE	BLACK
1. P—K4	P—K4
2. Kt—KB3	P—Q3
3. P—Q4	Kt—KB3

A better continuation than 3. . . . Kt—Q2, the " Hanham " variation, as then White can continue : 4. B—QB4, P—QB3 ; 5. Kt—B3, B—K2 ; 6. P × P, P × P ; 7. Kt—KKt5, B × Kt ; 8. Q—R5, and White is better placed for the End-Game. After our move, 3. . . . Kt—KB3, the continuation 4. P × P, Kt × P ; 5. B—QB4, P—QB3 presents no difficulties for Black.

4. Kt—B3	QKt—Q2
5. B—QB4	B—K2 (See Fig. 18.)

FIG. 18.—5. . . . B—K2.

5. Castles   . . .

Here 6. B × Pch., though tempting, gives Black the advantage; nor is the attack by 6. Kt—KKt5, any better, being premature, as the White pieces are insufficiently developed. If, however, White plays 6. P × P and Black replies 6. . . . QKt × P (*not* . . . P × P?) Black should have a quite satisfactory game.

          . . .   Castles

There is no urgency to castle at this point. The spirit of this Opening is, in the early stages, strictly defensive and 6. . . . P—KR3, etc., before Black starts his fight for the initiative, would conform to the general scheme.

   7. Q—K2   P—B3
   8. P—QR4   . . .

An essential move for White. Black's P—QKt4 must be prevented or he will free his game by . . . B—Kt2, with good prospects; while if he played 8. B—KKt5, Black could have an excellent game, as by 8. . . . P—KR3; 9. B—R4, Kt—R4; 10. B—Kt3, Kt × B; 11. RP × Kt, P—QKt4; 12. B—Q3, P—R3. As it is, White should have little difficulty in winning in view of Black's cramped defence.

Instead of 3. . . . Kt—KB3 or Kt—Q2 in reply to White's 3. P—Q4, Black may play 3. . . . P × P, thereby abandoning the centre—a hazardous procedure; the game might then go—4. Kt × P, Kt—KB3; 5. Kt—QB3: and whether Black played 5. . . . B—K2 or P—KKt3 he would have difficulty in freeing himself from his restricted position.

THREE KNIGHTS' GAME

In the *Three Knights' Game*, after 1. P—K4, P—K4; 2. Kt—KB3, Kt—QB3 (or Kt—KB3), White plays 3. Kt—B3, as in:

   1. P—K4   P—K4
   2. Kt—KB3   Kt—QB3
   3. Kt—B3   B—Kt5

4. B—Kt5	Kt—K2
5. P—Q4	P × P
6. Kt × P	Castles

Even game.

Black could have played, instead of 3. . . . B—Kt5, 3. . . . B—B4 or P—KKt3 ; but whatever the actual variation he may adopt he has small chance of a win against correct play.

FOUR KNIGHTS' GAME

This Opening arises by Black moving 3. . . . Kt—B3, the previous moves being as in the Three Knights ; it is converted into a Ruy Lopez if White plays 4. B—Kt5 ; and into a Double Ruy Lopez, if Black replies 4. . . . B—Kt5.

WHITE	BLACK
1. P—K4	P—K4
2. Kt—QB3	Kt—KB3
3. Kt—B3	Kt—B3
4. B—Kt5	B—Kt5

Here Black could have launched an enterprising counter-attack with 4. . . . Kt—Q5, to which White has several replies, of which the most promising are : 5. Kt × Kt, B—R4, and B—B4 ; beware of the obvious 5. Kt × P, it is dangerous for White.

5. Castles	Castles
6. Kt—Q5	Kt × Kt
7. P × Kt	P—K5
8. P × Kt	P × Kt
9. Q × P	. . .

If White had played 9. P × QP, Black's best reply would have been 9. . . . P × P, attacking the Rook ; if 9. P × KtP, Black replies 9. . . . B × KtP, with a promising attack.

. . .	QP × P
10. B—K2	B—Q3

Even game.

THE VIENNA OPENING

comes about by 1. P—K4, P—K4 ; 2. Kt—QB3. White thereby secures his KP and, above all, controls Black's Q4 ; but as it sets Black no real problem of opening strategy it is now not often played.

Of Black's defences—2. . . . Kt—KB3, B—B4, and Kt—QB3 (other possibles are not worth trying) the first is the strongest and most logical ; it bears on the centre, attacks White's KP, and ensures . . . P—Q4.

WHITE	BLACK
1. P—K4	P—K4
2. Kt—QB3	Kt—KB3
3. B—B4	Kt × P
4. Kt × Kt	P—Q4

If White on his 4th move had played B × Pch., then 4. . . . K × B ; 5. Kt × Kt, P—Q4 ; and in either case, Black has reached equality without any of the tribulations which a second player would expect in the opening.

If on his 3rd move White attacks the centre by offering the temporary sacrifice of his KBP —

THE VIENNA GAMBIT

is the result and, if Black takes the Pawn, White's game is promising indeed. He can, with P—Q4, assume full control of the centre and both Bishops are mobilized. The value of Black's second move, . . . Kt—KB3, is seen here ; he boldly contests the centre by . . . P—Q4.

1. $\dfrac{\text{P—K4}}{\text{P—K4}}$; 2. $\dfrac{\text{Kt—QB3}}{\text{Kt—KB3}}$; 3. $\dfrac{\text{P—B4}}{\text{P—Q4}}$; 4. $\dfrac{\text{P} \times \text{KP}}{\text{Kt} \times \text{P}}$;

5. $\dfrac{\text{Kt—B3}}{\text{B—K2}}$; 6. $\dfrac{\text{P—Q4}}{\text{Castles}}$; 7. $\dfrac{\text{B—Q3}}{\text{P—KB4}}$; 8. $\dfrac{\text{P} \times \text{P}e.p.}{\text{B} \times \text{P}}$;

9. $\dfrac{\text{Castles}}{\text{Kt—B3}}$ and Black has a satisfactory position. On his

eighth move (see Fig. 21, p. 406) he could have played . . . Kt × P, which, however, leads to complications.

THE SCOTCH GAME AND SCOTCH GAMBIT

1. P—K4	P—K4
2. Kt—KB3	Kt—QB3
3. P—Q4	P × P

Black is obliged to exchange Pawns ; for if 3. . . . P—Q3 ; 4. P × P, Kt × P ; 5. Kt × Kt, P × Kt ; Q × Qch., and Black's position is ruined. The idea underlying this opening is to challenge possession of the centre by 3. P—Q4, at this early stage, though it has the drawback that the plan is disclosed when Black's QKt only has been mobilized, enabling Black to take counter-measures in good time.

The Scotch Gambit, in which White does not recapture the Pawn on the 4th move, is precarious for White against sound play. Both openings have fallen into disfavour, but they provide good practice.

4. $\dfrac{\text{Kt} \times \text{P}}{\text{Kt—B3}}$; 5. $\dfrac{\text{Kt} \times \text{Kt}}{\text{KtP.} \times \text{Kt}}$; 6. $\dfrac{\text{B—Q3}}{\text{P—Q4}}$; 7. $\dfrac{\text{P} \times \text{P}}{\text{P} \times \text{P}}$;

8. $\dfrac{\text{B—Kt5ch.}}{\text{B—Q2}}$; 9. $\dfrac{\text{B} \times \text{Bch.}}{\text{Q} \times \text{B}}$; 10. $\dfrac{\text{Castles}}{\text{B—K2}}$; 11. $\dfrac{\text{Kt—Q2}}{\text{Castles K}}$;

And Black, with a Pawn in the centre, has at least as good a game as his opponent. Whenever Black in K-side openings can, without attendant disadvantages, force ... P—Q4, White will have lost the advantage of the first move.

THE SCOTCH GAMBIT

As has been said, the Scotch Gambit arises when White refuses to capture Black's Pawn on his 4th move. Repeat the first three moves of each side above :

4. $\dfrac{\text{B—QB4}}{\text{B—B4}}$; 5. $\dfrac{\text{P—B3}}{\text{P} \times \text{P}}$; 6. $\dfrac{\text{Kt} \times \text{P}}{\text{P—Q3}}$; 7. $\dfrac{\text{Q—Kt3}}{\text{Q—Q2}}$;

8. $\dfrac{\text{Kt—Q5}}{\text{KKt—K2}}$; 9. $\dfrac{\text{Q—B3}}{\text{Castles}}$ and White has no equivalent

for the Pawn he has given up.

THE CENTRE GAME AND THE DANISH GAMBIT

The remarks made in connection with the Scotch Game and Gambit apply here with even greater force, for White's attack on the centre by P—Q4, occurs here even earlier. They have little chance against sound and expert play by Black, and therefore have all but disappeared from the master's repertoire, but against weak play on his part these openings afford great scope for manœuvre.

WHITE	BLACK
1. P—K4	P—K4
2. P—Q4	P × P
3. Q × P	Kt—QB3

It is clear that White now loses a move, which in itself should equalize the game. However, he finds a suitable square for the Q at K3, in readiness for a K-side attack.

Moreover, he has a Pawn in the centre. Black must strive, as in so many other openings, to encompass the liberating move . . . P—Q4. It is evident that White will castle on the Q-side, which is part of his strategy in opening the Q-file. This fore-knowledge should greatly help Black in the choice of his moves.

4. Q—K3	Kt—B3
5. Kt—QB3	B—Kt5
6. B—Q2	Castles
7. Castles	R—Ksq.
8. Q—Kt3	Kt × P
9. Kt × Kt	R × Kt
10. B—KB4	Q—B3

Black has won a Pawn, which White cannot recover by 11. B × P, without endangering his position, as Black would cut off the B by . . . P—Q3, and occupy the QB file with a Rook after further development.

11. Kt—R3	P—Q3

and Black has the better chances.

As another example: After the first four moves as above, play 5. P—K5, and the game may proceed: . . . Kt—KKt5; 6. Q—K4, P—Q4; 7. P × P*e.p.*, ch., B—K3; 8. B—QR6, Q × P; 9. B × P, Q—Kt5ch. ; 10. Q × Q, Kt × Q—again with advantage to Black.

THE DANISH GAMBIT

In this offshoot of the Centre Game, White, after 2. . . . P × P, offers the sacrifice of a Pawn instead of recapturing : 3. P—QB3, and if Black accepts it he offers yet another by 4. B—QB4, P × P ; 5. B × P, and now, although White is two Pawns down, he has two Bishops bearing on Black's K-side, whereas Black is totally undeveloped. It looks as if White ought to win long before Black can marshal his forces ; but the old saving clause, . . . P—Q4 retrieves the position, for though Black gives back one of the Pawns he can hold the other and put up a sufficient defence. Any other method except perhaps 5. . . . Q—K2 ; is most hazardous, as is seen in the following variation, given to illustrate the basic idea of the Gambit.

WHITE	BLACK
1. P—K4	P—K4
2. P—Q4	P × P

3. P—QB3   P × P
4. B—QB4   P × P
5. B × P   Kt—KB3

If Black had played 5. . . . P—Q4 ; e.g. 6. B × P, Kt—KB3 ;
7. B × Pch., K × B ; 8. Q × Q, B—Kt5ch., he would win the
End-Game owing to his superiority on the Q-side ; while if 6. P × P,
Kt—KB3, he keeps one of the Pawns and has no positional difficulties to fear.

6. Kt—QB3   B—Kt5

Tempting but unsound. He cannot afford to neglect his Q-side
as he does. With every move, White improves his attacking
chances.

7. Kt—K2   . . .

Giving up yet another Pawn, which, however, Black cannot
afford to take.

. . .   Kt × P
8. Castles   Kt × Kt
9. Kt × Kt   B × Kt
10. B × B   Q—Kt4

Owing to his short-sighted
policy, Black has had to exchange
the few pieces which he had in
play. The sequel is brilliant and
instructive.

11. R—Ksq.ch.   K—Qsq.
12. P—B4   Q × P
13. B × KtP   R—Ktsq.
14. Q—Kt4   . . .

and Black is lost. If: . . .
Q × Q ; 15. B—B6 mate, and
if . . . Q—Q3 ; 15. B—B6ch.,
Q × B ; 16. Q × R mate.

FIG. 19.—10. . . . Q—Kt4.

Instead of giving all three
Pawns, White obtains a fine
attack by giving only two.
After the first three moves :
4. Kt × P, B—Kt5 ; 5. B—QB4, P—Q3 ; 6. Kt—B3, B × Kt
ch. ; 7. P × B, Kt—QB3 ; 8. Castles, Kt—B3 ; 9. P—K5,
P × P ; 10. Q—Kt3. But if Black takes only one he
obtains at once a positional advantage and avoids complications—as in : 1. P—K4, P—K4 ; 2. P—Q4, P × P ;
3. P—QB3, P—Q4 ; 4. KP × P, Kt—KB3 ; 5. Kt—B3
(if 5. P—QB4, then . . . P—B3), Kt × P ; 6. Q × P, Kt—
QB3 ; 7. B—QKt5, B—K2 ; 8. Castles, Castles ; 9. B × Kt,
P × B ; with the odds against White.

PONZIANI'S OPENING

The same idea of early aggression in the centre by P—Q4, obtains in this Opening 1. P—K4, P—K4 ; 2. Kt—KB3, Kt—QB3 ; 3. P—B3 ; but it fails, for Black can forestall his opponent by 3. . . . P—Q4 or Kt—B3 (P—B4, exposing his K, is too risky), and should have little difficulty in, at least, equalizing, owing to his superior opportunities for development.

PETROFF'S DEFENCE

Here, after 1. P—K4, P—K4 ; 2. Kt—KB3, Black, instead of defending the KP with 2. . . . Kt—QB3, plays Kt—KB3, attacking the opponent's KP. This mode of defence is sometimes adopted if the second player wishes to avoid the Ruy Lopez, Scotch Opening, or Evans Gambit. On the whole it yields a safe defence, although somewhat tame in the majority of variations.

THE KING'S GAMBITS

The object of a Gambit is twofold : by the sacrifice of a Pawn, a hostile Pawn is lured from the centre ; having command of the centre, the Gambit-player can develop his forces more rapidly than his opponent ; his threats multiply and, in reply, call for defensive instead of developing moves. In many cases he will regain his Pawn, developing yet another piece at the same time, and, moreover, he will derive benefit from the file thus opened ; and the cumulative effect will be a violent attack, frequently culminating in brilliant sacrificial combinations.

The only drawback to this picture is that the defender is under no compulsion to take the Gambit-Pawn. Indeed, he is often better off leaving it where it is, for then the object of the Opening has failed, the Gambit-Pawn is in the way of its own forces and, if answered by a full-blooded developing move, offering the Gambit actually is equivalent to a lost move.

It is also possible to accept the Gambit-Pawn, but to refrain from defending it, utilizing the time which the Gambit-Player will spend in recapturing it, in maturing one's own plans.

Gambit-play has fallen from grace, partly because defensive technique is stronger to-day than it was, and partly because the early disclosure of the player's intentions is foreign to the trend of modern Chess. Nevertheless, the student has much to learn from Gambits.

KING'S KNIGHT'S GAMBIT

WHITE	BLACK
1. P—K4	P—K4
2. P—KB4	. . .

THE KING'S GAMBIT.—Black has now a choice of policies. He can take the Pawn with a view to holding it by 3. . . . P—KKt4; or he can make the developing move 2. . . . B—B4 (King's Gambit Declined), or an attacking move 2. . . . P—Q4 (Falkbeer Counter-Gambit). In the first case he will have made two non-developing moves and, as White will be the first to castle, White will derive great advantage from the open file. Black will for long be strictly on the defensive; but, having taken the Pawn, he can make a pretence of defending it by developing moves so that White's preparation for a counter-attack is delayed.

	P × P
3. Kt—KB3	. . .

If White play 3. B—B4, the King's Bishop's Gambit results.

	P—KKt4

With 3. . . . B—K2; (threatening . . . B—R5ch.) the Cunningham Gambit arises; this is not favourable to the defence and is now rarely seen.

4. B—B4	. . .

If 4. P—KR4, Black is almost forced into a counter-attack by 4. . . . P—Kt5, which, in his undeveloped state, is extremely hazardous. He cannot play 4. . . . P—KB3, for it loses because of 5. Kt × P, P × Kt; 6. Q—R5ch. 4. . . . B—K2; is insufficient: 5. P × P, B × P; 6. P—Q4, P—Q3; 7. P—KKt3, and White's attack should prevail.

	B—Kt2
5. Castles	P—Q3
6. P—B3	. . .

Here 6. P—Q4, is equally good.

	Kt—QB3
7. P—Q4	P—KR3

an essential move for the defence.

Now, after . . . KKt—K2 or B3, and . . . Castles, Black

has a sound game with a Pawn ahead, though White still has the initiative owing to his command of the centre.

If Black plays ... P—Kt5 at his 4th move White adopts either the Muzio or Salvio Gambit, in the former of which although White sacrifices a whole piece, the resulting attack is of such violence that it has every chance to succeed.

THE MUZIO GAMBIT

WHITE	BLACK
1. P—K4	P—K4
2. P—KB4	P×P
3. Kt—KB3	P—KKt4
4. B—B4	P—Kt5
5. Castles	...

The Knight cannot afford to retire to Ktsq., consequently White must either give it up or play Kt—K5 (*see* Salvio Gambit, *below*).

...	P×Kt
6. Q×P	Q—B3
7. P—K5	...

FIG. 20.—5. . . . P×Kt.

A further sacrifice—to enable White to gain time for his development. After the capture of the KP, Black's K and Q will both be exposed to dangers on the open file.

...	Q×P
8. P—Q3	B—R3
9. Kt—B3	Kt—K2
10. B—Q2	QKt—B3
11. QR—Ksq.	Q—B4ch.
12. K—Rsq.	K—Qsq.

Black can hardly afford to castle in view of the open file, nor can the King stay at Ksq. leaving his KKt pinned.

13. QB×P	Kt—Q5
14. Q—B2	B×B
15. Q×B	Kt—K3
16. Q—B6	R—Ksq.
17. Kt—Q5	...

And White has maintained his advantage.

THE SALVIO GAMBIT

The first four moves as above.

5. $\dfrac{\text{Kt—K5}}{\text{Q—R5ch.}}$; 6. $\dfrac{\text{K—B1}}{\text{Kt—QB3}}$; 7. $\dfrac{\text{B} \times \text{Pch.}}{\text{K—K2}}$; 8. $\dfrac{\text{Kt} \times \text{Ktch.}}{\text{QP} \times \text{Kt}}$;

9. $\dfrac{\text{B} \times \text{Kt}}{\text{R} \times \text{B}}$; 10. $\dfrac{\text{Q—Ksq.}}{\text{P—Kt6}}$; 11. $\dfrac{\text{P—Q4}}{\text{P—B6}}$; 12. $\dfrac{\text{P—KR3}}{\text{B—Kt5}}$;

13. $\dfrac{\text{Q—K3}}{\text{R—Kt3}}$. Black has the better game.

THE KIESERITZKI GAMBIT

The first three moves are as above; then, 4. P—KR4, P—Kt5, and now White has the choice between 5. Kt—K5 (Kieseritzki Gambit), and 5. Kt—Kt5 (Allgaier Gambit).

5. Kt—K5, leads to an anxious time for the defence, which, however, with careful play should prevail.

5. $\dfrac{\text{Kt—K5}}{\text{B—Kt2}}$; 6. $\dfrac{\text{P—Q4}}{\text{Kt—KB3}}$; 7. $\dfrac{\text{B—B4}}{\text{P—Q4}}$; 8. $\dfrac{\text{P} \times \text{P}}{\text{Kt—R4}}$;

9. $\dfrac{\text{Kt—QB3}}{\text{Castles}}$; 10. $\dfrac{\text{Kt—K4}}{\text{Kt—Q2}}$; 11. $\dfrac{\text{Kt} \times \text{BP}}{\text{Q—Ksq.}}$; 12. $\dfrac{\text{Kt(B7)Kt5}}{\text{Kt—Kt6}}$;

13. $\dfrac{\text{Kt—Kt3}}{\text{Kt—K6}}$; 14. $\dfrac{\text{B—Kt3}}{\text{Kt} \times \text{P}}$; 15. $\dfrac{\text{B} \times \text{Kt}}{\text{B} \times \text{Kt}}$ and Black has the advantage.

THE ALLGAIER GAMBIT

In playing 5. Kt—Kt5, White in effect gives up a piece, as, after . . . P—KR3, he has no option but to take the KBP. Although the ensuing attack may not be sound, Black will have to find the *coup juste* every time, in order to escape unscathed, and in practical play White has a very good chance of winning.

The first four moves as in the Kieseritzki Gambit:

5. $\dfrac{\text{Kt—Kt5}}{\text{P—KR3}}$; 6. $\dfrac{\text{Kt} \times \text{P}}{\text{K} \times \text{Kt}}$; 7. $\dfrac{\text{B—B4ch.}}{\text{P—Q4}}$; 8. $\dfrac{\text{B} \times \text{Pch.}}{\text{K—Ksq.}}$;

9. $\dfrac{\text{P—Q4}}{\text{Kt—KB3}}$; 10. $\dfrac{\text{Kt—B3}}{\text{B—Kt5}}$; 11. $\dfrac{\text{B} \times \text{BP}}{\text{Kt} \times \text{B}}$; 12. $\dfrac{\text{P} \times \text{Kt}}{\text{Q} \times \text{P}}$;

13. $\dfrac{\text{Castles}}{\text{B} \times \text{Kt}}$; 14. $\dfrac{\text{P} \times \text{B}}{\text{Kt—B3}}$; 15. $\dfrac{\text{Q—Q2}}{\text{B—K3}}$; 16. $\dfrac{\text{QR—Ksq.}}{\text{K—Q2}}$

and Black has nothing to fear as he has an extra piece.

THE BISHOP'S GAMBIT

The opening moves are 1. P—K4, P—K4 ; 2. P—KB4, P×P ; 3. B—B4, after which . . . Q—R5ch., the formerly favoured continuation, forces White to forgo castling by 4. K—Bsq. The Black Queen, however, is in a much exposed position and provides an easy mark for White's attack. 3. . . . Kt—KB3 or P—Q4 are now the accepted continuations, or a combination of the two.

1. $\dfrac{\text{P—K4}}{\text{P—K4}}$; 2. $\dfrac{\text{P—KB4}}{\text{P}\times\text{P}}$; 3. $\dfrac{\text{B—B4}}{\text{Kt—KB3}}$; 4. $\dfrac{\text{Kt—QB3}}{\text{P—B3}}$;

5. $\dfrac{\text{Q—B3}}{\text{P—Q4}}$; 6. $\dfrac{\text{P}\times\text{P}}{\text{B—Q3}}$; 7. $\dfrac{\text{P—Q4}}{\text{B—KKt5}}$; 8. $\dfrac{\text{Q—B2}}{\text{Castles}}$;

9. $\dfrac{\text{B}\times\text{P}}{\text{P}\times\text{P}}$; 10. $\dfrac{\text{B}\times\text{P}}{\text{Kt}\times\text{B}}$; 11. $\dfrac{\text{Kt}\times\text{Kt}}{\text{Q—R4ch.}}$; 12. $\dfrac{\text{Kt—B3}}{\text{B—Kt5}}$;

13. $\dfrac{\text{B—Q2}}{\text{R—Ksq.ch.}}$; 14. $\dfrac{\text{K—Bsq.}}{\text{Kt—B3}}$ and Black has the better game.

THE KING'S GAMBIT DECLINED

Although, in the majority of Gambits, the Defence obtains, if not an advantage, at least an open game, some players prefer not to venture into the labyrinth of their endless variations, and therefore decline to accept the Gambit. Amongst the modes of refusing are 2. . . . B—B4 and P—Q4 (the Falkbeer Counter-Gambit) ; the first is a sound developing move ; but Black must keep in mind that White can play P×P—when the question will be whether White's open KB file will be balanced by Black's open Q file—or P—B5, which blocks the position, probably with adverse effect on the development of Black's QB.

The second method 2. . . . P—Q4, offers as it were a Counter-Gambit and is far more difficult to meet. In many openings . . . P—Q4 is for Black a liberating move ; that he should be able to play it thus early, and with advantage, is in itself a condemnation of this Gambit.

First Variation

1. $\dfrac{\text{P--K4}}{\text{P--K4}}$; 2. $\dfrac{\text{P--KB4}}{\text{B--B4}}$; 3. $\dfrac{\text{Kt--KB3}^1}{\text{P--Q3}}$; 4. $\dfrac{\text{Kt--B3}^2}{\text{Kt--KB3}}$;

5. $\dfrac{\text{B--B4}}{\text{Kt--B3}}$; 6. $\dfrac{\text{P--Q3}}{\text{B--K3}}$; 7. $\dfrac{\text{B--Kt5}}{\text{P--QR3}}$; 8. $\dfrac{\text{B} \times \text{Ktch.}}{\text{P} \times \text{B}}$;

9. $\dfrac{\text{Q--K2}}{\text{P} \times \text{P}}$; 10. $\dfrac{\text{B} \times \text{P}}{\text{Q--Ktsq.}}$; 11. $\dfrac{\text{Kt--Qsq.}}{\text{Castles}}$; 12. $\dfrac{\text{P--B3}}{\text{R--Ksq.}}$;

13. $\dfrac{\text{B--K3}}{\text{B} \times \text{B}}$; 14. $\dfrac{\text{Kt} \times \text{B}}{\text{Kt--Kt5}}$; 15. $\dfrac{\text{Castles K}}{\text{Q--Kt3}}$; 16. $\dfrac{\text{Kt--Q4}}{\text{Kt} \times \text{Kt}}$;

17. $\dfrac{\text{Q} \times \text{Kt}}{\text{P--QB4}}$.   The game is even.

Second Variation
(Falkbeer Counter-Gambit)

1. $\dfrac{\text{P--K4}}{\text{P--K4}}$; 2. $\dfrac{\text{P--KB4}}{\text{P--Q4}}$; 3. $\dfrac{\text{P} \times \text{QP}}{\text{P--K5}}$; 4. $\dfrac{\text{P--Q3}}{\text{Kt--KB3}}$;

5. $\dfrac{\text{P} \times \text{P}}{\text{Kt} \times \text{KP}}$; 6. $\dfrac{\text{Kt--KB3}}{\text{B--QB4}}$; 7. $\dfrac{\text{Q--K2}}{\text{B--B4}^3}$; 8. $\dfrac{\text{Kt--B3}^4}{\text{Q--K2}}$;

9. $\dfrac{\text{B--K3}}{\text{B} \times \text{B}}$; 10. $\dfrac{\text{Q} \times \text{B}}{\text{Kt} \times \text{Kt}}$; 11. $\dfrac{\text{Q} \times \text{Qch.}}{\text{K} \times \text{Q}}$; 12. $\dfrac{\text{P} \times \text{Kt}}{\text{B--K5}}$;

13. $\dfrac{\text{P--B4}}{\text{P--QB3}}$; 14. $\dfrac{\text{P} \times \text{P}}{\text{B} \times \text{Kt}}$; 15. $\dfrac{\text{P--B7}}{\text{Kt--B3}}$; 16. $\dfrac{\text{P} \times \text{B}}{}$.

White is two Pawns to the good ; his ragged Pawn position certainly gives Black some advantage, but not enough for a win

[1] Not 3. P × P because of . . . Q—R5ch. ; (4. K—K2, Q mates ; or 4. P—Kt3, again Q × Pch., winning a Rook).

[2] Again White cannot play 4. P × P, because of . . . P × P ; 5. Kt × P, Q—Q5 ; winning.   He could, however, instead of 5. Kt × P, play 5. P—B3, with play in the centre.

[3] 7. . . . B—B7ch. would lose, e.g. 8. K—Qsq., Q × Pch. ; 9. KKt—Q2, P—KB4 ; 10. Kt—B3.

[4] 8. P—KKt4, winning a piece, would lose the game as follows : 8. P—KKt4, Castles ; 9. P × B, R—Ksq. ; with a winning attack.

CLOSE AND SEMI-OPEN GAMES

As already explained (see p. 372) the Close games comprise all commencing with any other move than 1. P—K4, and the Semi-open all to which Black replies with any other move than 1. ... P—K4. They all require a considerable knowledge of Pawn-play, which is only to be acquired by long experience. In the Open Games the attack is mostly made with pieces, while in the Close and Semi-open the Pawns are pushed forward and the pieces posted behind

OPEN   CLOSE

Both after White's 8th move.

FIG. 21.   FIG. 22.
Vienna Gambit (see p. 396).   King's Indian : Grünfeld's
                                              Defence (see p. 411).

them in strategical positions, coming into action only after the dispositions of the plan of campaign are matured. Any attempt to go further than the opening moves of the more popular of the Close Games would therefore be out of place in an elementary treatise ; but the Semi-open lend themselves to more extended treatment. The chief of these are : the French (1. P—K4, P—K3), Sicilian (1. ... P—QB4), and Caro-Kann (1. ... P—QB3) Defences ; while the Centre Counter (1. ... P—Q4), Alekhine's (1. ... Kt—KB3), and Nimzowitsch's (1. ... Kt—QB3) are less frequently seen. The three first named are sound defences, and particularly suitable when Black wishes to avoid complications for which White, knowing what Opening he proposes to adopt, might have prepared.

THE FRENCH DEFENCE

WHITE	BLACK
1. P—K4	P—K3

Black's QB is temporarily shut in, but, on the other hand, he has none of the immediate difficulties of the Gambits or the Ruy Lopez.

2. P—Q4	P—Q4
3. Kt—QB3	Kt—KB3
4. P—K5	. . .

P—K5 on White's 3rd is not so good; it gives an interesting game, but favours Black.

| . . . | KKt—Q2 |
| 5. P—B4 | P—QB4 |

To break the centre—a laudable object, but better still is to prevent its formation.

| 6. P×P | Kt—QB3 |

The Pawn cannot be defended so Black uses his time to bring an additional piece into play.

| 7. Kt—B3 | B×P |
| 8. B—Q3 | P—B3 |

Again an attack upon the centre.

9. P×P	Kt×P
10. Q—K2	Castles
11. P—QR3	P—QR3

The game is so far even. For another French Defence see p. 365, and Fig. 6.

THE SICILIAN DEFENCE

WHITE	BLACK
1. P—K4	P—QB4

Black at once opposes the formation of a centre; his disadvantage—if it be one—is that he may find it difficult to play . . . P—Q4, and to prevent White's eventual P—QB4.

White's main lines of play are 2. Kt—QB3, with P—KKt3, in which case Black generally also adopts the Fianchetto development; or 2. Kt—KB3; or the Wing Gambit by 2. P—QKt4, which is inferior but dangerous in the hands of an attacking player.

Black's choice of second moves is 2. . . . P—K3; 2. . . . P—Q3; 2. . . . Kt—KB3; and 2. . . . Kt—QB3; according to White's second move.

1. $\dfrac{\text{P—K4}}{\text{P—QB4}}$; 2. $\dfrac{\text{Kt—QB3}}{\text{Kt—QB3}}$; 3. $\dfrac{\text{P—KKt3}}{\text{P—KKt3}}$; 4. $\dfrac{\text{B—Kt2}}{\text{B—Kt2}}$;

5. $\dfrac{\text{P—Q3}}{\text{P—Q3}}$; 6. $\dfrac{\text{KKt—K2}}{\text{Kt—B3}^1}$; 7. $\dfrac{\text{Castles}}{\text{Castles}}$; 8. $\dfrac{\text{P—KR3}}{\text{B—Q2}}$;

9. $\dfrac{\text{B—K3}}{}$ — and White has attacking chances, with P—KB4 at the proper moment.

In the following variation Black's 8. .... P—QR3 constitutes the " Paulsen Defence " to the Sicilian ; it is, however, usually played earlier, e.g. at his 4th move ; its main object is to prevent a hostile Kt occupying QKt5 and so forbidding her QB2 to the Black Q.

1. $\dfrac{\text{P—K4}}{\text{P—QB4}}$; 2. $\dfrac{\text{Kt—KB3}}{\text{P—K3}}$; 3. $\dfrac{\text{P—Q4}^2}{\text{P}\times\text{P}}$; 4. $\dfrac{\text{Kt}\times\text{P}}{\text{Kt—KB3}}$;

5. $\dfrac{\text{QKt—B3}}{\text{P—Q3}}$; 6. $\dfrac{\text{B—K2}}{\text{B—K2}}$; 7. $\dfrac{\text{Castles}}{\text{Castles}}$; 8. $\dfrac{\text{K—Rsq.}}{\text{P—QR3}}$

In the Wing Gambit—1. P—K4, P—QB4 ; 2. P—QKt4 —White offers the Pawn in order to build up a centre and confine his opponent's forces. The game may now proceed : 2. ... P×P ; 3. P—Q4, Kt—KB3 ; 4. B—Q3, P—Q3 ; 5. P—KB4, P—K4 ; 6. Kt—KB3, P×QP ; 7. Castles, Kt—B3 ; 8. Q—Ksq., B—K2 ; 9. B—Kt2, Castles ; 10. QKt—Q2 — and White will recover one of his Pawns and still have attacking chances. If White should tempt with 3. P—QR3 (instead of P—Q4) Black must not fall for it but counter in the centre at once, thus : 3. P—QR3, P—Q4 ; 4. P—K5, Kt—QB3 ; 5. P—Q4, Q—B2 ; 6. Kt—KB3, B—Kt5, and he is in a strong position.

THE CARO-KANN DEFENCE

As in the French, Black wishes to play . . . P—Q4, after his preparatory 1. . . . P—QB3, but without the disadvantage of cramping his QB. After the usual : 1. P—K4, P—QB3 ; 2. P—Q4, P—Q4, White has three

---

[1] Black could also play 6. . . . P—K3, followed by 7. . . . KKt—K2.

[2] Here 3. B—K2 is also good, e.g. 3. B—K2, Kt—QB3 ; 4. Castles, P—Q3 ; 5. P—Q4, P×P ; 6. Kt×P, Kt—B3 ; 7. B—B3, Kt—K4 ; 8. P—B4, with a good game.

main continuations at his disposal—(*a*) 3. P—K5 (which
has little object, as Black's QB is free to develop), (*b*) 3. Kt—
QB3 (the most natural follow-up), and 3. P×P, which
may lead to intricate play after Black has recaptured,
especially if White immediately attacks the centre with
4. P—QB4. Thus: 3. P×P, P×P; 4. P—QB4 (putting
the onus on Black to maintain a centre and at the same
time develop his QB), Kt—KB3; 5. Kt—QB3, Kt—B3;
6. B—Kt5, P×P (the obvious ... P—K3 would shut in the
QB—but is playable), 7. P—Q5, and Black has a difficult,
but not hopeless game.

The alternative, and quieter move for White is 4. B—Q3,
depriving Black's QB of his best square at KB4, and the
game could then proceed: ... Kt—QB3; 5. P—QB3,
Kt—B3; 6. B—KB4, B—Kt5—and now, 7. Q—Kt3
should lead to an even game, while 7. Kt—Kt3 should
result in a better position for White.

In the 3. Kt—QB3 variation 3. ... P×P; 4. Kt×P is
the only reasonable continuation (the Gambit offer, 4. P—B3
is amply met by 4. ... P—K4 or ... P—K6). In reply
Black should avoid 4. ... Kt—B3, as 5. Kt × Ktch. means
the disorganization of his K-side Pawns, though 5. Kt—Kt3
is more likely to lead to an even game; 4. ... Kt—Q2,
followed by the development of both K's Kts, may also be
played, and should lead to a quiet game rather in favour
of White; but Black's best move is 4. ... B—B4, forcing
the withdrawal of the Kt. In the following specimen
game Black achieves a slight advantage:

$$1. \frac{\text{P—K4}}{\text{P—QB3}}; \quad 2. \frac{\text{P—Q4}}{\text{P—Q4}}; \quad 3. \frac{\text{Kt—QB3}}{\text{P×P}}; \quad 4. \frac{\text{Kt×P}}{\text{B—B4}};$$

$$5. \frac{\text{Kt—Kt3}}{\text{B—Kt3}}; \quad 6. \frac{\text{P—KB4}}{\text{P—KR4}}; \quad 7. \frac{\text{P—KR4}}{\text{P—K3}}; \quad 8. \frac{\text{Kt—B3}}{\text{Kt—Q2}};$$

$$9. \frac{\text{B—B4}}{\text{B—K2}}; \quad 10. \frac{\text{Castles}}{\text{Q—B2 !}}; \quad 11. \frac{\text{Kt—K2}}{\text{Castles}}.$$

QUEEN'S PAWN GAMES

The Queen's Pawn openings divide naturally into those
which do, and those which do not, constitute the Gambit
(1. P—Q4, P—Q4; 2. P—QB4).

QUEEN'S GAMBIT ACCEPTED. 1. P—Q4, P—Q4;

2. P—QB4, P×P; 3. Kt—KB3 (if KtQB3 Black replies
... P—K4! or ... P—QB4), Kt—KB3; 4. P—K3,
P—K3; 5. B×P, P—B4; 6. Castles, Kt—B3, etc.

QUEEN'S GAMBIT DECLINED. Of the methods of declin-
ing the Gambit the best are: (a) the Orthodox,
(b) Tarrasch's Defence, and (c) the Slav Defence.
(a) Orthodox: 1. P—Q4, P—Q4; 2. P—QB4, P—K3;
3. Kt—QB3, Kt—KB3; (b) Tarrasch's Defence: 1. P—Q4,
P—Q4; 2. P—QB4, P—K3; 3. Kt—QB3, P—QB4;
(c) the Slav Defence: 1. P—Q4, P—Q4; 2. P—QB4,
P—QB3; 3. Kt—KB3, Kt—B3.

These Defences, the last of which is considered the best
(largely because it affords an outlet for Black's QB) lead
to very many interesting variations which the learner is
recommended to study in one of the books devoted to the
Openings.

The remaining QP Games (that is, all excluding the
Gambits) may conveniently be grouped under three heads
according to whether Black replies to 1. P—Q4 with
(a) P—Q4, (b) Kt—KB3, or (c) any other move.

(a) THE STONEWALL: 1. P—Q4, P—Q4; 2. P—K3,
Kt—KB3; 3. B—Q3, P—B4; 4. P—QB3, Kt—B3;
5. P—KB4, B—Kt5; 6. Kt—B3, P—K3.

COLLE SYSTEM: 1. P—Q4, P—Q4; 2. Kt—KB3,
Kt—KB3; 3. P—K3, P—B4; 4. P—B3, P—K3; 5. QKt
—Q2, Kt—B3; 6. B—Q3, B—Q3.

QUEEN'S KNIGHT: 1. P—Q4, P—Q4; 2. Kt—QB3,
Kt—KB3; 3. B—Kt5, B—B4; 4. P—K3, P—B3;
5. B—Q3, B—Kt3; 6. Kt—B3, QKt—Q2.

(b) This group includes the Indian Defences (those in
which Black does not play P—Q4 at an early stage) and
others.

QUEEN'S INDIAN: 1. P—Q4, Kt—KB3; 2. Kt—KB3,
P—QKt3; 3. P—KKt3, B—Kt2; 4. B—Kt2, P—K3;
5. P—B4, B—Kt5ch.; 6. B—Q2, Q—K2. The
" Bogolyubov Variation " may bring about a similar set-up,
minus the valuable fianchetto of Black's QB: 1. P—K4,
Kt—KB3; 2. P—QB4, P—K3; 3. Kt—KB3, B—Kt5ch.;
4. B—Q2, Q—K2; 5. P—KKt3, etc.

KING'S INDIAN: Here Black's fianchetto is on the K-
instead of Q-side, and there are numerous variations.
1. P—Q4, Kt—KB3; 2. P—QB4, P—KKt3; 3. Kt—QB3,

B—Kt2 ; 4. P—K4, P—Q3 ; 5. P—KKt3, Castles ; 6. B—Kt2, QKt—Q2 ; 7. Kt—B3, P—K4. On his third move Black can set up the strong Grünfeld Defence with 3. . . . P—Q4 with confidence, in spite of its giving White at least five reasonable continuations (4. P—K3, P×P, B—B4, Q—Kt3, and Kt—B3). As an example :

1. $\dfrac{\text{P—Q4}}{\text{Kt—KB3}}$; 2. $\dfrac{\text{P—QB4}}{\text{P—KKt3}}$; 3. $\dfrac{\text{Kt—QB3}}{\text{P—Q4}}$; 4. $\dfrac{\text{P×P}}{\text{Kt×P}}$;

5. $\dfrac{\text{P—KKt3}}{\text{B—Kt2}}$; 6. $\dfrac{\text{B—Kt2}}{\text{Kt—Kt3}\,!}$; 7. $\dfrac{\text{P—K3}}{\text{Castles}}$; 8. $\dfrac{\text{KKt—K2}}{}$;

(see Fig. 22).

The NIMZO-INDIAN is characterized, after 1. P—Q4, Kt—KB3 ; 2. P—QB4, P—K3 ; 3. Kt—QB3, by 3. . . . B—Kt5, to which White has the good replies 4. Q—B2 and Q—Kt3, with others, including Kt—B3, P—K3, and P—QR3. Black's move initiates a counter-offensive preventing White's P—K4 and preparing the break-up of his centre by . . . P—Q4 or . . . P—QB4. Thus, the game may continue :

4. $\dfrac{\text{Q—B2}}{\text{P—Q4}}$; 5. $\dfrac{\text{P×P}}{\text{Q×P}}$; 6. $\dfrac{\text{P—K3}}{\text{P—B4}}$;

7. $\dfrac{\text{P—QR3}}{\text{B×Ktch.}}$; 8. $\dfrac{\text{P×B}}{\text{Castles}}$; 9. $\dfrac{\text{Kt—B3}}{\text{P—QKt3}}$; or 4. $\dfrac{\text{Q—Kt3}}{\text{P—B4}}$;

5 $\dfrac{\text{P×P}}{\text{Kt—B3}}$; 6. $\dfrac{\text{Kt—B3}}{\text{Kt—K5}}$; 7. $\dfrac{\text{B—Q2}}{\text{Kt×B}}$; 8. $\dfrac{\text{Kt×Kt}}{\text{P—B4}}$;

9. $\dfrac{\text{P—K3}}{\text{B×P}}$, etc.

The CATALAN SYSTEM—a modern combination of the King's Indian and Queen's Gambit—is the most important Opening not yet treated, e.g. : 1. $\dfrac{\text{P—Q4}}{\text{Kt—KB3}}$; 2. $\dfrac{\text{P—QB4}}{\text{P—K3}}$;

3. $\dfrac{\text{Kt—KB3}}{\text{P—Q4}}$; 4. $\dfrac{\text{P—KKt3}}{\text{B—K2}}$; 5. $\dfrac{\text{B—Kt2}}{\text{Castles}}$; 6. $\dfrac{\text{Castles}}{\text{P—B4}}$;

7. $\dfrac{\text{P×QP}}{\text{Kt×P}}$; 8. $\dfrac{\text{P—K4}}{\text{Kt—Kt3}}$, etc. At his 6th move Black could play the less aggressive QKt—Q2 or P—QKt3 with excellent prospects.

In the BUDAPEST DEFENCE Black sacrifices a Pawn in the attempt to gain the initiative, but White's return of the Pawn is apt to lead to difficulties; for example:

$$1. \frac{\text{P—Q4}}{\text{Kt—KB3}} ; \quad 2. \frac{\text{P—QB4}}{\text{P—K4}} ; \quad 3. \frac{\text{P} \times \text{P}}{\text{Kt—Kt5}} ; \quad 4. \frac{\text{P—K4}}{\text{Kt} \times \text{KP}} ;$$

$$5. \frac{\text{P—B4}}{\text{KKt—B3}} ; \quad 6. \frac{\text{Kt—KB3}}{\text{B—B4}} .$$

(c) The DUTCH DEFENCE (1. . . . P—KB4) is one of the most popular in this group, its object being to prevent P—K4 and inaugurate an early attack on the King; White's best response is the K-fianchetto:

$$1. \frac{\text{P—Q4}}{\text{P—KB4}} ; \quad 2. \frac{\text{P—KKt3}}{\text{P—K3}} ; \quad 3. \frac{\text{B—Kt2}}{\text{Kt—KB3}} ; \quad 4. \frac{\text{Kt—KB3}}{\text{P—Q4}} ;$$

$$5. \frac{\text{Castles}}{\text{B—Q3}} ; \quad 6. \frac{\text{P—B4}}{\text{P—B3}} ; \quad 7. \frac{\text{P—Kt3}}{\text{QKt—Q2}} ; \quad 8. \frac{\text{B—Kt2}}{\text{Castles}} .$$

The BENONI COUNTER GAMBIT (1. . . . P—QB4) is not recommended to the beginner, though it still occasionally appears in tournament play:

$$1. \frac{\text{P—Q4}}{\text{P—QB4}} ; \quad 2. \frac{\text{P—Q5}}{\text{P—K4}} ;$$

$$3. \frac{\text{P—K4}}{\text{P—Q3}} ; \quad 4. \frac{\text{P—KB4}}{\text{P} \times \text{P}} ; \quad 5. \frac{\text{B} \times \text{P}}{\text{Q—R5ch.}} ; \quad 6. \frac{\text{P—Kt3}}{\text{Q—K2}} ;$$

$$7. \frac{\text{Kt—KB3 !}}{\text{Q} \times \text{Pch.}} ; \quad 8. \frac{\text{K—B2}}{\text{Kt—KB3}} ; \quad 9. \frac{\text{B—R3 !}}{} \quad \text{and Black must}$$

play 9. . . . K—Q1, or lose his Q.

The following, though little played to-day, are worth mention if only for the practice they can give the beginner:

The ENGLISH OPENING:

$$1. \frac{\text{P—QB4}}{\text{P—K4}} ; \quad 2. \frac{\text{Kt—QB3}}{\text{Kt—KB3}} ;$$

$$3. \frac{\text{P—KKt3}}{\text{P—Q4}} ; \quad 4. \frac{\text{P} \times \text{P}}{\text{Kt} \times \text{P}} ; \quad 5. \frac{\text{B—Kt2}}{\text{Kt—Kt3}} ; \quad 6. \frac{\text{Kt—B3}}{\text{Kt—B3}} ;$$

$$7. \frac{\text{Castles}}{\text{B—K2}} ; \quad 8. \frac{\text{P—Q3}}{\text{Castles}} .$$

BIRD'S OPENING:

$$1. \frac{\text{P—KB4}}{\text{Kt—KB3}} ; \quad 2. \frac{\text{P—QKt3}}{\text{P—K3}} ; \quad 3. \frac{\text{B—Kt2}}{\text{P—Q4}} ;$$

$$4. \frac{\text{Kt—KB3}}{\text{B—K2}} ; \quad 5. \frac{\text{P—K3}}{\text{QKt—Q2}} ; \quad 6. \frac{\text{B—Q3}}{\text{Kt—K5}} ; \quad 7. \frac{\text{Kt—K5}}{\text{Castles}} .$$

FROM'S GAMBIT—a reply to Bird's Opening in the hope, by the sacrifice of a Pawn, to build up a counter-attack:

$$1. \frac{P{-}KB4}{P{-}K4} \; ; \quad 2. \frac{P{\times}P}{P{-}Q3} \; ; \quad 3. \frac{P{\times}P}{B{\times}P} \; ; \quad 4. \frac{Kt{-}KB3}{P{-}KKt4\,!}$$

THE END-GAME

As before stated, the Middle part of the game, when the player is thrown upon his own resources, commences where the Opening ceases, and the End-Game where the Middle-Game ceases.

This stage of the game is a study in itself. In the majority of cases its treatment is a matter of intuition, but the student may be assisted by the knowledge of general principles, and by familiarity with certain standard positions which frequently occur in practice.

KING AND PAWN AGAINST KING

In many games one or the other player remains at the close with a Pawn, which has to be queened. Fig. 23 illustrates an ending in which White is a Pawn ahead and, with the move, would win with 1. R—KR2, checkmate. But as it is Black's move he is able to exchange both Q and R, and if he can prevent White's queening he may draw the game. There is a simple method of ascertaining this at a glance without calculation (by means of the imaginary "square" depicted in Fig. 24). Black forces the exchange of pieces thus:

FIG. 23.—Black to move and draw.

FIG. 24.—Black to move and draw.

WHITE	BLACK
1. . . .	Q—B3ch.
2. Q—Kt2ch.	Q × Qch.
3. R × Q	R—R8ch.
4. R—Ktsq.	R × Rch.
5. K × R	. . .

producing the position in Fig. 24; and Black draws; for the Black K can reach the P before the White K can approach to defend it. Consequently White can only advance the P; but the Black K will be able to stop it from queening, for his next move will bring him *within the square* (indicated above) in which the P stands, and in such case he can always overtake it. Thus—

5. . . .	K—Kt6
6. P—Kt4	K—B5
7. P—Kt5	K—K4
8. P—Kt6	K—Q3
9. P—Kt7	K—B2

And the P is lost. It will be seen that the Black K remains with every move *within the square* of the P.

FIG. 25.—White to move and win.

Fig. 25 illustrates a position in which the P can be supported by the K. Here if White were at once to advance the P, the Black K would move *within the square* of the P and capture it. Therefore the K must go to protect it.

1. K—Q2	K—B5
2. K—K3	K—Q4
3. K—B4	K—K3
4. K—Kt5	K—B2
5. K—R6	K—Ktsq.

6. P—Kt4	K—Rsq.
7. P—Kt5	K—Ktsq.
8. K—Kt6	K—Rsq.
9. K—B7	. . .

If Black had played 8. . . . K—Bsq., White would have played 9. K—R7.

                              ...   K—R2
    10. P—Kt6ch.   ...

And the P cannot be prevented from queening.

KING AND QUEEN AGAINST KING

The position being as in Fig. 26, the shortest way to
checkmate the Black K is as given below:

WHITE	BLACK
1. K—Kt2	K—Q4
2. K—B3	K—K4
3. Q—KKt6	K—B5
4. K—Q4	K—B6
5. Q—Kt5	K—B7
6. Q—Kt4	K—K8
7. K—K3	K—B8
8. Q—Kt7	...

Not 8. Q—Kt3, because Black would then be stalemate,
a contingency which White must carefully guard against
in similar positions.

         ...   K—K8
    9. Q mates at Ktsq.
       or Rsq.

FIG. 26.   FIG. 27.

TWO ROOKS AND KING AGAINST KING

Fig. 27 shows the most unfavourable position for White's
two Rooks. The shortest way to checkmate the Black
King is as follows:

WHITE	BLACK
1. R—Ksq.	K—Q5
2. R(Ktsq.)—Qsq.ch.	K—B6
3. R—K2	K—B5
4. R—B2ch.	K—Kt6
5. R—B8	K—R6
6. R—QKtsq.	K—R5
7. R—R8, mate	. . .

KING AND ROOK AGAINST KING

Fig. 28 represents the most unfavourable position for White. The shortest way to checkmate Black is:

FIG. 28.

WHITE	BLACK
1. K—B4	K—K5
2. R—Ksq.ch.	K—B4
3. K—Q4	K—B5
4. R—Bsq.ch.	K—Kt4
5. K—K4	. . .

It will be noticed that the White K always approaches at the distance of a Kt's move, whilst the Black K moves either on diagonals, or takes the "opposition" to the White K.

WHITE	BLACK
. . .	K—Kt3
6. K—K5	K—Kt4
7. R—Ktsq.ch.	K—R5
8. K—B5	K—R6
9. K—B4	K—R7
10. R—Kt3	K—R8
11. K—B3	K—R7
12. K—B2	K—R8
13. R—R3, mate	. . .

N.B.—The Rook can only checkmate on an outer row or file of the board.

KING AND TWO BISHOPS AGAINST KING

To checkmate with two Bs is comparatively easy.

Fig. 29 illustrates the most unfavourable position for White and the solution given is the shortest attainable.

White must be careful not to stalemate the Black King. For instance, if after 15. KB7 Black were to play K—Rsq., White could not reply 16. B—KB5; but must play 16. B—K3, K—R2; 17. B—B5ch., K—Rsq. ; 18. B—Q4 mate.

FIG. 29.—White to move and win.

WHITE	BLACK
1. B—Qsq.	K—K6
2. K—Kt2	K—Q7
3. B—QB2	K—K6
4. K—B3	K—B6
5. K—Q4	K—Kt5
6. B—Ksq.	K—B6
7. B—Q3	K—B5
8. B—K4	K—Kt4
9. K—K5	K—Kt5
10. B—KB2	K—Kt4
11. B—KB5	K—R3
12. K—B6	K—R4
13. B—K6	K—R3
14. B—Kt4	K—R2
15. K—B7 (see note above)	K—R3
16. B—K3ch.	K—R2
17. B—B5ch.	K—Rsq.
18. B—Q4, mate.	

KING, BISHOP, AND KNIGHT AGAINST KING

To checkmate with B and Kt is a very difficult process ; it can be forced only if the Black K is driven to one of the R squares of the same colour as the B. In the position shown in Fig. 30 the Black K must be driven either to QRsq., or KR8. Frequently the B and Kt are separated from the White K ; in that case the Black K cannot be prevented from moving to a R square of the opposite colour

FIG. 30.—White to move and win.

to the B. Then the forces must be brought together to act in concert with the White K ; when, by combined action, the Black K can be forced on to a corner square of the same colour as White's B, and checkmated as shown in the appended solution. Mate can be forced in the most unfavourable position (see Fig. 30) in about thirty or thirty-one moves.

WHITE	BLACK
1. Kt—Kt3ch.	K—B3

If 1. . . . K—B5 ; then 2. B—Qsq., K—B6 ; 3. K—Kt5, K—Q6 ; 4. K—B5, K—K5 ; 5. B—B2ch., K—K4 ; 6. Kt—Q4, K—B3 ; 7. K—Q6, K—B2 ; 8. Kt—B3, K—B3 ; 9. Kt—K5, K—Kt2 ; 10. K—K6, and the K is gradually forced on to the last rank.

2. K—Kt4	K—Q4
3. B—B3ch.	K—Q3
4. Kt—Q4	K—K4
5. K—B5	K—B3
6. K—Q5	K—B2
7. Kt—B5	K—B3
8. Kt—Q6	K—Kt3
9. K—K5	K—Kt2
10. B—K4	K—Ktsq.
11. K—B6	K—Rsq.

The K is now on the R square of opposite colour to the B, and must be driven to his KR8 or QRsq., in order to be checkmated.

12. Kt—B7ch.	K—Ktsq.
13. B—B5	. . .

Purposely losing a move (*coup de repos*) ; it is immaterial where the B moves to so long as it remains on the same diagonal, the object being to force Black to move, without altering White's position.

	K—Bsq.
14. B—R7	. . .

To prevent the K from returning to Ktsq. if the Kt moves.

	. . .	K—Ksq.
15.	Kt—K5	K—Qsq.
16.	B—K4	K—B2
17.	Kt—B4	. . .

The Black King is now gradually forced on to the fatal White corner.

	. . .	K—Q2
18.	K—B7	K—Qsq.
19.	B—B6	K—B2
20.	B—Kt5	. . .

Not to R4, because at Kt5 the B guards the additional square R6.

	. . .	K—Qsq.
21.	K—K6	K—Bsq.
22.	K—Q6	K—Qsq.
23.	Kt—R5	K—Bsq.
24.	B—Q7ch.	K—Ktsq.

If 24. . . . K—Qsq., then 25. Kt—B6, mate.

25.	K—B6	K—R2
26.	Kt—B4	K—R3
27.	K—B7	K—R2
28.	B—B8	K—Rsq.
29.	Kt—R5	K—R2
30.	Kt—B6ch.	K—Rsq.
31.	B—Kt7 mate	. . .

END-GAME WITH TWO KNIGHTS

The player should be very careful not to allow himself to be manœuvred into the position of being left with two Knights only on the board besides his King for, as has been mentioned (p. 370) he cannot do better than draw—unless his opponent makes a careless blunder.

Study of Fig. 31 will exemplify this point. White has succeeded in driving the lone King to his own QKt1 and checking him there, leaving

FIG. 31.—Two Knights v. King. A draw; but Black can lose through carelessness.

Black the choice between his R8 and B8 : if he is so mis-guided as to withdraw into the corner Kt—B2 mates him at once, whereas on B8 he would be perfectly safe.

FIG. 32.—Two Knights *v.* King and Pawn.
A win for White.

The case is altered, how-ever, if Black has one or more Pawns, for then—if White can eliminate all but one and effectively block that lone Pawn until the moment has arrived when he can set it free to Queen, and so give him the "time" wanted to achieve his object —White can win.

Fig. 32 shows a position in which White has the Black King where he wants him, and has got rid of the unnecessary Pawns and blocked the one necessary survivor: he now proceeds:—

WHITE	BLACK
1. Kt—Q6	K—R2
2. K—Kt5	K—Kt1
3. K—Kt6	K—R1
4. Kt—QKt5	K—Kt1
5. Kt—R7	K—R1

and the moment has arrived : he releases the Pawn with—

6. Kt—B4	P—R6
7. Kt—B6	P—R7
8. Kt—Q5	P—R8(Q)
9. Kt—B7 mate.	

Positions such as this very rarely occur, but it is just as well to know that they *can* be won when they do, granted sufficient care and foresight. If, for instance, the lone Pawn had been left at Kt5 instead of R5 this particular sequence of moves would have failed, as White King would have been checked on Black's queening.

A " TRICKY " FINISH

It is well known that it is not always policy to promote a Pawn to Queen—a Rook, Bishop, or Knight may be the only piece suitable for the occasion. The Rook *v.* Pawn position shown in Fig. 33—in which White turns what appears to be at best a draw into a surprising victory—furnishes, among other useful lessons, a pretty example of this.

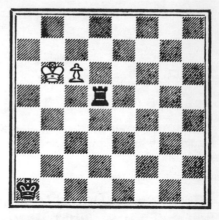

WHITE	BLACK
1. P—B7	R—Q2ch.
2. K—Kt5	R—Q4ch.
3. K—Kt4	R—Q5ch.
4. K—Kt3	R—Q6ch.
5. K—B2.	

FIG. 33.—Rook *v.* Pawn. White avoids stalemate and wins.

Note that White could not have ventured on to the QB's file before this point : for had he done so the Rook would at once have played to Q8 and from there to QB8, and captured the Pawn (or Queen) on the next move.

Black is now in difficulties : he cannot give another check nor stop the Pawn queening without the loss of both Rook and game ; but he sees a chance of stalemate, so he plays 5. . . . R—Q5, intending, when White has queened, to play 6. . . . Q—B5ch., in which case White has no option but to take the Rook and draw, the lone King having no move available and not being in check. White, however, instead of playing 6. P—B8(Q), plays 6. P—B8(R) ! The stalemate is definitely off, and Black's only means of postponing the evil day is 6. . . . R—QR5, whereupon White replies with 7. K—Kt3, and mates in a move or two.

DRAUGHTS

" In friendly contention, the old men
Laughed at each unlucky hit or unsuccessful manœuvre—
Laughed when a man was crowned, or a breach was made in the
   king-row."

LONGFELLOW—*Evangeline.*

THE game of Draughts is played on a board of sixty-four squares of alternate colours, and with twenty-four pieces, called men (twelve on each side), also of opposite colours. It is played by two persons ; the one having the twelve black or red pieces is technically said to be playing the *first side*, and the other, having the twelve white, to be playing the *second side*. Each player endeavours to confine the pieces of the other in situations where they cannot be played, or both to capture and fix, so that *none can be played*, the person whose side is brought to this state loses the game.

The essential rules of the game are as under—

The board shall be so placed that the bottom corner square on the left hand shall be black.

Then the men shall be placed on the black squares.*

The black men shall be placed upon the supposed first twelve squares of the board ; the white upon the last twelve squares (see Fig. I).

Each player shall play alternately with black and white men. Lots shall be cast for the colour at the commencement of a match, *the winner to have the choice of taking* black *or* white.

The first move must *invariably* be made by the person having the black men.

At the end of five minutes " Time " may be called ; and if the move be not completed on the expiry of another minute, the game shall be adjudged lost through improper delay.

---

* In all treatises on the game the men are, for typographical reasons, shown on the *white* squares. This involves a corresponding alteration of the position of the board, which is shown with a *white* bottom square on the left hand.

When there is only *one way* of taking one or more pieces, " Time " shall be called at the end of one minute ; and if the move be not completed on the expiry of another minute, the game shall be adjudged lost through improper delay.

After the first move has been made, if either player arrange any piece without giving intimation to his opponent, he shall forfeit the game ; but, if it is his turn to play, he may avoid the penalty by playing that piece, if possible.

After the pieces have been arranged, if the person whose turn it is to play *touch* one, he must either play that piece or forfeit the game. When the piece is not playable, he is penalised according to the preceding law.

If *any part* of a playable piece be played over an angle of the square on which it is stationed, the play must be completed in *that direction.*

A capturing play, as well as an ordinary one, is completed the moment the hand is withdrawn from the piece played, even though two or more pieces should have been taken.

When taking, if a player remove one of his own pieces, he cannot replace it, but his opponent can either play or insist on his replacing it.

Either player making a false or improper move shall forfeit the game to his opponent, without another move being made.

The " Huff " or " Blow " is, *before one plays his own piece,* to remove from the board any of the adverse pieces that might or should have taken. The " Huff " does not constitute a move.

The player has the power either to *huff, compel the take,* or to *let the piece remain on the board,* as he thinks proper.*

When a man first reaches any of the squares on the opposite extreme line of the board it becomes a

* A player may be huffed for not taking the full number of men he should have taken by the play adopted. Thus if he takes one man only, where by the same play, duly continued, he could have taken two, he is liable to the huff. If, however, he has the choice of two moves, by one of which he would take a larger number of men than by the other, he is under no obligation to adopt that move.

" King." It must be crowned (by placing a man of the same colour on the top of it) by the opponent, and can afterwards be moved backwards or forwards as the limits of the board permit.

A Draw occurs when neither of the players can force a win. When one of the sides appears stronger than the other, the stronger party may be required to complete the win, or to show a decided advantage

White.

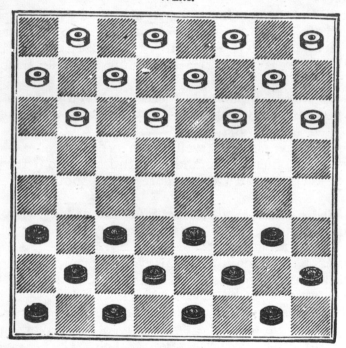

Black.

FIG. I.

over his opponent *within forty of his own moves*— counted from the point at which notice was given —failing in which, he must relinquish the game as a draw.

The above diagram (Fig. I.) shows the board set for play, and Fig. 2 shows the draught-board numbered for the purpose of recording moves.

The game is begun by each player moving alternately one of his men along the diagonal on which it is situated. The men can only move forward either to right or left one square at a time, unless they have attained one of the four squares on the extreme further side of the board (technically termed the " crown-head "). This done, they become Kings, and can move either forward or backward. The pieces take in the direction they move, by leaping over any opposing man that may be immediately contiguous, provided there be a vacant square behind it. If several men

White.

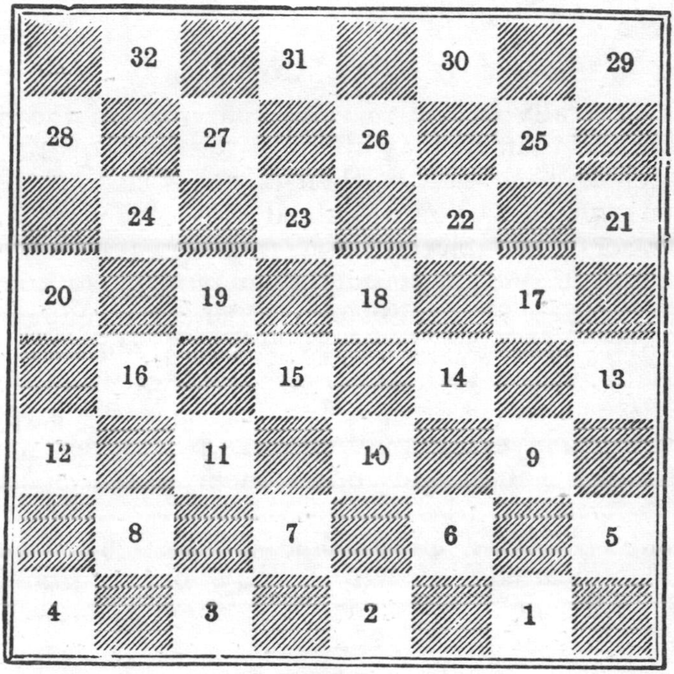

Black.

FIG. 2.

should be exposed by having open spaces behind them alternately, they may be all taken at one capture, and the capturing piece is then placed on the square beyond the last man.

To explain the mode of capturing by a practical illustration, let us begin by placing the men as for a game. You will perceive that Black, who always plays first, can only move one of the men placed on 9, 10, 11, or 12 ; supposing him, then, to play the man on 11 to 15, and White to answer this by playing 22 to 18, Black can take the White man on 18 by leaping from 15 to 22, and removing the captured piece from the board. Should Black not take the man on 18, but make another move—say 12 to 16, for instance—he is liable to be " huffed " ; that is, as penalty for not making the capture, White may remove from the board the man (on 15) with which Black should have taken. When one party " huffs " the other in preference to compelling the take, he does not replace the piece his opponent moved, but simply removes the man huffed from the board and then plays his own move.

General Advice.

It is generally better to keep your men in the middle of the board than to play them to the side squares, as in the latter case one-half of their power is curtailed.

When you have once gained an advantage in the number of your pieces, you increase the proportion by exchanges, but in forcing them you must take care not to damage your position. Open your game at all times upon a regular plan ; by so doing you will acquire method in both attack and defence. Accustom yourself to play slowly at first, and, if a beginner, prefer playing with better players than yourself. Note their methods of opening a game, and follow them when opportunity presents itself.

If playing against an inferior, it is as well to keep the game complicated ; if with a superior, to simplify it. Avoid scattering your forces ; as they get fewer concentrate them as much as possible.

Never touch the squares of the board with your fingers ; and accustom yourself to play your move off-hand, when you have once made up your mind.

Do not lose time in studying when you have only one way of taking, but take quickly.

Pay quite as much attention to the probable plans of your adversary as to your own.

Remember that the science of the game consists in so moving your pieces at the commencement as to obtain a position which will compel your adversary to give his men away. One man ahead with a clear game should be a certain *win*.

In conclusion, the student is strongly advised to

study and master the theory and practice of the play embraced in the First, Second, Third, and Fourth Positions (see *post*). These endings, in different forms, are of very frequent occurrence, and should be thoroughly mastered.

VARIOUS OPENINGS AND HOW FORMED.

1. The " Ayrshire Lassie " is formed by the first four moves (counting the play on both sides) : 11 to 15, 24 to 20, 8 to 11, 28 to 24.

2. The " Bristol " is formed by the first three moves : 11 to 16, 24 to 20, 16 to 19.

3. The " Cross " is formed by the first two moves : 11 to 15, 23 to 18.

4. The " Defiance " is formed by the first four moves : 11 to 15, 23 to 19, 9 to 14, 27 to 23.

5. The " Dyke " is formed by the first three moves : 11 to 15, 22 to 17, 15 to 19.

6. The " Fife " is formed by the first five moves : 11 to 15, 23 to 19, 9 to 14, 22 to 17, 5 to 9.

7. The " Glasgow " is formed by the first five moves : 11 to 15, 23 to 19, 8 to 11, 22 to 17, 11 to 16.

8. The " Laird and Lady " is formed by the first five moves : 11 to 15, 23 to 19, 8 to 11, 22 to 17, 9 to 13.

9. " The Maid of the Mill " is formed by the first five moves : 11 to 15, 22 to 17, 8 to 11, 17 to 13. 15 to 18.

10. The " Old Fourteenth " is formed by the first five moves : 11 to 15, 23 to 19, 8 to 11, 22 to 17, 4 to 8.

11. The " Second Double Corner " is formed by the first two moves : 11 to 15, 24 to 19 (so named because the first move of the *second* player is from the one double corner towards the other).

12. The " Single Corner " is formed by the first two moves . 11 to 15, 22 to 18 (each move being played from one single corner towards the other).

13. The " Souter " is formed by the first five moves : 11 to 15, 23 to 19, 9 to 14, 22 to 17, 6 to 9.

14. The " Whilter " is formed by the first five moves : 11 to 15, 23 to 19, 9 to 14, 22 to 17, 7 to 11.

15. The " Will-o'-the-Wisp " is formed by the first three moves : 11 to 15, 23 to 19, 9 to 13.

N.B.—The reader should observe, in studying the position following, that the numbering of the squares always starts from the *black* side of the board, whether black occupy the upper or the lower rows.

END GAMES

Two Kings to One

To win with two Kings against one in the double corner (see Fig. 3) is often a source of difficulty to

Position.
Black.

White.
Fig. 3.
[WHITE TO MOVE AND WIN.]

the learner and yet, once known, nothing is more simple. The following shows how to force the win :

Solution

22·18	9·6	15·10
5·9	18·14	1·5
11·15	6·1	10·6

5·1	5·9	13·17
14·10	1·5	15·18
1·5	9·13	17·13
6·1	10·15	18·22
		W. wins.

THREE KINGS TO TWO

This, again, is of very frequent occurrence, and the novice, even with the stronger game, may find the position difficult to deal with.

The proper course for White is either to pin one of Black's men, and then go for the other, or to force an exchange, so as to be left with two Kings to one, when the game, as we have seen, is a foregone conclusion. To avoid this, Black naturally endeavours to reach the two double corners, so as to have his men

Position.

Black.

White.

FIG. 4.

[WHITE TO MOVE AND WIN.]

as far apart as possible, and to divide the attacking force. Where Black adopts these tactics the proper play, on the part of White, is to get his three Kings in a line on the same diagonal as Black's two. Thus, if Black is at 32 and 5, White must manœuvre to place his man upon squares 23, 18, and 14. If Black occupies 28 and 1, White must secure 19, 15, and 10. In this position, however Black may play, he is compelled, on White's next move, to accept the offer of an exchange. White has then two Kings to one, and the game is practically at an end.

THE ELEMENTARY POSITIONS

There are four often recurring situations known as the First, Second, Third, and Fourth Positions. It is highly desirable that the student should make himself well acquainted with them.

FIRST POSITION.

Black.

White

FIG. 1.

[BLACK TO MOVE AND WIN.]

Solution

27·32	6·1	14·18	9·14
8·11	22·18	9·6	1·5
32·27	1·6	18·15	14·17
11·7	18·15	30·25	15·10—S
27·23	6·1	15·18	17·22
7·10	15·10	6·10	10·14
22·26	1·5	5·1	22·25
10·6—V. 1	10·6	25·21	5·1
26·31	5·1	1·5	25·22
6·9	14·10	10·6	1·6
31·26	1·5	18·15	22·25
9·6	6·1	21·17	6·10
26·22	5·9	5·1	25·22
6·10	1·5	6·9	10·15
23·18	9·13	15·18	22·25
10·6	10·14	17·13	15·18
18·14	13·9	18·15	25·21
			B. wins

VARIATION 1.

30·25	22·18	5·9	15·18
23·18	1·5	10·15	9·5
10·6	18·15	V 2—9·5	18·22
18·14	5·1	15·18	17·14
6·1	15·10	5·9	1·6
26·30	1·5	1·5	5·1
25·21	10·6	9·6	6·2
30·25	5·1	18·15	1·5
1·5	14·10	21·17	22·17
25·22	1·5	5·1	14·9
5·1	6·1	6·9	B. wins.

VARIATION 2.

9·14	17·13	Continue as
1·5	1·5	trunk at
21·17	14·17	S.
5·1	15·10	B. wins.

SECOND POSITION.

Black.

White.

FIG. 6.

[BLACK TO MOVE AND WIN.]

Solution

5·9	15·19	6·10
11·15	27·32	19·23
9·14	19·24	10·15
15·11	32·28	23·27
14·18	24·27	15·19
11·16	28·32	27·32
18·15	27·31	19·24
16·20	32·28	32·28
15·11	31·27	24·27
20·24	28·32	28·24
3·7	27·23	27·32
24·19	32·28	24·28
7·10	23·18	32·27
19·23	28·24	28·32
10·15	18·14	27·24
23·27	24·19	32·28

24·19	15·19	6·1
28·32	28·32	8·11
19·15	19·24	14·9
32·28	32·28	13·6
15·10	11·16	1·10
28·24	28·19	11·16
10·6	16·23	10·15
24·19	12·8	16·20
14·10	23·18	15·19
19·24	8·4	B. wins.
10·15	18·14	
24·28	4·8	

THIRD POSITION.

Black.

White.

FIG. 7

[BLACK TO MOVE AND WIN.]

Solution

13·9	18·22	21·25
22·18	6·1	18·15—V. 2
9·6	22·18—V. 1	1·6

14·17	10·14	22·26
6·2	31·27	27·24
17·14	18·22	26·22
25·22	27·23	24·20
15·10	22·25—V. 3	22·26
22·26	2·7	20·16
14·18	25·22	26·22
5·9	7·11	16·12
10·6	22·25—V. 4	22·26
9·13	11·15	12·8
6·10	25·22	26·22
26·31	23·27	8·3
		B. wins.

VARIATION 1.

14·18	10·15	26·31
5·9	30·26	18·22
18·23	15·19	31·27
1·6	26·30	21·17
23·26	19·23	27·31
6·10	22·26	9·14
26·30	23·18	B. wins.

VARIATION 2.

14·17	5·14	25·21
5·9	30·26	17·22
A—17·21	14·18	21·17
9·14	B. wins.	22·6
18·9	—.	1·19
1·5	A	B. wins.
21·30	18·15	

VARIATION 3.

14·10	10·14	14·9
23·19	19·15	15·10
		B. wins.

VARIATION 4.

22·18	22·26	22·26
23·27	27·24	20·16
18·22	26·22	26·22
11·15	24·20	16·12

B. wins. Very critical, and requires extreme care in forcing the win.

FOURTH POSITION.
Black.

White.
FIG. 8.

[BLACK TO MOVE AND WIN.]		[WHITE TO MOVE AND DRAW.]	
	Solution		
Black to Move.		**White to Move.**	
28·24	32·27	31·27	22·18
32·28	24·28	23·19	31·27
24·20	27·32	27·31	28·24
28·32	18·22	19·24	27·31
22·18	31·27	32·27	18·23
31·27	22·26	24·20	31·26
23·19	30·23	27·32	Drawn.
27·31	28·24		
19·24	B. wins.		

BACKGAMMON

BACKGAMMON is played by two persons, on a special
"board" with thirty "men," fifteen white and
fifteen black (or red), similar to those used for the
game of Draughts. The board (see Fig. 1) is square,
usually of wood, lined with leather, and is divided
into two equal compartments, each with a raised

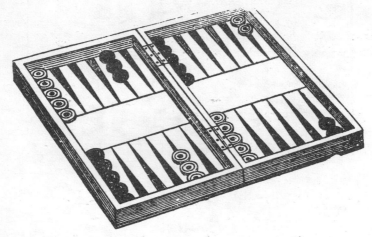

wall or border. It is usually made in two portions,
hinged so as to fold together and bearing on their
outward surfaces the necessary squares for draughts
or chess, so that the one board may answer both
purposes.

The board is so placed in use that the two compartments, known as "tables," shall lie longitudinally
between the players. One of these is known as the
"outer," the other as the "inner" or "home" table.
Which of the two is for the time being the inner and
which the outer table is governed by the arrangement of the men at starting. With the men placed
as Fig. 1, the right hand is the inner or home table, and
the left hand consequently the outer table. The portions

of the two latter nearest to each player are known as *his* inner and outer tables respectively.

Each table is marked with twelve " points," six at either end. They are alternately of black and white, black and red, or other distinctive colours. The two points in the inner table farthest from the dividing partition or " bar " are known as the " ace " points, and those next in order as the two or " deuce " points, followed in succession by the three or " trois " points, the four or " quatre " points, the five or " cinque " points, and finally the " six "* points, next the bar. The points in the outer tables are designated in like manner, but starting in this case from the dividing partition. The ace point in the outer table is more commonly known as the " bar " point.

A pair of dice (or sometimes a pair for each player) and a couple of dice-boxes complete the apparatus of the game.

The men are arranged at starting as shown in Fig. 1 —viz., two of White's men are placed on the ace point in Black's inner table, five are placed on the six point in Black's outer table, three on the deuce point in White's outer table, and five on the six point in White's inner table. Black's men are placed in like manner on the points immediately facing these.

PLAYING

The game is commenced by each player throwing on the centre of the board a single die, the higher throw of the two giving the right to begin. In the event of a tie, the players throw again. All subsequent throws are with both dice.

The thrower of the higher number may either adopt the points shown by the two dice as his own throw, or throw again. After throwing, he calls the number of the throw, the higher number first, as " six deuce," " cinque trois," " quatre ace," or as the case may be, and then proceeds to make his move in accordance with it. The movement of the men of each player is from the ace point in his opponent's home table towards the

---

* Pronounced *tray, kater, sank,* and *size,* respectively.

like point in his own, though for many purposes it suffices if he can play them into his own table, independently of their reaching any particular point therein the object of the game being first to get all the player's men into his own inner table, and then to play them out again, according to certain rules to be hereafter stated. The number uppermost on each die entitles the player to move one man forward a corresponding number of points. Thus if he threw "six trois," he is entitled to move one man six points onward, and then the same or another man three points onward. In the event of his throwing the same points with both dice (known as "doublets"), he is entitled to play the throw twice over. Suppose, for example, that he throws two aces; he may move one or more men forward to an aggregate extent of four points. If he throw double deuces, he may move to an aggregate extent of eight points; if double three, twelve points, and so on.

The right to move is subject to a certain qualification —viz., that a man can only be played to a point which is either vacant or occupied by one or more men of the player, or by one man only of the adversary. A player getting two men on a given point is said to "make" such point, and as he thereby secures such men from capture, and at the same time impedes the onward march of the enemy, it is always an object to do this. A single man on a given point is known as a "blot," and not only does not prevent the enemy playing to that point, but in the event of its being "hit"—*i.e.*, reached by an adverse throw, it is "taken up" (placed on the bar between the two tables), and, however far advanced it may have been, has to begin its journey anew from the inner table of the adversary. Nor can such man again start on its journey until its owner is fortunate enough to make a throw corresponding with a vacant point or blot in such table. Until he does this, the play of his other men is suspended. If the adverse player's home table is completely full—*i.e.*, each point occupied by two or more men, his play is altogether suspended, the adversary continuing to throw and move until the course of play again throws open one or more points in his table.

Any part of a throw which cannot be played is lost to the thrower, but every player is compelled to play the whole of his throw if it is possible to do so.

BEARING OFF THE MEN

When either player has succeeded in getting all his men into his home table, he proceeds to " bear them off "—*i.e.,* to remove them from the board. When the game has reached this stage, each throw entitles the player either to move forward a man or men (to the extent indicated by the throw) within the limits of his own table, or to remove men from the corresponding

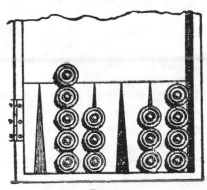

FIG. 2

points. Thus, suppose that the player's men are thus distributed in his table : five men on the cinque point, three on the quatre point, three on the deuce, and four on the ace point, the trois and six points being unoccupied (see Fig. 2). Suppose that the player throws " quatre trois." For the quatre, he may either remove a man from the quatre point or advance a man from the " cinque " to the " ace " point. In the case of the trois, he has no man on that point, and therefore *must* play forward, either by advancing a man from the cinque to the deuce, or from the quatre to the ace point. If, however, he throws a number which he cannot deal with after either of these fashions—*e.g.,* a six, he is entitled to bear off a man from his highest occupied point, in this case the cinque.

Doublets have, as in the earlier stages of the game,

a twofold value, and may be played either wholly by moving men forward, wholly by bearing off, or partly by the one method and partly by the other, as may be desirable. Suppose, for instance, that the player, having his men as shown in the figure, throws deuces ; having only three men on the deuce point, he can only bear off that number ; the fourth men must be played forward, either from the cinque or quatre point.

The player who first succeeds in removing all his men from the board wins the game, but the *value* of the game depends upon the stage reached by the adverse player, as follows :—

If the adversary has got all his men into his own home table, and has begun to bear off, the game of the winner is known as a " hit."

If the winner has borne off all his men before his adversary has begun to do the same, the game is known as a " gammon." The loser is said to be " gammoned," and pays double the agreed stake.

If the winner has borne off all his men while the adversary has still a man or men " up " (*i.e.*, on the bar) or in his (the winner's) home table, the game is a " backgammon," and the loser pays either thrice or four times (as may have been agreed) the amount of the single stake.

Where several games are played in succession, the winner of a " hit " throws first in the game next following. After a gammon or backgammon, the players throw again for the right to begin, as at starting.

Hints for Play

A leading principle is to " make points " whenever you fairly can, especially in or close to your home table. A second general principle is to avoid the leaving of " blots," particularly where they are likely to be " hit " by the adversary.* This latter principle is, however, subject to many qualifications. The advantages of spreading your men, in readiness to make

---

* This applies more particularly towards the close of the game. The leaving of a blot at the outset, when five out of six of the points in the adversary's table are still open, is a comparatively unimportant matter.

points, may more than counterbalance the risk, and in certain critical conditions of the game it is sometimes even desirable to be " hit," inasmuch as it enables you to make a fresh start from your adversary's home table and so get the opportunity in turn of taking *him* up.

At the opening of a game the men on both sides are in a uniform position, and it is, consequently, possible to lay down specific rules as to the best method of playing any given throw. We will go *seriatim* through all the possible throws. In some instances alternative methods will be given, according as the player aims merely at securing a hit, and is content, therefore, to play for safety, or elects to play a more risky game upon the chance of securing a gammon. This case often arises where the player has already lost the first hit of a rubber, in which case, if he loses the next game, he has lost the rubber also ; but if he can secure a gammon (reckoning as a double game), he becomes the winner of the rubber.

ACES.—(The best possible throw at starting.) Play two men on your " bar " point, and two on your cinque point.*

DEUCE ACE.—For a hit, play the deuce from the five men in your adversary's outer table, and the ace from the ace point in his inner table. For a gammon, play the ace from the six to the ace point in your own table

DEUCES.—For a hit, play two from the six to the quatre point in your own table, and the other two from the ace to the trois point in your opponent's inner table. For a gammon, play the second pair from the five men in his outer table.

TROIS ACE.—Make your cinque point.

TROIS DEUCE.—The approved play is to carry two

---

* This leaves a blot on the deuce point in your outer table, but this is a trifling disadvantage as compared with the gain of at once securing four points side by side. There are only three throws, six ace, cinque deuce, and quatre trois, that will enable the adversary to hit the blot ; and your next throw will in all probability enable you to place it beyond the reach of danger, either by playing another man on the same point, or by transferring the solitary man to one of the points already made.

men from the five in your adversary's outer table to
the quatre and cinque points in your own outer table.
This, of course, makes two blots. To avoid this some,
for a hit, play one man from the same point to the *deuce*
point in the above-mentioned table, but the bolder play
is to be preferred.

DOUBLE TROIS.—There are three ways of playing
this throw. Some players make the bar point. The
more usual play is, for a hit, to play two to the cinque
point in the player's own, and the other two to the quatre
point in the adversary's table. For a gammon,
play the last two from the six to the trois point in your
own table.

QUATRE ACE.—Play the quatre from the five men
in your opponent's outer table, and the ace from his
ace point. (Timid players, fearing to leave two
blots, sometimes play the whole throw from the
first-mentioned point, but the plan is not to be
recommended.)

QUATRE DEUCE.—Make your quatre point.

QUATRE TROIS.—Play two men from the five in your
adversary's outer table.

DOUBLE QUATRE.—Play two men from the ace to the
cinque point in the adversary's inner table, and two from
the five in his outer table. For a gammon, play two men
only, from the point last mentioned to the cinque point
in your own table.

CINQUE ACE.—Play the cinque from the five men in
your adversary's outer table, and the ace from the ace
point in his inner table. For a gammon, play the ace
from the six to the cinque point in your own table.

CINQUE DEUCE.—Play both men from the five in your
adversary's outer table.

CINQUE TROIS.—Make your trois point.

CINQUE QUATRE.—Move one man from your adversary's
ace point to the trois point in his outer table.

DOUBLE CINQUE.—Carry two men from the five in the
adversary's outer table, and make your trois point.

SIX ACE.—Make your bar point.

SIX DEUCE.—Move a man from the five in your
adversary's outer table to the cinque point in your own
table.

SIX TROIS, SIX QUATRE, SIX CINQUE.—Carry one man from your adversary's ace point as far as the throw will permit.

SIXES.—Place two men on your adversary's bar point, and two on your own.

Of the above throws (at the outset of the game), double aces are reckoned the best, and double sixes next best. Double trois comes third, followed by trois ace and six ace. Doublets, if playable, are good, as covering greater distance.

Any throw in which the higher of the two numbers is *two in advance of the other* (as cinque trois, trois ace) is also good, as enabling you to make a point in your table.

HALMA

HALMA is played on a board of 256 squares with little wooden " men " not unlike the Pawn at Chess. It is best played by two persons, but it is also arranged for four ; and even one player, if there is no opponent handy, can get quite a lot of interest out of the game by working out problems " on his own."

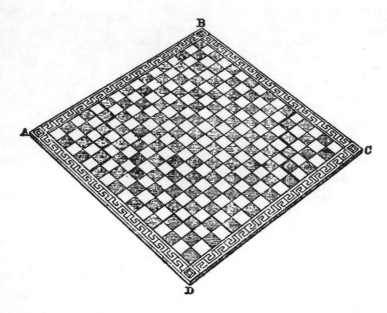

In each corner of the board is a " Yard " of thirteen squares enclosed by a black line ; in two of the corners— situated diagonally to each other—a heavier line encloses six additional squares, forming yards of nineteen squares each. The former are used when four players take part, and the latter when there are only two. We will describe first the game as played by two.

Each of the two players has nineteen men, coloured black and white respectively, and these he places in the nineteen-square yards, one man to each square. The object of each player is to get his men out of his own yard and into that of his adversary, and the first to achieve this wins the game. There are two kinds of move, viz., the " Step " and the " Hop " (hence the name, *Halma* in Greek signifying a leap). The Step is a simple move to an adjoining vacant square, and may be taken in any direction—forward, backward, sideways, or diagonally. The Hop is much farther reaching ; by means of it a man may jump over a man of either colour standing on any of the adjoining squares provided that the square on the other side of him *in the same direction* is vacant, and he may do this as often as opportunity allows all as part of one move. A Hop may consist of one jump or many, and may be straight, zig-zag, or winding, and, given the right conditions, in other words, a *ladder* being available, it is quite possible to get from one corner square to the corner diagonally opposite in one move.

There is no " taking " in Halma, the only object being to push the men forward as fast as possible, and to this end to place them so that they assist each other's progress and, so far as possible, obstruct that of the opponent. This object is attained by what we have already referred to as " ladders," *i.e.*, men so placed that another man can use them for a series of Hops. These may be in a direct line diagonally across the board, one empty square being between each man ; but, on the other hand, they may follow an intricate course, for, as has been already said, men may move in any direction, and it is often found that the best—and least obvious—ladder starts with one or two retrograde movements. The danger in the formation of ladders is that any ladder is equally open to one's opponent, in the reverse direction ; and for this reason it is often advisable to leave a break, so that the enemy shall be able to advance to that point and no further, his own man often supplying a link for a fresh advance.

When played as a four-handed game, each player has thirteen men only, coloured black, white purple, and green respectively, and places these in the smaller yards, of thirteen squares. Three different forms of the game may be played ; in the first each plays for his own hand, in which case the game is substantially the same as that for two ; in the second players at opposite angles are partners ; and in the third, the players sitting next to each other.

The object of the players in the second of these is entirely different from that in the ordinary game, as now the desire of the players at the opposite corners is to exchange pieces as rapidly as possible, and thus to aid each other in the construction and maintenance of ladders for each other's use. In the third the game is more like the first, as there is but limited opportunity for the players to help one another. The object in both is, of course, for one set of partners to " yard " their men before the other set, and when one player has all his men in the opposite yard, he drops out and his partner continues without him.

In the " Solitaire " game, the player usually sets himself a problem in which the object is to get a given number of men from a given position to a required position in a specified number of moves, for instance, to get the nineteen men out of one of the yards and into a symmetrical position in nineteen moves. There are many ways of doing this, and if one has discovered one of them it is interesting as well as improving to go on and discover some more. Another interesting " solitaire " is to arrange 37 men on the board in such a way that a man in a corner square can hop to the next before the opposite corner square diagonally, making 61 jumps in doing so.

When Halma was first introduced—some thirty or more years ago—it was permissible to take one step either before or after a hop in any one move ; but this was found to make the game so very easy that it was soon given up, and is no longer allowed.

REVERSI

REVERSI is a game for two players, and is played on an ordinary draught-board of sixty-four squares, no notice being taken of the difference in colour of the squares. Each player has thirty-two pieces, or " men," which are very like small draughtsmen but are coloured black on

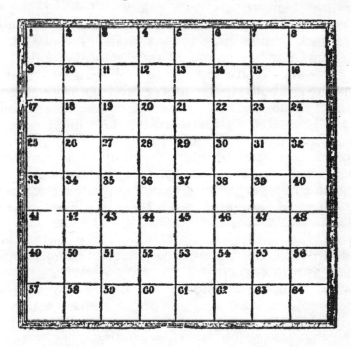

one side and red on the other. One player takes " Red," and the other " Black "; and the object of each is to capture and " reverse " as many of his opponent's pieces as he can, all of the sixty-four men being on the board at the conclusion of the game.

The game is started by the first player (whom we will suppose to be Red) placing a man in one or other of the four central squares marked in the diagram as 28, 29, 36, 37. His opponent places a black man in another of these squares, and the operation is repeated until the

447

four are filled. The precise placing of these men is optional, but it is generally considered to be bad play on the part of the first player if he places his diagonally.

The method of play now changes ; for henceforth each is bound to place every man he plays in juxtaposition to a hostile man, and in such a manner that another of his own men is in a straight line with it in the opposite direction ; any number of " the enemy " may intervene, so long as the line is unbroken. Such intervening men are " taken " by the last player ; he does not, however, remove them from the board, as at Chess or Draughts, but simply turns them over, or " reverses " them, thereby converting them to his own colour. This applies, not merely to a single line, but to any number of lines of adverse men converging to the man just placed, and having a man of like colour at their opposite ends.

To give an illustration ·—We will suppose that the fifth move is about to be made, Red having placed his men on Nos. 28 and 36, Black, of course, occupying 29 and 37. It is Red's turn to play ; he can place a man either at 22, 30, 38, or 46. In either of the two first-mentioned cases, he will turn the man on 29, and in the two last cases the man on 37, to his own colour. The turning of a number of lines cannot, of course, occur until a later stage of the game when there are more pieces on the board.

During the earlier stage of the game both players endeavour to keep within the central sixteen squares bounded at the corners by 19, 22, 46, and 43, and the first who is forced outside these limits is placed at a considerable disadvantage. Of these sixteen squares the most desirable to occupy are those at the angles, already named, the possession of these being a help towards the attainment of other desirable positions. The most important squares, however, lie on the outer limits of the board, the corners (1, 8, 64, and 57) being the best of all, and giving the holder a very good chance of winning the game. The next best after these are the squares next but one to them in the outer rows, viz., 3, 6, 17, 41, 24, 48, 59, and 62. On the other hand, the very worst squares to occupy are those diagonally next to the corners, viz., 10, 15, 55, and 50, for the occupation of either of these by the one player materially assists his opponent in obtaining possession of the corresponding corner square. The same objection holds, in a less degree, against Nos. 2, 9, 7, 16, 49, 58, 56, and 63 ; till one of the three adjoining squa es is occupied no man can be played into a corner square, hence the importance of avoiding these positions.

It must, however, be borne in mind that the terms " good " and " bad " are, as applied to squares, purely relative ; for much depends upon the state oi the game and upon the positions one's adversary has seized upon. A given square may be made desirable, o the reverse, according to the occupation of the neighbouring squares, and when a corner square is once occupied the objection to occupying the adjoining squares loses its force.

A piece once placed in position on the board is never moved off its square until the end of the game, but of course, it may be reversed again and again. Note also, that if a player is not able to place a piece in accordance with the rules, he loses his turn and his opponent goes on playing as long as he is so situated.

MERELLES or NINE MEN'S MORRIS

THIS is a very old English game. It used to be played on the village green (as evidenced by the allusion in Shakespeare's *Midsummer Night's Dream*, II., ii.), with black and white pebbles, the " board " being marked out with a trowel on the turf, and is still to be seen played by rustics in village alehouses on a chalk-marked table.

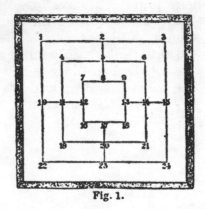

Fig. 1.

In the modern adaptation of the game a board ruled off into compartments as shown in the diagram is used; for convenience of reference the points of intersection are indicated by numerals, but these, of course, do not appear on the actual board.

Each player starts with nine counters, or " men," one taking black and the other white; these, at the outset, are all " in hand," and the first process is to place them on the board. Each player places one alternately on a point of intersection, and the object of each is to get three of his own men into a line, when he is entitled to " pound," *i.e.*, remove from the board, any one of his adversary's men. This right is, however, subject to one qualification, viz., that he cannot take one of three men already in line unless there is no other available, when one of the three must suffer.

When each player has had nine turns, all the men

450

will be on the board, and the game assumes a new character. The players now begin to *move* their men, the limit of a move being from the existing position of the man moved to any adjoining point of intersection which happens to be vacant. Thus, a man at 1 can move to 2 or 10 ; a man at 2 can move to 1, 3, or 5 ; at 21, to 14 or 20, and so on, always supposing that such points are vacant.

The game continues thus until one of the players is reduced by successive " poundings " to three men only, when a third stage begins. The moves of the player thus reduced are no longer restricted to adjacent points of intersection, but he can " hop " to any vacant point he pleases. This is a great advantage, and often enables one to recover a good deal of lost ground—until the adversary is likewise reduced to three men, when he becomes entitled to hop also. This is the final struggle ; for as soon as either becomes reduced to two men, he is defeated, and the game is over.

GO-BANG

GO-BANG was introduced into this country from Japan; it is extremely simple; there is no moving, and no taking, and yet it has a fascination of its own and affords ample scope for the exercise of judgment and skill.

It is played on a board of 361 squares—nineteen each way; and each man has his own coloured counters. There is nothing on the board to start with; the player having the first turn places one of his men on any square he likes, then his opponent does the same, and so on alternately. The object of each player is to place five of his men in a consecutive row, either vertically or diagonally, and when either succeeds in doing this the game is at an end.

The game may be played by either two, three, or four players, the counters of each being of a different colour; but the two-handed game is the best, the fact of three —or even two—antagonists being entitled to pose before one's turn comes round again tending to destroy the science of the game, and deprive the skilful player of his due advantage.

PART V

DART-BOARD GAMES

DARTS

DARTS ranks with Morelles (*see* p. 450) as one of the oldest of English games but, unlike it, Darts has been brought very much up-to-date and in its refurbished condition, with freshly designed targets—or " dart-boards," as they are now called, cunningly wrought darts, and well thought out though hardly as yet standardized rules for the various games that may be played with them, it would scarcely be recognized by our great-great-grandfathers as the game in which they indulged in the village inns of the time of George III, and earlier. It is still, *par excellence*, the game of the tavern, and many of its rites and ceremonies, and even its peculiar terms, have intimate connexions with beer and tankards ; but, as an indoor game, it has become so popular in Clubs, Institutes, and the like, and in the domestic circle itself, that *Hoyle's Games Modernized* would to-day fail to live up to its title were a guide to its play not included.

The old game, from which the modern varieties derive, was played with a dart consisting of a straight piece of stick, about six inches long, into one end of which was fixed, point outwards, an ordinary large-sized beheaded pin ; at the other end was a guide made of a square piece of paper folded twice from corner to corner and then inserted in cross-slits cut for the purpose. This was thrown at a target of soft-wood board having painted on it three or four concentric circles of different colours with a bull's-eye in the centre. The outer circle was numbered " 1 ", the next " 2 ", and so on, an extra allowance being made for the bull's-eye, and darts were thrown at it from some agreed distance, the scores being reckoned by the number of the circle in which they stuck. And that was all there was to it : no " doubles " or " trebles " ; no " Up in Annie's room " or " Madhouse ! "—which will be explained in due course ; no delicately radiating lines giving the board some resemblance to a bicycle wheel; and no " scoring backwards," as one has sometimes heard the subtraction method, which is obligatory in all modern Dart games, called. Indeed, Contract is not further removed from its great original, Whist, than is the Darts of to-day from the darts (with a small " d ") of yester-year : though there the parallel ends, for no card-player could admit that Whist was the jejune and feeble fore-runner of a now flourishing descendant as the old game of darts certainly was.

Darts is an indoor game of skill in which short arrow-like missiles—the " darts "—are thrown by hand at a specially marked board by opposing players (or sides) with the object of one player (or side) reaching, under the rules by which the particular game is governed, a specified score before the other. Unless otherwise prearranged a complete game consists of three " legs "—each leg being of the specified score—the first to win two out of the three being the winner. " Leg," by the way, is one of the many special terms that we shall come across ; a leg bears the same relation to a game as does a single hand of thirteen tricks at Whist to a rubber.

As befits a target every dart-board, or at any rate its playing area, is circular in shape ; it consists of a thick piece of wood cut across the grain (or sometimes of other material, as cork, plasticine, compressed bristles, fibre, or paper, etc.) ; the form in most common use, known as the " Clock " board, is marked by means of strong thin wires firmly fixed to the surface in concentric circles, these being crossed by similar radiating wires dividing the area into 20 sectors or triangles of equal size. There are other boards, marked somewhat differently and sometimes numbered somewhat differently, but this one (*see* Fig.) is the only one recognized for National, inter-district, and all regular competitions.

The board itself is about 18 inches across, and the playing area is bounded by the outermost of the concentric circles, which is $13\frac{1}{4}$ in. in diameter ; the space between this and the next inner ring is $\frac{3}{8}$ in. in breadth and constitutes the " doubles " ring, any dart landing in this portion of a triangle counting double the score shown for it. Within this ring the next circle ($8\frac{1}{4}$ in. dia.) forms the outer boundary of the " trebles " ring (also $\frac{3}{8}$ in. in breadth), where successful throws count three times the allotted score. In the plumb centre of the board is a $\frac{1}{2}$in. circle surrounded by one of $1\frac{1}{4}$in. ; a dart in the former, which in any other target would be called the " bull's-eye " but in the language of Darts is always referred to as the " dosser," counts 50 points, or " double 25 " (a distinction the reason for which will appear later), while one in the space between the two counts 25. Each triangle is numbered in the space between the boundary

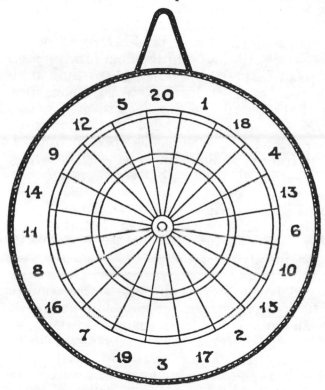

THE " CLOCK " BOARD

of the playing area and the edge of the board—technically known as " off the island "—and a dart sticking in any part of a triangle other than a " doubles " or " trebles " portion scores this number to the thrower. Darts " off the island " don't count, and nor do those that miss the board altogether or that, hitting it, merely drop.

The order of the numbering, which in the Clock Board is a " must," may seem at first sight to be a trifle erratic ; but this is merely an optical illusion. 20, the highest except for the inner circles, is always at the highest part of the board when in play, and 3 at the lowest—a purposeful arrangement, due to the fact that Newton's law of gravitation applies with equal force to darts in flight and to unsupported apples. It will further be noticed (*see* Fig.) that in each case the higher numbers, that is any over 11, are flanked by two lower ones, thus making it more than likely that a near miss of, say, the 20, 19, or 18 will entail a considerable drop from the anticipated score, especially if one were going for the double or treble.

The board is fixed to a perpendicular wall or partition with its centre 5ft. 8in. from the floor, and if playing at home it is advisable to have it backed by a protective surround such as 4 sq. ft. of plywood. Nine feet from the face of the board and parallel with it is marked the " hockey," *i.e.*, the line, not less than 18in. in length and otherwise as long as the available space permits, behind which both feet of the player must be when he is in action ; this line must on no account be overstepped, but it may, of course, be over-reached to any extent that the arm and agility of the player will allow.

The only other implement used in the game is the dart itself, and here the player—whether in Championship, League, or merely friendly events—has an absolutely free hand, for there is no restriction as to weight, length, thickness, material, or anything else. One result is that manufacturers have turned out quite a number of designs, but they all agree in having a sharp steel point, a shaft, and a flight : the shaft may be of loaded or unloaded wood, of brass, steel, or any other suitable material ; it may be shaped like a pencil, a small torpedo, a sort of tapered barrel, etc., while the flight may be made of stiff paper, feathers, celluloid, linen, or even tin. Weight and length (though attempts have been made to limit this to $6\frac{3}{4}$in.) are likewise matters of individual fancy : $\frac{1}{2}$oz. is light, $\frac{3}{4}$oz. seems to be about the average, and $4\frac{1}{2}$ to $5\frac{1}{2}$in. is about the usual length, with from $\frac{1}{2}$ to 1in. added for the projecting portion of the flight.

RULES

In the 1920's, in which period began what may be termed the game's " second time on earth "—for it had

long been moribund—a "National Darts' Association "
was formed by a group of licensed victuallers and issued
a set of "official" rules for use in competitions played
under its own auspices ; but, except for this specific
purpose, these have never been accorded the same sort
of recognition as have the Laws of Billiards, Chess, or
Contract, for instance, a remark that applies equally to a
code issued some years later by the London Darts Club.
As has been mentioned, Darts of to-day is essentially a
" public-house game," and in pretty nearly every inn,
club, or institute where it has a footing (and in which
has it not!) will be found minor variations in play and often
games that are peculiar to the locality or even to the
"school" itself.   So there are no hard and fast rules—
which is, perhaps, one reason why the game is so immensely
popular ; but there are certain main principles common to
all dart-board games and as rules of some sort are an
absolute necessity if a game is to be played at all we offer
the following code, which has been drawn up in accordance
with both of those mentioned above and after a fairly
extensive experience of play in many and varied haunts.
The code is in no way intended to supplant local custom,
and the stranger seeking a game in a strange land is advised to watch a leg or two before joining in, to enquire
as to any method of play or scoring that seems unfamiliar,
and particularly on no account to tell the " locals " that
they are doing it " all wrong ! " And in the domestic
circle, at all events, it is thought that this set of Rules
will prove a useful guide when taken in conjunction with
what has already been said as regards the board, its
position, the hockey-line, etc.

1.   A game shall consist of the best two out of three " legs " (*i.e.,*
rounds), each of the same total score.

2.   The side to take first throw shall be decided by the toss of a
coin, winning side (or player) to throw first in the first leg
and loser first in the second ; should a third leg be necessary
the sides toss again and winner starts.

3.   When sides consist of one against one the opponents shall
throw alternately ; in team competitions players of opposing
sides shall throw alternately.   No change shall be made in
the order of play during any one leg, and no new players or
substitutes may enter during the game.

4.   A single throw shall consist of three darts thrown in succession,
except when with the first or second dart the leg is finished
or the thrower has become " too hot," as defined in Rule
9 below.

P*

5. The score agreed upon per leg shall be marked at the top of the score-board before play commences, and the method of scoring shall be by subtraction from this total, the result of each throw being thus entered, at its conclusion, on the board.

6. In single play each opponent, and in team-play one player from each side shall score a double before that side shall be in play, which double shall count to the side making it (except that in League and Championship team matches of 1,001 up a " straight start "—*i.e.*, on a single—is the rule).

7. All legs shall finish on that double that brings the score to the exact total agreed upon, the winner being the side first to achieve this irrespective of which side had first throw. At any time that a leg can be finished with a double the thrower must, on his request, be informed which double is required.

8. For the purpose of Rules 6 and 7 the 50 ring (the " dosser ") shall count as double 25.

9. If when a final double is required the thrower, with any of his darts, becomes " too hot " by exceeding or scoring 1 less than the score agreed upon or, not having registered the required double, by equalling it, his throw comes to an end and he (or the next player on his side), when his turn next comes, throws for the double that was required at the time that the throw ended.

10. No dart can be re-thrown once it has been thrown ; all darts thrown count, but only those lawfully thrown and remaining stuck within the playing area at the completion of a throw shall score. A dart thrown unlawfully shall be forfeit, and any score made by such throw shall not count.

These simple rules cover all points that are likely to arise in play, but perhaps a little amplification may help the novice in applying them.

No. 1 calls for no comment, and nor does No. 2— except that if the players prefer to throw, instead of toss, for start the winner is usually he whose dart sticks nearest to the dosser, and not the highest scorer. In Rule 3 the last clause is not, at all events in " friendly " games, of the Medes and Persians' order ; if one of the players is obliged to fall out for some reason or other before the game has reached its appointed end a substitute *may* be called in—by agreement with the other side, of course.

Scoring by subtraction (Rule 5) instead of by addition as in all other games may seem a rather back-handed and roundabout way of doing things at first sight ; but it has the great advantage that at any stage of the game the players know exactly what score is to be aimed at, and one does not have to be a highly accomplished mathematician to get used to it.

Next to being able to plant a dart just where one wants it the chief qualification for successful dartsmanship is probably the faculty of knowing instinctively and almost without thinking whether it is possible to get out in one's next throw and, if it is, just how. The highest score that can be made in a throw is, of course, 180 (three treble 20's) ; but 170 (the dosser and two treble 20's— the dosser, it will be remembered, being reckoned as " double 25 ") is the highest with which one can get out, owing to the " finish on a double " rule. Therefore, as soon as this score is reached—if not before—the player should be figuring things out. For instance : Let us suppose that he is left with 89 to get and that his favourite finishing double (and all practised dartsmen have a favourite) is 20 ; he deducts the double 20 from the total, leaving 49 to be scored with his first two darts, and of course at once realizes that it can't be done without at least one double or treble—for the simple reason that the highest score in singles (two 25's) gives him 1 too many and the next highest 4 too few : also he sees that two doubles will be no use, because an odd number is called for. As a matter of fact, in this case he can get out in over a dozen different ways, finishing on his double 20 and without taking the rarely scored 25 ring into account. With any of the six doubles from 15 to 20 he can make his 49 with a single (19, 17, 15, 13, 11, and 9) ; with double 2, 5, 8, 11, and 14 he can do it with a treble (15, 13, 11, 9, 7) ; and with any of the trebles from 10 to 16 inclusive a single will suffice (19, 16, 13, 10, 7, 4, 1) to make his 49, though *not* to run out—because of the absence of the double. On the other hand, he will know also that if his first dart lands in any other double (1, 3, 4, 6, 7, 9, 10, 12, or 13) or treble (1, 2, 4, 6, 8, and 17 to 20) he will not be able to run out on a double 20, and will play his game accordingly.

Now it is not to be expected that every dartsman, however enthusiastic, should carry strings of figures like this in his head, just on the off-chance that he would be left with 89 ; but if those who aspire to the proficiency of the expert would study the *method* and make themselves familiar with the properties of the simple numbers that they have to use they would be surprised at the ease and rapidity with which they would soon be doing their

"mental arithmetic." The following Table will help—
if it is memorized.

No.	Double	Single + Double, or 1 Treble	2 Doubles, or Treble + Double	Single + 2 Doubles, or Treble + Double	Single + Treble + Double, or 2 Trebles
13	26	39	52	65	78
14	28	42	56	70	84
15	30	45	60	75	90
16	32	48	64	80	96
17	34	51	68	85	102
18	36	54	72	90	108
19	38	57	76	95	114

An examination of this skeleton Table (in which we
have not thought it necessary to include the multiples
of the numbers 1 to 12) will reveal quite a number of
useful and interesting facts. For instance ; any number
from 3 to 60 that is divisible by 3 can be got in one throw,
and with a double to finish with, by sticking to the
number resulting from that division, Thus : 18 wanted ;
3 into 18 gives 6—so single 6 + double 6 does it. Any
number from 4 to 64 if divided by 4 is in the same case,
and any number from 5 to 100 if divided by 5 ; so, if
you are left with 72 to run out on, two single 18's followed
by the double gives it you (4 into 72 = 18), or 55—treble
11 followed by the double, or the single followed by two
doubles, does the trick. Such points are worth noting,
especially in connexion with whatever number happens
to be one's favourite double.

While on the "mathematics" of the game it may be
as well—once for all, it is to be hoped—to put an end to
a quest that, in some dart circles, seems to be as alluring
and delusive as that for perpetual motion, namely, the
three trebles that will give you 101—for they simply
do not exist ! One can score 101 in one throw in any
number of ways : treble 7 + two double 20's, two treble
15's + single 11, or (without a double or treble at all)
two "dossers" + the 1, for instance ; but it is useless to
attempt to make any given score solely on *trebles* unless
the sum of the digits representing that score is divisible
by 3, and 101 does not fulfil this requirement (1 + 0 +

$1 = 2$) ; 102, on the other hand, does, and one can get it with the trebles of 7, 10, and 17, or 5, 11, and 18, etc., etc. Further, any score (not, of course, exceeding 180) that is divisible by 9 can be made with three trebles of the number obtained by that division (153, for instance, by three treble 17's), and any score (not exceeding 120) that is divisible by 6 by two trebles of the result.

Rule No. 6 is (with the one exception noted) invariably observed in all places where the game is taken seriously, and it would be a great pity if this were not so. It is certainly a bit heart-breaking when the opponents are forging ahead to find that the necessary double still eludes you and it is impossible even to start knocking bits off that 301, or whatever it may be ; but a game is never lost till it's won, and it is not at all uncommon for the side that is so far ahead to get hopelessly " stuck " in the attempt to score the final double, the while the perspiring opponents overhaul them and proceed to win ! That is where the excitement comes in.

Rules 7, 8, and 9 are all concerned with the finishing double, so we will take them together. No. 7 is perfectly plain ; it means just what it says, and applies to League and Championship games as well as to all others ; though, here again, local custom may have its fancy variations— more's the pity ; so if, when joining in a game among strangers, one finds that a " treble finish," or three darts in some particular double or treble, or even all three piled one on top of each other and still hanging precariously from the board, is recognized as a legitimate finale, one may deplore the fact that the true faith is not to be found among the " locals," but it's wise (and courteous) to say nothing about it and to let the home team have its way. Similarly, there may be a few haunts in which Rule 8 is not *de rigueur*, but they must be very few. Note that there is no double to the outer ring surrounding the dosser ; it can never count more than 25 per dart.

Rule 9 affords some scope for controversy ; and when meeting strangers the player had better make sure before the start whether they adhere to it, or play the " going back " game favoured by the National Darts Association for their team matches. Our rule works like this : if 20 is the number of points wanted and you get the single instead of the double 10—known as " splitting "—you now want double 5, and go for it ; but you miss, landing up, say, in the 12 triangle ; this makes you " too hot," and your throw is at an end.   Now under Rule 9 as here laid down your score is brought up to the single 10 that you have made, and you—or your partner—throws next time for the double 5, at which point you were " bust " ; but under the " going back " variation the single 10 you so well and truly made is not credited to you at all and the new throw begins with the score originally wanted, in this case 20.   There is a good deal to be said for both methods but, on the whole, the former makes the better game, and it does remove the temptation to introduce a bit of strategy which Darts is better without.   Take a neck-and-neck finish in which one side wants 14 and splits it with the first dart ; the player still has three chances of running out—1+d3, 3+d2, and 5+d1—not particularly pleasant combinations, any of them.   If " going back " is being played and the thrower is not quite sure of himself he now has to withstand the urge—slight, perhaps, but still there—purposely to make himself " too hot " so that he, or his partner, at the next throw has the simpler double 7 to go for.

One further word about this Rule : if you want, say, the double 8 to go out and get single 16 of course you are " bust," and so you are if you get single 15, because, much to the regret of many tyros, there is no " double $\frac{1}{2}$ " on the board ; if, however, you get single 14 or anything lower and have a dart left you are obliged to throw it.

The final rule, No. 10, makes it clear that a dart that falls off the board before the finish of a throw is a non-scorer, as also is one that is sticking in another dart and is not touching the board itself with its point.   An " unlawfully " thrown dart is one thrown out of turn or when either foot of the thrower projects beyond the hockey ; also—in most circles—one thrown other than by the unaided hand, with a catapult, for instance.

To return to the actual playing of Darts.   The usual game for a single, or for pairs, is three legs of 301 points each or, if time is short, a single leg of 501.   Three and four a-side games are also played, but these are not in much favour as they mean a lot of loose time on one's hands in between throws.   The Championships, however, are played between teams of eight, with legs of 1,001 up, straight start, best two out of three ; in League matches only two legs, also 1,001 up with straight start, is the usual thing, because of the additional interest through the possibility of a draw, a draw counting one point as against two for a win outright. By the way, there is always an odd "1" in the score ; the reason being that if it were not so it is feared that some super dartsman who is always certain of double 20, for instance, but of nothing else might be able to run out before the others had a chance, simply by plugging away at it !

SOME OTHER DART GAMES

QUITE a number of games are played on the dart-board beside the straightaway one (and still the best) that we have been describing ; they come in very well for a change, but as their rules vary with their locality and their popularity fluctuates with time they are best picked up through personal experience and by joining in the fun oneself. We cannot all do this, however, so here are directions for playing a few of the best ; variants can be added according to taste and ingenuity—for it's being done all the time !

ROUND THE CLOCK:

FOUR darts to the throw ; any number can play, all-against-all. Start on a double (obligatory), and then place in rotation one dart in each of the triangles from 1 to 20, followed by one in the dosser, and finishing on a treble. Except for the start and finale doubles and trebles are ignored ; a player scoring with the fourth dart of his throw has another throw of four—and again, each time on scoring with his fourth. A dart going into the wrong triangle of course does not count. The winner is he who first gets " round the clock."

SHOVE-HA'PENNY:

AN adaptation of the real game (*see* p. 468) ; played by one against one, two against two, or all against all ; whether pairs or sides, opponents play alternately. Each player throws three darts in turn, and each player (or side) has to score three points in each triangle from 1 to 9 inclusive, a single scoring 1, a double 2, and a treble 3 points. If an over-score is made in any " bed " this goes as a whole (doubles and trebles cannot be split) to the opponent, should he need it ; or, in an all-against-all game, to the next player or, if he does not want it, to the next, and so on. The winner is the first player to fill all the beds, but his winning shot must be *scored*, not received from an opponent.

Scores should be marked on a Shove-ha'penny lay-out chalked on the score-board and divided into as many columns as there are players, a stroke being made in the correct column for each dart placed.

SCRAM :

A GOOD game for two, one of whom is to prevent the other from scoring by himself occupying the triangles, the 25 and 50 rings being, as a rule, ignored. Toss for start ; winner as " stopper " and loser " scorer "—for the time being. Stopper aims his three darts to get the highest possible in three different triangles ; any triangle he gets is now out of play and scorer follows with three darts, scoring any number he makes, of course only from among those not occupied by his opponent. They take turn and turn about in this way until all the triangles are occupied, when the score is totalled, the players exchange rôles, and the former stopper seeks to beat his opponent's score as scorer. Doubles and trebles made by scorer count as such, but only if the sector is unoccupied.

In a variant of this game, sometimes known as " Brag," scorer starts first, having previously made a bet with his opponent that he will score over a certain number.

SHANGHAI :

QUITE one of the best games for a crowd. Any numde can take part, and the object is to amass the greatest possible total out of three shots at each number, in rotation, from 1 to 12, counting the actual scores made not merely the number of darts one gets home. Players throw three darts each in turn, first for the 1, then for the 2, and so on ; and once a number is passed, whether a score is made in that sector or not, there is no going back to it. Doubles and trebles count as such, so while 9 is a *possible* score in the 1 sector, 180 is equally possible in the 20 ; and the excitement of the game lies in this fact, for the high and low scorers in its earlier phases may well find their relative positions very thoroughly reversed in the later. Scores are entered on the board, the figures

1 to 12 being marked in a column to the left, and individual scores in a line with these in a separate column for each player.

Oxo:

A VARIANT of Shanghai, in which the sectors to be thrown for are those in which darts are sticking after the simultaneous throwing from the hand of two darts by each player in turn. A sector with no dart doesn't come into the game ; a sector with two or three (etc.) comes in two or three (etc.) times ; and if in the throwing any darts go " off the island," or miss the board altogether, then " zero," which is the space between the outer ring of the double and the board's edge, must be thrown for that number of times.

In the play there is an important difference : scoring is 1 point per number scored and *not* the score of the sector ; which means that whereas in Shanghai a player going for the 10 and getting the single, double, and treble scores 60 in Oxo he would score 6 only—and the same 6 for any other number, or for zero.

If less than five players are taking part it is usual to throw three darts simultaneously instead of two.

TECHNICAL TERMS

The language of Darts is really a study in itself, and can only be properly acquired by those who live, move, and have their being among its habitual users nightly ; but as some acquaintance with it is almost a necessity to the would-be player we give " translations " of such terms as not even a beginner should be without.

Many of the numbers have names of their own. " 1 " is known both as " Bill Taylor " and " Kelly's eye," but for what reason nobody seems to know ; " double 1 " is " Wagon and horses," but when this is wanted as a finale the thrower is said to be " Up in Annie's room," unless he is in the unfortunate position of having first to score the single 1, when he is " in the Madhouse," or, more simply, " Madhouse ! " " Double 20 " is " Top o' the house," for obvious reasons ; " 22 " is often called " Plenty too ! "—an example of Darts ' rhyming slang of which " Two Beehives " (" double 5's ") and " Two Jews " ("double 2's") are others. " Half-a-crown " is, of course, " 26," but this has other names, as " Bed-and-breakfast " (because in the faraway days this could be obtained for two-and-six at the village inns), and " Brewer." " 33 " is commonly " Feathers "—a reminiscence of the comic-cockney saying, " Firty-free fousand fevvers on a frush's froat," but in some parts is known as " Lord Sherborne " and in others as " Bull-calf "; " 40 " is " double top," " 42 " " Weaver's donkey," and " 45 " " Bag o' nuts " or " Cup and saucer "; " 57 " is, naturally, " Heinz," " 66 " " Clickety-click," and " 88 " " Connaught Rangers," the 1st Battalion of which was formerly the 88th Foot. " 99 " wanted is sure to bring the shout " Never won a game ! " but this is considered an unlucky number, so when it comes up the thrower is said to be " in the Wilderness." " 100 " is " Bill Harvey " (another mystery) or, more usually, " One ton "; " 111 " is invariably called " Lord Nelson "—for a reason that is probably known to most dart players—and " 222 " " Ducks in the pond."

A side that has failed to make its opening double before the other side has run out (a not infrequent occurrence) is said to be " Whitewashed," while a win of two legs out of three straight off is a " Dry wipe." " Leg-and-leg," by the way, is the correct expression when each side has won one—never " One-all " still less " Leg-all " ; similarly, one must not call " Game ! " when the game is won ; it is always " Office ! " " Cat's on the counter ! " " Ole lady ! " or " Hops ! " any of which call attention to the fact that it is time for a round of drinks ! " Turf," like " Island " (*see* p. 455) is a synonym for the playing area of the board, and " Bed," as in " three in a bed " or " in the wrong bed," for any sector. " Upstairs " and " Downstairs " mean the numbers in the upper and lower halves of the board respectively, while those on the left are, for some reason or other, collectively called " the married man's side."

Explanations of most of the other specialized terms are given in the description of the play, among them " dosser " (also known as the " pug," " bung-hole ," or " bull,") " going back," " too hot," " bust," and " splitting." A player who is " too hot " will very likely be greeted with the cry, " Come out ! " or " You've been ! " signifying that he must now make room for the next lucky man.

PART VI

TABLE GAMES

SHOVE-HA'PENNY

THIS famous old English game has been played in one form or another from at least Elizabethan times, but it is only since the Great War of 1914-18 that its rules have become more or less stabilized and that its popularity has become almost co-extensive with beer-drinking—for it is a strong favourite in taverns and workingmen's clubs.

In the early years of this century the " lay-out " consisted of a parallelogram, marked with chalk or otherwise on the bar table : it was some 12 to 14in. in breadth and as much as 3 or even 4ft. in length, and was divided transversely into nine equal partitions numbered progressively from 1 to 9.   Each player had a smooth ha'penny which he placed upon the edge of the table and struck with the palm of his hand, driving it towards these partitions and scoring the number allotted to that within which it came to rest : 31, which had to be made exactly, was usually game.   In some circles a tenth partition (numbered 10) was added, and then each player used four coins—which were considered equivalent to so many cards at cribbage— and the game was scored cribbage-fashion in fifteens, sequences, pairs, and pairs-royal.

To-day in the vast majority of places Shove-ha'penny is played under the conditions and rules—subject to slight local variations—here given. The board (*see* p. 468) is approximately 24in. long by 14½in. broad, divided by lines or incisions about 1/16in. broad into nine " beds," each of which is 1¼in., or sometimes a trifle more, in breadth.   The bed extends to within 1¼ in. of each edge of the board, the compartments so made being used for indicating the score ; both the semi-circular space at the top of the board and the four inches or so before reaching the first bed are also outside the playing area. The " board " may be of various materials—wood, slate, plate-glass, highly polished marble, etc.—it matters little which, so long as it is (and remains) perfectly smooth and perfectly " true." Slate has its patrons, chiefly on account of its non-liability to warp and its lasting qualities : but there are certain objections to slate, and most fans agree that nothing will beat a well-cared-for unvarnished piece of hardwood, such as mahogany, oak, or walnut. It should be of good thickness ($\frac{1}{2}$ to $\frac{3}{4}$in.),

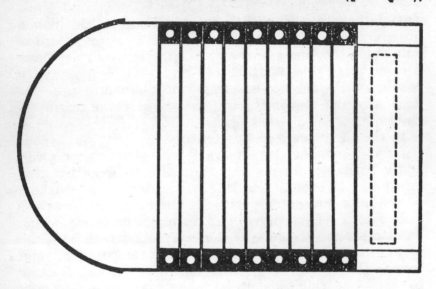

thoroughly seasoned, and cut with the grain parallel to its length ; to its under side is screwed a batten parallel with the bottom edge and about $1\frac{1}{2}$in. from it (shown in the Fig. by means of dotted lines) ; this, when the board is placed on a table, engages with the table-edge and so prevents movement during play. At the top a raised rim prevents a hard-hit disc falling off. The only other implements are the "ha'pennies"—five brass discs the exact breadth of a ha'penny, usually holed in the centre, having one side perfectly smooth and some design, or perhaps the maker's mark, on the other.

THE PLAY

The object of each opponent, or side of two players as the case may be, is to go game by winning two out of three " Horses," " Horse " being the technical term for a single filling of the board, that is, the placing, under he rules, of three discs in each of the nine beds."

The order of play having been decided by tossing, the first player starts by " shoving " three discs towards the beds : this is done by placing the discs, one after the other, so as to overlap the bottom end of the board and striking the overlap smartly with the ball of the thumb ; opponent follows with all five discs, and thereafter they play turn and turn about, each using all five, until one has his " Horse " complete. The loser starts the second Horse (with all five discs), and if a third is necessary the players toss for opening. There are various devices for recording the scores, but the usual method is by chalk marks in the spaces at the sides of each bed, one player taking the left and the other the right.

Unalterable rules are :—One disc one shove only. No score unless the disc lies wholly in the bed, there being an appreciable space between its edge and any boundary line. Scores must be taken on the completion of each turn and in accordance with the lie of the discs at that time. No disc that has been shoved may be touched or removed before all five have been played and the score recorded ; a player infringing this rule loses his score for the turn, but he may, at his discretion, either replay the disc or replace it where it lay if it has been moved by some other person. A disc that has hit the rim is out of play ; it cannot be used for cannoning, but if its rebound brings it fairly into a bed in which opponent needs a point or points opponent may score it for that bed ; further, if a player scores more points in any bed than he requires such points may be taken by his opponent (should he need them), but neither of these possible transferences apply to the last point for game.

These general rules are enforced in all variants of the game ; there are quite a number of these, mostly of local popularity and all very easily picked up—which latter remark applies also to the many terms peculiar to Shove-ha'penny. Although apparently such a simple game much skill and judgment are called for, as anyone who has watched a couple of experts for a few turns will readily admit : and it is only by watching such, and by plentiful practice, that one learns how to turn bad lies into good by skilful cannoning and acquires the many tricks of this most fascinating of pastimes.

DOMINOES

DOMINOES is a game properly for two persons (though it can be played by three, four, or even more, either as partners or all against all), played with a set of twenty-eight pieces, or " bones."

The pieces are usually of bone mounted on ebony, and are about 1⅞in. long by 1in. wide and ⅜in. thick; each has a central pin, slightly protruding from the face, to facilitate shuffling. They have on their faces the

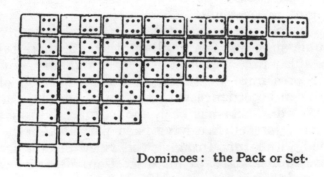

Dominoes: the Pack or Set.

permutations of the numbers from 6 to 9, taken two at a time. All with the same number at either end belong to the same " suit," the seven pieces with the blank forming the " blank " suit, the seven with the 5 the " five " suit, and so on; and every bone, except the doubles, is naturally in two suits, six-five, for instance, being in both the six and the five suit.

The spots on the different suits (see illustration) are :—

The " blank "	suit totals		21	spots
,, " one "	,,	,,	28	,,
,, " two "	,,	,,	35	,,
,, " three "	,,	,,	42	,,
,, " four "	,,	,,	49	,,
,, " five "	,,	,,	56	,,
,, " six "	,,	,,	63	,,

and the total number of spots in the set is 168, the difference in the two totals being, of course, due to the fact that the dominoes are—with the exception above noted—in two suits at once.

Of the large number of Domino games played we are, for reasons of space, able to describe only a few ; but the following general rules and hints will be found applicable to all.

Before playing the bones are turned out of the box face downwards on the table and are shuffled, both— or all—players having the right to shuffle. First play, or " the Down," as it is called, is then settled—usually by each player drawing a domino and the down going to the drawer of the highest ; another method is for one player to take a bone and his opponent to guess whether it is " odd " or " even " ; while in some games the matter if left till the drawing for the hands has taken place, when the holder of the highest double (and failing doubles, the highest domino) " downs."

When a definite score is to be played for this must be decided upon before play commences : when a hand is " blocked " or " closed " the hands are shown, the spots counted, and the player with the lowest number wins and scores the total of the two hands. A draw takes place when the spots of both sides are equal ; no score is awarded in such a case, and the " down " passes.

When dominoes are placed touching each other *lengthwise* the " doubles," *i.e.*, the bones having the same number of pips at each end, are placed *crosswise;* when the dominoes are laid side by side this is not done.

The dominoes remaining on the table after each player has drawn the number required for the game are left face down, and are known as the " stock," the " remainder," or—more poetically—the " boneyard." Players should sort their hands into suits, and then stand the bones, each on a long edge, on the table in a position that will make it impossible for an opponent to see their faces.

THE BLOCK GAME.

THIS is the simplest of all the Domino games, and we will therefore describe it first. Each player draws seven bones, and the one with the highest double downs, the down thereafter following in rotation, right to left, as in cards. The first down, if the player knows what he is doing, will be a domino from his longest suit, his object being to get the line back to this suit as often as possible so that he can get rid of the rest. Let us suppose that the first player has 4-0 and three other 4's with two other blanks and an odd suit in his hand ; he will play the 4-0. His opponent must now *match* this, *i.e.*, he must play a bone with either a 4 or a 0 on it ; if a 4 he places it endways against the 4 already down, if a 0 against the 0 ; and, of course, he will also play from his longest suit. This placing continues in rotation at either of the uncovered ends, until one player has got rid of all his pieces, when he cries " Domino ! " and scores the number of spots left in his opponent's hand. If at any time one player cannot down, he says so, and the other goes on playing till he can ; if neither can play, the game is said to be " blocked," the bones are laid face upwards, and the player having the smallest number of spots on the pieces he has left scores the total of both hands.

Skill in this game comes in in knowing which of two or more playable pieces to down, and especially in knowing when to block and when not to ; and these are points in which practice will soon make perfect—or nearly so. The game is usually played for either 50 or 100 points up, and stakes—if any—are settled for at so much a point for the difference between the two scores.

When the Block Game is played *four-handed* the players cut for partners, the two highest against the two lowest, the lowest having the first down. There is no difference in the play, but four bones only are drawn by each, and the game is over when one player has no pieces left, or when all four are blocked. In the *four-handed all against all* game a player may go on as long as he can follow suit at either end of the line.

THE DRAW GAME

THIS is really a variation of the Block Game, the only difference being that *after the first down* any player may, whether he is blocked or not, draw as many dominoes from the stock as he likes, provided that two are left on the table undrawn. If a player is blocked he is obliged to draw until he obtains a bone that can be played, or until he has drawn all but the last two. When playing *four-handed* six dominoes are drawn.

Drawing gives a great additional interest to the game,

and makes it considerably harder. One should always have an object in drawing, and should remember that a single bone too many may completely alter one's original plans. Before drawing, the second player should carefully note his hand, and, bearing in mind that the domino played is from the strong suit in his opponent's hand, he should form an opinion of what he is drawing for—whether to build up against his adversary or to strengthen his own hand.

MATADORE

MATADORE is another variety of the Block Game, but here the object is not to match the end but to play a domino the spots of one end of which, when added to the spots on the end of the domino it is played against, will total *seven*. The three bones whose pips amount to 7 (viz., the 6–1, 5–2 and 4–3) and the double blank are known as *Matadores;* these have all the force of trumps, and can be played at any time, at either end, and with either of their ends pointing outwards, whether the 7 is made by the placing or not.

Each player takes seven bones (except in the *four-handed* game, when five are taken), and any player may draw in his turn at any time, up to within two of the stock, and is obliged to draw if he is blocked until he has a playable bone or there are only two left. Bones are played side by side, not end to end, and doubles are not laid crosswise, but take their place in the line.

By way of illustrating the game, we will suppose that there is a 2 at one end of the line and a blank at the other. The only pieces that can be played are a 5 and a matadore—for only a matadore can be played to a blank. The player whose turn it is holds the double blank and three of the five suit (as well as others), the 5–0 being among them. He plays the 5–0 to the 2 ; there is now a blank at each end, and if his opponent does not have a matadore he has to draw till he gets one, or till there are only two bones left in stock. He draws, and we will suppose that at his third draw he obtains the 6–1, which he plays with the 6 pointing outwards. He plays it thus because it is to his advantage (on account of the scoring at the end) to prevent his opponent getting rid of his 6's, but before doing so he looks at his own hand and at the bones already placed to find out, if he can, whether or not his opponent holds either the double blank or the 1 blank; and as there are always at least two bones left in the stock he can never be *quite* certain. Now, if the next player holds the 1–0 he will play it; if not, he has to decide, taking into account what has been played and what he holds in his hand, whether he had better play his double blank to the 6 end—in which case knowing that his opponent has no matadore, he will force him to draw—or draw himself. It all depends on the state of the game; but, with such a leave, and no other conditions being given, the indications point to his playing the double blank. If all the matadores were out, and there were still some bones in the stock to be drawn, and the player had only one or two low ones left in his hand, of course, that is the only thing he would think of doing.

Matadore is decided and settled for as in the ordinary Block Game.

SEBASTOPOL, OR THE STAR

SEBASTOPOL is a game for four, and each player starts by drawing seven bones, there being none, therefore, left

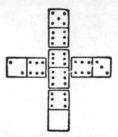

in " stock." The holder of the double six begins with this piece, and no player can go on unless he holds a six, which must be placed either at the end or side of the double, as shown in the illustration.

When the " star " is complete, play proceeds as in the Block Game, that is, the one whose turn it is to continue the lay-out shown in the above diagram would have to play a blank, 2, 5, or 3, and if he cannot play his turn passes to the player on his left. The scoring is done in exactly the same way as in the Block Game.

There are a number of varieties of this game, and among them may be mentioned the following, which is

not confined to four. If two, or three are playing, seven
bones are drawn, if four 5, and if six or seven 3. The
game must be begun with a double ; if first player does
not hold one he draws, and if he does not then obtain
a double the down passes to the player on his left, and
so on round the table till a double can be played. The
players in turn from the leader now play one of the
downed suit against each of the four sides of the double
until the " star " has been made, and play then proceeds
as in the Block Game, each in turn playing against one of
the four radii with a domino of the same suit, until one
of the party is " out."

DOMINO PATIENCE

THIS is a very old-fashioned game for one ; but it affords
excellent practice for the novice, so we do not hesitate
to give it.

Draw five bones from the pack haphazard, play one
of them, and then play as many to it, and the succeeding
dominoes, as possible. When you have finished, draw
as many fresh ones as you have played out, and again
play out all you can ; then draw again the number you
have played out, and continue thus until you have played
out the whole pack or have come to a dead stop. A
few turns at this will give one a very good insight into
" downing " for all domino games.

BERGEN

THIS is a game for two, and the object is to get the same
suit at both ends of the line. When this is obtained
it is termed a *double header*, and the player scores 2.

Each player takes 6 bones, and the highest double
starts, the player scoring his 2 points. Let us suppose
that it is 5–5 ; his opponent must now play a 5, and if
he does not possess one must draw one bone ; if the draw
is unsuccessful, first player plays again— or draws. But
we will suppose that second player brings out the 5—3 ;
first player can now reply with either a 5 or a 3 ; if he
has a five he will play it ; but, in our supposititious game
he hasn't, so he plays, let us say, the 3–6. His opponent
had 5–6, so he at once plays it and scores 3, as, with
a double 5 at one end and a single at the other this is

a *triple header*. If the first player had held a 5 he would have played it to prevent this happening.

The first player " out " adds one point to his score, and " game " is fifteen points. If both players become " blocked," spots are counted up, and the player having the smallest number *with no double in his hand* scores one point ; if he has a double his opponent scores one : and if both hold doubles the lowest number of pips wins the point.

BINGO

BINGO, the best of all the Domino games, is founded on Bézique, and, to play it well, requires a considerable amount of skill and a good memory. It is played by two players, each drawing seven bones ; " game " consists of being seven up, but to become one up one has to obtain 70 points in play.

After the down has been decided, second player turns up one of the stock, and the highest figure on that is trump, the blank counting seven. The trump is left face up, and the downer leads with any domino he likes. Second player plays to it, and *he need not follow suit;* the two bones form a trick, which is taken by the player of the higher domino, a trump, of course, taking any but a higher trump. The winner leads for the next trick, but before doing so draws one piece from the stock ; his opponent also draws, and replies, and the game proceeds thus until all the dominoes have been drawn, the turned-up trump being taken by the player who has the last draw.

Now the method of play alters, for second player must follow suit if he can : if he cannot, he must play a trump if he has one : and if he can do neither he must discard. The winner of a trick takes the trick, and counts any score it may contain.

The scoring dominoes are as follows : Apart from the trumps the only bones to count are all the doubles, which take their spot value, and the 6–4 and 0–3, which also score 10 whatever the trump. All bones of the trump suit score their spot value, except the double, which counts 28. Thus, double blank—known as " Bingo "—scores 14 when blanks are not trumps, but 28 when they are ; similarly, when sixes are trumps 6–6 scores 28, but in any other circumstances 12.

It follows from this that the total value of the scoring bones vary slightly according to the trump suit :—

When blank is trump, the total is				143
,,	1	,,	,,	135
,,	2	,,	,,	138
,,	3	,,	,,	131
,,	4	,,	,,	134
,,	5	,,	,,	129
,,	6	,,	,,	140

A player having two doubles in his hand and leading one of them, should show the other and announce "Double." If he wins the trick he adds 20 to his score ; if he holds three doubles, he announces "Triplets," and scores 40 ; if four doubles, he calls "Double doublet," and adds 50 if he wins the trick ; if he holds five doubles he says "King," and, winning the trick, takes 60 ; "Emperor" is the announcement should he hold six doubles, and 70 points (one towards game) are scored if the trick is won ; while if he holds seven doubles, he announces "Invincible," and scores three points towards game if he wins the trick. These combinations *must be announced* immediately the first double is played, otherwise their value is lost.

After either of the players has won a trick at any stage of the game, if he holds a hand by which he can be sure of scoring 70 points, he may, when it comes to his turn to play, turn the trump face down ; this stops all further drawing, and the second player has to follow suit, or play a trump, as stated above. If the player who has turned down the trump fails to make his 70 points in that hand, his opponent scores two points towards game, or, if he had not taken a trick before the trump was turned, three.

The scoring of 70 points by play gives the scorer one up towards game ; but when one's opponent has not scored 20 points this is increased to two, and if he has not taken a single trick, to three.

"Bingo" (double blank) takes any other piece, no matter what is trump, and if it takes the double of trumps the one who played it scores a point. All points must be claimed *as they occur;* otherwise they cannot be scored.

SOLITAIRE

SOLITAIRE is, as its name implies, a game for a solitary player ; and it has the great merit that it can be played with equal enjoyment and profit by children, by invalids, and—in their spare moments—by Professors of Higher Mathematics. At first glance it is the simplest game imaginable, consisting, as it does, in jumping marbles over each other ; but, just as in cricket there is a great deal more than—

Casting a ball at three straight sticks and defending the
same with a fourth—

so, in Solitaire, there is a great deal more than meets the eye, as will quickly become evident to any of our readers who would give a little time to studying the problems detailed in Ernest Bergholt's " The Game of Solitaire."

It is usually played on a board in which are scooped thirty-three hemispherical hollows arranged as in our diagram.

The numbering, of course, does not appear on the board, and is shown here merely for convenience of reference. Marbles fit into these hollows, and at the start of most games every hollow is occupied except one, the number of which is specified. For those who do not possess the solitaire board as usually sold, this diagram drawn on cardboard of suitable size, and Halma men or counters instead of marbles, will do equally well.

As has been said, the ordinary game of Solitaire commences with one hole left vacant; a series of moves is then made with the object of ending up with only one marble on the board. A move is made by any ball that can jump over another, either horizontally or vertically, never diagonally, into a vacant hollow on the other side; the ball so jumped over is *taken* and removed from the board, while the jumping ball remains in the hole to which it has arrived unless it can continue its move by jumping over another horizontal or vertical neighbour into another vacant hollow.

For example: suppose we start with No. 1 hole vacant; No. 3 marble can jump over No. 2, removing it in the process and landing on No. 1; 10 can now jump to 2, taking 5; 12 can go to 10, removing 11; and this gives the ball now in No. 1 a two-step jump to 11, taking 2 and 6 *en route*. If we now proceed 10-12, 13-11, 8 can jump over to 12, taking 9 and 11; 24 can then go to 10, capturing 17, which makes it possible for 27 to take four pieces at one move, viz., Nos. 20, 12, 10, and 4, landing up himself at 1. As a matter of fact he would stop short when he had taken 10, remaining himself in 9, for it is not at all desirable to get right away into No. 1's corner again. 25 now goes to 11, taking 18, whereupon 26 captures 19, 11, and 9, settling at hole No. 8. In these eleven moves seventeen balls have been removed, and it is possible in a few more moves to take off all but the final marble. This is known as *reducing*; certain combinations are irreducible, and these will soon become recognized, but when one plays with one hole vacant to start with—it does not matter *which* hole—it is possible, with careful play, to reduce to 1 every time. But care is necessary; for it is also possible for an unskilled player quite early in the game to make such a move that he leaves an absolutely irreducible group.

There are many interesting problems that the beginner can set himself for practice: for instance—

Take four marbles and set them at 5, 8, 9, and 10; reduce these to 1 in three moves.

Set seven marbles at 13, 18, 20, 24, 25, 26, and 27, and reduce them in five moves.

Reduce the *Small Square* (as 5, 6, 10, 11) in two moves; the *Anvil* (six balls placed as at 23, 24, 25, 26, 29, and 30) in three moves; and the *Right Angle* (five balls, as 9, 16, 23, 24, and 25) also in three moves. The " T " of five balls (9, 10, 11, 17, 24) can also be reduced in three.

Complications are introduced by many players, by employing what are known as " Balls on the Watch," and " Dead Balls." A " ball on the watch " is one that is compelled to remain stationary throughout the game, until, at the final move, it captures the remaining ball or balls, and becomes the sole survivor. Such a marble should be of a different colour or material from the others. A " dead ball " is one that is not allowed to be moved during any part of the game, and must be captured with the final move. One cannot have more than one " ball on the watch " in any game, but good players will frequently handicap themselves with as many as three, or even four, " dead balls," and every one of these must be taken with a composite move at the end.